Analyzing Literature-to-Film Adaptations

Analyzing Literature-to-Film Adaptations

Adaptations

A Novelist's Exploration and Guide

Mary H. Snyder

continuum

2011

The Continuum International Publishing Group
80 Maiden Lane, New York, NY 10038
The Tower Building, 11 York Road, London SE1 7NX

www.continuumbooks.com

Library of Congress Cataloging-in-Publication Data
Snyder, Mary H.
Analyzing literature-to-film adaptations: a novelist's exploration and
guide / by Mary H. Snyder.
    p. cm.
  Includes bibliographical references and index.
  ISBN-13: 978-1-4411-4998-5 (hardcover: alk. paper)
  ISBN-10: 1-4411-4998-8 (hardcover: alk. paper)
  ISBN-13: 978-1-4411-6818-4 (pbk.: alk. paper)
  ISBN-10: 1-4411-6818-4 (pbk.: alk. paper) 1. Film adaptations—
History and criticism. 2. American fiction—Film and video adaptations.
I. Title.
  PN1997.85.S59 2011
  791.43'75—dc22

                                    2010022592

ISBN: HB: 978-1-4411-4998-5
       PB: 978-1-4411-6818-4

Typeset by Pindar NZ, Auckland, New Zealand

Contents

Introduction

This book explores the adaptation of literature to film from the perspective of a novelist, or fiction writer. Admittedly, I would love to try my hand at a screenplay, as John Irving did, and successfully, for the film adaptation of one of his novels, *The Cider House Rules*. I even wonder how it would be to direct a film, although I'd probably end up tearing out all of my hair by the time I finished, if I made it that far. John Irving himself writes in *My Movie Business*, his memoir about the making of the film *The Cider House Rules*, that it's his job to give his notes to the director, ". . . but, in the end, there can only be one director . . . When I feel like being a director, I write a novel" (Irving 1999b, 152).

As much as I like to imagine partaking in the role of director, or screenwriter for that matter, the truth is the reality of doing so does not attract me. I love to write stories but without the necessity of collaboration or frequent interruptions by the perspectives of others as filmmakers must endure, and unfettered by a specific format as screenwriters must follow. In fact, I revel in making up stories about people in my spare time. I lie in my bed in the morning for at least an hour and think of hypothetical people, or characters, and their lives and their stories, and I let my imagination take over. I refer to them as waking dreams of a sort. And, when it seems time to capture these stories for the sake of posterity (and possible public display), the medium I slide into as if it were my favorite, comfortable chair, softly worn, cushiony, and inviting, is the written word, welcoming me to shape a narrative that best suits my subject, my characters, my story — or, my plan of my imaginary world.

Writers of novels, and short stories, always have a plan, a strategy. And, this plan unravels as they begin and continue in their process of creation. The plan and the process vary for each writer. John Irving, for example, explains his process:

> Most of my friends who are novelists have told me that they never know the end of their novels when they start writing them; they find it peculiar that for my novels I need to know, and I need to know not just the ending, but every significant event in the main characters' lives. When I finally write the first sentence, I want to know everything that happens, so that I am not inventing the story as I write it; rather, I am remembering a story that has already happened. The invention is over by the time I begin. All I want to be thinking of is the language — the sentence I am writing, and

the sentence that follows it. Just the language. (Irving 1999b, 156)

When I wrote my novel, I started with two short stories about two different women whose lives I began overlapping. I didn't know my beginning, my middle, or my end when I began. The novel grew as I grew with it. Irving employs the method above for writing each of his novels, he reiterated during a talk he gave at a writer's conference. I, on the other hand, am looking to another novel, beginning with a vague idea of a plan, and letting the subject matter and characters carry me along for a while. Then I'll know what to do. I rely on an inner guidance while Irving prefers to focus on the language of his work as he begins. Other writers have other processes. Michael Cunningham, for *The Hours*, began the novel as a contemporary version of Virginia Woolf's *Mrs. Dalloway*. He almost threw away his first attempt, until he considered adding a character based on his mother, changing the dynamics of the novel. When he came upon this revelation about the novel, he decided not to "kiss it goodbye," and explains that at this point all he had to do was write it.

Misconceptions of the creation of a novel, when looking at literature-to-film adaptation, seem to abound. Those who study film adaptation do not consider with much depth what goes into making a novel, while they are quite focused on defending the multitude of factors that go into making a film. I'm not disputing the latter, but I expend quite a bit of this book addressing the former. I do so not only to justify my own work, in elaborating on what went into creating my own novel and all the factors leading to its production, but also to justify the work of novelists and fiction writers, which it seems necessary to do. I've discovered that approaching literature-to-film adaptation from a novelist's perspective is a rather unique perspective, in that most of the scholars and experts on the subject that I've read began with some form of a literary training, and developed an educational and often experiential background in the art of film, and film theory and analysis. Some of these scholars are strictly trained in film studies. Many of these individuals teach film, and are referred to as film experts.

I hail from a literature department, but my interest in film is limited. And, primarily, it's limited to film adaptation. I appreciate film, and I respect the art and see it as art, but my focus is literature, and the dynamics of adaptation of the literary to the filmic have become fascinating to me. At first, I was intimidated by the concept, especially from the personal perspective that my novel could be made into a film. However, through my research and as my own thoughts on the topic have developed and evolved, I've become more comfortable with literature-to-film adaptation. I don't see the process as one medium hacking away at the other, or disrespecting the other, although that can occur if the process is mishandled. I also don't see the film adaptation process as requiring "fidelity" or "faithfulness" to the original text on no uncertain terms. I believe a literature-to-film adaptation process-to-product can be successful within parameters that are not necessarily narrow or limiting, but that are mindful, however, of the source text.

I've come to see literature-to-film adaptation as a form of intertextuality worthy of intense study and exploration, from many angles, allowing for critical study that can be made accessible not only to high school or undergraduate college students, but also to the layperson. By layperson, I refer to any individual with an inquiring mind, although not necessarily one with a scholarly mind who wants to probe the more intricate aspects of film adaptation, or who wants to write a book or make a movie. Perhaps the book clubs begun several years ago might even consider taking on discussions of film adaptations, once given the basic tools for doing so. What I want to do is make those tools available to those individuals interested in viewing literature-to-film adaptation from a more informed perspective. This book is for the student who would like to turn a more discriminating eye towards the practice and theory of adapting literature to film. Where does one begin to analyze the process? Where does one begin to analyze the production? Where does one begin to scrutinize the entire system of adaptation? Where does one begin and how does one continue?

The main objective of this book is to put forth a means to analyze literature-to-film adaptations, and from this point, I will refer to literature-to-film adaptations as lit-to-film adaptations, for the sake of writing and reading ease. I do not defend the film aspect of lit-to-film adaptation, but instead introduce specific critical approaches that can be applied to analyzing lit-to-film adaptation, contending that to do so fairly is to reinstate the importance of the literature in lit-to-film adaptation.

Since I am approaching lit-to-film adaptation from the perspective of a novelist who has written a text that could be considered for film adaptation and I examine the complexities that accompanies this action for a writer, I've taken note that in the midst of all the discourse surrounding lit-to-film adaptation, most attention by some quite fine minds has been focused on a defense of the film piece of lit-to-film adaptation. For example, film theorist Robert Stam in his introduction to *Literature and Film: A Guide to the Theory and Practice of Film Adaptation* devotes an entire section entitled "The Roots of a Prejudice" to an examination of how the literature has been privileged automatically in the discourse on the quality of its adaptation to film, due to its assumed superiority to film. Yet as he continues, his discussion of originality and source texts from a poststructuralist perspective signal to me quite problematic issues, especially for the novelist. Thomas Leitch, Brian McFarlane, Timothy Corrigan, among others, also present arguments concerning film adaptation studies that, even if subtly, spend a good amount of time and energy defending film and its quality and value, and its limitations and specificities, which I don't feel is necessary. (That is, they often contradict themselves by being almost overly defensive of film. If film needs to be so defended, does this not imply that it is not only seen as less, but that it might be less? I don't see film as less, but I also don't see it as more, or in need of so much protection.)

I am fair to both the literature and film in my presentation of lit-to-film adaptation, or at least that is my design. We've come to a point in our culture where film has become increasingly respected as a text and has begun to find its place in academia, to the point that perhaps its defense has been successful. However, now it's time to consider both literature and film and the parts they both play in a lit-to-film adaptation, in an equitable manner.

I've searched endlessly and have not found a book about lit-to-film adaptation from the perspective of the writer. A few writers have chronicled their personal experience with film adaptation, but these are not analytical approaches to the "discipline." I've wondered about that. It seems most scholars that speak to lit-to-film adaptation analysis and theory assume they understand unequivocally the creation process of fiction or assume that it's inconsequential to the adaptation studies discourse, while, as I've stated above, these same scholars have taken a defensive posturing towards their approach to film. What's alluring about film, I think, for scholars, is that in the realm of academia, it's relatively new, or thought to be. And scholars gravitate to what is new. What is new is rife with the endless possibility of originality, the requirement of any subject taken on by just about any scholar. Ironically, the subject of originality is at the root of much of the quagmire that envelops lit-to-film adaptation studies.

I concede that my actual undertaking of lit-to-film adaptation analysis is not original. Much of what I broach in this book has been broached before, perhaps only stated differently. However, what is original about my approach to lit-to-film adaptation studies is that I have engaged in the creative process of writing a novel, and I have studied and analyzed that process. Thus my perspective as a scholar of lit-to-film adaptation studies combined with my additional perspective as a fiction writer who has explored the creative process of writing a novel is original. I've researched film but can be more objective about the medium since I began this project seeing film as the enemy of my work, but relaxed into an appreciation of film, and lit-to-film adaptation, if carried out purposefully and carefully. I did my own work on my novel with care and purpose, and as I explain later, my novel was a long journey through a novel-to-novel adaptation, the process itself having raised many issues that concerned me as I completed my novel and the possibility of film adaptation began to hover around me.

I want to articulate specifically that not only am I approaching lit-to-film adaptation analysis from the perspective of a novelist, the creator of the source text, but also from the perspective of an instructor, desiring to make lit-to-film adaptation analysis understandable and accessible to students. Lit-to-film adaptation analysis is an explosive minefield of teaching possibilities, but in my endeavors to teach it, I haven't found one entirely useful text to utilize for doing so. I've taken bits and pieces from here and there, which say the same thing in different ways, and others that simply talk about how difficult lit-to-film adaptation is to discuss and explore. Often, the language is so obtuse, it confuses the scholar writing it. Robert Stam, in the section of his introduction entitled "Bakhtin, Gennette, and Transtextuality," applies a rather complex treatment of the concept of intertextuality broadened to a spectrum of "textualities" by Gerard Genette to film adaptation, and Stam himself begins to make mistakes that an editor didn't even catch. On page 27, he writes: "The first type of transtextuality is 'intertextuality' . . .." But on page 28, he writes: "Genette's third type of intertextuality is 'metatextuality' . . .." What Stam meant to refer to here was Genette's third type of transtextuality, yet this isn't the only mistake made in this section of his argument. Furthermore, when teaching this material to students, in its already convoluted state, these mistakes make for further difficulties in comprehension. Honestly, there has to be a better way, at least for introductory students.

Thus this is a book meant to teach the intricacies as well as the conflicts that make up lit-to-film adaptation and lit-to-film adaptation analysis, but my intention is to present the material in a way that is understandable and accessible to undergraduate students, high school students, and even laypeople. My design is to encourage changes in the pedagogy we use for literature classes for introductory students while also encouraging changes in curriculum that include film. My goal is to put literature and its directly associative film on equal footing, not that they are equal as texts, but that they are on equal footing in academia, at the most introductory level. To do so I will abandon the fierce defense of film in this relationship, and I will also shelve the stodgy insistence that if we don't only focus on literature we will end up with illiterate students who will gravitate towards film for sustenance simply because it's entertaining and easy. Literature and film can surprisingly work together in a culture that is becoming increasingly technologic while at the same time seems to dig its feet into what has been considered traditional all along. We don 3D glasses in front of a huge OMNIMAX screen and enjoy the rush of excitement it brings us, while at home we look forward to getting into bed with a good book to de-stress and fall into a peaceful sleep before the next hectic day begins. Lit-to-film adaptation studies offers a potential learning experience that could aid students in bringing their confused desires together in a satisfying, effective, and stimulating way that satisfies the pedagogy required of it at the introductory level.

I've written a novel, taught various genres of literature, and cultivated an understanding of what goes into making a film and analyzing a film. I've not had the personal experience of making a film, but I do know what goes into writing a novel. George Bluestone writes in his *Novels into Films*: "The reputable novel, generally speaking, has been supported by a small, literate audience, has been produced by an individual writer, and has remained relatively free of rigid censorship" (Bluestone 2003, vi). Bluestone goes on to state that: "The film, on the other hand, has been supported by a mass audience, produced cooperatively under industrial conditions, and restricted by a self-imposed Production Code" (vi). I disagree with Bluestone on both points since although the latter might have been the case more strictly in 1956 at the writing of his text, the restrictions on film have changed. I also disagree with his statement about the novel, not only from a generational perspective, but from the perspective of a novelist today, who has studied novels of the past, and has written one of today. Although a novel does claim an individual writer, there are many influences on that one individual writer, that result in a literary work being a collaborative work just as a film is, obviously not in all or as many ways but certainly in at least some.

My own journey as a novelist is addressed in this book. It's important to understand why a good number of people tend to favor the book over the film in a lit-to-film adaptation. It might seem to some that the book has been treated dismissively while the film has been privileged, although film experts have been determined to state otherwise. I see where the film experts are coming from, but I also understand the loyalty we harbor to the books we have read and imagined. I also sense a loyalty to the art of the text, or book, and the authorial process that produced the book when I'm involved in discussions about lit-to-film adaptations out of the classroom, that inevitably employ the word "better" in some manner. I've grappled with my own loyalty to the novel *Frankenstein*, and its captivating and quite teachable authorial process that we as scholars and students have been quite privy to, due to the author's journals and the writings of those surrounding her at the time of the novel's inception.

In fact, as I myself was writing my novel, I was aware of the many ways in which my work might be received and critiqued, examined and mined, for meaning and critical analyses of technique. As I approached my writing project with increasing fervor and tenacity, the shadow of literary analysis peered over my shoulder as I sat at my computer. My work would be held to the same standards that in graduate school I'd learned to hold other texts to, literary standards. And in graduate school, and as I moved into teaching, I not only held texts to literary standards and analyzed them against those standards, but insisted on pushing beyond those standards to analyze the complexities inherent in those texts. Thus, without complexities having been addressed and explored by the writer herself when writing the work, the text cannot be examined, and would not be considered, as Bluestone refers to it, a reputable novel by any means. As frightening as it is to know your text will be explored, analyzed and critiqued, it is what a writer most desires: to put a piece "out there" to be discussed or even fought over, based on arguments made, supported convincingly and with precision. To perform such analysis of a text is required of scholars and taught to and encouraged in students of literature. I expound on the basics of literary analysis in this book, and touch on the more complex methodologies for approaching literary texts.

Interestingly, it was as I was becoming immersed in the intricacies of literary analysis that I came upon a novel that spoke to me. Through its author, I felt as if I'd discovered an individual with whom I connected when I was feeling isolated. Books and the study of books had always been my solace, but this book was an explanation, that also asked questions I needed answered. The mother of the author of *Frankenstein* inspired my novel. Mary Wollstonecraft died ten days after giving birth to Mary Shelley, leaving a novel she'd been working on unfinished. Both Mary Wollstonecraft's prose and fiction inspired my novel, but it was her unfinished novel, *Maria, or The Wrongs of Woman*, that made the greatest impression upon me. And, it was Mary Wollstonecraft's treatment by scholars and critics that first inspired my resistance to my own work, if published, being interpreted for and adapted to film.

This book of lit-to-film adaptation analysis starts at my beginning. I discuss how my novel came to be. Interestingly, and appropriately, it was an adaptation itself, a novel-to-novel adaptation. My novel became an adaptation of Mary Wollstonecraft's novel written two hundred years ago. However, that had not been my initial plan. Wollstonecraft had left her novel incomplete at her death, yet finished enough for her husband, William Godwin, to publish it; I wanted to "finish" it for her, bring it to completion. After further exploration and study of what doing so might mean and entail, both theoretically and physically, I changed direction and chose to adapt the novel and its subject matter to contemporary society. As my novel grew into this adaptation, it became its own being, its own text, yet was inspired by that previous text, and wouldn't have come to be the way it was without that previous text, and that previous writer, and her previous thought and what went into her thought. My novel brought the ideas put forth by an author two centuries ago into a contemporary setting, and the result was revealing and at times troublesome. Often I found myself wondering, how far have we come as a society in two hundred years, really?

Once I discovered *Maria*, and Mary Wollstonecraft herself, and then decided to adapt her text, I found it necessary to do a thorough analysis of the text, as thorough an analysis as I could manage. Since the novel was published as a fragment, approaching the novel from a poststructuralist perspective proved advantageous to understanding the vicissitudes of the text, many of which would be given no consideration under a more traditional examination of the text. As I explain in this book, however, this entire process of my own adaptation, which was conducted in a responsible, respectful manner especially through the use of poststructuralist theory, contradicts the use of that same theory to justify haphazard and often careless adaptation practices as a whole.

Several theoretical issues were raised as I tackled this adaptation. Many of the same issues also prompted the adaptation as well, and I explore these issues in some depth. The writing of the novel itself is detailed and examined, the process documented. I liken the writing of my novel, and any novel, to Victor Frankenstein piecing together his creature, or monster. Writing a novel is a different experience for every writer, but for all writers it is a creative process that brings together many elements that go into the text's making. My novel proved to be experimental in nature, addressing difficult subject matter in as delicate a way as could be achieved. Distinct parallels between Wollstonecraft's 1798 novel and my new millennium novel were constructed in a purposeful manner. The question I put forth was how much has actually changed for women, children, and men in the past two hundred years, considering that patriarchy still reigns as the system we abide by, no matter how many revolutions have been and continue to be carried out against it.

Once I'd completed the first draft of my novel, I went away from it for a while, a long while. I'd done quite a bit of revision with it, which had taught me valuable lessons on crafting a work of fiction. However, I wasn't ready to "bid my hideous progeny go forth" as Mary Shelley claimed she was, although she writes that in the introduction to her third, and much revised, edition of *Frankenstein*. In her case, she was bidding her progeny go forth *again*, while I wasn't ready to put it "out there" (or forth) a first time. As my work on the novel had consumed me for a few years, I needed a respite from it. I continued to work on it in intervals, and often to talk about it. And that's when it came — the question that prompted the most direct route to this book: "Who will be in the movie?" I humored the speaker, but began to cogitate on this idea with horror.

The idea of my work, my baby, being adapted to film kept me up at night. First of all, would someone interpreting my work for film understand all that had gone into its production? And, would they take the care and time that a responsible interpretation would require? But more importantly for me, would someone be as careful with my work as I'd been with *Maria*, when I myself was almost careless, when I myself had had to step back from another writer's novel I'd been so enthusiastic about that I was going to redress it for her, finish it for her, polish it for her? Yet as I'd proceeded instead with an adaptation of her novel to write my own contemporary version, I'd been cautious and meticulous, questioning the process as I went, as I wrote. I'd had mentors and colleagues to guide me and also keep me in check. Would the same consideration be given my own work, if it were adapted to film? And could it be?

Mentioning my novel to interested parties as time went by resulted in one individual's interest in attempting a screenplay for my novel. He was a newbie screenwriter with a dream of one day being a director. I figured, if nothing else, working with him would give me an idea of how a film adaptation of my novel might work. It became a trial run of sorts. It was through this process that I started exploring the idea of a marriage of media, when it came to literature and film, especially novel or short story and film. Could the adaptation process be a type of exchange, not only after the film was complete and from an analytical approach to both novel and film, but as the process was ongoing? Perhaps the screenwriter's work on my novel, as I continued to work on and revise it, could allow for both creative undertakings to benefit from the other, as a good marriage allows each individual of the union to do. However, the project turned into a disaster. What were meant to be discussions of my novel and his work on the screenplay ended up with him operating merely from our discussions of my novel, and not even one read-through of my novel, to write the screenplay. He insisted on changing the point of view of the novel to its opposite in the film, moving so far away from the work I'd done that I didn't think I'd ever consider my novel for film. Yet I knew that the subject matter of my novel could be translated to film, and I also felt strongly that what I'd written could reach a film audience in a different but equally effective way as the novel could. I didn't want to give up on film. I did want to, and did, however, give up on this particular screenwriter.

I knew that literary analysis, and the study of literature, demands of anything written a certain standard of quality for it to be taken seriously as literary art. Thus it follows that literary analysis based on theoretical questions and critical approaches governs not only how literary fiction is received and analyzed, but also in many ways how it is written. Having the concept of film thrown into the mix as I considered my novel and how it would be received, not only by readers and critics, but possibly by filmmakers, I wondered what exactly keeps filmmakers in check. Working with this first screenwriter had me in a quandary. Does anything keep filmmakers in check? Sure, I'd read the movie reviews in the *New York Times* on a weekly basis. Admittedly, though, I didn't know much about film when I was first introduced to the idea that my work could be adapted to film, if I allowed it and then if someone desired to do so. This first experience with a screenwriter motivated me to understand film and its inner workings. How could I give my work over, with any kind of confidence in doing so, to a medium about which I knew very little? Thus my next step was to research and learn about film. I explore and relate my findings in this book.

I discovered how a film is made, and the intense collaborative process by which a film is conceived and produced. One important element of filmmaking that becomes crucial for understanding it in the process of a film adaptation, especially from a novelist's perspective, is the writing of the screenplay. A screenplay can be an original endeavor, an idea completely conceived by the screenwriter, or it can come from a source text, as in the case of lit-to-film adaptation. The screenplay is the step taken between reading and interpreting the novel to designing, planning, and making the film.

The film itself, regardless of whether or not it is an adaptation, can be put together in a myriad of ways, using a plethora of various methods, the creative process being different from how a novel is made but a creative process nonetheless. A film has a narrative structure comprised of many scenes, arranged in a purposeful way, from a particular point of view.

There is the making of the film, but more importantly, there is what is referred to as film studies, a discipline devoted to the study, analysis, and theoretical exploration of film. Thus film is analyzed beyond a movie review level, and is held to equally as rigorous standards as is literature. What's important to make of all of this, then, is that filmmakers do have standards hovering about them as they put a film together, just as authors do when writing a novel. However, most of the constraints for filmmakers are different, and one more than any other: money. Although a profit margin is an author's concern, it is often an enemy that must be banished as the author writes. For many authors, even writing to publish can be seen as an enemy of art.

Although money can be seen as the enemy of a filmmaker, and the art of film, I suppose as well, in many cases with film, a profit margin must be embraced right from the beginning, or a film won't have a chance of being made. Independent film markets have relaxed this constraint somewhat, but not enough to free filmmakers from their dependence on financial means, inhibiting the creative process in ways that do not inhibit a writer. It must be said, however, that a writer can't write any more easily than a filmmaker can film if she doesn't have the necessary resources she needs to do so. The writer might not need the exorbitant funding that is required to make a film, yet resources are still necessary to write a novel. No evidence can be gathered to effectively argue my point here, but I contend that as many writers who could be significant authors are stymied by financial constraints as aspiring filmmakers who never get to make their dream film. Often, the resources an emerging writer requires are reserved for those writers who have been previously published or have proved their profitable worth in some way. Thus such constraints can stymie the writer from being experimentally creative in the same way they can a filmmaker, and experimental creativeness is undoubtedly how we progress into the future, not simply march.

Film, although obviously newer than literature (although only somewhat newer than the novel and about the same age as the short story), has become established as a text that can be examined, studied, analyzed, and doing so has become a discipline taught in academia. The discipline only has potential for more growth as media and communication studies intensify their advancement in academia as well, and we move further into an explosively expansive technological era.

The conclusion is easily made then: both literature and film are held to rigorous analytical and theoretical standards. Then, it follows that a work in either medium must be of sufficient worth to be studied and explored, held to the standards developed for analysis, and approached from different perspectives. Most creators working to produce their creations in either literature or film want their work remembered or discussed, and know that they must satisfy certain requirements for their work to be considered from an academic or elevated analytical perspective.

So at this point in my exploration, I felt at ease with my understanding of film, especially film as art, and it being held to certain standards for determination of quality and complexity. However, I hadn't brainstormed an idea that I'd envisioned for film. I'd envisioned it as a literary narrative. I'd traveled all this way, took time and a great deal of energy and all the resources I could muster, to bring to life the story that had grown out of all my hard work. And I'd brought it to "life" in the form of a novel. The question "Who will be in the movie?" was huge. A movie? But my story was made for a novel; how could it be turned into a film? Could it be, without the story being compromised, cheated, or cheapened? All this work I'd done could be handed to someone else; what would they do with it? And then the questions arose: what, in fact, keeps a lit-to-film adaptation in check? The problem I encountered in addressing this question was that when we move into film adaptation, and I refer here specifically to lit-to-film adaptation, the dynamics of the academic discourse become radically altered from the way literature and film are discussed. The most remarkable changes that I observed seem to result largely from the vicissitudes of various scholars' perspectives concerning film adaptation. For example, the terminology used to refer to different elements of film adaptation varies to the point of confusion for the individuals trying to understand it. In many ways, what I found while attempting to understand film adaptation, and especially lit-to-film adaptation, grew to be problematic, so much so that the question changed for me. What, in fact, *can* keep a lit-to-film adaptation in check? In other words, since this is not an area of study that is as developed as literary analysis or film analysis, what standards of analysis should be used or applied to keep a lit-to-film adaptation in check? That way, an adapter has standards hovering about him or her, as novelists and filmmakers do. And that way, critics and scholars have a consistent theoretical means for analyzing lit-to-film adaptations. Finally, lit-to-film adaptation analysis can be taught to students at various levels of ability.

It's necessary here to define my focus. Although film adaptation is a broad field, and a mass of many types of adaptations can be studied, adaptations that go back and forth — exchanging — in a wide array of directions, my focus is strictly confined to literature, primarily novels but also short stories, adapted to film. I focus on literature that has been written (although not necessarily published yet when snagged for film), and then is adapted for film, or as David Hare, the screenwriter for the film *The Hours* (adapted from the novel of the same name), asserts, is "reconceived" for film. Adaptation consumes hundreds of textual/intertextual relationships, and I will not even begin to take on the almost overwhelming concept of adaptation. I will concentrate exclusively on the adaptation of a novel or short story to/for film.

So, first viewing the process from inside of it, rather than on the outside from an analytical perspective, I continued to pursue the idea of the marriage of media when considering lit-to-film adaptation. As I did, though, it began to seem too limited. I studied the adaptation process of *The Hours*, and although the book and film were married in a manner by which they are both teachable together, and brilliant companions of each other, I had to recognize that each lit-to-film adaptation is unique. Not all could be viewed as strictly a marriage of media. Some adaptations I studied were more conflictual and confrontational of each other than indicative of a peaceful marriage, but by viewing the two of them together, their separateness and their connections, invaluable insights could be gained. I began to move away from the idea of the marriage of media, because it didn't seem an adequate means to refer to lit-to-film adaptations and their intricacies and diversities. I also found myself agreeing with Robert Stam in that the terminology used to refer to lit-to-film adaptations grew out of a striking parallel to the language of marriage, and how good or bad a marriage is. The most common terms to describe the efficacy of a lit-to-film adaptation had become based on the concepts of fidelity and infidelity, faithfulness and unfaithfulness, betrayal, violation, even desecration. As Stam states, "the conventional language of adaptation criticism has often been profoundly moralistic, rich in terms that imply that the cinema has somehow done a disservice to literature" (2005, 3). I disagree with Stam's assumption that the terms stem from the view that film has disgraced the literature, although this view does persist in particular ways amongst certain populations. However, since my initial response to understanding lit-to-film adaptation was to see the conjoining as a marriage of sorts, perhaps it isn't difficult to understand why these terms have been used to describe the initial perceptual view of a combination of literature and film in a film adaptation.

Yet, how do we make the standards for analyzing lit-to-film adaptations at least somewhat consistent across the board, and how do we develop these standards for analysis when scholars can't decide on a language from which to develop such standards? But most importantly, how do we move beyond the tendency of most lit-to-film adaptation scholars either to fervently or almost insidiously defend the part film plays in film adaptation?

I will explore the adroit yet often contradictory scholarship that abounds concerning lit-to-film adaptation. My approach is from that of a novelist not as defensive of the film aspect of lit-to-film adaptation as the adaptation scholars, but at the same time not willing to privilege the literature simply because it is seen as steeped in tradition. I see lit-to-film adaptation as an invariably useful means to teaching especially introductory students both literature and film, and introducing them to the way not only that texts can intersect and exchange with each other, but as students they can study these intersections and exchanges from outside the process, once the product is placed in their domain. I work to elude any bias. I will not defend film. I will not defend literature. I will try to be fair to those who invent, those who construct a text. I will safeguard the work I've put into my own text, but also safeguard the work that a filmmaker would put into an adaptation of my text. This book is not a means to relegate the literature or film to some higher place using adaptation studies as the vehicle. It is meant to help students understand the books they read that become films, and be able not merely to see one as better than the other, but to view both as texts they can examine and analyze.

Although I do understand the tendency for lit-to-film adaptation scholars to defend film, I have to wonder at their need to do so. If it weren't for literature, and its effect on film through lit-to-film adaptation, film would not have the standing it does now in the academy, or anywhere for that matter. Although Timothy Corrigan, in his essay "Literature On Screen, A History: In the Gap," falls into the trap of defending film, he elucidates his reader on the history of film adaptation, explaining that the adaptation of literature to film helped to raise the quality of film, and the quality of its audience:

> Identified in the early years of the twentieth century primarily with working-class and immigrant audiences of music halls and vaudevillian stages, the movies begin to adapt literary subjects to suggest and promote a kind of cultural uplift that would presumably curb many of the social and moral suspicions about their power over children, women, and the putatively educated. (Corrigan 2007, 34)

Corrigan goes on to describe the development of lit-to-film adaptations in the late '20s and early '30s when they became more popular due to the introduction of sound in 1927. At the same time, censorship grew more rigid as controls were placed on which literature could be adapted, depending on their subject matter. Thus classic literary adaptations became more frequent since the canonical status of the literature was more apt to protect filmmakers from the censors. Yet as this was happening, there began to be a struggle for legal and artistic rights amongst authors and auteurs (directors, filmmakers), which may have begun the wrestling that continues to occur in the discourse on lit-to-film adaptation. And Corrigan himself is caught up in this wrestling. In the introduction to his informative book, *Film and Literature: An Introduction and Reader*, he makes it clear how far film has come as he writes of viewing literature and film together:

> Whether because of its massive social impact, because of the aesthetic development of film art, or because of shifts in cultural literacy, the cinema now demands equal time and attention when we argue the relative value and meaning of movies and literature. (1999, 3)

This statement made by Corrigan has been reiterated so many times that it has hindered progression in adaptation studies, yet scholars argue the opposite. Most argue that not respecting film is what has slowed the progress of lit-to-film adaptation studies. However, more recent scholarship in literature and particularly film theory has been evolving and as a result, lit-to-film adaptation studies is experiencing a change as well.

Corrigan is certainly not the only scholar to assert a defense for film when engaging in a treatment of lit-to-film adaptation. Thomas Leitch, Brian McFarlane, and most influentially, Robert Stam, all can be equally intimidating and angering to an author of a novel suspected of potential for lit-to-film adaptation. I've found myself becoming defensive in turn as I'm reading these scholars. What about my novel? What about my story? What about all the time I've spent developing my story? And what about the time I spent struggling through the lived experience and hearing others' lived experiences that inspired my story? Does that not count for anything? Is it that once I write it down, not even publish it but write it down, it's fair game for film, a text is a text, and it can be opened up, raped, manipulated, and turned into a film that other scholars will vociferously defend, before it's even been seen or evaluated? Perhaps this line of thinking isn't exactly rational, or at the least scholarly, but it is honest. And, my reaction might be helpful in understanding a large number of people who become just as defensive of their reading of a novel or story that they then view as a film adaptation.

Thomas Leitch sets out in his essay "Twelve Fallacies in Contemporary Adaptation Theory" to argue that "adaptation theory has remained tangential to the thrust of film study because it has never been undertaken with conviction and theoretical rigor" (2003, 1). Yet the fallacies he explains to his reader are rooted in the differences between literature and film that have not been bridged mainly because the thinking on lit-to-film adaptation is focused on validating the film contribution to lit-to-film adaptation. Unfortunately then, the differences, and not the interconnection that whether either side wants to admit it or not has happened inevitably in a literature-to-film venture, take center stage in Leitch's essay. It's understandable when George Bluestone, for the first major treatment of lit-to-film adaptation, *Novels into Film*, writes:

> Like the drama, the film is a visual, verbal, and aural medium presented before a theater audience. Like the ballet, it relies heavily on movement and music. Like the novel, it usually presents a narrative depicting characters in a series of conflicts. Like painting, it is (except for stereoscopic film) two dimensional, composed of light and

shadow and sometimes color. But the ultimate definition of a thing lies in its unique qualities, and no sooner do we attend to the film's specific properties than differentiating characteristics begin to assert themselves. (1957, v–vi)

It's not as understandable in 2003 when Leitch's essay was first published, forty-seven years after Bluestone's work, that the thrust of the argument is still essentially the same. We should be much further along in this debate than we are.

Leitch isn't alone in this continuing argument growing quite old. Brian McFarlane, in his essay "Reading Film and Literature," begins his essay claiming to "dispose of some of the shibboleths that hover about the discourse, both popular and scholarly, relating to film-literature connections" (2007, 15). His efforts to do so are informative and interesting, though not exactly cutting edge, but his efforts ultimately result in a subtle defense of what film can do that novels can't, or what film can do that its viewers, mostly uninformed viewers of film adaptation, believe it can't. He even concludes the essay rather defensively, writing that "the most helpful discourse surrounding [the literature-film connection] may be one which, respecting the specificities of each, is concerned to explore how they deal with each other, rather than which came first and which is 'better' than the other" (28). I agree with him here, but in his essay, he doesn't address how they deal with each other, only how film is discriminated against in this so-called connection as he refers to it.

Robert Stam has been the most influential and probably effective in defending the medium of film. He has done so in ways that taint film adaptation analysis, taint it to disregard the importance of the source text, often that source text being the literature contribution to the adaptation. His poststructuralist approach to lit-to-film adaptation has become problematic in that this approach undermines the importance of the literary text and its contribution to a film based upon it. In Stam and Alessandro Raengo's *Literature and Film: A Guide to the Theory and Practice of Film Adaptation*, Stam writes:

> The poststructuralist interrogation of the unified subject . . . fissured the author as point of origin of art . . . Unlike new criticism's notions of organic unity, poststructuralist criticism emphasized the fissures, aporias, and excesses of the text. And if authors are fissured, fragmented, multi-discursive, hardly "present" even to themselves, the analyst may inquire, how can an adaptation communicate the "spirit" or "self-presence" of authorial intention? (2005, 9)

Although I myself most often rely on poststructuralist approaches to texts, and did so as I analyzed the novel-to-novel adaptation project I completed, Stam has helped me see the limitations of poststructuralism, and when it can be taken so far as to broaden the concept of meaning, or dilute it, to the point where it is difficult to discern any meaning at all. Stam shows that poststructuralism can open up texts in an almost abusive manner, to the point of degrading that which is original, and unique, and that which comes from one's unconscious or imagination, but also from years of observation, reflection, and research. Stam's view of poststructuralism almost seems to take on a rather Buddhist or Native American view, that we are all connected and thus texts are as well, in an unconscious manner that makes all texts common property of a universal collective. To view literary texts this way, to excuse adaptations of their responsibility to the texts on which they're based, is simply to encourage irresponsibility. Stam states that "if 'originality' in literature is downplayed, the 'offense' in 'betraying' that originality, for example through an 'unfaithful' adaptation, is that much the less grave" (Stam and Raengo 2005, 9). To misuse a theoretical approach to justify freedom in how we choose to use texts is an erroneous application of such theory. And as a writer of fiction, it makes me very uneasy. As a scholar, I don't find it any more comforting.

Christine Geraghty, in her *Now a Major Motion Picture: Film Applications of Literature and Drama*, expresses her reservations concerning Stam's approach to lit-to-film adaptation:

> The openness of Stam's approach is indeed productive, but it might lead to textual accounts that deliberately seek to escape the interpretative and social processes that work to pin down meaning at a particular point. This not only makes analysis almost impossible, given the number and fleetingness of possible associations and connections between texts, but also does not necessarily help our study of adaptations. (2008, 4)

Yet, Geraghty continues to explain in her introduction that she will focus her study on specific adaptations, and not concern herself with fidelity in these adaptations. That is, she contends that her emphasis is not on the process of adaptation but on the work of "recall," a concept put forth by Catherine Grant:

> This work of "recall" positions an adaptation precisely as an adaptation, and studying it involves both textual and contextual analysis. The adaptation might draw attention to its literary origins in its presentation of its own material, but the act of comparison invited by an adaptation might also draw on memories, understandings, and associations with other versions of the original, in a variety of media. (2008, 4)

Here, Geraghty seems to be struggling with how to avoid sizing up the novel and the film side by side, and her clarity of analysis is compromised. I will discuss this further, but how closely a film adaptation is to its original is of importance, and reveals textual and contextual clues that aid in analyzing the adaptation. This apparent need to avoid fidelity rather than embrace it only seems to confuse and conflate the actual practice of lit-to-film adaptation analysis. My aim here is to clarify this confusion, and help clear a pathway for students — all students, not only graduate students — to analyze lit-to-film adaptations so that the language to which they are introduced is easily digestible, and the concepts to which they apply this language are easily understandable. Amidst this confusion created by scholars in the field, I don't see that path being forged.

Geraghty does make another important point about Stam's contradictorily expansive but reductive approach to lit-to-film adaptation. She states that Stam's dependence on cultural theory to explore adaptation theory means he runs the risk of underplaying important features of adaptation, features she claims to explore in her study. Stam does seem to rest his laurels too easily on cultural studies, at a time when a new trend in theory, which includes challenging the concept of theory altogether, is moving theory away from cultural studies, and embracing new thought on literary and multitextual theory.

Despite the problems scholars are confronting as well as creating as they tackle lit-to-film adaptation theory, other issues arise as well. Not only is adaptation studies rife with a bias towards film that only seems to preach to the choir while alienating further any of those who also appreciate and perhaps favor the literature through habit in a lit-to-film adaptation. It is also rife with lofty language difficult for introductory students to understand, and to make matters worse, the language is often inconsistent from scholar to scholar. Scholars seem to use terms that fit their analysis of lit-to-film adaptation while teachers find it difficult (based on personal experience) to use material from different scholars' perspectives because time must be spent explaining why different terminology is used by the scholars to mean the same thing. The lofty language combined with the inconsistent language, combined with the complexity of what is being studied, make the material difficult to teach, and very difficult to learn. In fact, I haven't felt confident about teaching students lit-to-film adaptation in a way that can help them view it impartially, encouraging them to examine their bias against film and their preference for the literature, which is what needs to be accomplished. Certainly, scholars would agree that this is clearly an important goal when teaching lit-to-film adaptation and analytical approaches to the subject.

The lofty language used by many scholars, making lit-to-film adaptation studies inaccessible to introductory students and actually most undergraduates much less lay-people, can be easily identified in writings by Robert Stam, Thomas Leitch, and Kamilla Elliott. Although all have contributed crucial insights into film adaptation studies and theory, their studies aren't helpful in teaching adaptation studies to students in a way that they can understand. I attempt to translate some of their conclusions in this book, but have found myself being selective about what I use, and have felt much like an interpreter. In his introduction to *Literature and Film: A Guide to the Theory and Practice of Film Adaptation*, Robert Stam discusses a plethora of approaches to studying lit-to-film adaptation. However, introductory students, many of whom are not English majors nor will they ever be, but who can benefit from learning analytical approaches to literature made into film, do not have the background to digest and process such concepts as Gerard Genette's five categories of transtextuality (which Stam himself confuses in his explanation), an explanation of narratology and characterization that employs terms like various forms of analepses to types of diegesis. As I'm reading his work to determine how to translate it, I'm wracking my brain thinking there has got to be an easier way to explain lit-to-film adaptation. I mean, it doesn't have to be this fancy. I'm thinking, also, if this is the material I have to work with, I'm going to lose my students, and they'll say to me simply, "I like just saying the book is better." And where will that have gotten me, them, and anyone who makes up a part of this discourse?

Thomas Leitch, in his essay "Twelve Fallacies in Contemporary Adaptation Theory," doesn't present his material in quite as difficult a manner for introductory students to process, but his work still requires an already existing background in literary and film analysis, which introductory students usually haven't acquired and might not ever master in even a small way. Kamilla Elliott, in her book *Rethinking the Novel/Film*

Debate puts forth engaging thought on the issue at hand, but once again, not in a way that is teachable to the student I'm trying to reach. The student I'm trying to reach is the one who has just told me they like the book better, or in some cases and increasingly more common, the movie better, in a component of a first-year writing or introductory literary analysis course designed to introduce students to a new way of looking at literature and film, and mastering a rudimentary language for doing so.

An even more frustrating problem I've encountered with trying to teach lit-to-film adaptation, and lit-to-film adaptation analysis, is working with the texts that are meant to be for teaching such material. The difficulty is that each text devoted to introducing students to lit-to-film adaptation relies on different terminology. For example, for my first-year writing students last year, after having previously used Leitch and McFarlane without great success in getting through to my students, I used excerpts from both Linda Castanzo Cahir's *Literature into Film: Theory and Practical Approaches* and John Desmond and Peter Hawkes's *Adaptation: Studying Film and Literature*. Although both texts provided me with teachable material that could complement each other, their differing use of terminology confused my students. Cahir refers to lit-to-film adaptation as translation; the chapter I used was entitled "The Nature of Film Translation: Literal, Traditional, and Radical." I used a section of Desmond and Hawkes entitled "Film Adaptation: The Case of Apples and Oranges." They define and support their choice of terminology, explaining the parameters they rely on to categorize a film as a close adaptation, a loose adaptation, and an intermediate adaptation (2006, 44). Although Desmond and Hawkes are in agreement with Cahir on the approach to take when studying lit-to-film adaptation, their inconsistency in terminology makes their material difficult to teach, at least together.

My dilemma, however, is do I dare introduce more terms that might be different from what's already in existence? But I do dare, because I explain why I do, and try to do so in a way that takes a middle ground, a stance somewhere amidst the debate (as Elliott refers to it), to attempt to keep students out of the debate, and into the practice of analyzing lit-to-film adaptations, in class and then for future use beyond my class. From my perspective as a novelist, it might seem selfish. But that would be too quick of a judgment call to make. As a novelist, chances are that I would be the creator of the preferred text in an intertextual endeavor to make my novel into a film. I don't want to be preferred. I want both texts, both my novel and the film, to be understood. And, I expect both my novel, and thus the film, to be worthy of a detailed, painstaking analysis.

What I want to do in this book is help students, at the most introductory level, even high school, and laypeople, push their analytical skills beyond whether the novel or film is better in a lit-to-film adaptation, and analyze the book they've read and the film they've viewed, in a way that is interesting and insightful. I propose approaching such critical thought by thinking of it as intertextual comparison. Although issues of "fidelity" and "faithfulness" are a part of the analysis, I also eschew the use of those words for something that is a positive combination of skills and creativity into an entire process whose product is multiplicitous by its very nature. Instead, I see lit-to-film adaptation as, whether we like it or not, an exercise in comparison/contrast, if one is in fact viewing the adaptation as an explicit connection between two mediums. (And, perhaps the terms fidelity and faithfulness can be retained, and viewed as intellectual terminology rather than representative of the moral implications we give them in everyday society.) Thus, if one analyzes the novel alone, then this is through literary analysis. If one analyzes the film alone, then this should be solely through film analysis. But if the film is acknowledged as a lit-to-film adaptation, then an intertextual comparison is being acknowledged and the analysis of such must follow suit.

This to me is a good thing. Julie Sanders, in her book *Adaptation and Appropriation*, seems to be in agreement (or I with her) when she refers to the comparative nature of analyzing both adaptations and appropriations:

> Intellectual or scholarly examinations of this kind are not aimed at identifying "good" or "bad" adaptations. On what grounds, after all, could such a judgment be made? Fidelity to the original? . . . it is usually at the very point of infidelity that the most creative acts of adaptation and appropriation take place . . . Adaptation studies are, then, not about making polarized value judgments, but about analyzing process, ideology, and methodology. (2006, 20)

I attempt in this book to take Sanders's approach to adaptation. It is about comparison and contrast of the two texts that comprise the entire process/product of lit-to-film adaptation. To try and circumvent this fact seems to benefit no one. To embrace this reality is to embark on a fascinating, and dare I say "fun" exploration into, in this case, two mediums working together to achieve a desired effect, which is often up to the reader/viewer/analyzer to recognize and/or reconcile. And I agree wholeheartedly with Sanders when she states that "it is the very endurance and survival of the source text that enables the ongoing process of juxtaposed readings that are crucial to the cultural operations of adaptation, and the ongoing experiences of pleasure for the reader or spectator in tracing the intertextual relationships" (25). That is, it's important not to dismiss the source text in approaching lit-to-film adaptation analysis, for purposes of analysis. Moreover, it's important that students be encouraged to explore the intertextual dynamics of adaptation study without feeling compelled to defend the literature due to its disappearance in methodologies some scholars encourage when approaching adaptation studies.

Note: At the writing, i.e. completion, of this book, I've summoned up the courage to put forth my novel, with trepidation, and allow it to be read and considered by various publishers. Whether it's published by an outside company or self-published, it will be available under my pen name, Merre Larkin, and excerpts will be available on my website: www.merrelarkin.com.

Part One

The Creation and Study of Literature

Chapter 1

Premeditation

That's where this story begins. Actually, that isn't where the story in my novel began. Most stories, when written, begin somewhere in the middle of it all; it's referred to as *in media res*. I began my novel somewhere towards the end of the actual story it would relate. But my story behind the novel began with "Premeditation," the title of a short story I wrote, and with no premeditation whatsoever as to its becoming the first step towards my novel.

My history as a writer is probably unusual, or maybe simply unique. I never was known to have said that when I grew up I wanted to be a writer. I read all the time, would hide in my room at twelve years old, away from my four younger siblings, and traditionally present parents. I was the only one with my own room, since I was a girl followed by two brothers, then two sisters, so it was a haven for escape, and convenient for reading. Yet with all the reading I did, I never said to myself, wow I want to write something like this someday.

My mother tells me that in second grade my teacher told her to keep me writing, that I was very adept at creative writing. Writing did always come easily for me, but I would dread sitting down to it so much that I thought it wasn't for me. (I didn't know this is how writing is, but it is. The pain is in sitting down, plowing through; the ecstasy is in knowing you've done so.) Unfortunately, or not, I also was quite proficient in math. I performed equally well in both my verbal and math SAT scores. I excelled in academics in all subjects, got accepted early decision to a prestigious college, and off I went into the engineering program at that school. With my father guiding me, I wasn't encouraged to think about what I loved to do (even though I wouldn't have chosen writing at that point anyway), but rather what I was skilled at that would give me the most financial security upon graduation.

I'm providing this information because this is, and I've found it to be effective when done thoughtfully and purposefully, how I teach. I let my students know where I'm coming from when I'm teaching them. It opens up an environment of sharing thoughts and ideas, and in a literature and/or writing classroom, this is a necessity. I am their conduit to the knowledge I'm disseminating. They deserve to know the terrain of that conduit, so they can navigate through it in a way that is comfortable for them. Since I view you as my student, I'm explaining the terrain through which you're moving.

I graduated from college in chemical engineering and sociology. As I continued through college, circumstances and yearnings guided me towards inputting more writing into my engineering curriculum. Basically, my dad was paying, and I had to stay in engineering because I was satisfying the requirements necessary to succeed in it. My desire for it was waning. A sociology course fascinated me, and I chose to do the five-year engineering and liberal arts program, my father agreeing so I'd stay with engineering. The writing for my sociology major, and the electives I could take, were what urged me to finish my degree with enthusiasm (I tolerated the engineering part of it).

I interviewed for a chemical engineering position in California. They liked me, but not for the job they had available. They told me I didn't want the job, they could tell (so different from my father). They sent me to another department in the company, and I got a job as a research analyst, writing reports for companies on various technologies. I liked it and learned a lot. When I left the job to parent full-time, I immediately became bored out of my mind and started writing in a journal, then going to the library with my daughter in a Snugli, supplementing my journal writing with books I would read and then write about in my journal. This led to freelance writing, private jaunts into poetry, and even a few stabs at starting a book, all nonfiction. One was going to change the world of politics in our country.

As my life continued, several things happened to me and around me, as is the case with all of us I suppose, but I couldn't speak about it. The words wouldn't come. Other words would, but not the ones that reached in to release what I needed to communicate, to express myself so that others would know me and recognize me. This was when, by some strange twist of fate inside myself, I began to write fiction. I didn't write autobiographical stories, either. I didn't simply turn incidents in my life into "fiction." What I did was gather up what was going on inside of me and what was going on outside of me, my reflections and observations etched quietly in the private recesses of my mind, and poured all of it out into stories. Some of them were quite awful. Some of them had potential. I see this now, but when I began, I wrote them to express myself. The only act I can compare it to is being given a bunch of tubes of oil or acrylic paints, a palette to mix them up on, and a ton of canvases, and going crazy with colors and shapes and images. Then you come to this realization that you might actually be kind of good at this, without meaning to be.

In October of 1998, I was at the height of processing a change in my life and inside myself, and couldn't explain it to anyone. I was seeing the world through new eyes, and I was discovering all that I'd been and hidden away was free to come out, but I didn't know how to do it. Although I was seeing the world through new eyes, the world was pretty much the same, only I was facing it head on. And in the midst of the turmoil that comes with facing the truth of a lie lived out a bit too long, I wrote the story, "Premeditation." This is how it began, again in the middle of things:

I haven't seen my mother in four years. I'm in the car, on my way to visit her. I'm scared. We write letters to each other. Sometimes, not too often, we talk on the phone. It's hard to hear her voice. It reminds me of all that I've lost, especially her. Sometimes I send her copies of these little tapes I make, my memoir tapes. She's the only one who knows about them. She always writes back how much she enjoys hearing my thoughts and reveries. It makes me feel good when she does.

Callie is the character who is narrating from the first person perspective. She's going to visit her mother in prison. This is the beginning of how my novel came to be. This is also the beginning of how I came to consider myself a novelist. The story I originally wrote was 1,500 words long, so full and unfocused though that it could only be handled by the scope of a novel. I'd written a very different story the year before for a creative writing workshop, and the members of the group and instructor liked the story but critiqued its inadequacy as a short story, all agreeing that it would only work as a novel because it had too much in it to satisfy the short story genre.

In that same workshop, I expressed to the group that I didn't know why I was there, since I wasn't properly trained to be a writer, but that I wanted to be there. I shared my chemical engineering background apologetically. The instructor quickly corrected me, with an enthusiasm that I have to say altered my stance considerably, "Engineering is excellent training for writing a novel!" She went on about formulas, equations, and flowcharts. Interestingly, she ended up being right. When I completed my novel, and a mentor began to examine it to decide how to guide me in revision, she told me the organization of the novel was impeccable. Nothing needed to be changed there, but the crafting of it was where I needed to direct my efforts.

Another short story followed quickly behind "Premeditation," which I entitled "Day After Night." It begins:

> I run. Faster than I thought I could. My adrenaline kicks in, on overdrive. Fear drives me, to an unknown destination I hope will be better than from where I have come. It has to be.

The narrator of this story, and main character, becomes the close friend and fellow inmate of the mother of Callie in "Premeditation." And from there, I created my novel as it came to me, and as I came to it.

I didn't plan to grow up to be a writer, or a novelist. I didn't even plan to be a teacher. But that's what happened. As Hélène Cixous encourages in her essay "Coming to Writing," sometimes we just have to let ourselves go. And we'll get *there*.

> Let yourself go! Let go of everything! Lose everything! Take to the air. Take to the open sea. Take to letters. Listen: nothing is found. Nothing is lost. Everything remains to be sought. Go, fly, swim, bound, descend, cross, love the unknown, love the uncertain, love what has not yet been seen, love no one, love whom you are, whom you will be, leave yourself, shrug off the old lies, *dare what you don't dare*, it is there that you will take pleasure, never make your here anywhere but *there*, and rejoice, rejoice in the terror, follow it where you're afraid to go, go ahead, take the plunge, you're on the right trail! (1991, 40)

Chapter 2

On Literary Creation

Invention, it must be humbly admitted, does not consist in creating out of void, but out of chaos; the materials must, in the first place, be afforded: it can give form to dark, shapeless substances, but cannot bring into being the substance itself . . . Invention consists in the capacity of seizing on the capabilities of a subject: and in the power of moulding and fashioning ideas suggested to it.

(Shelley 1992, 8)

I want to be clear about literary creation. It will be important for a full understanding and appreciation of lit-to-film adaptation. Although it seems to be assumed that the literary part of the transaction that occurs in lit-to-film adaptation is understood, as a novelist, I believe it deserves more time and attention than it's received in most lit-to-film adaptation discussions. There is no one way to write a novel, but all novelists or authors work diligently at it, and map out their own strategy for doing so. The maps might be vastly different, but they are maps nonetheless. They might be in the form of an ornate flow chart, or they could be notes on scrap pieces of paper. There's a strategy, and there's a process. To exemplify how complex and multiplicitous this process can be, I will discuss my own process in writing my novel. It is one of which I am intimately cognitive, although it will not be repeated when I write another novel. Even as each writer has a unique creative process, so each novel requires, and perhaps each piece of literature in circulation has required, a different literary creation process. I will detail my process for the novel that inspired the writing of this book in particular.

When I first began to take my writing seriously, I believed that the creative process came strictly from within myself. My imagination would conjure up an idea, and free-flow writing would allow my imagination to soar into a poem or short story. My naïve belief about the creative process of writing was dramatically altered when I began to write a novel. I discovered that creation does not only come from one's imagination, and we as writers and artists do not create in a vacuum. Yet to explain the creation of a novel or any work of art proves to be a complex endeavor. Just when it seems as if the concept of creation has been captured by language and explained, the inadequacies of the explanation begin to unravel. In attempting to capture the creative process in words, one can only come close to its full dimensions, and learn to accept that there will always be facets of creation that will seem unreachable and inexplicable.

However, words are all I have to chronicle an exploration into writing, so I will try. In the following, I explore the many elements of literary creation that I encountered in writing my novel, and the influences that affected its production: imagination, lived experience, literary influences, critical analysis, strategy, cultural influences, the determination of the novel's organization and structure, and revision.

Throughout the three years that I worked on my novel, consumed as I'd been with the conception and organization of the different elements of my work, I could well liken myself to Victor Frankenstein and the creation of his monster in Mary Shelley's novel. He stitched together different body parts that he gathered from various sources to create a human being, the perfect human being. My monster, this novel, rendered me at times almost as obsessed as Frankenstein was with his act of creation. I worked late into the night, with a passion I had never before experienced. Frankenstein's passion, though, grew into an unhealthy obsession:

> I pursued my undertaking with unremitting ardour. My cheek had grown pale with study, and my person had become emaciated with confinement. Sometimes, on the very brink of certainty, I failed; yet still I clung to the hope which the next day or the next hour might realise. One secret which I alone possessed was the hope to which I had dedicated myself; and the moon gazed on my midnight labours, while, with unrelaxed and breathless eagerness, I pursued nature to her hiding-places. (Shelley 1992, 53)

Frankenstein seemed to find creation painful; I found creation to be painfully blissful, much like giving birth to a child. I must confess, though, that when I completed the first draft of my novel, I thought I would feel a joy and immense sense of accomplishment, yet the process had been so draining, and the creation itself so overwhelming, that the novel went neglected for months upon its completion. I walked away from it, much like Frankenstein turned away from the being he had created. He was afraid of it, as he relates: "[The monster] might have spoken, but I did not hear; one hand was stretched out, seemingly to detain me, but I escaped, and rushed downstairs" (57).

When a mother gives birth and holds her infant for the first time, she is elated until it begins to cry and she needs to feed it. This is the beginning of the creator's fear — the fear that comes with responsibility for another life. I have been frightened by my own artistic hideous progeny, but while Frankenstein abandoned his creation in horror, most mothers do not abandon their children. They push beyond their fear to learn how to take care of the child. Similarly, I pushed past my apprehension about what I had created to begin to nurture it and craft it into a worthy piece of art. Trying to understand the process of creation, especially through critical analysis, helped me to continue with my writing and revision of the novel.

How does creation happen? How did my novel come to be? Just as Frankenstein's interest in creation led him to create a human being, my interest in the creation of words and sentences, narrative, a text, a being, prompted me to write my novel. Frankenstein began with his study of and fascination with the sciences. I began with the study of Mary Wollstonecraft's fragment, *Maria, or The Wrongs of Woman*, which was left unfinished at the time of her death. It is perhaps no surprise that *Frankenstein* should come to mind as the most immediate metaphor for my own act of creation, for not only did Wollstonecraft leave *Maria* behind after her death, but she also left behind a new-born. Perhaps Mary Shelley was left as a "fragment" as well after her mother's death, and thus later pursued an understanding of creation and the consequences of neglecting that creation through the writing of *Frankenstein*.

My first inclination was to heal such wounds by an attempt to "complete" Wollstonecraft's *Maria*. Many writers and even editors have done this with none of the qualms I developed as I thought more seriously about finishing a work that wasn't mine to finish. Decidedly, I did not feel justified in performing this task, and instead, chose to adapt Wollstonecraft's novel to my own, bringing the subject and a similar structure to contemporary society and writing. Thus began my novel-to-novel adaptation.

I still wasn't sure as to how I would go about this adaptation. Once I'd decided to write my own novel, my next plan of action was to intersperse chapters of *Maria*, finished, with my own chapters, and interconnect them, showing how the present reflected the past. I was discouraged by a more experienced writer, a mentor, from attempting this endeavor as the product would have been too long and disjointed.

As I've said, my novel grew out of two short stories, each portraying two women in each story who become friends in my novel. This friendship became the driving force of the plot, in a quiet, unobtrusive manner. These two short stories that began the novel, however, played only a small role in the creation of the entire text. The text became a Frankensteinian patchwork of many different parts that led to a whole.

My final plan for my novel became, then, to write my own novel with a contemporary setting, adapting it from Wollstonecraft's *Maria*, and using excerpts from *Maria* to enhance my own writing. In using *Maria*, I also desired to bring *Maria* into fuller view of academicians and critics. However, what began as an adaptation of *Maria*, as well as a combination of my work with Wollstonecraft's work, also developed into my own quest to understand the process of creation. I intended to embark on a new way to create a novel, and in so doing, discover the many intricacies of creation, not only by writing a novel, but by studying the work of a novelist before me to more effectively and adequately adapt her story to the contemporary setting of my story. I hoped, along with my Romantic predecessor, Victor Frankenstein, to ". . . [tread] in the steps already marked, [and] . . . pioneer a new way, explore unknown powers, and unfold to the world the deepest mysteries of creation" (Shelley 1992, 47).

What I discovered throughout this project were the infinite means available for creating a work. We as writers are often unaware of the influences affecting the creation of our texts. I mapped out a strategy for my work by outlining each chapter of the novel, proceeding in various order, and filling in the gaps as I wrote. I often consulted with objective, experienced mentors who would help me uncover gaps I had missed in my work and continue on the path to accomplishing my creation. But while I had a clearly defined strategy, my lived experience not only as a woman but predominantly as a human being, influenced my work. This included my lived experience as a student, a writer, a mother, a daughter, a friend, a woman, and a person. Yet as I was writing, and working on an analysis of Wollstonecraft's writing as well, I encountered contemporary critics who questioned the quality of Wollstonecraft's work using her lived experience as a weapon against her. It was an awakening for me in the twentieth century to stumble upon contemporary critics with unjust demands of women's writing and writings. I began to find that women writers were often held up to impossible standards in their writing. If women's lives did not reflect their writing, then their writing was considered ineffectual and inaccurate. However, if women's writing was judged to reflect their lives too closely, it was then discredited for its lack of originality, and dismissed as autobiographical.

This is a subject I will explore in some depth, to represent the vulnerabilities of marginalized populations represented in writing, and marginalized populations writing, women being only one of these populations, but an important one in that they do constitute half of the human race, yet seem to proffer still today much less consideration from the outset as men attain as writers. And this is a subject that has great bearing on adaptation. I was a woman adapting another woman's work, and I had to be attentive to what I was doing, due to the discrimination that occurs with women's writing, a much newer phenomenon than men's writing. Adaptation is a complex operation and cannot be simplified and minimized as it has been allowed to be. It must be fully examined, and held up to the light to do so. It can be done in lesser degrees but when one extensive project taken on by someone is then re-taken on by another, for a different purpose or medium, it must be done with care, thoughtfulness, responsibility, and a respect for the originator and source text.

The unfair expectations that I encountered in the criticism of women's writing seemed to stem from a lack of understanding about women's lived experience. Women's lived experience is as full and broad as men's lived experience, but it is often assumed that one woman's experience is so similar to another's as to simply link them together as the same. I also found in the world of literature, even today, a tendency to disregard women's ability to reason, and to strategize. Thus, to defend women's writing against a hegemonic thinking that continues to dismiss or diminish it, my quest for understanding the underworld of creation became a greater concern for me. All writing has a strategy, I reasoned, even women's writing. Because of the limited knowledge perhaps of women's lived experience, women's writing can seem to mirror their lived experience; yet as I have said, all lived experience is much too complex to be replicated. Even creative nonfiction represents a writer's perception of their own lives, still open to interpretation. To dismiss a fictional novel as simply a writer's personal experience seems ludicrous to me. Lived experience is part of the stitching together of a creation of fiction, a piece of the monster.

My own strategy was based on my reading of Wollstonecraft and other writers. As I would sit down to write with my strategy outlined and lying next to me, my imagination, or unconscious, would dominate at times and lead me in directions I had not planned to take. Wollstonecraft's life and philosophy, other women's lived experiences, other men's lived experiences, research on sexual abuse, rape, and murder, and my critical analysis of *Maria* and *Frankenstein* filtered into the creation of my work. In short, my lived experience as well as my imagination contributed to the creation of my novel. Throughout the writing of the novel, and its continued revision, I worked from a strategy and had a vision of what I wanted the novel to achieve. Part of the strategy of the creation, for me, was to remember that each reader will bring her or his lived experience to the reading of the novel, and I wanted to encourage as diversified and individual an interpretation of the text as I could. I did not begin this way. In the beginning, I wanted the reader to see it my way. However, through my study of creation, I realized that even the creator of a text cannot fully control how the text develops. Once a creator accepts this, her creation does not seem so overwhelming. Victor Frankenstein shows us that controlling another being or a text proves to be an elusive and often dangerous endeavor. Arguably, it was Frankenstein's need to control his monster without providing the nurturing and care that it required, and his fear of his creation, that led to the destruction of so many lives, and his deep regret for ever having created such a beast.

Interestingly, after completing my novel, I felt more of an affinity with the creator of the novel *Frankenstein*, Mary Shelley, than with the fictive Victor Frankenstein. Although I was initially overwhelmed with my creation upon completion, I soon returned to it with an open mind, nurturing and caring for what I had done. The most important aspect of creation neglected by Victor Frankenstein was the revision of his "project." If he, perhaps, had spent the time beyond the initial creation, and crafted his creation into a refined, accomplished being, Frankenstein's monster might have been a benevolent "monster," and an asset to society. In the final stage of my project, I began necessary but tedious re-visioning of my creation — revisions that attempted to reach my acquired vision of excellence. This might be the most crucial element of literary creation. I believe the reckless actions of Frankenstein's monster signal a great need for continued creation beyond the first sparks of life in a creative project, and this was indeed one of Shelley's "points" in her work.

When my novel has reached what I consider to be its completion, like Shelley, I will "bid my hideous progeny go forth and prosper" (Shelley 1992, 10), for despite the fears and anxieties encountered in its production, I too "have an affection for it" (Shelley 1996, 10). However, I must add here a point that I will explore further as I move forward, that the possibility of my own work being adapted unnerves me and I question today what our contemporary understanding is of allowing our work to "go forth and prosper." I also must wonder as to what Shelley's views would be on how her *Frankenstein* has been brought forth and led others to prosper.

Chapter 3

Before the Beginning: Understanding the Study of Literature to Understand the Role of Literature in Our Lives

It's important to understand how we've gotten to here, where we are today with literature and its impact on our lives. There was a time, for centuries in fact, when only a select few studied literature, and by very loose rules, if any. We went through a time when the rules became quite rigid, and then towards the latter part of the twentieth century these rules gradually were challenged and opened up into a myriad of ways of looking at and studying literature. Literary theory, as it's called, burgeoned until perhaps a decade ago, and we're currently in a quandary of where to go from here. Yet what I mean by quandary is mostly how to incorporate all that has gone before into a comprehensible study for today's needs and desires.

What is literary theory? Although it sounds intimidating, and literary theory itself can be quite intimidating, it most simply represents the body of knowledge that examines how we look at literature, how we study literature. And, thanks to the literary theorists, the term literature itself has come to encompass more than the "greats" and has been opened up to include a multitude of different forms and genres of texts. Terry Eagleton, in the preface to his anniversary edition of *Literary Theory: An Introduction*, explains the use of theory, and the distinction between literary theory and literary criticism:

> Rather than simply providing new methods for the study of literary works, [theory] asks about the nature and function of literature and the literary institution . . . Its aim is not just to help us to see what literary works mean, or how valuable they are; instead, it queries our commonsense notions of what it is to "mean" in the first place, and poses questions about the criteria by which we evaluate literary art. (2008, viii)

Steven Lynn, in his *Texts and Contexts*, agrees and puts it much more simply, "Theory enables practice" (1998, xviii). Theory provides us as literary analysts or critics the

31

means by which to look at literature and approach it in an effort to interpret it and understand what it might be saying to us. Even seeing a work as boring, Lynn says, is taking a stance on it, one based in how entertaining the work is, but a stance nonetheless. That stance probably won't get one far in writing a sound analytical paper. However, it is a place to start, a beginning to a response that can lead to an analysis based in theoretical stances that push beyond entertainment to uncovering intricacies of the text and its contexts. And, when pushed further, the exploration can become increasingly interesting.

Before English and the study of literature became an established discipline, and surprisingly to most, this didn't occur until the end of the nineteenth century, philosophers, critics, educators, and authors were writing about writing since ancient times, long before it was considered "theory." A few key individuals need to be mentioned since their work helped to guide the incipience of literary theory and its progression.

Aristotle's *Poetics* (fourth century BC) is considered the earliest work of theory. It questions the nature of literature itself, and puts forth famous definitions of tragedy. In this work Aristotle insists that literature is about character and that character is revealed through action. He identifies what he considers to be the required stages in the progress of a plot. Aristotle was first to develop an approach to literature that was focused on the reader, which stemmed from his preoccupation with drama and how it was viewed from the perspective of the audience and how it moved them.

Sir Philip Sidney's *A Defence of Poesie* (1580), also called *An Apology for Poetry*, was the first work in English writing to address literature. Sidney draws from Ovid (43 BC–AD 17), who believed in teaching through delighting or by giving pleasure, and from Horace (65–8 BC), who believed that a poem was a "speaking picture" meant to instruct and delight at the same time. Interestingly, the idea of a poem being referred to as a speaking picture in the time of Horace foreshadows quite long ago the idea of literature-to-film adaptation, or so it can be seen as such. As we are moving through an understanding of literature and literary study, I will point out the language that foreshadows and even might explain why, when film arrived on the scene, it wasn't much of a leap to begin adapting already established literature to that medium. Yet it's crucial to explore where that simple notion has led us.

In his *A Defence of Poesie*, Sidney privileges literature above other forms of writing, and his defense of literature is very convincing. He criticizes the beliefs of his time that learning was best achieved through the study of history, philosophy, law, and medicine, and instead insists that literature teaches through example. The poet shows while the philosopher tells, and we remember what the poet showed us while we forget what the philosopher told us. Sidney also believes in learning best while having fun, or being moved, doing so. Poetry, or literature, is as Sidney puts it, "delightfull teaching." Those resistant to learning through study, those not destined to be scholars, can learn what is important through poetry and literature. Sidney then privileges active learning over passive learning, and considers literature an exercise in active learning.

It's important to note that since Sidney is writing about literature in general, and doesn't write about individual works or writers, his work is considered to be critical theory. Writing about individual texts began after Sidney. Thus critical theory came before practical criticism. Samuel Johnson, a British writer of the eighteenth century, was the first to publish detailed commentary on the work of a single author. Before him, only the Bible and other religious texts had been subjected to any kind of intense examination.

However, after Johnson, the Romantic writers ushered in a burgeoning preoccupation with critical theory, or the study of how literature is created and received. They also dabbled, and effectively, in literary (or practical) criticism, analyzing the works of each other and those outside of their circle as well. William Wordsworth's preface to the *Lyrical Ballads* in 1800 is considered to be, according to Peter Barry in *Beginning Theory*, "one of a number of significant critical works in literary theory whose immediate aim is to provide a rationale for the critic's own poetic work, and to educate audiences for it" (Barry 2009, 22–3). Wordsworth's poetry directly challenged what had previously been considered the accepted style and subjects for poetry, and he wrote his preface to prepare his audience for his revolution in poetics, claiming to be a "man writing to men" and justifying the use of a more accessible language for readers of his poetry.

Although Samuel Taylor Coleridge worked closely with Wordsworth as they began their literary careers, later in their lives Coleridge began to disagree publicly with Wordsworth, claiming that literature should entertain through its fictional, or fantastical, qualities, and should produce an aesthetic effect. He didn't believe in Wordsworth's insistence that poetry should be closer to the language of prose.

The younger Romantic poet, Percy Shelley, following on the heels of Wordsworth and Coleridge, put forth his *A Defence of Poetry* in 1821, which emphasizes that poetry "compels us to feel that which we perceive, and to imagine that which we know" (quoted in Barry 2009, 23). He focuses on not only how poetry is created but the nature of the poet. He privileges poets as the "best and happiest minds," and the "unacknowledged legislators of the World" (Damrosch and Dettmar 2006, 876). In many ways, he is in agreement with Sidney, but arguing against his own generation as "a culture now dominated by science and industry" (872) that doesn't give poets their just due. The poet, he says, is a "nightingale, who sits in the darkness and sings to cheer its own solitude with sweet sounds" (870). Although Shelley never finished his essay, it anticipates future work in literary theory, most interestingly, Freud's notion of the mind made up of conscious and unconscious elements.

T. S. Eliot's "Tradition and the Individual Talent" continues Shelley's thoughts, bringing them into the foray of critical theory as it's begun to be recorded and discussed, and argued amongst not merely a select few any longer. Eliot's piece distinguishes between the author, or the person behind the work, and the writer, or the person in the work. Eliot believes that the greater the separation can be between these two aspects of the individual who creates the work, "the more completely separate in him will be the man who suffers and the mind which creates" (2000, 94). We will return to this piece quite often as we proceed through literature and film and then make our way into lit-to-film adaptation. It's interesting, though, to note that Eliot responds to the thoughts of Shelley, a hundred years earlier, who states in his *A Defence* that

the mind in creation is a fading coal, which some invisible influence, like an inconstant wind, awakens to transitory brightness; this power arises from within, like the

colour of a flower, which fades and changes as it is developed, and the conscious portion of our natures are unprophetic either of its approach or of its departure. (quoted
in Barry 2009, 24)

John Keats, another Romantic poet, and friend of Percy Shelley, didn't write literary theory in the way Wordsworth, Coleridge, and Shelley did, but he pondered the
nature and dynamics of literature in his letters. He inserts his thoughts on the unconscious, much like Shelley had, in a letter to Bailey of November 22, 1817, stating how
"the simple imaginative Mind may have its rewards in the repetition of its own silent
Working coming continually on the Spirit with a fine suddenness." Keats also wrote of
the concept of negative capability, which we now associate with the unconscious, or as
he put it, "when a man is capable of being in uncertainties, mysteries, doubts without
any irritable reaching after fact and reason" (quoted in Barry 2009, 24).

Thus the critical writings of the Romantics exerted a considerable influence on the
concerns of critical theory as they developed into where we are today, as can be seen
in the essay by Eliot mentioned above. Eliot, then, a pioneer of literary theory locating
its place in the academy, draws from the critical theory written before it was so named.
The history of the study of English had been developing for centuries before it began
to be institutionally situated, towards the end of the nineteenth century.

The Rise of English, Leading to the Rise of Literary Theory

Liberal humanism, or humanism, is the term given to refer to the kind of criticism that
was used to approach literature before theory. This type of criticism is closely related to
other forms of criticism, including formalism and New Criticism. But first, it's helpful
to know how English developed as an academic subject to be able to understand how
liberal humanism came to be, which led to literary theory, comprising many different,
and often opposing, kinds of criticism used to view literature.

In their introductory texts to literary theory, both Peter Barry in *Beginning Theory*
and Terry Eagleton in *Literary Theory* explain the development of English as a discipline. How the discipline began and evolved isn't only important to understand how
literary theory came to be considered an entity all of its own, but it also shows how a
discipline comes into being, and the arbitrary nature of how that occurs, with several
outside influences working at it. This process of a discipline being established has
also occurred in the much younger discipline of film studies, and we will be exploring
that as well when we come to film. A new discipline might also be in development,
although it is difficult to know that now, since we are in its midst, and that might be
lit-to-film adaptation studies.

Higher education in England up until the first quarter of the nineteenth century was
what Barry refers to as a Church of England monopoly. There were two universities,
Oxford and Cambridge, divided into smaller colleges that were run like monasteries.
Only men could attend, and obviously then only men could be instructors, who were
ordained ministers, unmarried, and residents of the college. Thus, up until the 1820s,
the way higher education was organized hadn't changed since the Middle Ages.

Not that there weren't attempts to change it, but they were met with conservative forces working against them, until 1826 when the University College was established in London, "with a charter to award degrees to men and women of all religions or none" (Barry 2009, 12). The study of the English language was first taught in 1828. English literature was first taught in 1831, the same year that the third and final edition of Mary Shelley's *Frankenstein* was published. Interestingly, the 1831 version was taught most often in the twentieth century, but many instructors have now returned to the first edition of the novel, published in 1818. Besides the delay in the text of a woman being given the credit it was due by literary scholars, perhaps its placement in history prior to the official teaching of English literature contributed to the delay as well.

F. D. Maurice was appointed Professor in 1840 of the recently established King's College in London, and his inaugural lecture incited the humanistic view of looking at literature. He stated in his address that the study of English would "emancipate" individuals from their own time period, the one in which he was speaking, and connect them instead with "what is fixed and enduring." Maurice saw literature as the property of the middle class and the expression of their values. For him, the middle class was where the heart of society lay, the aristocracy were part of an international elite and the poor had to focus on everyday survival. He believed a middle-class education should focus on English, and thus English literature, and in so doing, encourage a sense of belonging, a sense of country (Barry 2009, 13).

In many ways, the study of English literature began to serve as a substitute for the way in which religion united — and controlled — people, but no longer was able to do so. In fact, as Terry Eagleton states, "If one were asked to provide a single explanation for the growth of English studies in the later nineteenth century, one could do worse than reply: 'the failure of religion'" (2008, 20). However, Barry doesn't accept

> the simplistic view that the founders of English were motivated by a desire for ideological control. This was undoubtedly one of their motives, but the reality was much more complicated. There was, behind the teaching of early English, a distinctly Victorian mixture of class guilt about social inequalities, a genuine desire to improve things for everybody, and a kind of missionary zeal to spread culture and enlightenment, and a self-interested desire to maintain social stability. (Barry 2009, 13)

Regardless of the motivations, English as a discipline was gaining support, even though the first attempt to establish a Chair in English was defeated in 1887. A speech against the Chair being granted was given by the Professor of History, Edward Freeman, and was a leading factor in the defeat. Freeman stated in his speech:

> We are told that the study of literature "cultivates the taste, educates the sympathies and enlarges the mind". These are all excellent things, only we cannot examine tastes and sympathies. Examiners must have technical and positive information to examine. (quoted in Barry 2009, 14)

Barry writes here that this is a problem that really hasn't been solved in English, so Freeman had a point. The concession for the English Chair to be established was that the study of literature had to include the study of language as well. So even though

Oxford and Cambridge were suspicious of English as a discipline, an English course at Oxford was begun in 1894, and at Cambridge in 1911.

In the 1920s, changes and developments in the study of English began to take place, and were greatly inspired by three men: I. A. Richards, William Empson, and F. R. Leavis. Richards founded a method of studying English that we still follow today, although it has grown into what it is today through the thought of several other critics and theorists. Richards broke up the connection that had been established between literature and language, and encouraged a close reading of the text in his book, *Practical Criticism*. William Empson was a student of Richards and took the Richards method of close reading to the extreme in his book, *Seven Types of Ambiguity*. Leavis combined efforts with his wife — they'd met and married in 1929 — and in 1932, founded a journal called *Scrutiny*. In his dissertation, Leavis had focused on the connection between journalism and literature while his wife had written hers on popular fiction. *Scrutiny* then "extended the 'close-reading' method beyond poetry to novels and other materials" (Barry 2009, 15), and this was considered to be revolutionary in practice.

So, with the work of this group of people, the study of English went through a crucial transformation that warranted it heightened respect. Eagleton writes: "In the early 1920s it was desperately unclear why English was worth studying at all; by the early 1930s it had become a question of why it was worth wasting your time on anything else" (2008, 27). Out of this movement, then, came liberal humanism, or traditional literary criticism, the first of its kind to be put to paper and discussed and developed in the context of academia. Barry lists the ten tenets of liberal humanism, and since these are the basis from which literary theory builds, they are important to note.

1. Good literature is of timeless signficance.
2. The literary text contains its own meaning within itself and doesn't require placing it in a certain context.
3. To understand the text well it must be detached from any socio-political, literary-historical, and autobiographical contexts and studied in isolation.
4. Human nature is essentially unchanging . . . It follows that continuity is more important and significant than innovation.
5. Individuality is something securely possessed within each of us as our unique "essence." This transcends our environmental influences, and though individuality can change and develop (as do characters in a novel), it can't be transformed.
6. The purpose of literature is essentially the enhancement of life and the propagation of humane values, but not in a programmatic way.
7. Form and content in literature must be fused in an organic way, so the one grows inevitably from the other.
8. Sincerity (comprising truth-to-experience, honesty towards self, and capacity for human empathy and compassion) is a quality which resides within the language of literature.
9. What is valued in literature is the "silent" showing and demonstrating of something, rather than the explaining, or saying of it.
10. The job of criticism is to interpret the text, to mediate between it and the reader. (Barry 2009, 17–20)

This track of literary criticism, based on these tenets, followed from Samuel Johnson to Matthew Arnold (who saw literature as a possible replacement for religion and insisted on close reading as a means for literary criticism's goal being to attain pure, disinterested knowledge) to T. S. Eliot to Leavis. Russian formalism and New Criticism are closely related to liberal humanism. The formalists attempted to treat each work as its own distinct piece, free from its environment, era, and author. Formalism, though, was essentially the application of linguistics to the study of literature, so although it focused on the text, it did so in a very programmatic, prescribed manner. New Criticism is basically the American version of Richards's practical criticism, which both follow the tenets above. I know this seems very confusing, but for the most part, liberal humanism lumps together all of these earlier forms of criticism that take literary theory from the 1920s into the '60s. New Criticism in its simplest terms is like liberal humanism, focused on the text itself. It gives attention to the work itself and exposes its unity. It functions from the perspective that in a unified work, every element works together toward a theme, and this type of criticism shows how the various elements of a great work unify it. It all begins with a close reading. In the next section of the book, this methodology to analyze a text will be discussed, and we will combine these closely-related criticisms into one, calling it Close Textual Reading Criticism, to circumvent the confusion.

The second track of literary criticism follows from Phillip Sidney to Wordsworth, and Coleridge to George Eliot and Henry James, and it approaches the text as a means to understanding questions and ideas beyond the text itself. It asks "big picture" questions: How are literary works structured? How do they affect readers and audiences? What is the nature of literary language, or is there a language that is specifically "literary"? How does literature relate to our contemporary world and to matters of politics and gender? What can be said about literature from a philosophical point of view? What is the nature of the act of literary composition? (Barry 2009, 25). The literary theory we use today comes from both of these tracks, the one focused entirely on the text, and the one that focuses on the text as well as its contexts. However, the latter track grew in popularity during the postwar period. Critical theory began to come in "waves" with each specific decade, all working against the traditional literary criticism, or liberal humanism, or the close textual reading schools of thought.

In the 1960s, the rival approaches of Marxist criticism and psychoanalytical criticism emerged. At the same time, linguistic criticism and early forms of feminist criticism appeared on the horizon as well. The 1970s saw the introduction of controversial new approaches to literature: structuralism and poststructuralism. This movement was so powerful, it was as if a civil war had erupted in the English discipline (Barry 2009, 52). The 1980s saw a shift that reinstated the inclusion of history, politics, and context into the literary-critical agenda. New historicism and cultural materialism emerged, as well as reader-response and reader-reception theory. In the 1990s, postcolonialism arrived on the scene, along with postmodernism, and a broader approach that addressed feminist issues now referred to as gender studies, which included queer theory, or lesbian and gay studies.

The next section will list and treat the various theoretical approaches that can be used to analyze literature, and as you will see, some of these approaches can themselves be adapted for approaching both film, and lit-to-film adaptation. However, to comprehend fully the intricacies of lit-to-film adaptation, it is necessary to gain working knowledge of the literature aspect of the process that leads to the product. Literature is where the process begins. Appreciating how the creation of literature unfolds but also how literature itself works and how to interpret its meanings are all crucial to an understanding of lit-to-film adaptation, leading to an understanding of how to approach lit-to-film adaptation from an analytical perspective.

Before we move on, it's important to be able to simplify some of the basics of literary theory so as to recognize what these foundational elements have in common, and what their connecting threads are (keeping in mind that these are very simplified and much more involved than the list given here).

1. Many of the notions that we would usually regard as the basic givens of our existence (including our gender identity, our individual selfhood, and the notion of literature itself) are actually fluid and unstable things, rather than fixed and reliable essences — no overarching fixed truths can ever be established.
2. There is no such thing as objectivity, and all thinking and investigation is necessarily affected and largely determined by some prior ideological commitment. That is, everything one thinks or does is in some way influenced by one's past experiences, one's beliefs, and one's ideology. Every practical procedure presupposes a theoretical perspective of some kind. While liberal humanists insist they can do this by only focusing on the text, they are denying their own ideological commitment, their biases, their own interests that motivate them.
3. Language is the most important factor shaping our conceptions about life, ourselves, literary texts, and the world. "Language itself conditions, limits, and predetermines what we see . . . Language doesn't record reality, it shapes and creates it, so that the whole of our universe is textual. Further, for the theorist, meaning is jointly constructed by reader and writer." Thus, rather than being creators of language, we are products of language.
4. "Any claim to offer a definitive reading would be futile . . . all texts are necessarily self-contradictory . . . There is no final court of appeals in these matters, since literary texts, once they exist, are viewed by the theorist as independent linguistic structures whose authors are always 'dead' or 'absent'."
5. There is no such thing as a "total" theory, one which explains every aspect of an event . . . Thus, the appeal to the idea of a generalized, supposedly inclusive, human nature is likely in practice to marginalize, or denigrate, or even deny the humanity of women, or other disadvantaged groups. (Barry 2009, 33–5, and Klages 2001)

So, to quote from the end of Barry's "Theory Before 'Theory'" section, where he reduces these fives basic tenets of literary theory into what might be a rather cool bumper sticker, although too long and might give away a touch of nerdiness in the driver/owner of the car: "Politics is pervasive, Language is constitutive, Truth is provisional, Meaning is contingent, Human nature is a myth." And, so, we continue.

Chapter 4

Literary Criticism/Analysis: Putting Theory into Practice

Although literary analysis, or putting into practice a theory or combination of theories to present an interpretation or reading of a text, might seem somewhat of a drudgery, maybe because it's a requirement of most literature-based classes, it can be a fascinating exploration into the depths of a text. It can be informative and illuminating, not only in terms of the text, but in terms of how one sees the world and oneself. Analyzing a literary text, and other kinds of texts, expands the mind and one's understanding of the world. It's not required in classes as a form of torture. It has many benefits, amongst them learning to view the world from a more analytical perspective, and not simply accepting what is on the surface of any text or experience.

That being said, we're going to start here with literature, and how to explore a literary text. Many of these methods can be adapted and used for other texts besides literary texts, and we'll be delving into the use of theory to understand film, and lit-to-film adaptations, so this beginning is meant to lead us far beyond here. Yet it is an apt place to begin.

The most effective way to approach a literary text is to expect to read it more than once in order to understand it and form a sound interpretation of it. The first reading should be an experiential read, letting yourself appreciate the text, follow the story, and notice the intricacies of the writing of the story. Underline or note which aspects of the story move you, and impress you. Note which parts of the story confuse you or are difficult to comprehend. (These are the places you'll want to return to once you've read it the first time through.) Also, be mindful of your emotional response to the text. Although you can't rely on only this response as your sole means to analyzing the text, it's an important aspect of experiencing the text and then approaching it from an analytical perspective.

Regardless of the interpretation you're beginning to form of the text, and which critical approach or approaches you're leaning towards using to analyze and even write about the text, it's prudent to conduct a close textual reading of the text. As I discussed in the section on literary theory, close textual reading is effectively an encapsulation of liberal humanism, Russian formalism, and New Criticism. Liberal humanism grew out of the literary theory that preceded English becoming a subject of study (before it was called literary theory), explained in great detail in the preceding chapter. Russian formalism flourished in Moscow and St. Petersburg in the 1920s, and the Russian formalists based their theories on those of Ferdinand de Saussure, the Swiss linguist. The work of these formalists is more related to that of the structuralists, which will be addressed below. The Russian formalists argued that literature was a systematic set of linguistic and structural elements that could be analyzed. That is, literature from their perspective was a self-enclosed system studied for its form not its content (Dobie 2009, 35).

New Criticism is related to Russian formalism but remains its own school of thought. It put forth that a reader should understand and value a work for its own inherent worth, and came about in many ways as a reaction to the attention of scholars and teachers of the early twentieth century on the biographical and historical context of a work. The New Critics, T. S. Eliot one of the most well known of the bunch, didn't like that the text itself seemed to be diminished by the attention paid to its externalities. So, the New Critic's real interest would be in the finished work, not how the work was finished. Yet today, when we look at a text for its intrinsic properties, it's often referred to as a formalist approach. As I've mentioned before, I find this to be confusing in light of all the different schools of thought that have gone into developing this approach, one of them being Russian formalism, so I'll refer to this approach as a Close Textual Reading of the text. And, regardless of the text and the approaches that will be applied to that text to formulate a complex and engaging critique of it, one should always begin with the close reading approach, since it focuses the reader first and foremost on the text itself, and this is important. To push forth into other approaches before a focus on the text itself can distract the reader from the text itself, and the textual elements that make up its whole.

A Close Textual Reading, and Stylistics

Basic questions asked of a text when reading it closely include how the various elements of the work reinforce its meanings, and how these elements are related to the whole. The work's organizing principle needs to be identified, as do the issues that the work raises. How the structure of the work resolves those issues is crucial to this reading as well. So, in approaching the text in question from a close textual reading perspective — the text in question being either a short story or novel here — the following questions, which help to arrive at a theme and a starting point from which to continue exploring this text, need to be addressed.

1. Plot: Does the plot conform to a formula? Is it predictable? What are the conflicts within the story? Is the story told chronologically? Are there flashbacks, foreshadowing? Where is the climax? Are the conflicts resolved at the end? Outline the plot, and how events unfold, being very specific. How does the structure of the plot affect your reading of the text?
2. Character: Who is the main character and why? Who are the other characters in the story and how are they used? How does the author reveal characters? How are they described? Make a list of the characters and describe them, from their physical attributes to how they're portrayed (based on the information given in the text).

3. Point of view: Who tells the story? Is it one narrator? Is it first person or third person? If it's third person, is it third-person omniscient, limited omniscient, or objective? How much does the narrator know? Does the point of view change during the course of the story? Is the narration reliable and objective? Or, does the narration appear innocent, emotional, or self-deluded? Does the author directly comment on the action? How does the point of view affect your reading of the text?

4. Setting: Is the setting important? How is it used to flesh out the characters, and/or develop the characters? Is the setting used symbolically? Is the setting vital enough to the story to be considered a character? Describe the setting, giving as many details as you can, especially if it changes, and if so, as it changes, throughout the text.

5. Symbolism: Are there symbols used in the story and how do they contribute to one's understanding of the story?

6. Style, tone, and irony: Is the style consistent throughout the text? Do all the characters use the same language, or are there different voices? Is the level of diction formal or informal? How are the sentences structured? How does the author's use of language contribute to the tone of the story?

7. Title: How does the title relate to the story told?

8. Theme: What are the themes running through the story? What is the text saying to the reader? What messages are being conveyed? Explain the main theme that you see in the text in one sentence.

9. Now, go back through questions 1 to 7, and explore how each of the fictional techniques used in the text as you've explained them helps to bring out this main theme.

These are the questions a reader asks of a short story or novel, in order to move beyond the first response to the text. What techniques has the writer applied to the text to convey meaning? How has that meaning been conveyed? And what is the meaning that is being conveyed? Once an examination of the text has been performed, you can now push forward to explore the text from a more specific critical approach or combination of critical approaches that seem appropriate to the text, as you the reader views it. The techniques that the author has employed in writing the text will prove instrumental in supporting your particular approach or approaches to the text.

A stylistic approach to a text is an extension of close textual reading, and although I will mention it here, it's a cumbersome approach to a text, and one used by those who are well versed in the study of linguistics. It's important to mention, however, since it shows just how complex and intricate a reading of a text can be. Stylistics focuses greatly on the linguistic minutiae of a text. According to Peter Barry, stylistics "uses the methods and findings of the science of linguistics in the analysis of literary texts." Linguistics is the "scientific study of language and its structures, rather than the learning of individual languages" (Barry 2009, 196). Stylistics identifies the linguistic details of a particular work and how they contribute to the text's overall meanings and effects. For example, a stylistics approach would examine the grammatical structure of the sentences and what their structure contributes to the text's meaning. Thus stylistic critics

- describe technical aspects of the language of the text,

- provide objective linguistic data to support existing readings or intuitions about a literary work,
- often try to establish a new reading of the text,
- but mainly, try to show that literature has no ineffable, mystical core which is beyond analysis. (Barry 2009, 207)

A stylistic approach can lead to an interesting exploration into the linguistic aspects of the text, since as Barry insists, "this body of practice is the product of very specific theories about literary language and how it works" (196). It can be quite helpful in delving into how the language works in a text to bring out its meanings.

Although for the previous readings of the text, we've kept the author and any other externalities of the text out of it, now we can begin to look at other critical approaches that view the text from a more extensive perspective. First, we will look at biographical criticism, and then its alter ego, reader response and reader reception criticism, the former focusing on the author of the work, and the latter focusing on the reader of the work.

A Biographical Approach to the Text

Biographical strategies take into account the author's life and its influence on the text. This strategy, of course, requires knowledge of the author's life. Events in a work might follow actual events in a writer's life just as characters might be based on people known by the author, or at least in knowing the writer's life, such claims can be made and supported. Critics who espouse a focus on the text, like the New Critics or the formalists, insist that one can never know a writer's intention, and that an interpretation should be based solely on internal evidence rather than on any biographical information. However, biography can serve as a control on interpretation, keeping readers from misinterpreting a text by having knowledge of the author's life. Biographical information can be very helpful in understanding texts that are written by individuals of marginalized populations, because often we do not have a full enough understanding of the context in which they're writing. This type of criticism combined with historical criticism can be illuminating when analyzing a text that isn't as familiar to us as the texts we've been accustomed to studying, the texts of a hegemonic tradition based predominantly in white male dominance.

Reader Response Criticism

Reader response and reader reception criticism is an approach to the text from the reader's, or your, perspective. As Terry Eagleton writes in *Literary Theory*:

Reception theory examines the reader's role in literature, and as such is a fairly novel development. Indeed one might very roughly periodize the history of modern literary theory in three states: a preoccupation with the author (Romanticism and the nineteenth century); an exclusive concern with the text (New Criticism); and a marked shift of attention to the reader over recent years. (2008, 64)

Reader reception criticism looks at a text not only from the current reader's perspective, or your perspective, but takes into account readers of the text from various historical periods and how the time period and contextual situation of a reader might affect the reading, or interpretation of a text. "Receptionists" look for what the leading theorist of this concept, Hans Robert Jauss, called the "horizon of expectations" of the reading audience, depending on what readers value and look for in a work at a particular point in time, and history (Dobie 2009, 133). Thus, if viewing the text from the reader reception approach, one would need to be aware of where they are placed in history and how that might affect their reading of the text. This type of reader-based criticism isn't as focused on one's individual response to the text, but requires the reader to step back, examining their own place in history and how their reading of the text in this place and time might affect how they interpret the text.

Reader-response criticism is more focused on the reader's response to the text itself, not as much about where the reader is placed as they're reading it but more on a direct response to the text as they're reading it. Reader-response criticism is probably one of my most preferred approaches to a text, when it can be used appropriately. A reader-response approach assumes that a text is always unfinished, and does not have a fixed meaning. Whereas formalist, or close textual reading, critics assume that a literary work is finished with fixed formal properties, reader-response critics perceive a literary work as an "evolving creation of the reader as he or she processes the characters, plots, images, and other elements while reading." Michael Meyer explains:

> Some reader response critics argue that this act of creative reading is, to a degree, controlled by the text, but it can produce many interpretations of the same text by different readers. There is no single definitive reading of a work, because the crucial assumption is that readers create rather than discover meanings in texts. Readers who have gone back to works they had read earlier in their lives often find that a later reading draws very different responses from them. (Meyer 2008, 1552)

So, perhaps you have read a text in high school, and encounter it again in college. Your life has changed, you've read other works since, and you've matured in your acquisition of knowledge. You can now achieve a different, more developed reading of the text that you can fuse with your previous reading, and thus enhance your reading of the text in so doing.

The focus of any reader-based criticism is inevitably on context, since it stems from who is reading the text, and affirms that the reading of the text changes with each reader. In Stanley Fish's essay "Is There A Text in This Class?," a discussion of reader response criticism, he writes:

> [I]t is impossible even to think of a sentence independently of a context, and when we are asked to consider a sentence for which no context has been specified, we will automatically hear it in the context which it has most often been encountered. (1999, 46)

Therefore, each reader will come to a text with their own understanding of the subjects it broaches, and this will influence their reading of that text. Admittedly, I often rely on a reader-response approach to literary texts in order to explore the diversity of their meanings. I am not comfortable with the idea that a text can be reduced to one fixed meaning, as the formalists and New Critics insisted. The meaning of a text grows and changes as the reader grows and changes. The critic of a text reads it over and over again, and a more thorough, intensive meaning may result from this process, but finite meaning is elusive. In my experience, each time I read the same text in an attempt to further explore and analyze it, I feel as if I'm approaching the text as a different person. Fish states:

> The change from one structure of understanding to another is not a rupture but a modification of the interests and concerns that are already in place; and because they are already in place, they constrain the direction of their own modification. That is, in both cases the hearer [or reader] is already in a situation informed by tacitly known purposes and goals, and in both cases he ends up in another situation whose purposes and goals stand in some elaborated relation (of contrast, opposition, extension) to those they supplant. (1999, 50–1)

A first reading of a text, then, isn't entirely supplanted by a second or third reading, but enhanced. A critic of a text can push beyond their initial understanding of a text during a second and third reading to achieve an even fuller understanding of the text, or perhaps a new perspective from which to see the text, which can be melded to the first reading. This type of criticism will be explored and shown in practice in the sample critique detailed later in this book.

Structuralism, Semiotics, and Narratology

Reader-response criticism is considered a theory under the poststructuralist umbrella of literary theory. But before discussing poststructuralism and its often celebrated (as well as despised) offshoot, deconstruction, it's important to understand what led to the revolution in theory that became poststructuralism. It began with structuralism in the 1950s and '60s with a return to Ferdinand de Saussure, the Swiss linguist, on whom the Russian formalists had based much of their theory as I mentioned above. Saussure's ideas laid a foundation for many significant developments in the study of linguistics, including the work of the structuralists. Saussure was writing at the turn of the twentieth century, and is considered one of the fathers of twentieth-century linguistics.

Saussure is also referred to as the founder of semiotics, a science designed to investigate meaning through signs observable in cultural phenomena. Saussure believed it was entirely possible to develop a science based in the study of signs in everyday life. (His notes on this science were compiled for the *Course in General Linguistics*, published after his death.) Thus Saussure based his theory of language on the idea that we live amongst signifying systems, though not necessarily all involving words. As Ann Dobie explains in her book *Theory into Practice*, "any organized, structured set of signs carries cultural meanings, making it possible to 'read' a culture by examining those signs" (2009, 155). Saussure saw linguistics as a branch of semiology, involving how words are used as signs.

First of all, the concept of "sign" needs to be understood here. According to David Chandler, in his updated web version of his book, *Semiotics for Beginners*, we are a species "driven by a desire to make meanings . . . [and] we make meanings through our creation and interpretation of 'signs'." Chandler states that "anything can be a sign as long as someone interprets it as 'signifiying' something — referring to or standing for something other than itself" (2009, 1). Most often, we interpret signs unconsciously, without even realizing we are, by relating them to other familiar systems that we use to understand ourselves and the world around us. Semiotics is wrapped up in this purposeful use of signs.

Saussure introduced a two-part model of the sign, and it's important to be aware of the following terms because they frequently arise in discussions of literature and other media, and especially in discussions involving the analysis of texts. Saussure defined a *sign* as being composed of a *signifier*, the form which the sign takes, and the *signified*, the concept the sign represents. The sign, then, according to Saussure, is the whole that results from the association of the signifier with the signified. And, a sign must have both a signifier and a signified, because it is "a recognizable combination of a signifier with a particular signified" (Chandler 2009, 1). Chandler offers the example of the word "Open" put outside a shop. This then is the signifier that represents that the shop is open for business in that moment the person walks towards it. However, the same word could be used to represent a myriad of other specific concepts, or different signifieds. It could be on the top of a box, representing that the box needs to be opened from that particular end.

Imagine teaching a young child the signs of our world. My daughter (now in college), when she first began walking, also began taking note of the world going on around her, as if she was an official part of it and needed to know about everything, and what everything "meant." One morning, we go out for her toddling walk down the sidewalk, and an airplane flies over us (we live near an airport). She points up at it, and I say, "Airplane." She tries to imitate my pronunciation of the word. We keep going, and a bird flies above us. She points and tries to say, "Airplane." I shake my head, and say, "Bird." In her newly forming mind, she associates something that flies above us as the first word I label it with, but then I distinguish them from each other by calling each concept or object something different. She is learning the use of signs to understand the world around her, but also to communicate the world around her to others. I'm teaching her how to function in our particular world of an organized, structured set of signs.

This example shows how semiology works in everyday life, and why for Saussure, semiology was "a science which studies the role of signs as part of social life" (Chandler 2009, 1). Yet semiotics is often used in the analysis of texts. Chandler refers to a text as referring to "a message which has been recorded in some way . . . so that it is physically independent of its sender or receiver. A text is an assemblage of signs (such as words, images, sounds, and/or gestures) constructed (and interpreted) with reference to the conventions associated with a genre and in a particular medium" (1). Chandler refers to a medium as including "such broad categories as speech and writing or print and broadcasting" or more specifically, "forms within the mass media (radio, television, newspapers, books, photographs, films, and records) or the media of interpersonal communication (telephone, letter, fax, email, video-conferencing, computer-based chat systems [and to add, any form of social networking])." However, for our treatment here, in discussing literary analysis, we will focus on the language of literary texts, and Saussure's theories that led to the development of structuralism which grew out of semiology.

To understand how Saussure fits into the more specific study of literature, what might seem quite established and taken for granted by us today, wasn't, during the time in which he was developing his ideas about the study of language, and the use of words. Saussure's thought went against what had previously been accepted about the concept of language. First, Saussure stressed that words are always arbitrary and that the meanings of words are maintained by the ways in which they're used. The structuralists became fascinated by this arbitrariness of language that Saussure insisted upon, and believed that it followed "that language isn't a reflection of the world and of experience, but a system which stands quite separate from it" (Barry 2009, 49).

Saussure also emphasized that the meanings of words were relational, in that no word could be defined in isolation from other words, that words derive their meanings from their relation to other words. Saussure pointed out that we understand the meaning of one word by how it compares to other words, in what ways it is different from other words. Saussure is quoted as saying: "In a language there are only differences, without fixed terms" (Barry 2009, 41). This concept of difference will be revisited when we discuss deconstruction, since the structuralists worked with difference and especially opposites, which they referred to as binary opposition.

In addition, for Saussure, language constitutes or creates our world, not only records or labels it. We as individuals assign meaning to an object or idea with our own mind, so that meaning is constructed by and expressed through language. Meaning is not contained within the object or idea; we assign it meaning with our knowledge of language. Saussure put forth a concept of language as a system of signs. Signs are composed of two parts, he stated: a written or sound construction, known as the signifier, and its meaning, called the signified. The spoken or written form of tree, for example, is a signifier. What comes into your mind when you hear or read that word is the signified. Thus, with the introduction of these terms, Saussure made it impossible to speak of a word as a symbol representing something outside of us, which is how language and the word had been thought of before Saussure. According to Saussure, then, language not only allows us to record and label it, but mediates our reality and structures our experience.

Structuralists built on Saussure's theories and also the anthropologist Claude Levi-Strauss's work on the interpretation of myths. Levi-Strauss developed the idea of stories rooted in basic oppositions like animal/human, relation/stranger, husband/son, especially in his study of the Oedipus myth. Structuralists wanted to figure out how meaning was produced. Their goal was to identify what in the underlying structures of a text produced the meaning that led to the creation of a reader's experience. Roland Barthes seized upon the work done by both Saussure and Levi-Strauss to apply the structuralist method to the general field of modern culture. This step in theory led to the eventual inclusion of popular culture as a field worthy of study and analysis. So, as Barry states:

For the structuralist, the culture we are part of can be "read" like a language . . . since culture is made up of many structural networks which carry significance and can be shown to operate in a systematic way. These networks operate through "codes" as a system of signs; they can make statements, just as language does, and they can be read or decoded by the structuralist . . . (2009, 46)

To simplify structuralism here, a structuralist critique is looking for parallels, echoes, reflections, repetitions, contrasts, and patterns in a text, usually a prose narrative, and examines these factors in the following elements of the narrative: plot, structure, character/motive, situation/circumstance, and language/imagery.

It would follow then that narratology, the study of narrative structures, is considered a branch of structuralism. Those who study narratology examine "how narratives make meaning, and what the basic mechanisms and procedures are which are common to all acts of story-telling" (214). Narratology is not the study of the narrative structure of individual stories but the study of the nature of narrative and storytelling. Aristotle is the first scholar associated with the development of narratology since he identified three essential elements of plot in his *Poetics*: the concept of the fault or tragic flaw (the hamartia), the moment when the protagonist realizes the truth of the situation (the anagnorisis), and a turn-around or often when the hero falls from greatness (the peripeteia). Aristotle saw all three elements as focused on the hero or heroine, or the protagonist. A second scholar associated with narratology is the Russian formalist, Vladimir Propp (1895–1970), who studied recurrent structures and situations in Russian folk tales, and discussed his discoveries in *The Morphology of the Folktale*. He identified that a tale could be told using any number of thirty-one functions that can make up that tale, although no tale can be constructed of all of them. Only a selection could be used, but he insisted they had to be used in the order in which he had them listed. What limited the scope of his theory on narratology, though, was that he didn't address any aspect concerning how the story was presented, through whose perspective or using what style.

The most prominent narratologist besides Roland Barthes, who wrote profusely albeit often quite esoterically on narrative, is Gerard Genette. Genette's focus has been on how the narrative or story is told, or its process of telling itself. Genette distinguished between mimesis in storytelling, which is "slow telling," or a staging of the story, showing the reader the story rather than telling the reader in exposition style. Diegesis, on the other hand, is "telling" or "relating," when part of the narrative is summarized to the reader rather than given in scenes that display the story unfolding. Diegesis gives essential linking information between scenes — "the narrator just says what happens, without trying to show it as it happens" (Barry 2009, 223). In any fiction workshop or class, but also now in any creative nonfiction class (and I've been a student and an instructor of both), the key to balancing a narrative is how much a writer shows, and how much a writer tells. The most effective balance is determined by the story itself, and what the writer wants to convey to her reader. Yet telling a story seems to come more easily to students, whereas a more experienced writer begins to revel in the showing aspect of writing, when one can get a message to one's reader that they need to recognize, rather than giving it to them by telling them, which can be seen as a giving away of the story.

Genette also focused on the point of view from which a story is told, and who is narrating the story. He explored the management of time and duration within a story, how it flashes back or forward, the use of foreshadowing to hint at what's to come, and where the story begins, which is usually somewhere in the middle (*in media res*). So most often a story begins *in media res* with information given about what went before, and devices hinting at what's to come, all pushing forward the narrative to some conclusion. Genette focused as well on how a story is presented, in terms of the framework of the story. Is one story embedded into another? He referred to the main story as the primary narrative, and the stories contained within that story, embedded or secondary narratives. Finally, Genette looked at the way speech and thought are represented in stories, since the way both are presented develops both the characters and the momentum of the story.

Narratology is an important field of study with which to be familiar when studying both literary narrative and film narrative. We'll be addressing the concept of narratology later in this book, since the connection between narrative in written form and narrative in filmic form requires exploration when considering lit-to-film adaptation.

Poststructuralism and Its Famous/Infamous Byproduct, Deconstruction

Structuralists sought to understand how language doesn't only reflect or record the world; it shapes it, so that how we see is synonymous with what we see. Structuralism purported to explore how a work gives meaning to the reader, how it gets its meaning across to the reader, how it moves the reader, what it does to achieve that. As Jonathan Culler explains, structuralism sought "not to produce new interpretations of works but to understand how they can have the meanings and effects that they do" (1997, 120). However, Culler claims that once structuralism became more established as a school of thought, theorists began to distance themselves from it: "It became clear that works by alleged structuralists did not fit the idea of structuralism as an attempt to master and codify structure" (121). A handful of theorists began to challenge structuralist practices, and these individuals began what was considered a controversial movement called poststructuralism. The poststructuralists claimed that, like structuralism itself, theories get caught up and "entangled" in the phenomena they try to explain, and that texts create meaning by going against any conventions that structural analysis identifies. "They recognized the impossibility of describing a complete or coherent signifying system, since systems are always changing." (121)

According to Peter Barry, poststructuralism asserts that "we have no access to any fixed landmark which is beyond linguistic processing, and hence we have no standard by which to measure anything. Without a fixed point of reference against which to measure movement you cannot tell whether or not you are moving at all" (Barry 2009, 59). This is what poststructuralists call the decentered universe; there are no intellectual reference points because they're always changing. Just when you think you've nailed them down, they've changed.

Terry Eagleton explains this instability of language in terms of signifiers and signifieds, by describing what happens when you look up a word in the dictionary:

> If you want to know the meaning (or signified) of a signifier, you can look it up in the dictionary; but all you will find will be yet more signifiers, whose signifieds you can in turn look up, and so on . . . [This process] is not only in theory infinite but somehow circular: signifiers keep transforming into signifieds and vice versa, and you will never arrive at a final signified which is not a signifier in itself. (2008, 111)

This example shows the instability of language that the poststructuralists were determined to expose. The anxiety about language that poststructuralists identified and explored is not that remote from our own understanding of and experience within language. Barry says, and I agree, that we experience "anxious feelings at any level beyond that of casual daily exchange with people we know very well and whose status is the same as our own" (2009, 60). We worry about how we come across to those we're not familiar with, and that we'll be misinterpreted. Students often express to me that what is in their head doesn't come out on the paper, so what does come out on the paper isn't necessarily what they meant to say. That is, often language is elusive, and inadequate for expressing ourselves. Eagleton uses his own expression of himself as an example that demonstrates quite well this inadequacy inherent in language:

> [I]t is an illusion for me to believe that I can ever be fully present to you in what I say or write, because to use such signs at all entails that my meaning is always somehow dispersed, divided and never quite at one with itself. Not only my meaning, indeed, but *me*: since language is something I am made out of, rather than merely a convenient tool I use, the whole idea that I am a stable, unified entity must also be a fiction. Not only can I never be fully present to you, but I can never be fully present to myself either. I still need to use signs when I look into my mind or search my soul, and this means that I will never experience any "full communion" with myself. It is not that I can have a pure, unblemished meaning, intention or experience which then gets distorted or refracted by the flawed medium of language: because language is the very air I breathe, I can never have a pure, unblemished meaning or experience at all. (2008, 112–13)

Eagleton goes on to compare the difference between speaking and writing, saying that at least in speaking, there's the possibility of representing oneself more purely. He suggests that "in the act of speaking I seem to 'coincide' with myself in a way quite different from what happens when I write." When he speaks, his words are right there in front of him, and they are intimate and spontaneous. However, in writing, he says, "my meanings threaten to escape from my control." He puts his thoughts into print, and "since a printed text has a durable, material existence it can always be circulated, reproduced, cited, used in ways which I did not foresee or intend" (113). Writing is speech in our minds, that isn't spontaneous, and becomes recorded, revised, adapted. Eagleton calls writing "a second-hand mode of communication . . . always at one remove from my consciousness" (113). Thus if the writer him or herself isn't immediately present in what they write, the reader or critic can't assume that what is written isn't without contradictions in meaning and unconscious maneuvers that the writer him or herself is unaware they've made. Poststructuralism delves into this inadequacy we experience in expressing ourselves, approaching texts from this perspective, that language — and meaning — are not as stable or discernible as previously thought.

Poststructuralism is an important school of thought to understand, although the ideas on which it is based prove themselves to be as elusive as they claim language and meaning to be. Yet it's worth trying to understand. Barry provides an informative discussion of the distinctions between structuralism and poststructuralism (condensed below), which helps to locate poststructuralism in how we view literature today.

1. Structuralism derives ultimately from linguistics, and looks at language from a more scientific perspective based on the "science" of linguistics. Structuralism believes in method, system, and reason as being able to establish reliable truths. Poststructuralism derives from philosophy, a discipline which has always tended to stress the difficulty of achieving secure knowledge about things. Philosophy's "procedures often begin by calling into question what is usually taken for granted as simply the way things are . . ."

2. Structuralist writing tends towards abstraction and generalization: it aims for a detached, "scientific coolness" of tone. Poststructuralist writing, by contrast, tends to be much more emotive. Often the tone is urgent and euphoric, and the style flamboyant and self-consciously showy . . . it aims for an engaged warmth rather than detached coolness.

3. Structuralists accept that the world is constructed through language, in the sense that we do not have access to reality other than through the linguistic medium. All the same, it decides to live with that fact and continue to use language to think and perceive with . . . by contrast, poststructuralism is much more fundamentalist in insisting upon the consequences of the view that, in effect, reality itself is textual . . . We are not fully in control of the medium of language, so meanings cannot be planted in set places . . . they can only be randomly scattered or disseminated . . . the meanings words have can never be guaranteed one hundred percent pure . . . words are always contaminated by their opposites . . .

4. Structuralism questions our way of structuring and categorizing reality, and prompts us to break free of habitual modes of perception and categorization. "Poststructuralism is more fundamental: it distrusts the very notion of reason, and the idea of the human being as an independent entity, preferring the notion of the 'dissolved' or 'constructed' subject, whereby what we may think of as the individual is really a product of social and linguistic forces — that is, not an essence at all, merely a 'tissue of textualities'." (Barry 2009: 60–3)

To further distinguish structuralism from poststructuralism, Eagleton explains that structuralism would view a text by examining its binary oppositions and how they worked, while poststructuralism, through the practice of deconstruction, "tries to show how oppositions, in order to hold themselves in place, are sometimes betrayed into inverting and collapsing themselves" (2008, 115). Thus the poststructuralists, according to Eagleton, view language as "a much less stable affair" than the structuralists had. Eagleton states that through the poststructuralist view, rather than language

being a well-defined, clearly demarcated structure containing symmetrical units of
signifiers and signifieds, it [looks] more like a sprawling limitless web where there
is a constant interchange and circulation of elements, where none of the elements is
absolutely definable and where everything is caught up and traced through everything else. (112)

Officially, or unofficially, poststructuralism emerged in France in the late 1960s, with
the writings of Roland Barthes and Jacques Derrida. Roland Barthes began his association with literary theory as a structuralist, but with his 1968 essay "The Death of the
Author," it was clear he was moving away from structuralism to a new way of looking
at texts. His pivotal essay makes a case for the independence of the text, and that it's
not the author who is important any longer, but the reader. He felt it was not only time
to stop seeing the Author as a kind of God figure, but the Critic as well. Ultimately,
he said, the text is meant for the reader. Barthes states in his essay: "To give a text an
Author is to impose a limit on that text, to furnish it with a final signified, to close the
writing" (Barthes 1977, 147). The idea of the Author limits how we see a text, and
closes it off to the multiplicitous meanings that could be found in it otherwise. Barthes
says in the essay that: "Once the author is removed, the claim to decipher a text becomes
quite futile" (147), meaning it can't be held down to one or a closed number of readings that are based on the identity of the author.

   Instead he claims, "a text is made up of multiple writings, drawn from many cultures and entering mutual relations of dialogue, parody, contestation, but there is one
place where this multiplicity is focused and that place is the reader, not . . . the author"
(148). Barthes here is not referring to just any reader, nor is he encouraging that a
reader bring himself or herself to the reading. He's referring to a reader, a witness, a
group of witnesses, that the work is meant for. In effect, he's pointing out that a text
doesn't exist if it doesn't have a reader. It's similar to the question commonly asked,
If a tree falls in the woods, and no one is there to hear it, does it make a sound? If a
text is written but is never read, can it ever have any meaning at all? Barthes states
that the

   reader is the space on which all quotations that make up a writing are inscribed without any of them being lost; a text's unity lies not in its origin but in its destination. Yet
   this destination cannot any longer be personal: the reader is without history, biography, psychology; he is simply that someone who holds together in a single field all
   the traces by which the written text is constituted. (148)

Barthes concludes his famous essay by stating that "the birth of the reader must be at
the cost of the death of the Author" (148).

   In 1971, shortly after his "Author" essay, Barthes pushed further in another essay,
"From Work to Text," to rename and relocate the "work" of an author as instead a
"text," opening up the text to textual relations, rather than limiting the work to that of
one person as if they own that work and they in many ways are that work, defining its
identity. The concept of the "text" allows the writing once again to stand alone, and in
relationship with other texts. In this essay, he reiterates the importance of the reader to

a text, the general reader, any reader. To see a work as a text, he says, "requires that one abolish . . . the distance between writing and reading, in no way by intensifying the projection of the reader into the work but by joining them in a single signifying practice" (162). Michael Payne comments on Barthes's perception of the reader and reading in this essay when he explains that "Barthes's purpose here is not to disparage informed or cultural reading but rather to point out the richness and significance in all reading experience" (Payne 1997, 7). Barthes seems not only to expand and delineate how we should perceive the role of the text, but also how we should perceive the role of the reader, in the interchange of language and meaning.

In *Literary Theory*, Eagleton discusses how Barthes's view of the reader changes how we see the critic as well. The critic, he says, "shifts from role of consumer to that of producer." Of course, it's not as if any interpretation at all can be made with reference to a text, but literature is now seen as less of an object "to which criticism must conform than a free space in which it can sport" (2008, 119), and thus criticism can open onto new frontiers with less restrictive guidelines holding it back. Eagleton sees the movement from structuralism to poststructuralism paralleled in part by Barthes's own movement from "work" to "text." He states that

> it is a shift from seeing the poem or novel as a closed entity, equipped with definite meanings which it is the critic's task to decipher, to seeing it as irreducibly plural, an endless play of signifiers which can never be fully nailed down to a single center, essence or meaning. (120)

The concept of the "center" brings us directly to Jacques Derrida. His lecture which later was transcribed into essay form, "Structure, Sign and Play in the Discourse of the Human Sciences," is considered by many as the incipience of the poststructuralist movement. In this essay, Derrida puts forth that in modern times, an event has occurred which represents a radical break from the past ways of thought, a rupture as he refers to it. Prior to this event, it was simply accepted that there was a norm or center in all things, all structures. The center that dominated most pervasively was the concept that man was "the measure of all other things in the universe" (Barry 2009, 64). However, Derrida insists that in the twentieth century, the centers as we'd known them were destroyed, by historical events, scientific discoveries, and intellectual and artistic revolutions. Thus, according to Derrida, the "center is not the center" any longer (Derrida 1978, 279). In the reconceived universe of the twentieth century, there are no absolutes or fixed points; in fact, the universe has become decentered and relativistic (everything relates to each other, nothing stands for itself unequivocally). As Barry states, Derrida is saying in this essay that now, all we have is "free play" (Barry 2009, 65).

As Derrida embraces in this essay the idea of the decentered universe of free play as liberating, Barthes celebrates the demise of the idea of the author as ushering in "an era of joyous freedom" (Barry 2009, 65). Yet what does this mean for how we view literature? And, what does this have to do with literature, and other texts in various mediums? Well, as Barry explains, poststructuralism as thought is more of an attitude of mind than a practical method of criticism. But what Derrida begins to put forth in his essay is the idea of applying this new thought to textual analysis. Although in his essay he discusses the application of his newly-formed thought to opposing philosophical entities and how one is understood fully only in terms of the other, he's putting forth the means to apply the same practice to textual analysis. In his essay, Derrida writes: "It is a question of explicitly and systematically posing the problem of the status of a discourse which borrows from a heritage the resources necessary for deconstruction of that heritage itself. A problem of *economy* and *strategy*" (1978, 282). The concept of deconstruction is introduced here for the first time. The poststructuralist literary critic is engaged, then, in the task of deconstructing the text; deconstruction is the method by which poststructuralist thought is carried out. Barry explains that deconstruction "can roughly be defined as applied poststructuralism." He continues by stating that "a deconstructive reading can be said to uncover the unconscious rather than the conscious dimension of the text, all the things which its overt textuality glosses over or fails to recognize" (2009, 68).

So, whereas structuralists focused their energies on showing a unity of purpose within the text, as if every element in the text was directed towards this end, deconstructionists explore how a text is at war with itself, looking for how elements of the text show the text's disunity. Barry provides the following diagram to show the difference between what the structuralist looks for as opposed to the deconstructionist, or poststructuralist critic:

The structuralist seeks	The poststructuralist seeks
Parallels in the text	Contradictions in the text
Balances	Shifts
Reflections/repetitions	Conflicts
Symmetry	Absences/omissions
Contrasts	Linguistic quirks
Patterns	Aporia (a textual knot that resists disentanglement)

(2009, 70)

Eagleton further adds to the explanation of deconstruction as he states:

> The tactic of deconstructive criticism . . . is to show how texts come to embarrass their own ruling systems of logic; and deconstruction shows this by fastening on the "symptomatic" points, the aporia or impasses of meaning, where texts get into trouble, come unstuck, offer to contradict themselves. (2008, 116)

Barry processes through an example of deconstructive criticism in his book, which I will paraphrase here, since it offers easily understandable guidelines for carrying out a deconstructive critique of a text. In the example of literary criticism and pre-treatment for an adaptation that I give later in this book, you will see how this type of criticism can be performed in actual practice. But for our purposes here, I will give the basics that can be applied to any text being critiqued in this fashion.

Barry refers to the three stages of the deconstructive process as the verbal, the textual, and the linguistic. The verbal stage is similar to that of more conventional forms of close reading; it involves looking in the text for paradoxes and contradictions. A deconstructionist wants to show the signifier at war with the signified. This first stage turns up useful material for use in the later stages. The textual stage of the method moves beyond individual phases and takes a more overall view of the text. The critic looks for shifts or breaks in the continuity of the text: these shifts reveal instabilities of attitudes, and thus the lack of a fixed and unified position. They can be shifts in focus, time, tone, point of view, attitude, pace, or vocabulary. Omissions are important, too — when a text doesn't tell us things we would expect to be told. The linguistic stage, then, involves looking for moments in the text when the adequacy of language itself as a medium of communication is called into question, like when there is implicit or explicit reference to the unreliability or untrustworthiness of language. This might be a point in the text when the text itself seems to go against what's actually happening or meant (Barry 2009, 71–3).

This is, very technically, how deconstruction is done. Yet the nature of deconstruction, not to be held down to any strictly held methodology or law, invites a variation on this process of any kind. And thus we have the beauty of deconstruction. To conclude this discussion, it's important to look at the Yale school of deconstruction, which included such critics as Paul de Man, J. Hillis Miller and Harold Bloom. Eagleton in his *Literary Theory* is careful to include the American study of deconstruction, and these critics put forth a fascinating yet disconcerting view on literature and its texts. Paul de Man especially focused his criticism on "demonstrating that literary language constantly undermines its own meaning . . . All language is ineradicably metaphorical . . . it is a mistake to believe that any language is literally literal" (2008, 125–6). Yet the problem with literature is that it's already figurative and ambiguous; its fiction is meant to bring out a meaning it doesn't say directly. However, de Man says other works are just as figurative and ambiguous, but "pass themselves off as unquestionable truth" (126). So, de Man points out, the reader of a literary work "finds herself suspended between a 'literal' and a figurative meaning, unable to choose between the two, and thus cast dizzyingly into a bottomless linguistic abyss by a text which has become 'unreadable'." The Yale critics believed that "literature does not need to be deconstructed by the critic: it can be shown to deconstruct itself, and moreover is actually 'about' this very operation" (126). Thus literary works are ironic in nature. What we expect to get from them by analyzing literary works and interpreting them in some way, what they seem designed for, just such interpretation, becomes elusive in that the writing can't be assumed to be meaning what we identify it to mean, no matter how careful or thoughtful we try to be. Eagleton states, then, that:

> Literary criticism thus becomes an ironic, uneasy business, an unsettling venture into the inner void of the text which lays bare the illusoriness of meaning, the impossibility of truth and the deceitful guiles of all discourse. (126)

This might make more sense when we look at psychoanalytic criticism and how Freud's concept of the unconscious influenced the poststructuralist movement, so that we now challenge any writer's intent in that their unconscious drive might be overtaking their conscious mind so that they themselves might not understand from where their words and thoughts have come. However, I'm not convinced these approaches, that open up the text to be thought of as almost writing created out of an "unconscious" vacuum, are necessarily and entirely appropriate for viewing literature, since the unconscious is heavily influenced by an individual's experiences and their means of handling those experiences. And an individual's unconscious is distinct from another individual's unconscious, which seems to be discounted, or ignored, by a good number of critics, several in lit-to-film adaptation studies, and by others, including adapters.

Eagleton brings up one last point concerning deconstruction that I want to address with reference to lit-to-film adaptation. He says that "you can be sure that if your own critical account of someone else's critical account of a text has left the tiniest grains of 'positive' meaning within its folds, somebody else will come along and deconstruct you in turn" (2008, 127). However, if we view a film adaptation as a type of critical commentary of a literary work, because in many ways it could be seen as such, how can that adaptation be challenged? First of all, if you traverse mediums, is that still considered deconstructing? Is it possible to traverse mediums? Is lit-to-film adaptation a form of critique and interpretation of another text? How do you challenge a deconstruction done in a different medium, do you challenge it from the medium it's been deconstructed in, or in the medium of the one that was deconstructed? And if we're talking about language, and the expression of it, and how elusive it is, isn't the expression of film language distinct and incompatible with the language of literature, since language in the *same* form or medium has its own innate differences? How do we navigate through these choppy waters? We continue.

Postmodernism

Although postmodernism isn't actually a type of literary analysis, it is important to understand how it fits into the way we look at literature today, as well as at other texts, including of course film. Distinguishing postmodernism from modernism, as well as poststructuralism, helps to understand a bit about not only the history of literature, but the history of literary theory and criticism. Michael Payne says in his essay "The Survival of Truth after Derrida" that deconstruction and poststructuralism are often mistakenly associated with postmodernism. He states, though, that postmodernism "is a cultural style, like classicism and romanticism; and like those styles, it can never be securely defined, though it can be described" (2000, 128).

It's best to begin by describing modernism, which was the name given to the movement in the arts and culture of the first half of the twentieth century. It was a movement that reevaluated and reconceived the way art and culture were practiced, so that all the previous elements were challenged and rejected. In literature, this meant "a rejection of traditional realism (chronological plots, continuous narratives relayed by omniscient narrators, 'closed endings', etc.) in favour of experimental forms of various kinds" (Barry 2009, 78–9). High modernism constituted the time from 1910 to 1930 and among the big names were T. S. Eliot, James Joyce, Virginia Woolf, Gertrude Stein, Franz Kafka, and Rainer Maria Rilke. Literary modernism placed emphasis on impressionism and subjectivity — on *how* we see not *what* we see; a movement away from objectivity; a blurring of genre styles, a new appreciation of fragmentation, discontinuous narrative, and collage-style writing; and a reflexive quality in the writing itself about just that, writing. This pushed literature into more experimental styles and innovation. It retreated after the 1930s only to resurge in the 1960s, but not with the fervor it had in its earlier run (79).

Postmodernism is seen as oppositional to modernism rather than sequential. It didn't simply pick up where modernism left off; it was a reaction to modernism in a sense, retaining some of the elemental aspects of modernism while rejecting others. The distinctions begin with the postmodernist view of fragmentation as opposed to the view taken by modernists. Barry states that postmodernism views fragmentation as "an exhilarating, liberating phenomenon, symptomatic of our escape from the claustrophobic embrace of fixed systems of belief . . . the modernist laments fragmentation while the postmodernist celebrates it" (81). Second, while modernism eschewed the ornate and elaborate art forms of the nineteenth century, "postmodernism rejects the distinction between 'high' and 'popular' art which was important in modernism, and believes in excess, in gaudiness, and in 'bad taste' mixtures of qualities" (81).

Payne makes it clear that postmodernism and poststructuralism, although they are confused with each other, are more unrelated than related. Both schools of thought challenge modernism. However, "poststructuralism works within the ideology of modernism, calling into question its suppositions, examining the grounds of truth, meaning, and value in the interests of providing the truth, meaning, and value with a more stable and thoughtful foundation in the modern world" (Payne 2000, 129). Payne states that postmodernism "is a more radical break with modernism, although it is often not carefully distinguished from poststructuralism, especially by those who are in reaction against any questioning of the modernist aesthetic or by those most radical advocates of postmodernism who enjoy chaos in all its forms" (129).

What seems to be the greatest distinction that I see between postmodernism and poststructuralism is that postmodernism seems more focused on how art, including literature, is created, or how it should be created, and the elements that go into making it what it is, whereas poststructuralism seems more focused on how texts, including literary texts, are read and viewed and interpreted, and how they mean what they only mean right now because meaning is unstable and temporary.

Psychoanalytic/Psychological Criticism

Psychoanalytic criticism, or psychological criticism as it is referred to more broadly, is strongly based in the theories of the Austrian, Sigmund Freud (1856–1939). Other psychoanalytical theories grew out of Freud's that have extended the practice of psychoanalysis considerably, and its use in offering a deeper understanding of a text, its writer, and its reader. Yet it all began with Dr. Freud.

Psychoanalysis is a form of therapy that was developed to cure mental disorders, and its foundation rests on the interaction between the conscious and the unconscious elements of the mind and how they work together (or don't). The method used for understanding how an individual's mind works is to encourage a patient to talk freely, so that the patient is unwittingly at times invited to explore the deep recesses of their unconscious, to get to what they are repressing. It's believed that what patients are repressing in their unconscious leads to the problems manifested in their conscious mind. Facing these issues, according to the theories of psychoanalysis, brings about healing of the conscious mind. Psychoanalysis is based upon "specific theories of how the mind, the instincts, and sexuality work" (Barry 2009, 92), and these theories were introduced by Freud. Although the work of Freud has been rigorously challenged and disputed, he "remains a major cultural force, and his impact on how we think about ourselves has been incalculable" (92).

Freud's theories changed our notions of human behavior by investigating uncharted territory, so to speak, in such controversial areas as wish fulfillment, sexuality, the unconscious, and repression. In fact, according to Barry, "all of Freud's work depends upon the notion of the unconscious, which is the part of the mind beyond consciousness which nevertheless has a strong influence upon our actions" (92). Although Freud didn't discover the unconscious, he put forth theories about it that placed it at the heart of our lives. Repression, he believed, went hand in hand with the unconscious. What we don't want to remember, we bury in our unconscious, and thus we repress those memories. Eventually, though, what we repress begins to seep out into our behavior based on our consciousness, usually in ways that are not appropriate or healthy. Pushing beyond the idea of the conscious and the unconscious, Freud later developed a three-part conceptualization of the mind that included the ego, the superego, and the id. These corresponded to the consciousness, the conscience, and the unconscious. The superego is considered the part of us that adheres to all the rules, and is our moral compass inside our minds, and thus is the conscience. The id represents our desires, and holds the libido, or the energy drive associated with sexual desire. Freud believed we are not consciously aware of these desires. The ego is the aspect of the mind, according to Freud, that balances the superego and the id. If one of the two begins to become too stringent in its control of the mind, the ego is the part that is supposed to bring the mind back into an equilibrium, that is indicative of a healthy mental state. Obviously, from the way these three elements are described, this balance can be thrown off, and when it can't return to a healthy state, psychoanalysis is considered necessary.

Freud is known to have relied on literature to explore the workings of the mind. His literary studies supposedly influenced the development of his theories as much as his clinical work. In so doing, he "expanded our sense of how language and symbols operate by demonstrating their ability to reflect unconscious fears or desires" (Gioia and Gwynn 2006, 887). Freudian psychoanalytic criticism, then, gives central importance to the conscious and unconscious mind, looking at the text's more obvious content and also its more hidden content, or the meanings that might be seen as subverted within the text, so that even the author wasn't aware that they were conveying this meaning. Much of Freud's work undermines authorial intention and encourages poststructuralist thought. Freudian critics pay close attention to unconscious motives and feelings, of both the author and the characters in the text. Such critics also identify "the presence in the literary work of psychoanalytic symptoms, conditions, or phases, such as the oral, anal, and phallic stages of emotional and sexual development in infants" (Barry 2009, 100), leading to Freud's concept of the libido. This critical view might include identification of the Oedipus complex in the work, which Freud is famous, and maybe infamous, for having developed: the son as an infant conceives of the desire to get rid of his father so he can be the sexual partner of his mother, meant to explain the conflicts that drive these relationships as the son matures. This type of criticism can be taken further at times to make "large-scale applications of psychoanalytic concepts to literary history in general" (101). Barry mentions Harold Bloom's work as an example. His *The Anxiety of Influence* explores the idea of writers inhibited in their writing by the greatness and influence of those who have written before them. Sandra Gilbert and Susan Gubar push this idea further in their chapter of "The Anxiety of Authorship" (Gilbert and Gubar 1984) when they discuss the idea of women experiencing anxiety when picking up the pen to write, since it was not considered their domain.

And, in fact, Freudian theories didn't bode well for how we think about women, and their mental wellbeing, and feminist critics have spent a good amount of energy revoking his theories, challenging his perceptions of women, not always based on sound research. Although their arguments against his work are understandable and valid, it also needs to be understood that gender relations were drastically different during the time in which Freud was developing his theories. It would be nice to think he could have been light years ahead of his time, and in developing his theories, he was. But when it came to applying those theories to individuals, he was as caught up in the perceptions of his time period as most everyone else. Still, his theories continue to be useful today, even in contesting them.

Freud had many colleagues and followers who elaborated on his work and continued his work, in many different directions. One, though, who is to be most noted, especially in terms of literature, is Jacques Lacan (1901–1981). Lacan was a "French psychoanalyst whose work had an extraordinary influence upon many aspects of recent literary theory" (Barry 2009, 104). The Freudian approach to literature began to wane in the 1960s, but Lacan revived Freud's theories by updating them. In the mid-1950s, Lacan began to challenge his field, and started placing increased emphasis on the unconscious but in very different ways than Freud had. As Ann Dobie explains,

> Freud's concept of the unconscious as a force that determines our actions and beliefs shook the long-held ideal that we are beings who can control our own destinies; Lacan further weakened the humanist concept of a stable self by denying the possibility of bringing the contents of the unconscious into consciousness. Whereas Freud wanted to make hidden drives and desires conscious so they could be managed, Lacan claimed that the ego can never replace the unconscious or possess its contents for the simple reason that the ego, the "I" self, is only an illusion produced by the unconscious. (2009, 64)

Lacan, then, was fascinated by how humans develop this illusion. His interest in the unconscious went beyond Freud's, and he saw the unconscious as the core of one's being, and he also believed that the unconscious was structured like a language. So, whereas Freud believed that the unconscious could "slip" into language arbitrarily and provide clues this way as to its inner workings, Lacan believed "the unconscious, the very essence of the self, is a linguistic effect that exists before the individual enters into it, making it possible to analyze the unconscious" (65). In essence, there is a language of the unconscious that is unique and that helps to form the individual, without the individual's conscious awareness.

So, Lacanian critics, when analyzing a text, pay close attention to the unconscious motives and feelings, not of the author or characters as Freudian critics do, but those of the text itself. They look for Lacanian symptoms or phases in the literary work. For example, Lacan studied and put forth a theory of the "mirror stage." This is the stage in a child's life when he becomes aware that he is in fact separate from the mother. When a child is born, he feels as one with the mother, in a dyadic union with the mother. At about six months of age, he sees himself in the mirror with his mother, and begins to realize he is separate from the mother. This realization that develops from six to eighteen months alerts him to the fact that he is no longer one with the mother, and, according to Lacan, is what creates the concept of lack and desire in individuals. Basically, we spend the rest of our lives trying to fill this void of not being one with the mother. When this idea can be identified in a text, Lacan's work can be invoked to explain how it's working in that particular text.

Lacanian critics also look at a text in terms of Lacan's broader implications, like the idea of lack and desire, beyond its supposed origin in childhood experience. Finally, these critics "see the literary text as an enactment or demonstration of Lacanian views about language and the unconscious" (Barry 2009, 110), which has been explained as a view that insists the unconscious is much more pervasive in the text, as it is in language, than Freud felt it to be.

Putting psychoanalytic or psychological criticism in simpler terms, then, it can be broken down into three approaches. First, "it can investigate the creative process of the arts. What is the nature of literary genius, and how does it relate to normal mental functions?" (Gioia and Gwynn 2006, 888). Secondly, one can explore the psychology of the particular artist or writer. With reference to a literary work, how does it reflect the author's personal psychology? The third common approach is an analysis of the fictional characters in a text. What do the emotions and behaviors of the characters reveal about their psychological states? One can examine the personalities of the characters and study how their personalities guide their actions. Also, in viewing a literary work, one can identify how dreams, repression, and desire are presented consciously or unconsciously by the author, and then move beyond Freudian and Lacanian theories to explore more current psychological disorders exemplified by the characters, or even the author in their writing of their text. What's interesting is to apply a more recently studied psychological disorder and apply it to a character of a book written long ago. For example, I've had students who have analyzed and developed the idea of Victor Frankenstein in Mary Shelley's *Frankenstein* exhibiting symptoms of social anxiety disorder, which might have led him to create the disaster he does, mainly by rejecting his creation, more than in creating it. Psychological criticism can be quite illuminating and interesting to use for exploring a text.

Feminist, Masculinist, Lesbian/Gay — Or Just Gender — Criticism

The feminist movement of the 1960s wasn't the beginning of feminism. Many writers, and activists, had already written and expressed the condition and oppression of women in society. Mary Wollstonecraft wrote *A Vindication of the Rights of Woman* in 1792, as the intellectual thought surrounding the French Revolution began to move towards freedom for all, or "Liberty, equality, fraternity!" Wollstonecraft believed that same slogan should include women in its purpose. She encouraged her readers, most of whom she knew would be male, to give women an education, and her strategy was to insist that women needed such an education in order to raise children well and handle their responsibilities as manager of the household. Virginia Woolf also wrote on women's education in 1929 in her book, *A Room of One's Own*, trying to subdue her anger at the fact that she, due to being a woman, could not enter the library at Oxford without a male escort. Ironically, her father's manuscripts were housed in the library, but she could not enter the library on her own. She writes in her book that more women would be writing and able to express their genius if they had the same quality education as men, and the same comforts, including a stipend and a room of their own. Simone de Beauvoir wrote *The Second Sex* in 1949, which argued against inequality and enforced "otherness," or the marginalization of women in society. The French version of the book is much more accurate in depicting all that Beauvoir meant to convey to her reader, and only in 2009 has an English version finally been published that adequately translates the original text since the only other English translation dates back to 1952 and was done by H. M. Parshley, a zoologist, with very little feedback from Beauvoir. Although her limited help was the excuse used to justify the negligence of the translation, its published inadequacies should have behooved the publisher, or another major publisher, much more expediently to option another, better qualified, more committed translator to do the honors. That way, American women would have experienced sooner a closer translation to the book that European women experienced.

In all three of these books, the writers make reference to male writers, and their influence on the continued inequality of women. However, as Barry states, there were also "male contributions to this tradition of feminist writing . . . John Stuart Mill's *The Subjection of Women* (1869) and *The Origin of the Family* (1884) by Friedrich Engels" (2009, 116). But, although the feminist movement stretches back to the nineteenth century and even a bit before, the modern attempt to look at literature from a feminist perspective began to develop only in the early 1960s, and this criticism was the direct product of the women's movement of this time period.

One issue that began to surface during this time period was women's identity based in the language used to refer to women, and woman. Toril Moi, a prominent literary theorist especially in feminist theory (and one of the proponents who advocated for a new English translation of Beauvoir's *The Second Sex*), distinguished between the terms, "feminist," "female," and "feminine." Moi "explains [that] the first is 'a political position', the second 'a matter of biology', and the third 'a set of culturally defined characteristics'" (Barry 2009, 117). Looking at these terms was only one of the manifestations of the new exploration into the way language conditioned and socialized women in society into the roles they were expected to perform. And it follows, then, that literature, and especially the representation of women in literature, "was felt to be one of the most important forms of [socialization], since it provided the role models which indicated to women, and men, what constituted acceptable versions of the 'feminine' and legitimate feminine goals and aspirations" (117).

In the 1970s, feminist criticism became about bringing to light the ways in which patriarchy worked to inform the cultural perspectives on gender, perpetuating sexual inequality as a result. In the 1980s, just as in other critical approaches, things took a turn. Feminism became more interested in other critical approaches and how they affected the feminist perspective and how they could strengthen this perspective. Feminism began to focus more on how women lived and their outlook on the world, rather than "attacking male versions of the world" (117). Most importantly for the field of literature, feminism began to place more attention on the established canon and its absence of women writers, and "the need to construct a new canon of women's writing by rewriting the history of the novel and of poetry in such a way that neglected women writers were given new prominence" (117).

It seemed as though, finally, the words written by Virginia Woolf in *A Room of One's Own* were being given their just due and being taken seriously, whether intentionally or unintentionally, but justifiably:

> Indeed, since freedom and fullness of expression are of the essence of the art, such a lack of tradition, such a scarcity and inadequacy of tools, must have told enormously upon the writing of women. Moreover, a book is not made of sentences laid end to end, but of sentences built, if an image helps, into arcades and domes. And this shape too has been made by men out of their own needs for their own uses. There is no reason to think that the form of the epic or of the poetic play suits a woman any more than the sentence suits her. But all the older forms of literature were hardened and set by the time she became a writer. The novel alone was young enough to be soft in her hands — another reason, perhaps, why she wrote novels. Yet who shall say that even now "the novel" (I give it inverted commas to mark my sense of the words' inadequacy), who shall say that even this most pliable of all forms is rightly shaped for her use? No doubt we shall find her knocking that into shape for herself when she has the free use of her limbs; and providing some new vehicle, not necessarily in verse, for the poetry in her. For it is the poetry that is still denied outlet. And I went on to ponder how a woman nowadays would write a poetic tragedy in five acts — would she use verse — would she not use prose rather? (1929, 77)

Thus feminist criticism began to focus on the writing of women, and critics such as Elaine Showalter began to examine women's writing from the past and critique it from a feminist perspective. Also, feminist critics and theorists began to look deeper into women writing, and the way they'd written, and the way they could write, now that they were "coming to writing," as Hélène Cixous, a French feminist/theorist (although she would probably refer to herself more as theorist than feminist), called it. Cixous wrote her controversial essay "The Laugh of the Medusa" to put forth the question of whether or not there is a writing that is essentially "woman," and this "category" of writing began to be known as *écriture feminine*, or feminine writing.

At about this time, a distinction began to be made between Anglo-American feminism and French feminism. The Anglo-Americans were skeptical of the current theory coming into practice, such as poststructuralism and psychoanalytic criticism. However, the French feminists were embracing it, and using it as the basis for much of their theoretical work. So the Anglo-Americans were focused on the close reading of texts, although relying on historical texts and other non-literary research to guide them. The British feminists relied on a Marxist perspective of looking at texts, or looking at texts from a more "socialist feminist" approach. But, the French feminists became quite theoretical, "taking as its starting-point the insights of major post-structuralists, especially Lacan, Foucault [Michel, who will be introduced in the Historical Criticism section], and Derrida" (Barry 2009, 120). These French feminists went beyond literature to derive their theories: "they write about language, representation, and psychology as such and often travel through detailed treatments of major philosophical issues of this kind before coming to the literary text itself" (120). Three of the most important of these theorists are Julia Kristeva, Hélène Cixous (mentioned above), and Luce Irigaray.

These theorists focused much of their efforts on feminism and language, examining how women fit into writing and literature, as writers, since the use of language in literature had been until more recently dominated by men and male writers and their perceptions of life, the world, women, and themselves. The question became how does a woman fit into this tradition, and can she, as it is currently constructed. To address this question, Cixous wrote the essay I mentioned above, "The Laugh of the Medusa," and the concept of *écriture feminine* (feminine writing) began to cause quite a stir. Kristeva pushed beyond *écriture feminine*, beyond Cixous's emphasis that there is a writing from the body, from the female body, that is essentially feminine writing, and essentially female. Kristeva used the concept of *écriture feminine* to explore further psychoanalytic theories of how language operates within us as humans. She identified the symbolic and the semiotic to distinguish two different aspects of language. She discusses these aspects in her essay, "The System and the Speaking Subject." According to Kristeva, the symbolic aspect of language is associated with authority, logic (and order), fathers, repression and control. It is linked with the paternal, it is fixed and unified, it represents the conscious mind, and Kristeva sees it as prose. The semiotic aspect of language is not ordered, or fixed, but is expression that seems displaced, slippery, condensed. It's looser, more random in how connections are made. It is considered maternal, representing the unconscious mind, and Kristeva sees this aspect of language in poetry. Both of these aspects of language are in any given sample of writing, so that they are not two different kinds of language, but two different facets of language, that are also related in their oppositional nature to each other. The symbolic then is the ordered, structured aspect of language, while the semiotic is the randomly connected, improvisational, accidental aspect of language, the latter fitting with the poststructuralist view of language. So, deconstruction can be explained as "the 'unconscious' of the text emerging into and disrupting the 'conscious' or 'surface' meaning" (Barry 2009, 124). Finally, the semiotic aspect of language for Kristeva represents the feminine in language, and the symbolic the masculine. However, both are present in all representations of language in some way or another, which counters what Cixous puts forth in "The Laugh of the Medusa."

In other aspects of psychoanalysis, many feminist critics have disagreed with each other along the way, although this is how theory and criticism tend to play out, and it's also how ideas are introduced, through intellectually-based arguments against theories and ideas of others. Kate Millett's well-known text *Sexual Politics* condemned Freud and his theories due to the patriarchal attitudes from which they grew. Rejection of Freud continues in feminism, but there have been feminists as well who have defended Freud. Some feminist critics have simply viewed Freud's theories differently, more metaphorically, by stepping back. For example, Freud's concept of penis envy in women doesn't have to be taken literally. It might reflect that women aren't envious of the body part, but what having that body part means in our patriarchal-structured, male-dominated world. Gilbert and Gubar take Freud's ideas a bit further when they suggest that the woman writer is seen as castrating the man when she picks up the pen, the pen being the penis. Men are cultural reproducers, and women are biological reproducers, so if they pick up the pen to insert themselves into the role of cultural reproducer, they are stepping on men, and metaphorically, castrating them by taking the pen from them. Gilbert and Gubar use this theory to explain the practice of many women writers in the eighteenth and nineteenth centuries, often in their introductions or prefaces, to apologize for writing, for inserting themselves into the cultural sphere through writing, where they felt they didn't belong.

According to Barry, the defense of both Freud and Lacan has been more welcome among French and British feminists than American feminists. I'm with the French and the British on this one; the theories of both men are much too useful and fascinating to shrug off due to their inability to treat women in a way that is acceptable to modern women. For me, this is one of my most frustrating conflicts with other feminists, and feminist critics: the refusal to acknowledge the limitations and influences of a past writer's environment, understandably resulting in their writing not being as progressive as our more contemporary thinking. Often these same critics fail to identify what might be a subverted underlying text hidden within a text; that suberted text has more to tell us than the surface text does. Frequently, there is a strategy used depending on who past (especially women) writers figured their audience would be. Sometimes they held back with good reason, and sometimes they wrote in a way that would be published. Also, they were victims of their environment, not privy to the knowledge we have today. And the same goes for Sigmund Freud and Jacques Lacan. I do not believe in throwing the baby out with the bathwater, so to speak.

So, finally, feminist critique involves challenging the canon and established male writers, and rediscovering texts written by women. The revaluing of women's experience is a focus of feminist critics. Feminist criticism analyzes literature by both men and women in an effort to understand literary representations of women as well as the writers and cultures that create them. It places literature in a social context, and its analyses often have sociopolitical purposes — explaining, for example, how images of women in literature reflect the patriarchal forces that have impeded women's efforts to achieve full equality with men. Feminist critics examine the idea of essentialism, that women and men are different because of biology, or whether social construction creates that difference. They explore the question of a female language and its availability to men.

It needs to be pointed out that emerging alongside feminist criticism was a movement toward queer theory, which reached a critical point in the 1980s. Queer theory in practice is gay and lesbian criticism. Gay and lesbian critics focus on how homosexuals are represented in literature, how they read literature, and whether sexuality and gender are culturally constructed or innate. Although gay and lesbian readings often raise significant interpretive controversies among critics, they have opened up provocative discussions of seemingly familiar texts. Gender criticism is now the term that includes both feminist and gay/lesbian criticism, since both schools of thought expand categories and definitions of what is masculine and feminine and tend to regard sexuality as more complex than merely masculine and feminine, heterosexual and homosexual.

A smaller, less visible masculinist movement has evolved along with feminist criticism, yet it seems to have as much difficulty agreeing on a plan of action as feminism often does. When I graduated from college after finishing my undergraduate work, in 1987, I was very interested in a program at the University of Southern California called the Study of Women and Men in Society. I had done a fifty-page research report for Bucknell University (the college I attended) on women's studies programs across the nation and locally, to help Bucknell get such a program off the ground. I liked the idea of the study of women and men in society, though, at USC. And, I still believe that until men are involved in working towards establishing perceptually, systemically, and institutionally the equality of women and men, doing so will be difficult to achieve. The National Organization for Men Against Sexism (NOMAS) has as their statement of principles what the masculinist movement began with as a purpose:

> NOMAS advocates a perspective that is pro-feminist, gay affirmative, anti-racist, dedicated to enhancing men's lives, and committed to justice on a broad range of social issues including class, age, religion, and physical abilities. We affirm that working to make this nation's ideals of equality substantive is the finest expression of what it means to be men.

Although rarely is it found in literary criticism much mention of the way men are portrayed, and how this has helped to create their association with what it means to be male, in a way that is not only detrimental to women, but is also detrimental to them in ways they don't always see, it is an area I would like to see developed. I understand the precarious nature of encouraging such study in literature, since literature has been dominated by men for centuries. Yet, maybe for that reason alone, we should be. How has it benefited men to achieve such dominance, and has it benefited them, more than in economic and authoritative ways? What about quality of life, including quality of relationships with women, with children, and between and among men? I think this is an area of literary study worth pursuing, with caution and thought, but with progress.

Historical/Cultural Criticism

History can be used as a means for understanding a literary work more fully, and using historical tools can be done in a myriad of ways that have been investigated and explored by many theorists. Historical approaches to a text view the text as a document reflecting, producing, or being produced by the social conditions during the time in which it was written, giving equal attention to the social environment of the time and the work itself. Four historical strategies have been especially influential in reading texts from a historical perspective, and they include: literary history criticism, Marxist criticism, new historicist criticism, and cultural criticism. Names of different types of historical criticism have been used to mean basically the same thing, and I will address those in this section. In many cases, the British theorists have called one type of approach by a particular name, and it is similar to an approach called by another name according to American theorists. It will help to know these, so as not to be confused.

Literary history criticism puts the emphasis on the period in which a work was written more than on the work itself. Although a literary text is assumed to have transcended time so that it addresses universal, human concerns of its readers over a span of decades, even centuries, the literary historian researches and examines the part of the past in which the text was composed, which can bring out more fully the language, ideas, and purposes of the text. Literary historical criticism moves beyond the author's personal life and the text itself to find the relations between the text and the social and intellectual events and attitudes of the time in which the author was writing it. Literary history positions the text in the context of its own time, and often makes literary connections with other literary works that might have had some bearing on the writing of the text being studied. As Michael Meyer writes in *The Bedford Introduction to Literature*, "The basic strategy of literary historians is to illuminate the historic background in order to shed light on some aspect of the work itself" (2008, 2090–1). So one might ask of a text if approaching it from this perspective how the work reflects the time period in which it was written and how this affects the text itself. One could explore the literary or historical influences that help to shape the form and content of the text. All of this can be done once it is determined that the historical context will be useful in interpreting the work, and more importantly, is readily available.

New historicism takes the idea of literary historical criticism that much further. The term was given to this type of criticism by the American critic Stephen Greenblatt, and his book *Renaissance Self-Fashioning: from More to Shakespeare* (1980) was considered its starting point. Barry defines new historicism as "a method based on the parallel reading of literary and non-literary texts, usually of the same historical period . . . [and it] refuses to 'privilege' the literary text" (2009, 166). That is, the literary and non-literary texts are given the same attention and are thought to both "constantly inform or interrogate each other" (166). New historical criticism will most often examine a literary text within the frame of a parallel nonliterary text; "the text and co-text used will be seen as expressions of the same historical 'moment', and interpreted accordingly" (167). The main difference between new historicism and literary historicism is that new historicism gives equal weight to literary and nonliterary texts, whereas literary historicism centers on the literary text as its focal point. Also, new historicism is more about how history is written in texts, rather than the details or facts of the historical events or moments themselves. Barry states it simply: "the word of the past replaces the world of the past" (169). And so, how the past was written is most important to the new historicist.

Barry also explains Derrida's influence on new historicism as he writes: "New historicism accepts Derrida's view that there is nothing outside the text, in the special sense that everything about the past is only available to us in textualised form" (169). So that even history written during the time it was occurring is biased, influenced by the ideological thinking of the time, the political atmosphere, and the placement of the writer within that historical moment. It doesn't change as we rewrite history, trying to understand it. We try to sift through the writing on that time, which is often the writing of that time, and then we rewrite it, analyze it, within our own context, with its own ideologies encircling us, with the political and social environment influencing us, all of this needing to be taken into account. So, "new historicist essays always themselves constitute another remaking, another permutation of the past, as the play or poem under discussion is juxtaposed with a chosen document, so that a new entity is formed . . . [the aim being] to present a new reality by re-situating it" (169).

Poststructuralist cultural historian Michel Foucault needs to be mentioned here, and his influence on new historicist thought. Foucault introduces a focus on "discursive practices" or the way discourse is carried out in society, any society during any time period. Discourse, he believed, was influenced by the power structure in society, and he investigated "the way power is internalized by those whom it disempowers, so that it does not have to be constantly enforced externally" (170). So Foucault believed that language itself, texts themselves, were able to keep the power structure in place. Barry explains:

> Discourse is not just a way of speaking or writing, but the whole "mental set" and ideology which encloses the thinking of all members of a given society. It is not singular and monolithic — there is always a multiplicity of discourses — so that the operation of power structures is as significant a factor in (say) the family as in layers of government. (170)

So, new historicists are focused on juxtaposing literary and nonliterary texts, trying to give equal attention to both to bring something new to the literary text. They focus their attention on how issues of power emanate from both texts and in so doing, maintain that power and its structural organization. They draw from the poststructuralist way of looking at texts, opening them up, seeing them as new, but also focusing on their inescapable textuality, and that "every facet of reality is textualised" (173), so that everything in essence that we know has been captured in texts, and thus is textual, and thus open to interpretation with a multiplicity of meanings, constantly changing.

Marxist criticism was an important development in literary analysis that led the way to the theories I've explored here that question and challenge the canon, and its privileging of the male gender, the upper class, and whiteness. Karl Marx (1818–1883), a German philosopher, and Friedrich Engels (1820–1895), a German sociologist, founded this school of thought. Barry explains Marxism in a clear and concise manner (and it is a school of thought that is not always easy to comprehend and is often mis-interpreted or expressed in a convoluted fashion) when he writes:

> The aim of Marxism is to bring about a classless society, based on the common ownership of the means of production, distribution, and exchange. Marxism is a *materialist* philosophy: that is, it tries to explain things without assuming the existence of a world, or of forces, beyond the natural world around us, and the society we live in. It looks for concrete, scientific, logical explanations of the world of observable fact. (Its opposite is *idealist* philosophy, which *does* believe in the existence of a spiritual "world elsewhere" and would offer, for instance, religious explanations of life and conduct.) (150)

Marxism is most different from other philosophies in that it doesn't only seek to understand the world, it also seeks to change it.

Marxist literary criticism obviously has its roots in Marxist philosophy, and "maintains that a writer's social class and its prevailing 'ideology' (outlook, values, tacit assumptions, half-realized allegiances, etc.) have a major bearing on what is written by a member of that class" (152). The Marxist view of authors then is that they are influenced by their place in society, and they cannot escape this fact as they write, so their writing reflects it. And, it isn't only the content of their work that is affected but also the form in which it's written. More recent developments in Marxist criticism have been influenced by the work of French Marxist Louis Althusser (1918–1990). His influential essay "Ideology and Ideological State Apparatuses" argued that power is maintained in a society through the acceptance of that power by the members of that society, often through internal resignation to that power, whether conscious or unconscious. Althusser referred to the ideological structures in society which achieve this consent to power:

> [T]hese are such groups as political parties, schools, the media, the churches, the family, and art (including literature) which foster an ideology — a set of ideas and attitudes — which is sympathetic to the aims of the state and the political status quo. Thus, each of us feels that we are freely choosing what is in fact being imposed upon us. (158)

What Althusser is saying is that the state doesn't necessarily need to use violence or military force to keep its citizens in line; it has other ways of insisting on their acceptance of the power structure, and it's through "the internal consent of its citizens" (158). Basically, we are tricked into obedience, not rising up against the system, but striving to function within it. Althusser's thinking is closely linked with the concept of hegemony. What is passed down through history, we accept as truth, as the way it is, and we continue it, even if it makes no sense and has no bearing on our lives now. Often, it never made sense. Hegemony is "like an internalized form of social control which makes certain views seem 'natural' or visible so that they hardly seem like views at all, just 'the way things are'" (158).

So, Marxist critics distinguish in a text what's on the surface and what's hidden underneath, and they relate the subverted meanings within the text to Marxist themes. Perhaps there is a class struggle going on under the surface of the text, and thus a Marxist critic would point out where this is hidden in the folds of the text. Marxist critics also "relate the context of a work to the social-class status of the author" (161). Marxists will also look at a literary genre with reference to the social period it came out of, or that produced it (since Marxists believe that a text is produced not only by the author but the author's particular social standing during a particular time in history, and that particular social class itself). Marxists also relate the work to the "social assumptions" of the time in which it was read, or "consumed" (161). Finally, Marxists believe that a text is influenced by the political environment in which it was written and examine the implications of the politics of the author's time and how it affected the writing of the work (161). Questions that you would ask of a text if approaching it from a Marxist perspective might be:

1. How are class differences presented in the work? Are characters aware or unaware of the economic and social forces that affect their lives?
2. How do economic conditions determine the characters' lives?
3. What ideological values are explicit or implicit?
4. Does the work challenge or affirm the social order it describes? (Meyer 2008, 2122)

I will mention only briefly cultural materialism, which is related to Marxist criticism, but in many ways is considered to be the British version of new historicism, in that they are very similar. However, there are differences. Cultural materialism

> takes a good deal of its outlook (and its name) form the British left-wing critic Raymond Williams. Instead of Foucault's notion of "discourse" Williams invented the term "structures of feeling": these are concerned with "meanings and values as they are lived and felt". Structures of feeling are often antagonistic both to explicit systems of values and beliefs, and to the dominant ideologies within a society. (Barry 2009, 177)

Thus, according to Williams, cultural materialism focuses on the values put forth in a novel, through the characters or the narrator, or in some other way, and shows those values are in opposition to the values of the time period in which the work was written. In this way, cultural materialism represents a more optimistic type of criticism, showing that it believes literature can go up against what it is writing within, to write against, and be successful at it. Although cultural materialism like new historicism doesn't place its main focus on only the literary texts of a particular time period, it broadens its scope to all forms of culture, including television and popular music. This allows cultural materialism to use the past to help us understand the present. When we are researching a literary text, the nonliterary texts don't have to be limited to texts of the time period in which the literary text was written, but can be texts and other media in culture, from other time periods including the present, that have a connection with the literary text in some way. Cultural materialism, then, "involves using the past to 'read' the present, revealing the politics of our own society by what we choose to emphasize or suppress about the past" (Barry 2009, 178).

Cultural studies includes cultural materialism, or as it can be referred to, cultural historicism, since unlike new historicism, it not only focuses on the historical contexts of a literary work, it also is particularly attentive to "popular manifestations of social, political, and economic contexts" (Meyer 2008, 2093), and is not limited to only those of the time period in which the work was written (as explained above). A critic would look at popular culture during the time period in which a text was written to gain a fuller understanding of the writer's environment as she was working on her text. However, a cultural materialist critic might also examine a representation of the text in current popular culture to show how the text from the past is interpreted in today's society, and why. We will revisit this type of criticism when we come to litto-film adaptation analysis.

Another type of cultural criticism, and a very important one, is postcolonial criticism, which emerged only in the 1990s. It looks at the works of postcolonial writers but is in no way limited to them. Postcolonial criticism focuses on both how the colonized came to accept their situation and values of the more powerful culture yet also how the colonized would resist, and so this criticism analyzes both canonical texts as well as postcolonial texts. Michael Meyer describes postcolonial criticism as

> the study of cultural behavior and expression in relationship to the formerly colonized world. Postcolonial criticism refers to the analysis of literary works written by writers from countries and cultures that at one time were controlled by colonizing powers . . . the term also refers to the analysis of literary works written about colonial cultures by writers from the colonizing country . . . many of these kinds of analyses point out how writers from colonial powers sometimes misrepresent colonized culture by reflecting more their own values. (2008, 2093)

It's important to note that postcolonial critics enter a text realizing it might be contradicting itself, and that the writer may have written it this way, aware that they were contradicting themselves, or the text may reveal these contradictions without the author realizing they're there.

Postcolonial critics, then, "reject the claims to universalism made on behalf of Western literature and seek to show its limitations of outlook." They analyze the representations of other cultures in literature, and "show how such literature is often evasively and crucially silent on matters concerned with colonization and imperialism" (Barry 2009, 192). They look at cultural difference and diversity and examine how these differences play out in certain literary works. Most importantly, "they develop a perspective, not just applicable to postcolonial literatures, whereby states of marginality, plurality and perceived 'Otherness' are seen as sources of energy and potential change" (192).

So, as you can see, there are a myriad of critical theories that can be put into practice when developing an in-depth interpretation of any body of literature. Most often, these approaches can be combined to produce a full-bodied exploration into a text, and use of these critical theories is not limited to literature, as you will discover as we discuss film analysis. Many of these critical theories examined here represent ways to approach literature, but can be applied to all texts, including film when a film is viewed as a text. Although it is a text in a different medium than that of literature, you will see that it makes use of language through a various array of the elements and techniques that make up a film. And likewise, this same way of approaching one text can be broadened when approaching two texts, one that is a source text that has been adapted for another medium and one that is the adapted text in this other medium.

Before moving on, though, it's important to see how a critique of a text is carried out in a good deal of depth. It's difficult to learn the various methods of critiquing a text without seeing them put into action. The next section of this book will be an exploration into Mary Wollstonecraft's *Maria, or The Wrongs of Woman*. Various critical methods are used to analyze this text, and the critique itself puts forth several issues important to the subject of this book.

One, this critique examines and exposes the complications that arise from critics who analyze texts while much too deeply entrenched in their own agendas and what they want to accomplish in their own work with the use of the text at hand. Often, a text tells us what we don't want to "hear," and it is perhaps that our own perceptions of the text are not what we had originally believed to be the case. Some scholars proceed, not heeding to the text and what it is clamoring to say, and the result is sloppy scholarship. This is important to this book, because the same thing can happen when a source text is adapted to another medium, and in this book the focus is adaptation to film.

However, in the following critique, the premise for carrying it out was to explore the idea of adapting a novel from two hundred years ago into a contemporary novel of today, and the implications of what that would mean to the text of the past and the text of the present. And, although this isn't a term commonly used, the question asked of the entire process was, basically, is this literarily ethical? (When the time came to consider a novel for film in my own experience, the question became, is this textually ethical?) So, the second reason for including this critique in the book is to show an exploration into the idea of adaptation and its ethical boundaries — its problems and overlaps, and penetrations. How are these issues to be managed?

Third, this critique delves into a study of literary creation itself, and what goes into the making of a novel. So, the critique views the writing of a work from inside the process, as the critique discusses the writing of the novel of the present, adapted from the novel of the past. The critique continues by viewing the text of the past from outside the process, as the "product," and analyzing its implications and "meanings."

The critique of *Maria, or The Wrongs of Woman* begins with a close textual reading of the novel, the first reading I did of the novel. This is how I believe any approach to any text should begin. Look at it closely, then step back. That is why I've expounded upon critical theory and literary criticism, so it can also be seen how they can be put into practice. Although the theorists fought amongst themselves over which critical practice was the best and most "ethical" to use, the most "accurate" and "just" way to look at a text, the bottom line is that it's up to the reader and analyst how they wish to approach the text, having all of these tools at their disposal. These critical approaches are tools, tools that can be used to understand and outline that understanding through writing or other means (e.g. a film adaptation).

The in-depth investigation of *Maria*, novel-to-novel adaptation, and the process of literary creation are what follows. To locate the investigation in the process of the writing of my novel, adapted from Mary Wollstonecraft's novel, much of the initial stages of this critique were going on during the writing of the first draft of my novel. However, the first draft was written before I put together the deep exploration into her novel and my work. Intense revisions of my novel were being performed while this exploration of the adaptation process was ongoing. And although to write this is a bit premature since we haven't reached lit-to-film adaptation and its complexities and problems, I will be resuming revision of the novel, and completing the novel once I finish this exploration into lit-to-film adaptation. (I will continue to address my current thoughts on my novel and its being adapted in much the same way although with not so much care and depth as I did with Wollstonecraft's novel.)

What is important to remember as you read through this critique, and noting the points about adaptation, is that this adaptation was novel to novel. The adapted text remains within the same medium as the source text. Since this is so, my novel, adapted from *Maria*, would be subjected to the same close scrutiny as any literary text would, and as *Maria* has been. In this way, critics can argue within defined parameters, even though loosely defined, and in doing so, a critic who perhaps puts forth a conclusion about the literary adaptation that is baseless, can be challenged by another critic, in a common language that allows for a discourse to proceed. However, when an adaptation occurs across mediums, how to challenge the adaptation's efficacy becomes uncertain. Yet, just as a literary adaptation of a literary source text must be able to be challenged and explored based on methodological inquiry, so must a film adaptation of a literary source text.

This becomes a crucial element of critical practice when marginalized writers or creators are involved in any part of the adaptation process. There needs to be in place a means to challenge an interpretation of a source text, and I fervently maintain that a film adaptation of a literary source text is an interpretation of that text. When I took on the exploration of *Maria*, what I began to find was that as a woman writer, Mary Wollstonecraft was discriminated against and thus misinterpreted, as was her work, but not by male scholars as much as by female scholars. And I, as a woman writer, writing about subjects that perhaps go against the grain of society in that addressing them isn't usually seen as welcome to begin with, but then must follow a sort of formulaic representation to be considered as literary, am quite concerned about the fate of my work should it be adapted to film, especially by someone who is not qualified to handle such an adaptation. Let's just say that Roman Polanksi would not be a good choice to direct a film based on my novel, since a 13-year-old in my novel is raped by her father, and the father doesn't meet with a particularly pleasant fate, which is the basis really for the entire novel. I will leave it at that for now, and return to this point once I've established parameters for viewing lit-to-film adaptations, that I hope will call into question some of the current practices of lit-to-film adaptation, and the further marginalization of populations that continues rather than is abetted, even today, ten years into the new millennium. (There is an extensive list of names of the many individuals in the film industry who support Roman Polanski, a list published as I was working on this book. At the publishing of this list, my concentration happened to be focused on the character, Lexi, whose life is irreparably compromised and damaged by another character in my novel who eerily resembles Polanksi and whose crime resembles that of Polanksi's as well, although Seth was conceived ten years prior to me knowing who Polanksi even was.)

So, as you're reading the sections of the critique that follow, be thinking of the various points that are being put forth, because they are intermixed, and they overlap each other. This is how criticism works, and this is why we can apply different theories to one text that relate to each other, and in so doing, bring out facets of the text that one does not see upon simply a first reading or even a close reading.

Chapter 5

The List

I'm providing here a list of helpful books and essays, many of them mentioned in the previous section, for approaching a text from an analytical perspective. Reading these should help you feel as if you're becoming a more active participant in the practice of analyzing texts, and the more you read and try to understand these readings, the more comfortable you will be with applying the concepts in these readings to texts. I've listed the readings according to their approximate order of mention in the previous section.

Aristotle. 400 BC. *Poetics*.

Sidney, Sir Phillip. 1580. *An Apology for Poetry* in *The Norton Anthology of Theory and Criticism*. Vincent B. Leitch (ed.). New York: W. W. Norton & Company, 2001.

Wordsworth, William. 1800. "Preface" in *Lyrical Ballads. British Literature 1780–1830*. Anne K. Mellor and Richard E. Matlak (eds.). New York: Harcourt Brace & Company, 580.

Shelley, Percy. 1821. *A Defence of Poetry* in *British Literature 1780–1830*. Anne K. Mellor and Richard E. Matlak (eds.). New York: Harcourt Brace & Company, 1167–78.

Eliot, T. S. 1919. "Tradition and the Individual Talent" in *The Best American Essays of the Century*. Joyce Carol Oates (ed.). New York: Houghton Mifflin Company.

Fish, Stanley. 1980. "Is There a Text in This Class?" in *The Stanley Fish Reader*. H. Aram Veeser (ed.). Malden, MA: Blackwell Publishers, 38–54.

Tompkins, Jane. 1980. "An Introduction to Reader-Response Criticism" in *Reader-Response Criticism: From Formalism to Post-Structuralism*. Jane Tompkins (ed.). Baltimore, MD: The John Hopkins University Press.

Tompkins, Jane. 1980. "The Reader in History: The Changing Shape of Literary Response" in *Reader-Response Criticism: From Formalism to Post-Structuralism*. Jane Tompkins (ed.). Baltimore, MD: The John Hopkins University Press.

Tompkins, Jane. 1987. "Me and My Shadow" in *Feminisms: An Anthology of*

Literary Theory and Criticism. Robin R. Warhol and Diane Price Herndl (eds.). New Brunswick, NJ: Rutgers University Press, 1103–16.

Foucault, Michel. 1979. "What Is an Author?" in *The Foucault Reader*. Paul Rabinow (ed.). New York: Pantheon Books, 1984.

Greenblatt, Stephen. 1989. "Towards a Poetics of Culture" in *The New Historicism*. H. Aram Veeser (ed.). New York: Routledge, 1–14.

Barthes, Roland. 1968. "The Death of the Author" in *Image, Music, Text*. Trans. Stephen Heath. New York: Hill and Wang, 1977.

Barthes, Roland . 1971. "From Work to Text" in *Image, Music, Text*. Trans. Stephen Heath. New York: Hill and Wang, 1977.

Barthes, Roland. 1974. *S/Z*. Trans. Richard Miller. New York: Hill and Wang, 1974.

Derrida, Jacques. 1978. "Structure, Sign and Play in the Discourse of the Human Sciences" in *Writing and Difference*. Chicago: University of Chicago Press, 278–93.

Derrida, Jacques. 1974. *Of Grammatology*. Trans. Gayatri Chakravorty Spivak. Baltimore, MD: Johns Hopkins University Press.

Harold Bloom, 1973. *The Anxiety of Influence: A Theory of Poetry*. New York: Oxford University Press.

Freud, Sigmund. 1900. *The Interpretation of Dreams*. New York: Random House, 1978.

Lacan, Jacques. 1977. *Écrits: A Selection*. Trans. Alan Sheridan. New York: W. W. Norton & Company.

Wollstonecraft, Mary. 1992. *A Vindication of the Rights of Woman*. Barbara Taylor (ed.). New York: Alfred A. Knopf.

Woolf, Virginia. 1989. *A Room of One's Own*. New York: Harcourt.

Beauvoir, Simone de. 1989. *The Second Sex*. Trans. H. M. Parhsley (1952). New York: Vintage Books.

Kristeva, Julia. 1986. "The System and the Speaking Subject" in *The Kristeva Reader*. Toril Moi (ed.). New York: Columbia University Press. 24–33.

Kristeva, Julia. 1986. "Stabat Mater" in *The Kristeva Reader*. Toril Moi (ed.). New York: Columbia University Press, 160–86.

Kristeva, Julia. 1986. "Women's Time" in *The Kristeva Reader*. Toril Moi (ed.). New York: Columbia University Press, 187–213.

Cixous, Hélène. 1975. "The Laugh of the Medusa" in *Feminisms: An Anthology of Literary Theory and Criticism*. Robin R. Warhol and Diane Price Herndl (eds.). New Brunswick, NJ: Rutgers University Press, 347–61.

Cixous, Hélène. 1991. "Coming to Writing" in *Coming to Writing and Other Essays*. Deborah Jenson (ed.). Cambridge, MA: Harvard University Press.

Gilbert, Sandra M. and Susan Gubar. 1979. *The Madwoman in the Attic: The Woman Writer and the Nineteenth-Century Literary Imagination*. New Haven, CT: Yale University Press.

Miller, J. Hillis 1979. "The Critic as Host" in *Deconstruction and Criticism*. Harold Bloom (ed.). New York: The Seabury Press, 217–53.

Moi, Toril. 1985. *Sexual/Textual Politics: Feminist Literary Theory*. New York: Routledge.

Moi, Toril. 1999. *What is a Woman? And Other Essays.* Oxford, England: Oxford University Press.

Butler, Judith. 1990. *Gender Trouble.* New York: Routledge.

Sedgwick, Eve. 1985. *Between Men: English Literature and Male Homosocial Desire.* New York: Columbia University Press.

Marx, Karl and Friedrich Engels, 1848. *The Communist Manifesto.* New York: Oxford University Press, 2008.

Althusser, Louis. 1971. "Ideology and the Ideological State Apparatuses" in *Lenin and Philosophy and Other Essays.* New York: Monthly Review Press, 127–86.

Spivak, Gayatri Chakravorty. 2006. *In Other Worlds: Essays in Cultural Politics.* New York: Routledge.

Bhaba, Homi. 1974. "The Commitment to Theory" in *The Location of Culture.* New York: Routledge, 2004.

Said, Edward. 1994. *Orientalism.* New York: Vintage.

Genette, Gerard. 1972. *Narrative Discourse: An Essay in Method.* Ithaca, NY: Cornell University Press, 1983.

Chapter 6

A First Close Reading — *Maria*: The Injustices of Being a Woman

Mary Wollstonecraft's *Maria, or The Wrongs of Woman* reflects continuously on the injustices of being a woman as opposed to being a man. Both Jemima and Maria express sentiments, Jemima in the telling of her story and Maria in her memoirs, indicating their acknowledgment of the extreme inequality that exists between women and men in the society in which they live. Both characters express their indignation and frustration with what they perceive as men's ability to do what women could also do yet are not able to, only because they are, in fact, women. Maria goes further than Jemima in relating repetitively that what is acceptable behavior for men is unacceptable and reprehensible in women, and that the standards set for women far exceed the standards set for men. Maria perceives the injustices of being a woman at the same time she realizes there is little she can do to fight these injustices, injustices deeply embedded in the social system in which she lives.

Jemima tells her story and it seems the misfortunes that have befallen her stem more from her gender than from her class. Had she been a man of her class she still would have been able to find work. As a woman trying to find work, she had to fight against almost insurmountable odds. Prostitution was the only occupation she found easily. She found a position of servitude but was always worried about being dismissed. She derides the assertion made by people that anyone who is willing to work can find a job. She claims this is true for men, but not so for women, unless they want to do the most grueling jobs available and even these jobs are out of reach for many women whose reputation has been ruined in some way, most often by the victimization of a man. Although Jemima believes poverty to be a helpless condition in life, it is her womanhood that keeps her from supporting herself in a respectable manner. She states that "a man with half my industry, and, I may say, abilities, could have procured a decent livelihood, and discharged some of the duties which knit mankind together; whilst I, who acquired a taste for the rational, nay, in honest pride let me assert it, the virtuous enjoyments of life, was cast aside as the filth of society" (Wollstonecraft 1975, 89). Despite the fact that Jemima, poverty-stricken though she was, had found a way to improve herself, it was her gender that kept her from reaping the benefits of her improvements.

After hearing Jemima's story and reflecting on her own past, Maria regrets having given birth to a daughter. Jemima's story combined with her own haunts her night and keeps her from sleeping. It's as if Jemima's story has given her more reason to lose hope in escaping her prison sentence. And she must wonder if perhaps there is no other life for a female but some form of a prison sentence. Yet Maria is a feisty, indignant woman who refuses to give up her search for justice once she has cleared her mind of the doubts Jemima's story raises as to the fate of any woman. She regains her fortitude and beseeches Jemima's help in raising her daughter to be forewarned of the evils of the oppressors. Soon after, Jemima returns with the news that the child is dead. Hope leaves Maria, and her story unfolds.

As the story is told, the reader begins to wonder if the child, as a girl, was saved from a life that had the potential to become tortuous. Maria's story continuously relates the injustices of being a woman and although she ultimately fights against her oppressor and oppression, as we read her memoirs we also know where she now takes up residence. Fighting her oppressor has led her here. This is unnerving. Maria is portrayed as a woman who can see through to the oppression that holds her captive not just in the insane asylum but in her marriage. Yet her true lack of power to fight against this latter captivity results in her incarceration. In her memoirs to her daughter, Maria hones in on how the behavior of men and women is interpreted differently, and how men have rights that women don't, including rights to control the women they "own," their wives and daughters, even nieces.

Husbands, Maria relates to her daughter in her memoirs, can do whatever they please and not be reproached for it. Wives, on the other hand, must remain true and virtuous or be cast out onto the street with a sullied reputation. It is a woman's job to keep the attention of her husband, and rightly so, Maria feels, but she questions why the same standards are not held up for men. She writes ". . . women who have lost their husband's affection, are justly reproved for neglecting their persons, and not taking the same pains to keep, as to gain a heart; but who thinks of giving the same advice to men, though women are continually stigmatized for being attached to fops" (109).

Maria focuses on what we in modern society call the "double standard." An example of this today is women who have sex with many different men and are coined promiscuous (or worse) with a reputation that precedes them at every fraternity party they attend. However, men who sleep with many different women are partaking in acceptable behavior. A man who "sleeps around" is thought of as no less than any other man, if it is even noticed. If it is noticed, he is most likely to be more esteemed than his buddies who are more conservative in their sexual behavior. In eighteenth century society, women were to endure the "double standard" at every turn. They were, in fact, the property of their husbands. This kept the "double standard" intact. For example, Maria relates that ". . . a man would only be expected to maintain; yes, barely grant a subsistence, to a woman rendered odious by habitual intoxication; but who would expect him, or think it possible for him to love her? And . . . it would be thought equally unreasonable to insist . . . that he should not love another; whilst woman, weak in reason, impotent in will, is required to moralize, sentimentalize herself to stone, and pine her life away, labouring to reform her embruted mate" (114).

When Maria writes her memoirs, does she think she is doing her daughter a favor in opening her eyes to the oppression by those her daughter may not be able to fight against? By her daughter knowing of this oppression, might it not make it that much more impossible for her to endure, which could result in a fate similar to Maria's own? Is this what she wants for her daughter? Yet Maria seems to believe education will be the answer to all her daughter's problems with oppression by men and that her memoirs are a step towards this education. But even with the memoirs, and education, would her daughter have stood a fighting chance? I am left at the end of Maria's story wondering if it was better as a woman of the eighteenth century to be ignorant of the oppression surrounding her. Maria proves that being bright and perceptive could not save a woman from the violent oppression by which she was victimized and controlled. Perhaps being unaware of this oppression would have made life easier for Maria. Today women have choices. They may be painful at first, but a woman can make her own way once she leaves the shackles behind for good. At the end of the eighteenth century, wasting away in an insane asylum seemed a woman's only alternative to submitting to oppression, which could be equally as harmful if not more so than incarceration in an insane asylum, as can be seen in *Maria*. Sadly, death may have represented the only true course to freedom.

Chapter 7

Beginning *Maria*, Beginning *Sentences*, Beginning Literary Creation

Writing my novel began with *Maria*, a text that grabbed me so powerfully it impelled me to analyze its emotional appeal. Soon my emotional response to *Maria* grew into an intellectual admiration for the text with the analysis that followed my first reading of it. However, my fascination with the novel was challenged by many critics' lack of respect for this text. And, the writing of my novel, *Sentences*, became increasingly substantiated by the neglect of *Maria* by critics who exhibited sloppy scholarship while representing Wollstonecraft from their biased view of her as a writer, and by the marginalization of women's lived experience that pervades literature and our society even today. The writing of *Sentences* also was motivated by an attempt to bring *Maria* to the forefront of literature, to get it noticed for its literary quality despite its fragmentariness, and noticed for its depiction of the reality of women's lived experience in the late eighteenth century, all despite the critical denunciation of the personal in *Maria*.

As I've previously mentioned, my novel began as two short stories I wrote close to the time I first read *Maria*. I wrote those stories in reaction to the injustices inherent within women's lives. Just as Wollstonecraft's *Maria* has been criticized for its autobiographical nature, critics of my work who evaluated it in the context of a creative writing workshop seminar initially assumed my writing was also autobiographical. However, just as Wollstonecraft had never been in an insane asylum or married a tyrant of a husband, but had witnessed the lives of other women being subjected to these cruelties, I chose to write about a woman's life without talking about myself. I've experienced similar injustices to those experienced by the characters in my novel, but not the *same* ones. Thus my being a woman clearly influenced my writing, but my imagination influenced my writing as well. In his treatise, *A Defence of Poetry*, Percy Shelley writes:

> But poetry defeats the curse which binds us to be subjected to the accident of surrounding impressions. And whether it spreads its own figured curtain or withdraws life's dark veil from before the scene of things, it equally creates for us a being within our being. It makes us the inhabitants of a world to which the familiar world is a

chaos. It reproduces the common universe of which we are portions and percipients, and it purges from our inward sight the film of familiarity which obscures from us the wonder of our being. It compels us to feel that which we perceive, and to imagine that which we know. (1996, 1176–7)

As I wrote, then, I was a being within my being. I wrote of a world that was apart from the outside world, but also in ways connected to it, through me, the writer. In other words, a writer half creates her work using her imagination, and half creates from outside influences that channel through her. The short stories upon which I built my novel reflected my own life, and thus my lived experience as a woman, but also that of a human being exposed to the world outside of my imagination. Once I began my novel, drawing from my imagination and cultural influences, I started planning out my writing, devising a strategy to effect the purpose of my work.

After I mapped out my strategy, my imagination grew more instrumental to the development of the novel than my own lived experience. Also, extensive research of both *Maria* and the issues surrounding the characters became imperative to the writing of the novel. Excerpting passages from *Maria* and researching Wollstonecraft's life heavily influenced the writing of *Sentences*. Stephen Greenblatt, in his essay, "Towards a Poetics of Culture," a discussion of the analysis of literature from the new historicist perspective, reiterates Shelley's belief that writing is partly created from one's imagination. However, Greenblatt places less emphasis on an artist's imagination and more on her external influences than Shelley does. Greenblatt believes that most of the work of creators is inspired by what they experience outside of themselves, referring predominantly to cultural influence and exchange. He writes:

> an understanding that the work of art is not itself a pure flame that lies at the source of our speculations. Rather the work of art is itself the product of a set of manipulations, some of them our own . . ., many others undertaken in the construction of the original work. That is, the work of art is the product of a negotiation between a creator or class of creators, equipped with a complex, communally shared repertoire of conventions, and the institutions and practices of society. In order to achieve the negotiation, artists need to create a currency that is valid for a meaningful, mutually profitable exchange. It is important to emphasize that the process involves not simply appropriation but exchange, since the existence of art always implies a return, a return normally measured in pleasure and interest. (1989, 12)

Thus *Maria* can be assumed to be a work of the imagination combined with a strategy that has originated from experiences and both literary and cultural influences. These influences on Wollstonecraft's writing of *Maria* included feedback from other writers (predominantly her husband), what she was reading or had read, her previous writing or texts, and the political debate preoccupying her social sphere. I agree with both Shelley and Greenblatt that any creation is a reflection of the writer's lived experience, and perhaps a distortion of reality, in a positive or negative sense, through the aggrandizement or reduction of elements from that reality. Shelley writes that poetry, a category during his time in which we today include fiction, "is the creation of the actions according to the unchangeable forms of human nature, as existing in the mind of the creator, which is itself the image of all other minds" (1996, 1170). The creator or writer, then, interprets a certain aspect of lived experience in an original way.

However, when that lived experience is minimized and often ignored in society, it must follow that the interpretation of that lived experience in literature might be subject to the same neglectful treatment by both readers and critics. (I am speaking here of women's lived experience, but this statement can be applied as well to the experiences of people oppressed due to race, class, and sexual orientation, among others.) Based on many critics' attacks on Wollstonecraft and their neglect of *Maria*, which I will discuss further in the next chapter, it can be seen that women's lived experience becomes highly generalized by even the most contemporary critics. There is a tendency to assume that any text about women by a woman writer must invariably reflect that particular woman's life. As Julia Kristeva emphasizes in her essay "Women's Time," it is time for women to be seen as singular, and multiplicitous in their singularity. That is, women are individuals, and among women, experiences vary considerably from woman to woman, from human being to human being.

In her essay, Kristeva expresses a concern about feminism, and its privileging at times of the "Woman" experience. She believes that with this practice, feminism risks becoming a religion. If women's lived experience is placed on a pedestal by feminists, will women simply continue to be marginalized? Or, instead, will emphasizing the difference in women's lived experience from men's allow validation of their experiences as women and as human beings? Kristeva discusses this dilemma:

> Certain contemporary thinkers consider . . . that modernity is characterized as the first epoch in human history in which human beings attempt to live without religion. In its present form, is not feminism in the process of becoming one? Or is it . . . that having started with the idea of difference, feminism will break free of its belief in Woman, Her power, Her writing, so as to channel this demand for difference into each and every element of the female whole, and, finally, to bring out the singularity of each woman, and beyond this, her multiplicities, her plural languages, beyond the horizon, beyond sight, beyond faith itself? (1986d, 208)

Women's lived experiences do vary from woman to woman. And that one woman's experience is assumed to be almost identical to another's simply because they are both women neglects women's ability to imagine an alternate world of women beyond their own personal world. If a woman writer is incapable of "half creating" a text chronicling women's lived experience, then the text comes simply from her own experience, and it is not imagined with such a view in mind. It must follow that women create completely from outside of the imagination. My combined project of reading *Maria* and writing my own novel, my lived experience as a critic and a novelist, allows me to speak with some authority on imagination, upon which I relied heavily to write my novel.

In fact, I must add here that I, like Percy Shelley, believe that we as writers half create, and thus our writing is half created. Greenblatt, for me, doesn't give enough credit to an artist's imagination. Since my work began with an *emotional* response to Maria, and my critical and creative writing grew from there, my view of writing relies heavily on the British Romantic ideal of writing documented by William Wordsworth in his preface to the *Lyrical Ballads*:

> I have said that Poetry is the spontaneous overflow of powerful feelings: it takes its origin from emotion recollected in tranquillity: the emotion is contemplated till by a species of reaction the tranquillity gradually disappears, and an emotion, similar to that which was before the subject of contemplation, is gradually produced, and does itself actually exist in the mind. (1996, 580)

That emotion that is recollected in tranquility may come from a myriad of sources and most likely does, and many of them we may never be able to pinpoint as an origin. However, some we can. For me, at least one of those origins for my work was *Maria*.

Maria focuses on women's lived experience: marriage (and the oppressive marriage laws of the time), marital rape and coercion, motherhood, emotional abuse, domestic violence (through fear and intimidation), friendship between women, infatuation versus love, and how infatuation can be physically harmful to women who perceive it mistakenly as lasting love. Such traumatic and even "normal" maturation experiences in a woman's life are often not seen as important or valid in our society, or in literature. Women's subjectivity is perceived as trivial or perhaps even unspeakable because it is too embarrassing or upsetting. Wollstonecraft challenged the silence of her generation, as I do with mine. As such, my own novel is also consumed with women's lived experience. My strategy was to expose the dangers of the patriarchal structure of society, and the hegemonic thinking embedded in a patriarchal culture. The dangers are most pronounced for women, whom I believe have not come as far in the past two hundred years as we would like to believe.

As I continued to write my novel, the character of Annie began to grow into what I wanted her to represent based on my strategy for her and for my book. Annie is not a reflection of my life. She is not Maria nor is she Wollstonecraft. She is Annie, serving a strategic purpose in my novel. Choosing to bring Maria into contemporary society, I give her a new name, identity, and a modern attitude. Annie is educated at college, and has more legal rights than Maria, but she still suffers from the continued oppression of women, as does her daughter.

What I try to show in my novel is that women have been taught to heroicize the men they fall in love with, to their own detriment and that of their children. Men are taught to choose a woman who they can raise up on a pedestal while they live their lives around her. This pedestal and the reasons for the woman being put on it are defined differently according to the individual preferences of the man, yet greatly influenced by what are considered the ideal traits in our society for a woman to have. A relationship built on these limited parameters cannot work. Women and men need to be able to count on each other as trusted friends. Wollstonecraft herself promoted this for husbands and wives in *A Vindication of the Rights of Woman* in 1792. She writes:

> Friendship is a serious affection; the most sublime of all affections, because it is founded on principle, and cemented by time. The very reverse may be said of

love. In a great degree, love and friendship cannot subsist in the same bosom; even when inspired by different objects they weaken and destroy each other, and for the same object can only be felt in succession. The vain fears and fond jealousies, the winds which fan the flame of love, when judiciously or artfully tempered, are both incompatible with the tender confidence and sincere respect of friendship. (1992, 79)

Two hundred years later, women and men still become ensnared in hero worship and pedestals, and for the most part, the friendship between women and men to which Wollstonecraft refers remains elusive.

Working on *Sentences* opened my eyes to the hegemonic thinking that we assume we have transcended, but that we have not. The more research I did on women who kill, women in prison, and women recovering from all forms of abuse, the more I adjusted my strategy. I attempted to find a way to expose the lies perpetuated by a patriarchal society, lies that we are still taught to believe as truths. Yet I refused to invent a woman embracing victimhood. Instead, I constructed the woman of strength. Annie's daughter, Lexi, writes in her notebook about seeing her mother in prison:

I saw Mom! She looked tired and pale. She tried to smile but it didn't look like Mom. It was sad to see her. But she held me for a long time, tightly. That hug made up for the past few months of not seeing her at all. It was a free hug. A hug with no secrets, no lies, no anger. Well, not as much anger. I'm still trying to figure all that out. (You know, the book.) I talked to Mom alone, and asked her what she thought of me telling the truth. At first, she shook her head and wouldn't stop. But I told her I have to do this. (Larkin [this author's pen name], "Life and Death")

Annie is a woman of inner strength, unwilling to reveal that she is a strong woman. Perhaps she cannot reveal that she is strong; she has been taught to be silent and appear weak. Strong women are not accepted in our culture without castigation, because they are seen as castrating and masculine; they are seen as threats to the patriarchal order. Women of strength know how to be strong in their silence. They endure like martyrs. Thus women retain their dignity, but how will it help their daughters? Hélène Cixous, who greatly influenced my thinking and thus the direction of my novel, believes that women must end their silence. They must write and speak. Martyrdom and self-sacrifice serve to keep women marginalized and vulnerable to the horrors of oppression. Cixous writes:

It is by writing, from and toward women, and by taking up the challenge of speech which has been governed by the phallus that women will confirm women in a place other than that which is reserved in and by the symbolic, that is, in a place other than silence. Women should break out of the snare of silence. They shouldn't be conned into accepting a domain which is the margin or the harem. (1997, 351)

In my novel, writing and speech contribute to the end of women's silence, and the revelation of the truth. Healing begins to occur, and hope is restored. A future that didn't seem possible becomes attainable. At the end of the first draft of my novel, Lexi visits Annie in prison after turning 18 years old, the required age for visitation with her mother. This last chapter in its current form is from Lexi's point of view, and one passage reads:

> "Oh, Mom, I almost forgot. I wrote an ending to *Maria*." I hand her the folder I've been carrying.
> "You did it?" She smiles. "I didn't know if you'd get a chance, or really want to. Tamika has mine. Let's get it." She's still so into this literature stuff. I guess that's good. Yeah, it's good. (Larkin, "Time Waits")

What's "good" is not necessarily the text as a material artifact, but as evidence of a new freedom — the end of the "snare of silence."

Chapter 8

Critics on Women's Creations

Ending the silence, and silencing, of women must be achieved in a responsible, intellectual, rational, and thorough manner. As contemporary critics continue to destroy the reputation of Mary Wollstonecraft, I wonder at the accepted recklessness of some critics, women and men alike. It is not enough that Wollstonecraft has been mercilessly attacked since the courageous writing and subsequent publishing of her treatise, *The Vindication of the Rights of Woman*, in 1792. That this critical witch-hunt has continued to the present day is disturbing. In *Vindication*, Wollstonecraft single-handedly challenges the patriarchal structure of her society and the negative effects of that structure on women. At Wollstonecraft's time, most intellectuals did not challenge the oppression of women; they thought the position of women in society to be in keeping with their abilities and capabilities as human beings. Wollstonecraft challenged this thinking, and in her radicalism, became vulnerable to attack. Her credibility came under careful scrutiny, and eventually, her personal life was held up as evidence that the reforms for which she fought in *Vindication* must not be necessary. She herself did not live the life she espoused. It was thought that her emotions dominated her and she did not exhibit reason or rational thought in her personal life. Thus her philosophy became maligned along with her reputation.

One critic of Wollstonecraft's time, Horace Walpole, referred to the writer as a "hyena in petticoats" and a "philosophical serpent" (Taylor 1992, xii) after the publishing of *Vindication*. She was routinely described as caustic and abrasive in her personality. These were clearly gendered, pejorative terms used to refer to a woman who was highly intelligent, outspoken, and headstrong. Similar invectives would not be used to describe the insolent, aggressive behavior of an intellectual man at the time; this type of behavior was accepted and often expected of men of such stature. This perception imbalance of gender roles continues today, and explains why even contemporary critics insult Wollstonecraft. Her texts are frequently misread and some grossly ignored. And yet while her actual texts might be ignored, the well-known history of her personal life is regularly appropriated by critics to disparage her texts.

With the release of a new biography about Mary Wollstonecraft in 2001, Judith Shulevitz, a writer for the *New York Times*, seized the opportunity to discuss Wollstonecraft in her essay "Ahead of Her Time," for the book review. Her essay exhibits an inexcusable lack of research about the woman and her writing, and it exemplifies the practice by certain literary critics of using a woman writer's life to degrade her work. Shulevitz begins her essay:

> In *A Vindication of the Rights of Woman* (1792), feminism's founding document, Wollstonecraft asked for what, two centuries later, we got — the same education as men, legal equality, professional opportunity — as well as what we're still trying to get, such as an end to objectification. (2001a, 23)

Shulevitz fails to mention that *Vindication* became virtually ignored after Wollstonecraft's death due to her personal life being held up as evidence that this text should not be read. This neglect of a brilliant text may be why it has taken women two centuries to achieve what they have, and are still trying to obtain what they don't have. Women can pick up the pen, so to speak, without being made to feel as if they are out of their realm — the domestic realm that is. Yet women's writing, both past and present, continues to be easily discredited. In fact, Shulevitz herself repeats the same mistakes as the critics who defamed Wollstonecraft's character and writing two hundred years ago.

Although she begins her essay with a positive statement of the value of Wollstonecraft's text, Shulevitz then delves into the negative aspects of the writer's life, and of her personality. She describes Wollstonecraft as "a woman so blindly self-absorbed and unheroically in need of constant reassurance we can't figure out whether her accomplishments stemmed from courage or a maniacal effort to deflect despair" (2001a, 23). Never does Shulevitz consider the impact on Wollstonecraft's life of writing a treatise such as *Vindication*. Wollstonecraft wrote *Vindication* quickly, seizing the opportunity to improve women's position in society at a time when oppression in general was being questioned by intellectuals sparked by the passions ignited by the French Revolution. Although she wrote her text carefully, and strategically, she realized the chance she was taking in writing such a revolutionary work. Wollstonecraft herself, in her introduction to *Vindication*, states:

> This is a rough sketch of my plan; and should I express my conviction with the energetic emotions that I feel whenever I think of the subject, the dictates of experience and reflection will be felt by some of my readers. Animated by this important object, I shall disdain to cull my phrases or polish my style. I aim at being useful, and my sincerity will render me unaffected; for, wishing rather to persuade by the force of my arguments than dazzle by the elegance of my language, I shall not waste my time in rounding periods, or in fabricating the turgid bombast of artificial feelings, which, coming from the head never reach the heart. I shall be employed about things, not words! and, anxious to render my sex more respectable members of society, I shall try to avoid that flowery diction which has slided from essays into novels, and from novels into familiar letters and conversation. (1992, 4)

In this explanation of her writing style, Wollstonecraft protects herself from her readership. She does not want to be dismissed as a "gushing" female novelist. Yet she also does not want to trample on the egos of male writers; she insists that she is not trying to compete with their rhetorical style. She traverses somewhere in between these two extremes of writing during her time. She was not unaware of the backlash that could be awaiting her upon the completion of the text.

To explain Wollstonecraft's justification of her language style, it's helpful to mention the work of Isobel Armstrong. In her essay "The Gush of the Feminine," Armstrong argues for a rereading and renewed literary respect for women's poetry written during Wollstonecraft's time. However, that Armstrong must call for this rereading implies the dismissal of women's "flowery," "gushing," and perhaps over-emotional language in their writing. Armstrong contends: "The rhythm of revolution and reaction . . . that shapes the work of male writers is different for women" (1995, 16–17). She ends her piece claiming ". . . the gush of the feminine is a fallacy. Read for its analytical power, the intricacy and self-consciousness of women's poetry become self-evident" (32). This essay was written in 1995, two hundred years too late to relieve Wollstonecraft of her anxiety over the use of emotive, and thus disparagingly feminine, language.

Shulevitz doesn't excuse Wollstonecraft of the limitations within the context of her time period, however. She continues, implying that Wollstonecraft wrote *Vindication* recklessly, wanting to express herself and all the travails of her life. She writes:

> In an age that prized discretion, she [Wollstonecraft] blurted out the secrets of the affair to anyone she thought might pity her. Twice she attempted suicide — complete with notes. Had she succeeded, she would have left her infant daughter utterly alone. (2001a, 23)

Wollstonecraft led a difficult, deeply disappointing life, which is chronicled meticulously in her memoirs written by her husband, William Godwin. She grew up with an abusive father. Her mother favored the eldest brother, but it was Wollstonecraft who nursed her mother while she was dying. She was left to care for an illegitimate daughter after she discovered the father, whom she loved, was involved with another woman. Wollstonecraft relentlessly tried to find or create work so that she could function independently, but the boarding school she founded with her sisters failed, a governess position became unbearable, and her writing was her only means for (meager) financial support. In many ways, Wollstonecraft attempted to live the life that she espoused in her *Vindication*, but was constantly thwarted in her efforts. Shulevitz exhibits no consideration of this fact.

In fact, Shulevitz attacks *Vindication* using Wollstonecraft's personal life of which she has carefully revealed only the negative, damning parts and has conveniently omitted the efforts Wollstonecraft made to help those she loved, and women in general. Shulevitz writes of *Vindication*:

> Taken in its entirety . . ., the book turns out to be as abrasive as its author . . . Most of all it becomes clear that, though Wollstonecraft fought vigorously for women, she didn't like them much. (23)

Shulevitz's carelessness in making the last statement is shocking. Wollstonecraft remained loyal to her sisters, had a close relationship with a woman friend whom she followed to Italy to nurse while she died, and as was mentioned above, nursed her own mother as she died. Wollstonecraft did not approve of the way women were forced into roles in which they had no power except to connive and falsify themselves to the men in their lives in order to retain their position in society. Shulevitz believes the question Wollstonecraft set out to answer in *Vindication* is as follows: "Why are women so awful — so shallow, insipid, manipulative and morally unreliable?" (23). However, to reduce *Vindication* to one shallow question displays Shulevitz's irresponsibility in her attack on Wollstonecraft. Barbara Taylor, scholar and author of *Wild Words: Mary Wollstonecraft and Feminism*, writes in her introduction to *Vindication*:

> [I]ts continuing importance to us, I want to argue, is due to the way in which, in that text, Wollstonecraft identified the dilemma at the centre of all feminisms, past and present: how is it possible to be both a woman and a full and equal human subject? (1992, viii)

Taylor does not reduce *Vindication* to Wollstonecraft's attempt to answer one question, but she believes that Wollstonecraft exposed a dilemma that still resonates in the lives and thoughts of women today.

In fact, Wollstonecraft set out to raise and address several issues, and women are still grappling with many of these issues today. Wollstonecraft, as Shulevitz claims in her title (and nowhere else in the essay), was ahead of her time. Yet Shulevitz disparages *Vindication*, insisting that Wollstonecraft spent most of the text putting down women:

> [H]er catalog of women's failings is reiterated so often, and with such ferocity, that the reader can't help suspecting that Wollstonecraft was driven to this rhetorical device by an agenda that was darker and less calculated than mere persuasion. *Vindication* can also be read as autobiography, as the inadvertent expression of an exquisite personal anguish — the ambitious intellectual's guilty embarrassment at her own inclusion in the ranks of disrespected womanhood. (2001a, 23)

Vindication does not detail any aspect of Wollstonecraft's life. In fact, most of the disappointments and embarrassments to which Shulevitz surely refers occurred after *Vindication* was published. Here we encounter the crux of the issue. What Shulevitz really faults Wollstonecraft for is her autobiographical mode of writing. Her text is too "personal." In her essay "I Am a Woman," from her book *What Is a Woman?*, Toril Moi distinguishes between two forms of the personal that can be detected in theoretical texts. Writers will provide narrative directly from their lives, inserting themselves and their personal experiences directly into the text. However, the personal is also believed to inevitably exist in a theoretical text without being mentioned simply because the author writes from their lived experience. As Moi states, "Some think that only the first person singular is personal, others see the self or subjectivity transfusing the scholar's text whether she knows it or not" (1999, 153).

Wollstonecraft's subjectivity dominates her text, but she does not draw from personal narrative to defend her argument. Shulevitz purposefully misinterprets Wollstonecraft's subjectivity in her text, and uses it to disparage the writer's theory by claiming the text is simply too autobiographical. Yet Shulevitz contradicts herself at the end of her essay:

> Orderly and exact is exactly what Wollstonecraft wasn't. She couldn't be. She didn't have the education, to begin with, but more important, she had to trust her impulses, because they were the basis of her philosophy, the first to be grounded on a woman's experience. (23)

Simply because a text is grounded on an individual's experience does not make it autobiographical, nor arguably, irrational. Jean-Jacques Rousseau is not considered irrational in his writing of *Emile*, although it is based on his experience as a man. It is Wollstonecraft's lived experience as a woman, and observation of other women's lives, their actions and living conditions, that necessitated in her mind the writing of *The Vindication of the Rights of Woman*. It was not her need to "gush" into the public limelight.

Shulevitz ends her essay with an attempt to understand Wollstonecraft's predicament as a woman and writer ahead of her time, yet the accusatory tone of the passage cannot be ignored:

> She all but harassed people with copious correspondence and got her letters back when a relationship was over, which is why she left for posterity documents used to tarnish her reputation. How could she be sure what was worth preserving and what wasn't? Everything was new and might be meaningful. Besides, as we like to say these days, Wollstonecraft had no positive role models to emulate. She was making herself up as she went along. She paid dearly for that creation, and she is paying for it still. (2001a)

In fact, Shulevitz blames Wollstonecraft for the tarnishing of her own reputation, by leaving behind her letters to be read after her death. She didn't publish those letters; her husband did. William Godwin misjudged the reception of those letters by the public, and in so doing, ruined his wife's reputation. Perhaps he misconstrued his own freedom as a male philosopher — and his writing not to be judged in association with his personal life — assuming it would be extended to his wife. However, he grossly erred in releasing his memoirs of Wollstonecraft's life and her letters, and his error resulted in the disappearance of her texts for a century.

Shulevitz seems almost determined to find fault with Wollstonecraft as a person, and use her "discoveries" to malign her writing. Yet the lack of skill and self-restraint on her part only further sullies the reputation of a brilliant woman writer. Ironically, Shulevitz's essay on Wollstonecraft in the *New York Times Book Review* was succeeded by her essay two weeks later entitled, "The Wound and the Historian," a defense of Joseph J. Ellis, the historian and writer accused of lying to his college students about his past. Although Shulevitz believes that Wollstonecraft's invention of herself as a person is responsible for her dismissal as a writer, she believes that Ellis's invention of his past should not affect the reception of his writing. Shulevitz's essay begins with indepth background information about Ellis's work. Not until a third into the essay does Shulevitz write:

> Ellis's strengths as a writer bear keeping in mind as we consider his weakness as a man, recently exposed in the news as a penchant for making up war stories about himself. Ellis belongs to a generation of American historians that is turning away from critical social history — "history from below" — and reverting to the "great man" approach to the past. (2001b, 31)

Not only does Shulevitz minimize that Ellis "routinely embellished his undergraduate lectures with lies about serving in Vietnam" (Eakin 2001, 3), Shulevitz again sacrifices her literary critiquing credibility, but this time for a blind defense of Ellis. In much the same way she defends Ellis, she attacked Wollstonecraft. The personal is not political for Ellis, and yet the personal is *very* political for Wollstonecraft. Shulevitz defends Ellis's lying as necessary for his books to be as well written as they are. He needs the ability to lie to be a good writer? Yet, if he lies to his students, couldn't he have contrived at least part of his writing? Isn't his writing of John Adams and Thomas Jefferson at least somewhat suspect now? Shulevitz claimed *Vindication* was autobiographical; hence, Wollstonecraft was perhaps too much in her text. Why is the same criticism of Ellis not extended? Why would Shulevitz so readily denounce the writing of a brilliant woman, while defend the writing of a brilliant man, while both human beings exhibited human error? Why would she sacrifice her reputation as a literary critic to do so? In both cases, it seemed as if she hadn't done the research necessary to make her bold statements.

Shulevitz, unfortunately, is not the only contemporary critic to rely on poor judgment and insufficient research when discussing Wollstonecraft. Elaine Showalter makes a similar mistake in her book, *Inventing Herself: Claiming A Feminist Intellectual Heritage.*

This book gives brief biographies of several literary women. One chapter is dedicated to Mary Wollstonecraft, entitled "Amazonian Beginnings." Showalter shows herself to be an insensitive or naïve critic when she, like Shulevitz, accuses Wollstonecraft of not living her life according to the precepts set forth in *Vindication.* After Showalter discusses Wollstonecraft's relationships with Henry Fuseli and Gilbert Imlay she writes: "All of her brave, ignorant words in the Vindication about the stoic indifference of an intelligent and educated woman must have returned to mock her" (2001, 32). Yes, in 1791, Wollstonecraft entered into a friendship with Henry Fuseli, "the recently married bisexual painter and philosopher . . . for whom she felt, in Godwin's words, 'a Platonic affection'" (Todd 1992, xi). This relationship ended when "to the Fuselis she [Wollstonecraft] suggested a ménage à trois with herself as intellectual friend, but her offer was rejected by the wife marked out for the fleshly part" (xi). And yes, late in 1792, Wollstonecraft set out for Paris, "leaving behind one failed love-affair . . . and heading straight into another, with an American entrepreneur named Gilbert Imlay. Imlay introduced her to sex, fathered her first daughter, and eventually left her — precipitating two suicide attempts" (Taylor 1992, xiii).

Yes, Wollstonecraft fell prey to the same society and women's position in it as she had written against and to reform. This practice is by no means uncommon amongst writers and philosophers, male and female. However, as Shulevitz tried to do in her essay, Showalter uses Wollstonecraft's personal life to discredit her text. We know specifically of male philosophers throughout history who did not live the way they theorized life should be lived, yet this is accepted. Wollstonecraft, however, must live the words she wrote. She must defy the influences of her culture. We know that the purpose of theory is to move a society forward through thinking and rethinking. It is to document a means to better living. Theory is not the answer; it is the question. Wollstonecraft posed the questions. Yet her life was expected to provide the answers, and since it didn't, her text becomes diminished in quality? I think not.

Showalter doesn't only diminish the brilliance of *Vindication*; she completely ignores *Maria*. Ironically, Showalter makes suppositions about the end of Wollstonecraft's life that blatantly reveal the critic's sloppy scholarship. She did not do all of her research in exploring Wollstonecraft's life. In the beginning of her chapter, she writes that Wollstonecraft "died just as she had begun to realize in her own life the happiness and satisfaction she imagined in her fiction" (2001, 21). Showalter could not have read *Maria, or The Wrongs of Woman*. Wollstonecraft's fiction at the end of her life depicted the depressing and hopelessly dark life of Maria Venables. Thus what Wollstonecraft imagined in her fiction was not happiness and satisfaction. In fact, one of the possible endings Wollstonecraft left behind was that Maria commits suicide. And, much of the novel centers on Maria's incarceration in an insane asylum to which she was committed by her alcoholic, tyrannical husband, but Wollstonecraft portrays the asylum as a more appealing place to be than in her marriage!

Showalter is so determined to make a point about Wollstonecraft's character that she neglects the writer's texts. One must wonder why it is important to Showalter that she draw certain conclusions about a woman, her life and her writing, at the expense of thorough, in-depth scholarship.

Perhaps then it is *critics* who need to be cautious of their personal agenda when writing about the lives and texts of women writers. As a woman writer and creator witnessing critics who draw from a woman's personal life to attack her text, I am intimidated by this practice. How do I continue writing with indestructible confidence when I must wonder if my text will be carefully critiqued based on its literary merit, or if my personal life, or my gender, will be held up as a measure of its quality? (One such "critic" is an adapter. Thus the same concerns arise when I consider my work being adapted as well, by irresponsible consumers/interpreters of my work.)

Chapter 9

Women Writers and Strategy

If women's texts seem particularly vulnerable to sloppy and manipulative scholarship by reviewers and critics, we need to discover "why?." Many indicators point to a lack of respect for women writers' abilities to strategize. For example, *Frankenstein*, a complex and multidimensional text, represents one recipient of such disrespect. Mary Shelley's strategy for her novel is often overlooked in discussions of creativity, with critics focusing instead on the dream that supposedly inspired the writing of the novel. However, any novel, or work of art, that is as complex and innovative as *Frankenstein* simply could not be created without a working strategy. In fact, Shelley states in her introduction: "At first I thought but a few pages — of a short tale; but Shelley [Percy] urged me to develop the idea at greater length" (1992, 10). Thus what came together in Mary's imagination grew longer and more developed through the aid and use of a strategy.

Her strategy will never be fully known, but that the novel is misinterpreted as having been written either solely from her imagination, or alternately from her tragic experiences in life, is a common misconception of the creation of women's texts, rooted in a centuries-old belief that women are incapable of reason. Shelley may have written *Frankenstein* from her imagination, or a dream, her life experiences and the literary and historical influences that affected her work, but she needed to adopt a strategy in order to conjoin these elements of creation.

Shelley's own mother, Wollstonecraft, fought against the notion that women weren't reasoning beings, and in fact, wrote *A Vindication of the Rights of Woman* to expose this fallacy about women. Yet still today, critics deride *Vindication* for its lack of a coherent strategy. In fact, that a woman writer has relied on a carefully constructed strategy to write a text is often ignored by critics. But all writers strategize when they write their work, whether or not it is carefully organized and outlined on paper before the actual writing of a text, or it is an internal plan they have designed before writing.

In the criticism of both Judith Shulevitz and Elaine Showalter, Wollstonecraft's plan for writing *Vindication* is ignored altogether. Shulevitz claims the book was "dashed off in three weeks," and that "it took 200 pages to say what needed only 50" (2001a, 23). Wollstonecraft did write *Vindication* quickly, in six weeks; however, this in itself may have been strategic. The intellectual atmosphere was charged with revolutionary writing, and Wollstonecraft may have sensed a clearing for her daring philosophy.

Shulevitz fails to recognize that Wollstonecraft wrote to a predominantly male audience at a time when women were not given much credit for thought. In fact, she blatantly misreads Wollstonecraft's strategy, insulting the writer's genius by implying that she wrote her book to justify her own shame in being a woman:

> *Vindication* can also be read as autobiography, as the inadvertent expression of an exquisite personal anguish — the ambitious intellectual's guilty embarrassment at her inclusion in the ranks of disrespected womankind. It is hard not to hear in her aside to women, "My own sex, I hope, will excuse me, if I treat them like rational creatures, instead of flattering their *fascinating* graces, and viewing them as if they were in a state of perpetual childhood, unable to stand alone," a defensive self-justification of her condescending treatment of her dependent sisters. (23)

Perhaps Shulevitz cut Wollstonecraft's work from 200 pages to 50 in her own copy, and in doing so "missed" the writer's next statement in *Vindication* following the one quoted above:

> I wish to persuade women to endeavour to acquire strength, both of mind and body, and to convince them that the soft phrases, susceptibility of heart, delicacy of senti-ment, and refinement of taste, are almost synonymous with epithets of weakness, and that those beings who are only the objects of pity, and that kind of love which has been termed its sister, will soon become objects of contempt. (Wollstonecraft 1992, 3)

Wollstonecraft strategizes to convince her female readers that without an education, they will become vulnerable to the contempt of men when men no longer have use of them as objects of desire. For her male readers — the majority of her audience — she strategizes in ways that will gently challenge the way men think of women as mere com-modities, incapable of reasoning and deep thought. The passage Shulevitz quotes from *Vindication* is a direct attack on men's view of women, and the way they infantilize women. It is irresponsible on Shulevitz's part to take one sentence of Wollstonecraft's book and use it to frame her argument against the writer. Wollstonecraft isn't conde-scending to women; she's telling them to wake up, and she needs to be forceful about it. She's refusing to treat women as if they're children, as men in her society did. She recognizes that women can reason and think, as she herself is sitting at her desk, pen-ning a work of great thought dependent upon her ingeniously subversive strategy.

Elaine Showalter similarly critiques *Vindication* as rambling and too emotional for a philosophical text in her chapter on Wollstonecraft's life in her book, *Inventing Herself.* She never mentions Wollstonecraft's strategy, and in fact, claims that Wollstonecraft's contemporary readers saw her book as incoherent. Showalter writes:

> In Wollstonecraft's case, the feelings and desires she was working so hard to repress surfaced in her writing, "accounting," one critic comments, "for its apparent disor-ganization, digressiveness, sporadic examples, apostrophes, and outbursts . . . The resulting earthquake is the prose tempest of the *Vindication*." (2001, 28)

Ironically, the work, especially during the time in which it was written, has also been accused of being too masculine in its diction. Wollstonecraft was determined to remain objective, interjecting no personal information except her objective observations of women. Why, if *Vindication* is accused of subverting the feminine, must critics then accuse the writer of somehow exerting the feminine into the text, as if it's a disease one cannot escape?

In fact, Showalter undermines her own criticism of *Vindication* when she writes: "Wollstonecraft opposes 'flowery diction' but takes many of her images of women from gardening and flowers" (2001, 28). Showalter, as an eminent critic of women's litera-ture, appears silly as she writes this passage, all in an attempt to undermine the writer of *Vindication*? Flowery diction does not refer to the language of flowers. Wollstonecraft writes that she will "try to avoid that flowery diction which has slided from essays into novels, and from novels into familiar letters and conversation" (1992, 4). She disdains emotive language for her text, and tries to remain free of adornment. She was in one sense referring to the language of women novelists at the time, who romanticized life through the use of grandiosity. However, that she wasn't going to use flowery diction did not mean she wouldn't refer to flowers. Wollstonecraft relied on the metaphori-cal use of flowers in a few passages of her text, but this was a common strategy for a writer during this time, directly preceding the impending Romantic period of litera-ture. Wollstonecraft used a simple language, not a "flowery diction," but also added some poetical devices to her writing of the text, hence the few references to flowers that Showalter aggrandizes: "Women in the eighteenth century, she [Wollstonecraft] writes, are like 'flowers which are planted in too rich a soil, strength and usefulness sacrificed to beauty" (2001, 28). Showalter's misinterpretation of "flowery diction" prompts a questioning of the critic's need to make a point at the expense of erudite literary criticism. (This also refers back to Armstrong's "The Gush of the Feminine," and the more recent attempt at validating emotive language, which will be discussed later in this chapter.)

Showalter continues to deride *Vindication* in much the same way that Shulevitz does in her essay. Showalter writes: "A first-time reader of the *Vindication* will be surprised at how critical it is of women's timidity, laziness, lack of discipline, 'infantine airs,' petty vanity. And Wollstonecraft does not mince words or try not to offend her readers" (28–9). Again, it is difficult to understand how a leading critic of women's literature could overlook Wollstonecraft's need to strategize simply to get her text read. She didn't write this book to women; her "readers" were predominantly men, since they were the avid readers of philosophical texts during her time. They most likely were not offended by what she wrote as much as dismissive of it.

I detail the cursory and inaccurate treatment of *Vindication* and Wollstonecraft by contemporary critics to show that still today the strategy of women writers is easily dismissed by critics when it becomes more important to make a point. (And, if crit-ics dismiss the writing of women, and other writers who veer from the white male establishment of the literary canon, how are adapters expected to be held account-able?) That women's reasoning capabilities are still questioned render women writers vulnerable to the mishandling of their texts by irresponsible critics (and adapters). We can attribute this vulnerability to hegemonic thinking that continues to thrive even today. Wollstonecraft identified it two hundred years ago.

In *Vindication*, Wollstonecraft's expresses admiration for Catherine Macaulay, a woman of letters, whom Wollstonecraft claims "was an example of intellectual acquirements supposed to be incompatible with the weakness of her sex." She continues:

> I will not call hers a masculine understanding, because I admit not of such an arrogant assumption of reason; but I contend that it is a sound one, and that her judgment, the matured fruit of profound thinking, was a proof that a woman can acquire judgment in the full extent of the word. (1992, 113)

Wollstonecraft here begins her attack, albeit gently, on the writings of Jean-Jacques Rousseau. She is careful about her criticism of Rousseau, but she clarifies her disagreement with his "philosophy" on women. Rousseau represents one of many philosophers and writers who inspired people to believe that women were incapable of reason. Rousseau's thoughts on women were damaging to women for two centuries, and continue to be.

Shulevitz and Showalter are women, proving that women can reason, yet these same women often do not credit the women whom they critique with the same ability. How far entrenched within us all have Rousseau's ideas on women's capacity to think become? Rousseau was a widely-read and respected philosopher of his time (his *Emile* was published in 1762), which was, relatively speaking, Wollstonecraft's time. Wollstonecraft herself had difficulty dissenting with his work, since she concurred with his revolutionary politics, but disdained his treatment of women, in his work and in his life. Wollstonecraft's reservations about Rousseau's thoughts on women were well-founded. He has effected a hegemony that arguably has been sustained in the minds of people even today, rendering a woman's ability to reason suspect. In fairness to Rousseau, other philosophers have maligned women's reasoning capabilities, but it was his revolutionary reputation that brought his thinking greater notoriety.

Nonetheless, reading Rousseau confounds the modern female reader who has achieved prominence in both analytical subjects and critical thinking skills equal to or far beyond that of many men. Yet Rousseau writes in his text *Emile* of

> the first assignable difference in the moral relations of the two sexes. One ought to be active and strong, the other passive and weak. One must necessarily will and be able; it suffices that the other put up little resistance. Once this principle is established, it follows that woman is made specially to please man. If man ought to please her in turn, it is due to a less direct necessity. His merit is in his power; he pleases by the sole fact of his strength. This is not the law of love. I agree. But it is that of nature, prior to love itself. (1979, 358)

Rousseau establishes that women exist to please and cater to men. Men have the privilege, by nature, to be men only at certain moments, when they choose. Women, he contends, are always women. Women are always to please, never think. He writes: "The male is male only at certain moments. The female is female her whole life or at least during her whole youth" (361). In fact, Rousseau believes that men deserve to make servants of women, and that women must, in accordance with their vast insufficiencies as human beings, comply. He states that

> nature wants them to think, to judge, to love, to know, to cultivate their minds as well as their looks. These are the weapons nature gives them to take the place of the strength they lack and direct *ours*. They ought to learn many things but only those that are suitable for them to know. (364, my emphasis)

Wollstonecraft was not the first woman to exhibit critical thinking skills that Rousseau claims women cannot do. Although Wollstonecraft was three years old when *Emile* was published, there were many women who wrote and exhibited genius during Rousseau's time.

To read Wollstonecraft's *Vindication* written only thirty years after Rousseau's *Emile* should result in a loss of credibility for Rousseau. Instead, though, that so many critics of today neglect Wollstonecraft's need, but also ability, to strategize only shows that the thoughts on women that she adamantly refutes remain entrenched within our society. In her text, Wollstonecraft writes:

> "Educate women like men," says Rousseau, "and the more they resemble our sex the less power will they have over us." This is the very point I aim at. I do not wish them to have power over men; but over themselves. (1992, 67)

Here, Rousseau tries to convince his readers that women should not be educated like men or they won't have the power over men that they need. Wollstonecraft desires women to have power over themselves, exactly what Rousseau does not want. He also does not believe this possible, according to his writing. Wollstonecraft adamantly disagrees yet realizes that her society and its organization has been constructed according to Rousseau's assumption. She wouldn't have been motivated to write *Vindication* if one, Rousseau's assumption was accurate, and two, it was being misused to keep one half of the human species controlled by the other half.

Wollstonecraft herself proves that women writers can strategize. Yet her critics prove that even today intellectuals can become trapped within the hegemonic thinking promoted by Rousseau, and others, that women are incapable of reason. Contemporary women writers can be as vulnerable as Wollstonecraft was and is to the neglect of critics. One such writer and theorist is Hélène Cixous. Let me first point out, before I begin this section, that Cixous encouraged women to write emotive language, a language from the body. This might seem in opposition to Wollstonecraft, who promoted women's restraint of their bodily desires and expressed disdain for overemotional expression. However, what I find similar in the theories of both women is their strategic maneuvers. Both strategize in ways that mark their writing as contradictory and controversial. They are radical in their thoughts on women for their time, but they both write to achieve reform of women's lives and the end of oppression within a patriarchal system.

In 1975, Cixous published her ground-breaking essay "The Laugh of the Medusa," which fervently urged women to write, and more specifically, to write "woman."

Cixous had tired of her admittedly self-motivated restriction from writing. Yet she was more disturbed by the external constraints placed on women, effectively but almost silently encouraging their exclusion from literature and writing. In "The Laugh of the Medusa," she writes: "I know why you [women] haven't written. (And why I didn't write before the age of twenty-seven.) Because writing is at once too high, too great for you, it's reserved for the great — that is for 'great men'" (Cixous 1997, 348). Cixous claims that women need to find a "writing that inscribes femininity" (349). She believes that there is a writing for women that comes from the body, and that women have been inhibited from discovering this writing by the male world of literature and writing. She writes:

> To write. An act which will not only "realize" the decensored relation of woman to her sexuality, to her womanly being, giving her access to her native strength; it will give her back her goods, her pleasures, her organs, her immense bodily territories which have been kept under seal; it will tear her away from the superegoized structure in which she has always occupied the place reserved for the guilty . . . (351)

Cixous urges women to write in order to reconnect with themselves, and claim a space that is their own. She names this space *l'écriture feminine*, or feminine writing.

Cixous's strategy for her theoretical work and fiction was carefully organized and planned. Her strategy is apparent in "The Laugh of the Medusa," as her first paragraph proclaims:

> I shall speak about women's writing: about what it will do. Woman must write her self: must write about women and bring women to writing, from which they have been driven away as violently as from their bodies — for the same reasons, by the same law, with the same fatal goal. Woman must put herself into the text — as into the world and into history — by her own movement. (347)

Cixous's strategy, however, becomes neglected in the fear that she evokes among many feminists as she encourages women to write themselves, and is interpreted as primarily insisting women write from their bodies. Perhaps it is Cixous's concentration on women's bodies that prompts the dissension of the critics. She writes:

> I have been amazed more than once by a description a woman gave me of a world all her own which she had been secretly haunting since early childhood . . . I wished that that woman would write and proclaim this unique empire so that other women, other unacknowledged sovereigns, might exclaim: I, too, overflow; my desires have invented new desires, my body knows unheard-of songs. Time and again I, too, have felt so full of luminous torrents that I could burst — burst with forms much more beautiful than those which are put up in frames and sold for a stinking fortune. (347–8)

At a time when women, especially feminists, were challenging the oppression inherent in women being linked with their bodies, Cixous's theory of feminine writing seemed dangerous. Feminists did not want women to be essentialized and thus defined by their bodies. Essentialism implies that women relate to society according to the natural functioning of their bodies. Anti-essentialists believe in social construction; it is the culture in which a woman lives that determines her functioning within that culture. In the Introduction to her book *Essentially Speaking: Feminism, Nature and Difference*, Diana Fuss explains the opposition intrinsic to the concept of essentialism:

> Essentialism is most commonly understood as a belief in the real, true essence of things, the invariable and fixed properties which define the "whatness" of a given entity. In feminist theory, the idea that men and women, for example, are identified as such on the basis of transhistorical, eternal, immutable essences has been unequivocally rejected by many anti-essentialist poststructuralist feminists concerned with resisting any attempts to naturalize human nature. (1989, xi)

The essentialism inherent within Cixous's theory was believed by many feminist critics to encourage marginalization, and they had fought hard against the silencing that accompanies marginalization. However, did the critics consider that Cixous's supposed championing of essentialism, and thus marginalization, might have been her strategy? Cixous's strategy grew out of a desire to challenge marginalization. She attempted an experimental writing, a free-flowing form, that was designed to magnify the marginalization of women's writing in ways that hadn't been recognized. Her work may be seen as lacking a discernible strategy, and her writing could appear aimless, but Cixous deeply questioned the male establishment of literature, and did so through her style as well as her words:

> If woman has always functioned "within" the discourse of man, a signifier that has always referred back to the opposite signifier which annihilates its specific energy and diminishes or stifles its very different sounds, it is time for her to dislocate this "within," to explode it, turn it around, and seize it; to make it hers, containing it, taking it in her own mouth, biting that tongue with her very own teeth to invent for herself a language to get inside of. (1997, 356)

Evidence of Cixous's strategy reveals itself in the essay "Writing the Body: Toward an Understanding of L'Écriture Feminine," by Ann Rosalind Jones. Jones writes of the criticisms of a feminine writing:

> But *féminité* and *écriture feminine* are problematic as well as powerful concepts. They have been criticized as idealist and essentialist, bound up in the very system they claim to undermine; they have been attacked as theoretically fuzzy and as fatal to constructive political action. I think all of these objections are worth making. What's more, they must be made if American women are to sift out and use the positive elements in French thinking about *féminité*. (1997, 374)

Is a feminine writing idealist and essentialist? Or is it a concept created out of a desire to explode the binary system that it appears to adhere to? Could it be that Cixous deconstructs essentialism and marginalization by turning them in on themselves? In Derrida's essay, "Structure, Sign and Play in the Discourse of the Human Sciences," he writes of deconstruction:

> It is a question of explicitly and systematically posing the problem of the status of a discourse which borrows from a heritage the resources necessary for the deconstruction of that heritage itself. A problem of *economy* and *strategy*. (1978, 282)

Cixous appropriates a purposeful essentialist methodology for strategic purposes; she discusses a writing from the body that will free women. Yet she herself writes with a strategy, which does not come from the body but the reasoning mind. Thus, does a writing from the body really exist? Can it? Does Cixous believe in a writing from the body that will free women, or is her concept of feminine writing based on a strategy to convince women to write and find a place in the literary world that is "theirs?"

Cixous exemplifies in her own writing the impossibility of writing from the body. In fact, the idea of "invention" is frequently mentioned throughout Cixous's essay on writing entitled "Coming to Writing," and is also mentioned in "The Laugh of the Medusa." Invention involves planning and devising. One cannot invent a writing from the body if one must *invent* it. Invention does not imply an unconscious letting go of women's libidinal drives and allowing these drives and desires to guide their writing. In "Laugh," Cixous writes: "Women must write through their bodies, they must invent the impregnable language that will wreck partitions, classes, and rhetorics, regulations and codes . . ." (Cixous 1997, 355). In "Coming to Writing," which was published in 1977, two years after "Laugh," Cixous writes:

> The more you let yourself dream, the more you let yourself be worked through, the more you let yourself be disturbed, pursued, threatened, loved, the more you write, the more you escape the censor, the more the woman in you is affirmed, discovered, and invented. (55)

Cixous discusses inventing a language of woman, and of women inventing themselves. I believe that Cixous is trying to find a way for women to socially construct themselves, and their writing, in a space where they can be free from the patriarchal structure in which they and their writing become ensnared. However, does the search for such a space constitute a viable alternative to writing within the patriarchy? Is it even possible? Perhaps it is Cixous's search for this space that is important, and not the as yet unreachable utopia for women, which would allow women to write without being overshadowed by patriarchal influences. And the question must be asked of contemporary women writers: would we really want to achieve this utopia?

In "The Laugh of the Medusa," Cixous claims to believe in a return to nature for women, an expression by women of their biological body's natural rhythms and cycles, and drives and desires. Yet, Cixous, and Luce Irigaray and Monique Wittig, determine how a woman's body might express itself if it accurately reflected its rhythms, cycles, and drives. They purposefully design the writing of women that comes from the body.

Thus essentialism functions as a tool for Cixous to dispute women's limited space in literature and expose the marginality of women's writing. In "Laugh," she writes:

> Write, let no one hold you back, let nothing stop you: not man; not the imbecilic capitalist machinery, in which publishing houses are the crafty, obsequious relayers of imperatives handed down by the economy that works against us and off our backs; and not *yourself.* (348)

The idealism inherent in the theory behind *écriture feminine* seems so clear here that it must be interpreted as strategy. How can women fight against forces as large as "machinery" and the constant messages relayed to them every day that in some way they are less? Cixous isn't sure perhaps, but she proposes taking what is used against them, which is to say their bodies, to work *for* them.

In fact, Cixous's strategy may have included a desire to expose women's disconnection from their bodies as she writes:

> We've been turned away from our bodies, shamefully taught to ignore them, to strike them with that stupid sexual modesty; we've been made victims of the old fool's game: each one will love the other sex. I'll give you your body and you'll give me mine. But who are the men who give women the body that women blindly yield to them? Why so few texts? Because so few women have as yet won back their body. (355)

Cixous believes that women can win back their bodies by writing themselves into their work. She attempts to traverse the chasm between what women have been taught to believe of their bodies (which in many ways is to hate them) and what women should begin to believe of their bodies, which should be to appreciate all the fascinating intricacies hidden within the body's own memory. Cixous writes: "Men have committed the greatest crime against women. Insidiously, violently, they have led them to hate women, to be their own enemies, to mobilize their immense strength against themselves . . ." (349). Cixous believes the answer for women is just to write. And it will come.

Jones, at the end of her essay identifying the criticisms of *écriture feminine*, defends the deconstructive nature of a feminine writing as she writes:

> It takes a thorough-going familiarity with *male* figureheads of Western culture to recognize the intertextual games played by all these writers; their work shows that a resistance to culture is always built, at first, of bits and pieces of that culture, however they are disassembled, criticized, and transcended. (1997, 380)

Cixous incites women to write from the body in a natural, free-flowing manner, but she herself did not. Instead, she strategized for women writers to invent a writing for themselves that did not reflect the patriarchal foundations of the literary world. In her fiction, she challenges the preconceived notions of how a novel should be written. The presentation of *l'écriture feminine* as a women's writing that comes naturally from the body failed; its failure was intentional, exposing the need for women to find their place as writers in a world denying them ownership of such a place. Cixous in "Laugh," Wittig in her essay "The Mark of Gender," and Irigaray in her text *The Sex Which Is Not One*, pushed beyond the boundaries erected by men within which women were simply expected to write. Cixous proclaims in "Laugh:" "And why don't you write? Write! Writing is for you, you are for you; your body is yours, take it" (1997, 348). To Cixous, writing represents women's inscription on the world. In what appears to be a theory based in essentialism and marginalization if neglecting Cixous's ability to strategize instead becomes a brilliant theory, especially from a feminist perspective, if it is interpreted as driven by a clear and precise strategy.

All writing has a strategy, and strategy is gender neutral. It is crucial to the efficacy of a work. However, critics who deny or neglect the use of a strategy by women writers undermine and misrepresent their texts. In fact, as was seen with Wollstonecraft, women writers often must double-strategize. They must strategize to have their writing read, and then they develop the strategy for the work itself. Women have more freedom today to write with less inhibition about the reception of their work, but still today, a woman's text, especially one that ventures into new territory, is more vulnerable to harsh, and often harmful, criticism than such a text by a male writer. Most importantly, it's also still more vulnerable to misinterpretation since what women write about and the perspective from which they're writing isn't the dominant view from which we are taught to see and perceive the world.

Another contemporary writer and theorist accused of a lack of strategy is Jane Tompkins, in her essay, "Me and My Shadow." Just as Cixous adopts a free-writing style to demonstrate and strategize a writing that is "woman," Tompkins chooses to include her personal life and thoughts in a theoretical essay. Both women engage in strategic attempts to undermine the current practice of dispensing theory.

Tompkins influenced a controversy among critics concerning the inclusion of the personal in critical work. In her essay, she discusses the need for the personal to have a place in critical writing, especially in order to cater to the writing of women.

> What is personal is completely a function of what is perceived as personal. And what is perceived as personal by men, or rather, what is gripping, significant, "juicy," is different from what is felt to be that way by women. For what we are really talking about is not the personal as such, what we are talking about is what is important, answers one's needs, strikes one as immediately interesting. For women, the personal is such a category. (1997, 1113)

Returning to Wollstonecraft and her theory in *Vindication*, she would wholeheartedly disagree with Tompkins's insistence on including the personal in critical writing. She stipulated that the body and emotions should be separate from critical thinking, especially for women. Studying "Me and My Shadow" leads one to believe that Wollstonecraft might have had a point. Tompkins intersperses her observation of what a beautiful day it is in North Carolina with discussions of epistemology and semiotics. Does including the personal cloud one's argument, muddle it, or maybe even weaken it? Tompkins seems self-indulgent in her critical writing, and critical writing should steer clear of self-indulgence. Critical writing should be focused on the text, or texts being studied, and not the writer. Tompkins takes center stage and her critical work becomes lost in her "shadow." However, it is not necessarily ineffective to appropriate the personal for use in critical work. It depends on how it is managed. Cixous includes the personal when it enhances her strategy, and the use of the personal is much more controlled in "Laugh" than Tompkins's is in "Shadow." Perhaps if inclusion of the personal is purposeful, it can enhance a writer's strategy, and thus the message being conveyed.

Toril Moi, in her essay "I Am a Woman," expresses her discomfort with Tompkins's essay. She finds it to be "a very angry text" (1999a, 131). However, Moi feels that an issue has surfaced through Tompkins, and other critics, that needs to be addressed. Moi writes:

> I actually agreed that Jane Tompkins had identified a major problem in contemporary theory; namely the tendency to produce alienating, obfuscating, and off-putting language. (132)

Moi believes that emotions are important in critical writing, and that we have emotional responses to texts that need not be ignored. Yet she doesn't feel that Tompkins's privileging of the personal is the right way to solve the problem of the way theory is being written. Tompkins does tend to ramble in her essay at times, to the detriment of her strategy. Tompkins argues for the feminization of critical writing, and although she attempts it, her effort falls short of what is required of critical writing. The critical thought is absent, and, in fact, she allows her emotions and her body to guide her writing. Yet Moi does assert:

> Although Tompkins's solution (to turn her back on theory) was wrong, I thought, her sense that there was a problem was right. There is something wrong with the way a lot of theory is written these days. An increasing number of intellectual women from different disciplines tell me that they have given up reading feminist theory because it seems obscure, abstruse, and removed from their interests and experiences. (133)

So what is the solution? Moi insists that "the personal is not the enemy of serious thought" (136), and I'd agree. Moi writes of critical writing:

> Instead of worrying about whether a certain insight is 'impersonal' because we assume that it therefore must be masculinist and falsely universalizing, we would be better off asking whether the mode of knowledge employed is suitable for the case at hand, and whose purposes the information thus gathered serves. (160)

Moi here recognizes the importance of a strategy, and the employment of a strategy that best complements the task at hand. Wollstonecraft wrote impersonally due to her audience, but also primarily due to the nature of the message she was attempting to convey. She was consistent in her critical work; she argued that women should not draw from their emotions or their bodies to reason, or make judgments. So she did not do so in her writing. She remained as objective in her argument as she could. Ironically, she has been attacked for writing in too masculinist a style, while she has also been attacked for including too much of her lived experience in her writing of *Vindication*. Moi suggests that a writer of theory ask this question of their work:

> Are we engaged in discussing a question where personal insights are relevant and useful? Whose interests does the deployment of the personal serve in the case at hand? (160)

Perhaps the increasingly common use of the personal in theorizing will allow critics to distinguish between the purposeful use of the personal and the inevitable autobiographical component inherent in all writing.

Inclusion of the personal in theory by Jane Tompkins in "Me and My Shadow" and Hélène Cixous in "The Laugh of the Medusa" may signal a deep-rooted resentment that women writers harbor within them. It is not necessarily the absence of women's lived experience in literature that seems to be at the root of their discomfort; it is the absence of that lived experience being taken seriously, and studied. The following inquiry needs to be addressed: If "John" Tompkins had written a similar essay to Jane's, including his personal life and entitled "Me and My Shadow," would it have caused such dissension among other critics? Or would it have been heralded by many critics as a new way to "do" theory, upstaging the old way? Would it have signaled a male critic expressing his need to include the personal in his theory, and finally, a man expressing himself? Wouldn't it have been welcomed? That male experience is the norm of all human experience prompts one to believe that John's essay may not have been as abhorrent to so many people as Jane's was, and considered such a direct challenge to the way theory is supposed to be disseminated.

Men's lived experience is privileged, and thus, so is their theory. However, many women critics are actively attempting to legitimize women's lived experience, and going about it in very different ways. Moi herself uses Simone de Beauvoir to validate women's lived experience, and women as critics and philosophers. Yet she seems careful in presenting her argument that Beauvoir only recently has been considered (not declared) to be a philosopher in her own right. That is, Beauvoir is finally being considered a philosopher apart from her lover Jean Paul Sartre, the founder of existentialist thought, who in fact is always mentioned when speaking of her. When he is being spoken or written about, though, she is rarely mentioned. Decidedly, Moi focuses on the work of Beauvoir more than her life, a prudent strategy in attempting to validate the writing of this philosopher. Moi seems to understand the delicate nature of bringing women's lived experience into the arena of theory.

In fact, Moi herself seems careful not to insert the personal into her own theory. This may be her style, but she also may have learned to be more cautious in her theoretical writing due to her intensive study of Beauvoir which exposes the dismissal and mishandling of a brilliant woman's work. In fact, Moi unveiled a tragic mistranslation of Beauvoir's *The Second Sex* (which will be discussed in greater depth in Chapter 11). Reading Sartre's philosophy on existentialism and the concept of the individual human being experiencing a choice in the way "he" chooses to lead his life, it is apparent that Beauvoir's *The Second Sex* was a reaction to this theory. This theory didn't work for women. Women didn't have choices. Their lives were predetermined for them by culture, and Beauvoir tries to show that women should have choices, but these choices have been confiscated from them by the hegemonic thinking of society. Despite Beauvoir's brilliant and radical writing, it is her personal life that is still today exposed and often under merciless attack, in an almost underhanded means to discredit her writing. Due to her years embroiled in the study of Beauvoir, Moi then may be even more sensitized to the potential attack on her own work just for being the work of a woman. She may not even be conscious that her prose is armored in style and content.

What Moi does exhibit in her writing, however, is a conscious effort to strategize, as if she is quite cognizant of the threat of marginalization that hovers over women's theoretical endeavors waiting to abolish the work if it is not within the certain confines of accepted rhetoric or literature, oftentimes rendering it meaningless and dismissed. Cixous is often criticized as avant-garde, or "out there," as many critics fail to see she writes with a strategy in mind. She challenges previously held notions of women's writing. Tompkins is criticized as too confessional and breezy in her essay, "Me and My Shadow," but it must be assumed that based on her previous theoretical work, she purposefully sat down to write this essay, in order to question the way theory is done. Her essay had theorists reeling, including Moi. Moi found Tompkins's essay to be irresponsible, but admitted it raised the question of how to make theory more accessible to writers and readers alike.

Moi's style itself is more accessible and less esoteric than the writing of other theorists, yet she still conveys the message to "fellow" women theorists to play the game begun by men. She may play that game, but her content is every bit as revolutionary and radical as that of Beauvoir and Wollstonecraft. Moi is much more subtle than Cixous and Tompkins in presenting her theory, and perhaps more effective. She actively refuses to be ignored or discarded. In fact, Moi continues in the style begun by Wollstonecraft in *Vindication* and Beauvoir in *The Second Sex*: write in phallocentric language to challenge constrictions, neglect, and misrepresentation of women written in that language.

However, even when women writers adhere to the standards placed on both theoretical and creative writing, their ability to reason can be stripped away from them by invasive and disrespectful critics. My admiration for Mary Wollstonecraft's brilliance as a writer inspired my defense of her work after witnessing the cursory, inaccurate and often mean-spirited attack on her work by certain critics. My defense of Wollstonecraft grew into a defense of the ability of women writers, even contemporary writers like me, to think, reason and strategize. I was deeply involved in the construction and creation of my own novel, and as I tediously mapped out the strategy for my own work, I was appalled at how easily critics can ignore the strategy of a woman writer.

It is necessary to require of all critics the respect for the writing of all writers, both women and men, and to demand of critical writers responsible and fastidious scholarship. Critics are intellectuals who must educate themselves about the hegemony to which we are all susceptible, if they are not already aware of its dangers. Critics need to be mindful of the devastating damage they can do to a text's and a writer's reputation with inexcusable, sloppy scholarship and a neglect of a writer's strategy, or even a writer's ability to strategize. The damage isn't limited to the text and the writer. As can be seen with Mary Wollstonecraft, a writer and a text were ignored for over a century. Millions of people were denied the intellectual growth that may have been acquired by reading Wollstonecraft. Shouldn't critics begin to be held more accountable for insufficient analysis? And, in the new millennium, can we please assume women writers organize and conduct their work according to their own predetermined strategy? Moreover, if critics can do such damage with inadequate scholarship, the damage that other "interpreters" can do, such as adapters, is staggering. The work of adapters in the form of film that often draws large audiences is of great concern.

After this clarification of women writers' abilities to strategize, I still feel the need to insist that although *Sentences* exposes some of the harsh realities of a woman's lived experience, my novel is not autobiographical.

In writing the novel, the strategies on which I most heavily relied included the structure of the novel, a mix of genres, an experimentation with various creative techniques, deconstruction of other texts and within the novel itself, and intertextuality (direct influence by other texts, excerpting from *Maria*, and editing/revision from outside sources). Here I will discuss the structure of the novel and the interspersing of different genres and creative techniques.

I organized the novel to depict the many influences, whether hidden or conspicuous, that press on individuals as they try to conduct their lives in a way that seems feasible in alignment with their values and belief systems. I created news articles, magazine interviews, English papers, court transcripts, personal narratives and journals from different characters, excerpts from *Maria*, and excerpts from contemporary, factual sources in order to position the reader as an individual is positioned in society. That is, every day, we as individuals are exposed to many different types of information and perspectives outside of us that necessitate some form of interpretation, whether that interpretation is expressed formally or informally, or remains internalized. I wanted the reader to experience the story in a conglomeration of fragments, and piece together their interpretation.

The mixing of genres was used to discomfort the reader, and to attempt to keep the reader alert and searching for clues and missing pieces. Many novels ease the reader into the message it is attempting to convey. This is a strategy that works well for certain subjects. It might have worked for this novel, had I wanted the reader to think over what had occurred and let it absorb gradually. However, my design for this novel was to unsettle the reader. I decided to make it difficult to piece the story together, and this strategy was meant to reflect the need for individuals in society to do the same with information they receive. I wanted to instill in the reader the need to look beyond what appears to be on the surface. When provided with knowledge, one must sift through it, interpret it mindfully, applying critical thinking skills that become more developed as they are exercised. I desired to encourage the exercise of the reader's critical and interpretive skills.

The story of the novel unfolds not only with the use of various media sources, but predominantly through the voices of four different characters. Tamika is the prison guard who first talks about why she is working at the prison, and provides the introduction of Annie, the main character. Lindsay advances the reader's view of Annie through a journal entry that she lets Annie read. One chapter gives the account of the same period of time from the point of view of four different characters: Annie, Lexi and Sammy (Annie's daughters), and Seth (Annie's ex-husband). The novel then delves into the journals of Lexi while her mother's trial is ensuing. To bridge this part of the novel into Annie's memoirs, the part of the novel that is most closely linked to *Maria*, I used the genre of drama, and set up a discussion among Annie, Tamika, and Lindsay in the form of a play.

The creative techniques I used for the novel were meant to complement the inter-mixing of genres. Self-conscious narration and interior voices play a large role in this novel; the story unravels as each woman, or girl, relays their experiences or thoughts in different ways. Collage was the creative technique I drew from most heavily as I interspersed the various genres among created media representations, and other unusual contemporary sources, both fictional and factual.

The most experimental attempt at intertextuality comes at the end of the novel. In the beginning of the novel, Annie has written a letter to her daughter, Lexi, and asks her to finish one of the two endings of *Maria* left unfinished by Wollstonecraft when she died. The last section of the novel gives my ending to my novel, Lexi's version of a finished ending of *Maria*, and Annie's version of another ending of *Maria*. The novel ends with a poem written by Lexi.

The main purpose of my strategy was to depict the harmful effects of the way our society is structured, to show that no one can escape these negative effects, and to demonstrate how easy it is to become a victim of the insidious and destructive messages disseminated in our culture. I wanted the novel to demand the reader to develop her or his critical thinking skills; I wanted the reader to be uncomfortable, and search for a sense of resolution. If we as individuals refuse to develop the proper critical thinking skills necessary to defend ourselves against the subverted messages being promoted in not only a patriarchal but also capitalistic society, we will fall victim to its promulgation of power and accumulation of wealth as the way to achieving happiness. I don't know if I achieved my purpose, and I know readers, and critics, could see the novel differently. Actually, I'm aware of how the experimental and multiplicitous nature of the novel could leave it vulnerable to a vast array of interpretations, but also, the sensitivity of the subject matter and my being a woman writer could leave it open to incorrect and even inappropriate interpretations. And, with this study I've done, I know it can happen.

Chapter 10

Deconstruction and Monsters

As I've been navigating a path between my critical work and my creative work, I've struggled with the assertion of my emotional involvement with my work. Since, as I have noted, my attraction to Wollstonecraft's *Maria* began with an intense emotional response, I experienced a sense of relief when reading Toril Moi's following passage:

> I would say that emotional responses to texts, whether literary or theoretical, are good starting points for further investigation, in which we go on to work hard to widen and deepen the emotional response through deeper understanding. By deepening our thought we can also deepen our feelings. To respond emotionally to a text is to care about it. If the response is boredom, that is also an emotion, and usually signals disengagement from the text. As such it is as analysable as rage or delight. Some texts deserve an enraged or a bored response, others do not: the intellectual challenge is to show why or why not. (1999b, 132)

As I read *Maria* the first time through, I knew it would be the basis for my future work. In fact, my emotional response to the text was so strong that I stopped at the end of Chapter 2 of *Maria*, and could go no further. I raged to my daughter that I wondered how much had actually changed for women in the last two hundred years. I agonized over the last paragraph at the end of the chapter:

> She started back, trembling, alarmed at the emotion a strange coincidence of circumstances inspired, and wondering why she thought so much of a stranger, obliged as she had been by his timely interference . . . She found however that she could think of nothing else; or, if she thought of her daughter, it was to wish that she had a father whom her mother could respect and love. (Wollstonecraft 1975, 23)

My emotional response to the novel at this point was that I and many other contemporary women can relate to a character in a two-hundred-year-old novel, and share her pain and anguish.

This passage, and my continued emotional response to the rest of the novel, signaled to me the need for further investigation, and the more I explored *Maria*, the more I found my research warranted by the lack of attention this novel has received. This in-depth study has allowed me to witness firsthand the contradiction between the quality of the novel and its inadequate reception or complete neglect. *Maria* is a fascinating, well-written, and important historical novel, not only for women but for all human beings, yet the novel has been ignored and derided. Judith Shulevitz in her criticism of Wollstonecraft never mentions *Maria*, although *Maria* shows the writer's maturity of thought beyond *Vindication*. Elaine Showalter in her brief biography of Wollstonecraft also fails to mention *Maria*, despite the novel representing a very important last chapter in Wollstonecraft's life. A professor of English to whom I spoke about studying *Maria* stated: "*Maria* isn't really very good, is it? There is too much of her [Mary Wollstonecraft] in it."

Maria cleverly misleads the reader by beginning as a gothic novel would, but the reader soon learns that Maria's reality is far more gloomy and horrific than the imaginings in a gothic novel. Wollstonecraft's aim in writing *Maria* is outlined in her preface:

> In writing this novel, I have rather endeavoured to pourtray passions than manners. In many instances I could have made the incidents more dramatic, would I have sacrificed my main object, the desire of exhibiting the misery and oppression, peculiar to women, that arise out of the partial laws and customs of society. In the invention of the story, this view restrained my fancy; and the history ought rather to be considered, as of woman, than of an individual. The sentiments I have embodied. (5)

To contest the belief of the professor I mentioned above that Wollstonecraft is too much in *Maria*, it needs to be stated that the writer herself explains her connection to the novel in her preface. She declares that she is writing of women's lived experience, and that her scope is limited to this purpose. Her distance from her character in stating her purpose seems to convey that this novel is not autobiographical, but that she has experienced similar emotions and sentiments to Maria's.

Before I proceed with my analysis of *Maria*, it is important to dispel the assumption that Wollstonecraft based *Maria* predominantly on her own life, because that assumption will interfere with the validity of the novel as well as my analysis of it in my own work. Often, if a novel concentrates on women's lived experience and is written by a woman, it is branded that dreaded term that implies the author is devoid of imagination: the autobiographical novel. I am not inferring that novels termed by their authors as autobiographical are invalid texts. I am referring here to novels that are criticized for their autobiographical nature when the author's intention is clearly unknown.

Maria does not directly reflect Wollstonecraft's life. Wollstonecraft was never in an insane asylum. She did not have a tyrant of a husband who tried to prostitute her (pregnant) body to one of his friends as Maria's did, although Wollstonecraft was pregnant at the time she was writing *Maria*. Wollstonecraft had a strategy for her novel, as is apparent in her preface. She requested and received feedback from her husband, William Godwin, concerning versions of her novel. In order to make a statement that Wollstonecraft was too much in her novel, one would need to compare *Maria* to Godwin's memoirs of her life. The two texts read dramatically different. In fact, in Godwin's memoirs, he discusses the creative process behind the writing of *Maria*, revealing Wollstonecraft's involvement with her strategy:

> She was sensible how arduous a task it is to produce a truly excellent novel; and she roused her faculties to grapple with it. All her other works were produced with a rapidity, that did not give her powers time fully to expand. But this was written slowly and with mature considerations. She began it in several forms, which she successively rejected, after they were considerably advanced. She wrote many parts of the work again and again, and, when she had finished what she intended for the first part, she felt herself urgently stimulated to revise and improve what she had written, than to proceed, with constancy of application, in the parts that were to follow. (1987, 264)

My own reading of *Maria* grew into admiration for an experimental novel written in an attempt to challenge the novels being written during Wollstonecraft's time by and for women. With subsequent readings of *Maria*, I began to move beyond my emotional, reactionary perspective into the difficulties presented to women writers on writing about women's lives. I uncovered aspects of *Maria* that reveal Wollstonecraft's brilliant and extremely shrewd strategy, which was not haphazard or self-absorbed. In fact, in the novel's fragmented form, Wollstonecraft's strategy is more visible than it might have been had she been able to finish the novel.

Much of my reading of and critical experience with *Maria* can be illuminated by a consideration of reader response theory, and especially Stanley Fish's work with this approach to literature. In his essay "Is There A Text in This Class?," discussing reader response criticism, Fish writes:

> [I]t is impossible even to think of a sentence independently of a context, and when we are asked to consider a sentence for which no context has been specified, we will automatically hear it in the context which it has been most often encountered. (1999, 46)

Fish's essay begins with a student asking a professor the simple question (which is the title of the essay), "Is there a text in this class?" The professor assumes she's referring to the book he's assigned to the class, but she's recently taken a course with Fish, and says, to clarify what she means, "No, no . . . I mean in this class do we believe in poems and things, or is it just us?" Fish follows this antidote with his confession that he believes in "the instability of the text and the unavailability of determinate meanings" (42), but that this is not such a frightening concept. In fact, in his essay, he details how liberating it can be and illuminating.

I agree with Fish's theory on reader response and interpretation of the meaning of a text. It is impossible to reduce a text to one fixed meaning. The meaning of a text grows and changes as the reader grows and changes. The critic of a text reads it over and over again, and a more thorough, intensive meaning may result from this process, but finite meaning is elusive. As noted, my first reading of *Maria* elicited primarily a personal, emotional response; my second reading of *Maria* furthered and changed in certain ways my original interpretation of *Maria*. Thus each reading of *Maria* was based on a new situation, as Fish refers to it:

> The change from one structure of understanding to another is not a rupture but a modification of the interests and concerns that are already in place; and because they are already in place, they constrain the direction of their own modification. That is, in both cases the hearer [or reader] is already in a situation informed by tacitly known purposes and goals, and in both cases he ends up in another situation whose purposes and goals stand in some elaborated relation (of contrast, opposition, extension) to those they supplant. (50–1)

Reading *Vindication* allowed me to see *Maria* as a fictional sequel to the theory presented in *Vindication*. In *Maria*, Wollstonecraft challenges her original work on the oppression of women, and challenges the patriarchy's imprisonment of women within their lives. Reading *Frankenstein* helped me to identify the many parallels between two works written by mother and daughter.

A brief sketch, then, of my continuing journey of "response" follows. I read *Maria* closely for the third time as I was finishing the rough draft of my novel. As I planned and strategized the work of my own novel, I began to see more clearly the strategy inherent in Wollstonecraft's text. In my first two readings of *Maria*, I harbored an unintentional bias against a woman's novel, not giving much consideration to Wollstonecraft's strategy. After I'd written my own novel, recognizing my ability to reason and strategize, I began to see that all writers contemplate and plan out their strategy in order to produce their work.

At this time, I was also struggling with Cixous's theory, and its profound effect on the way I viewed women's writing. My third reading of *Maria* caused me to privilege the novel because it was women's writing. Since Cixous was fresh on my mind, as well as Julia Kristeva, and I was fumbling with the controversial concept of *écriture feminine*, I was asking myself, is there a feminine writing? Do women write "woman," the question posed and addressed by Cixous's theory in her essay "The Laugh of the Medusa?" I wondered, if women do write woman, then am I writing woman? Did Wollstonecraft write woman? I struggled with this question until I realized the importance of strategy in any writer's work, women or men. Cixous encourages a freestyle, open way of writing that she considers feminine, and this is detailed in her essay. As I discussed before, Cixous operated with a strategy, which was to motivate women to move beyond the patriarchy, and to begin doing so by considering themselves as different writers from men.

At the same time I was conflicted with Cixous's theory and her strategy, I was drawn to Kristeva's thinking in "Women's Time" that indirectly challenges Cixous's theory. Kristeva states that we must not think of women as Woman. It is time for women to be considered and to consider themselves as multiplicitous in their singularity. Women are individuals who think and act differently from each other. To regard women as Woman allows us to continue seeing men as Man. As I continued with my study of Wollstonecraft's *Maria* and my own novel, I began to see the structure of the patriarchy as the enemy and not the people within the system who either embrace or reject its mores.

As I moved into my fourth reading of *Maria*, having settled into the strategy and thus efficacy of the theories of Cixous and Kristeva, and as I was revising my own novel, I began to read *Maria* as a novel by a writer on the lives of women, and men. I realized through my defense of Wollstonecraft against neglectful, damaging critics how easy it is to become trapped in the autobiographical connections within women's texts. Instead of focusing on the way women write and surmising about their insertion of themselves into their texts, all critics, including myself, need to be vigilant about the way we view a woman writer's text that portrays or analyzes the experiences of women. The patriarchal system in which we live demands us to evaluate ourselves as critics of women's writing, but especially of women's writing about women's lived experience.

It is for this reason that reader-response theory is advantageous to women's writing. It is easy to dismiss a novel chronicling women's lived experience, because that experience is minimized in our patriarchal society. To read and reread such novels allows for the validation of the subject matter of these novels, as well as the quality of the writing. As critics we harbor biases, as do other members of our society. Fish's theory seems applicable to this problem inherent within literary criticism:

> What I have been arguing is that meanings come already calculated, not because of the norms embedded in the language but because language is always perceived, from the very first, within a structure of norms. That structure, however, is not abstract and independent but social; and therefore it is not a single structure with a privileged relationship to the process of communication as it occurs in any situation but a structure that changes when one situation, with its assumed background of practices, purposes, and goals, has given way to another. (1999, 52)

Thus with several readings of a text one can destabilize each reading before, and open up the text to being viewed from a less biased perspective, one not steeped in the "norms" to which Fish refers above. Fish here offers a solution to the sloppy scholarship and almost blind reductions of women's writing not to one meaning but to insignificance in the literary world. Critics, including myself, must reevaluate our practices, purposes and goals in order to step out of what we have previously held to be true, usually unconsciously, into a new way of thinking that grants women's writing (and the writing of other marginal writers, writing based in marginalized subject matter, and experimental writing) the same critical treatment as men's or "traditional" writing.

Since I use deconstruction as a tool in my analysis of *Maria*, and also indirectly in the writing of my novel, understanding this complex theory proved to be important to my work. Deconstruction focuses on the opposition between specific constructs. To simplify the theory behind deconstruction, that which is being deconstructed can be referred to as the "old," and that which is trying to replace the old is the "new." Deconstruction involves entering into the old in order to understand it, and break it down to form the new. However, the most important aspect of deconstruction is that the new is never free of the old. That is, opposites are never free of each other. Jonathan Culler explains:

Deconstruction is most simply defined as a critique of the hierarchical oppositions that have structured Western thought: inside/outside, mind/ body, literal/metaphorical, speech/writing, presence/absence, nature/culture. To deconstruct an opposition is to show that it is not natural and inevitable but a construction, produced by discourses that rely on it, and to show that it is a construction in a work of *de*construction that seeks to dismantle it and reinscribe it. (1997, 122)

In its handling of oppositions, deconstruction seems to blend the oppositions into each other, resulting in the formation of a sort of middle ground, which of course leans more towards the new since deconstruction is the understanding of the old in a quest for the new. Jacques Derrida states that a relationship "always already" exists between that which is being deconstructed, and that which is replacing what is being deconstructed.

Derrida writes of deconstruction:

Within the closure, by an oblique and always perilous movement, constantly falling back within what is being deconstructed, it is necessary to surround the critical concepts with a careful and thorough discourse — to mark the conditions, the medium, and the limits of their effectiveness and to designate rigorously their intimate relationship to the machine whose deconstruction they permit; and, in the same process, designate the crevice through which the yet unnameable glimmer beyond the closure can be glimpsed. (1997, 14)

In this passage, Derrida contradicts his own writing on deconstruction in that the glimmer is presented here as what deconstruction is always working towards, but never quite reaches. It is the pure opposition, untainted by the old. Although Derrida insists that nothing can be created out of the old into something new without containing some of the old, and the pure new is never attainable, the theory of deconstruction itself claims that there is no pure new, or truth. There is always play at work, so that there is constant movement and as Derrida states: "The center is not the center" (1978, 279). However, Derrida's focus in the passage above may be the designation of the crevice, or the part within the closure that leads to something new, which represents the most important and inescapable element of deconstruction.

Wollstonecraft's *Vindication* and *Maria* exhibit deconstructive qualities, although they are not in strict adherence to the theory. I will explore the deconstruction I see in Wollstonecraft's work, because I then perform my own deconstruction of her work, and apply this to the creation of my novel. Deconstruction plays a large role in the making of the "monster," since the novel itself is a growth out of an "old" towards a "new." I endeavored to replicate *Maria*'s mixing of genres and experiments with intertextuality, and also its treatment of the mother–daughter bond, but I also was in opposition to elements of the novel, primarily due to my being a contemporary writer. Thus I needed to forge an updated version of an old text.

Thus, to deconstruct *Maria* for my own work necessitated an exploration into Wollstonecraft's deconstructive techniques. In *Vindication*, Wollstonecraft functions as a deconstructive critic as she challenges and opposes Rousseau's philosophy with her own philosophy. In his essay "The Critic as Host," J. Hillis Miller discusses the concept of the critic as parasite, feeding off the original work. Yet in the realm of deconstruction, the critic is both parasite and host. The text is both parasite and host as well. The critic feeds off the original work, but the original work also feeds off the critic, and is illuminated further by the critic's treatment of the text. This element of deconstruction is what dominates Wollstonecraft's criticism of Rousseau.

Wollstonecraft explains her method of opposing Rousseau as she writes:

> I shall begin with Rousseau, and give a sketch of his character of woman in his own words, interspersing comments and reflections. My comments, it is true, will all spring from a few simple principles, and might have been deduced from what I have already said; but the artificial structure has been raised with so much ingenuity that it seems necessary to attack it in a more circumstantial manner, and make the application myself. (1992, 84)

Wollstonecraft and Rousseau are in opposition to each other concerning the rational intellectual capabilities of women, but their philosophies are also conjoined. This is unavoidable. Miller writes of deconstruction: "The place we inhabit, wherever we are, is always in this in-between zone, place of host and parasite, neither inside nor outside" (1979, 231). As Wollstonecraft attempts to clarify her opposition to Rousseau, she cannot do so without drawing from his philosophy. And Rousseau's text becomes changed by Wollstonecraft's opposition to it. The critic and text interchangeably function as parasite and host.

Although Wollstonecraft limits the intensity of her argument against Rousseau, she takes a more tenacious stance in her deconstruction of the patriarchy in *Maria*. In *Maria*, the deconstructive elements inherent in Wollstonecraft's critical technique have gained strength as she turns the fairy-tale romance that society subscribes to (being written by both women and men during her time) on its head. Also in the novel, she deconstructs the patriarchal structure of her society. She draws from the structure she is opposing to form a newly structured society designed for the liberation of women.

Derrida contends that when introducing a new way of thinking in opposition to another way of thinking, or deconstructing a heritage to introduce its opposition, the opposition must always borrow from that which it is opposing. As was quoted previously, Derrida writes:

> It is a question of explicitly and systematically posing the problem of the status of a discourse which borrows from a heritage the resources necessary for the deconstruction of that heritage itself. (1978, 282)

To deconstruct the patriarchy within her fiction, Wollstonecraft has her characters use the tools men have relied on to achieve power in society and consequently over women, and these tools provide her characters with a means to challenge the patriarchy and women's oppressive living conditions. For example, Maria picks up the pen and writes her memoirs for her daughter, in an effort to keep her from making the mistakes she did. Maria writes:

Addressing these memoirs to you, my child, uncertain whether I shall ever have an opportunity of instructing you, many observations will probably flow from my heart, which only a mother — a mother schooled in misery, could make . . . For my sake, warned by my example, always appear what you are, and you will not pass through existence without enjoying its genuine blessings, love and respect. (1975, 58–9)

Writing during Wollstonecraft's, and thus Maria's, time was a predominantly male endeavor. Women's writing often included romance or gothic novels in which the "girl" and the hero lived happily ever after. Maria picks up the pen to write against the conduct lessons written for women by men, and women, and she also writes against the fairy tale. She educates her daughter on how women are impelled in a patriarchal society to believe in a man's honesty, generosity and ability to care based on one simple gesture, only to find out too late that this same man is capable of deception and greed.

Maria's act of educating her daughter represents another way in which Wollstonecraft opposes the patriarchal culture of her time. As Wollstonecraft saw it, mothers often came to resent their daughters for being young and desired, and so instead of mentoring their daughters, mothers would sabotage their maturation and refuse to parent them. In *Vindication*, Wollstonecraft attributed this tension to the patriarchal system and women being instructed to please and submit to the men in their lives. Wollstonecraft believed that women needed to be educated intellectually, and exercise their capability to reason. In this way, they would be caring, nurturing mothers, able to guide their children based on their knowledge and experience. Maria's attempt to educate her daughter challenges the same belief that Wollstonecraft challenged — that girls should be concerned only with their beauty and not their intellectual advancement. Also, Maria's memoirs represent a bond between two women, mother and daughter, which is a tool Wollstonecraft borrows from men — the male bonding that occurs within a patriarchal system, heightening the power of men within that system.

Wollstonecraft further exploits this bond by replicating it through the friendship of Jemima and Maria. Forging this bond between two women, Wollstonecraft writes against the competition between women, and also portrays women working together to achieve a desired goal — power through independence. This friendship offers hope in one sense. Wollstonecraft provides multiple endings to *Maria*. In one ending, Maria commits suicide. But, in a second, and the most developed, ending, Jemima's friendship saves Maria's life; Jemima brings back Maria's baby, and it is assumed that they will raise her together. Jemima enters the room just as Maria has swallowed laudanum; she throws it up, and must choose whether or not to fight for her life. The child, having been tutored by Jemima on their journey, says, "Mamma!" to Maria. Maria remains silent for several minutes and then states, "The conflict is over! — I will live for my child!" (1975, 137). The loyal bond between Jemima and Maria has possibly saved all three of them.

Although *Maria* does not leave the reader with much hope for the existence of healthy heterosexual relationships, perhaps this is Wollstonecraft's purpose. She challenges the patriarchy and exposes the harm it imposes on everyone who falls into its trap. Wollstonecraft uses the tools that keep the patriarchal system intact to oppose this system and turn it back in on itself. In *Maria*, heterosexual relationships defined by the patriarchal structure of society are shown as not having a chance at being healthy and mutually beneficial for each partner, especially the woman. Wollstonecraft exposes the inefficacy of the relationship between a man and a woman, and especially marriage, within a patriarchal system and in her ending abolishes this relationship, allowing women the only means to freedom from oppression that she can devise — a bond, instead, between women.

In many ways, I deconstruct *Maria* in much the same manner that Wollstonecraft deconstructed the patriarchy in *Maria*. What I do in my novel is to also challenge the patriarchy, but I challenge Wollstonecraft's *Maria* as well. As much as I use *Maria* as a guide for my novel, I also use elements of it that are problematic to guide my novel. Derrida writes of opposing metaphysics (the branch of philosophy that, in extremely simplified terms here, examines the nature of reality) to arrive at something "new": "There is no sense in doing without the concepts of metaphysics in order to shake metaphysics" (1978, 280). I had to read and reread *Maria* in order to understand the components of the novel that I was trying to "shake" in my own work. Derrida also writes: "We can pronounce not a single destructive proposition which has not already had to slip into the form, the logic, and the implicit postulations of precisely what it seeks to contest" (280–1).

How then does my novel contest parts of *Maria*? And does this make me an irresponsible critic as well as writer? Referring again to Miller's "The Critic as Host," a critic is often seen as the parasite feeding off of the text to enhance their own work. A creation that grows out of an older (or source) text might be viewed as a parasite as well. As a deconstructive critic, and also as a deconstructive novelist, I find that my work is neither the parasite feeding off of *Maria* nor the host inviting *Maria* as its guest, but rather it is both. My work is enhanced by entering *Maria*, and consequently *Maria*, I would argue, gains clarity and definition, or perhaps redefinition, through my work. As Miller writes on the relationship between a critical text and the text it critiques, he constructs the following methodology that can also be used to validate the intertextual relationship between a new novel and an earlier text. Miller discusses the relationship between a new poem and earlier poems that have influenced it:

> The previous text is both the ground of the new one and something the new poem must annihilate by incorporating it, turning it into ghostly insubstantiality, so that the new poem may perform its possible-impossible task of becoming its own ground. The new poem both needs the old texts and must destroy them. It is both parasitical on them, feeding ungraciously on their substance, and at the same time it is the sinister host which unmans them by inviting them into its home. (1979, 225)

My novel grows out of Wollstonecraft's subtle attack on the patriarchy in *Maria*, but much of Wollstonecraft's negative portrayal of women shown through the character of Maria is discarded in my own work.

In my novel, I preferred a deconstruction of the patriarchy that provided an opposition rooted in the equality of women and men, and recognition that the patriarchal structure of society hurts everyone. In Wollstonecraft's novel, Maria can easily be blamed for the predicaments in which she finds herself. My aim in my novel was to portray a character who made mistakes just as Maria did, based on her place in society as a woman. However, Annie, Maria's successor, learns how to navigate through that system, and exhibits more strength and skill than Maria does for functioning within this system, which she grows to see as biased against her.

In *Maria*, Maria's hero worship of Darnford becomes uncomfortable. She has been deeply scarred by her relationship with her husband, yet she enters into another relationship, perhaps needing to hope in the existence of a hero. This hope, however, becomes her downfall since it undermines her newfound confidence and knowledge based on her recent experiences. This discomfort for the reader may have been Wollstonecraft's design. Maria's memoirs to her daughter also reveal her naiveté. She believes that by telling her daughter what she has experienced at the hands of the patriarchy she will preclude her daughter from making the same mistakes. Yet she herself who has written these memoirs for her daughter does not heed her own warnings. Then, in the trial scene, Maria reads a letter to the court in which she demands the "respect I owe myself" (1975, 132) by divorcing her husband. Not only does Maria enter the courtroom without a strategy (unlike her creator, Wollstonecraft herself, when she entered the intellectual forum on equality in 1792 with *Vindication*), but instead of focusing solely on her own defense, she also defends the man with whom she is accused of having an affair. The judge dismisses Maria's lengthy defense with a quick blow as he "alluded to 'the fallacy of letting women plead their feelings, as an excuse for the violation of the marriage-vow" (133).

Although Maria's conduct can be attributed to the society in which she lives, it also can be connected with her inability to process the realities of that society. Wollstonecraft's design may have been to present the oppression inherent within a patriarchal system as a pervasive force against which not even an intelligent, critical-thinking woman could fight. Two hundred years later, I decided to show that despite patriarchy's limitations placed on women, and its continued oppression of women, hope can emanate from a novel without making the story appear to be an unbelievable fairy tale.

Chapter 11

The Multiplicitous Nature of Intertextuality: *Maria* and *Sentences*

Intertextuality is a term proposed by Julia Kristeva "to indicate a text's construction *from texts*: a work is not a self-contained, individually authored whole, but the absorption and transformation of other texts, 'a mosaic of quotations'" (Payne 1997, 258). An offshoot of deconstruction theory, Kristeva's ideas borrow from Mikhail Bakhtin's theory of dialogism to develop her concept of intertextuality. She writes:

> [A]n insight first introduced into literary theory by Bakhtin: any text is constructed as a mosaic of quotations; any text is the absorption and transformation of another. The notion of *intertextuality* replaces that of intersubjectivity, and poetic language is read as at least *double*. (1986e, 37)

In the same essay, Kristeva expounds on the idea that all written texts are in some way influenced by other texts. However, she seems to be referring not to Harold Bloom's "anxiety of influence," which is concentrated on one text being influenced by one author or one work contributing to another, but rather to the almost unconscious inclusion of texts into another text. Mary Wollstonecraft, in *Maria*, undoubtedly was influenced by the work of those who had gone before her, and the texts of those writing at the same time that she was. That is, *Maria* reflects Wollstonecraft's involvement with many other texts that she was reading or studying at the time. Kristeva believes we "could thus posit and demonstrate the hypothesis that *any evolution of literary genres is an unconscious exteriorization of linguistic structures at their different levels*. The novel in particular exteriorizes linguistic dialogue" (37). Thus, according to Kristeva, *Maria* is the unconscious exteriorization of not only texts that Wollstonecraft was studying, but also observations she was making of the world around her, including the use of language.

We are reminded here of Greenblatt's concept of new historicism, and that literary creation is the product of a negotiation between a creator and or class of creators, equipped with a complex, communally, shared repertoire of conventions, and the institutions and practices of society. (1989, 12)

Percy Shelley's *A Defence of Poetry* is in agreement with Greenblatt, but allows room in the creation equation for the creator's imagination, which perhaps is untouched by culture. Shelley's belief in the imagination of a writer is apparent as he juxtaposes it to reason:

Reason is the enumeration of the quantities already known; imagination is the perception of the value of those quantities, both separately and as a whole . . . Reason is to Imagination as the instrument to the agent, as the body to the spirit, as the shadow to the substance. (1996, 1167)

Imagination is where the creative process begins, then is touched and shaped by the externalities, and expressed through reason. Intertextuality represents the touching and shaping. However, intertextuality can be unintentional or intentional while the intertextuality that Kristeva refers to is inevitable. A writer can be influenced by texts without realizing it, through the author's research into her topic, or texts she has studied previous to her work. However, a writer also can choose texts purposefully, desiring their influence on her work, and she can guide that influence.

Writers can further experiment with intertextuality by directly excerpting passages or lines from the texts of other writers. Poets appropriate lines from previously published poems and prose in their own texts. In her book *Fashioning the Female Subject: The Intertextual Networking of Dickinson, Moore, and Rich*, Sabine Sielke posits that intertextuality can go much further than simply appropriating lines. Sielke writes of Adrienne Rich and her intertextual relationship with Emily Dickinson's work:

Part of Rich's strategy is to construct her own identity and history by engaging with other women's texts, and Dickinson has played a major part in her dialogic identity. In fact, Dickinson's texts have served Rich as a kind of matrix, a ground against which she projected her own poetic figures. (1997, 17)

These writers do not change the texts of the poets with whom they interact; their experimentation with intertextuality is non-invasive to the work they appropriate. Yet the use of intertextuality in their work is carried out intentionally, and purposefully, and serves to enhance their work while it often functions as a guide in their evolution as poets as well.

However, just as the literary world must demand that critical analysis be responsible and accurate, the same requirements must be placed on intertextual writing. We return to Miller's "The Critic as Host." The critic is often viewed as a parasite of the work she critiques, and some critics deserve this label. Miller writes:

The host feeds the parasite and makes its life possible, but at the same time is killed by it, as criticism is often said to kill literature. Or can host and parasite live happily

together, in the domicile of the same text, feeding each other or sharing the food?
(1979, 217)

Critics and texts can coexist peacefully; the new work enhances the old text by giving
it attention in a respectful, responsible manner, and the old text inspires and guides the
writing of the new work. In an act of intertextuality, this same respectful relationship
between new text and old text needs to be required of the writer who draws from an
old text to create a new one. Enhancement of each text involved in the process of intertextuality, I believe, needs to occur. The contemporary author must respect — rather
than "kill" as Bloom would have it — the author that precedes her. I chose a mutually
enhancing intertextuality for my novel, and decided on this practice due to my questioning of the completion of a text by another writer.

It is important, however, to address a form of intertextual writing that by its very
nature tends to be problematic, and must be performed with caution and respect for
the text in question. It involves the editing by a writer or editor of the work or text of
another writer. This includes the editing that is involved with translation as well as
the strict editing, which includes deletion and addition, of the work of another writer.
William Godwin edited Wollstonecraft's *Maria*; he states in his preface that he inserted
brackets where he has added to the text. It is not clear whether or not he deleted any
of the text, although he does state that he attempted to leave the majority of the text as
close to how the writer had left it as he could. Godwin writes:

> In revising these sheets for the press, it was necessary for the editor, in some places,
> to connect the more finished parts with the pages of an older copy, and a line or
> two in addition sometimes appeared requisite for that purpose. Wherever such a
> liberty has been taken, the additional phrases will be found inclosed in brackets . . .
> (Wollstonecraft 1975, 4)

Although Godwin may have had good intentions, and his connecting of the different
parts of the novel that Wollstonecraft had left behind at her death seem to be done in
an effective manner, he insists on inserting himself into the text where it often is not
necessary. Godwin succinctly states that it is his "most earnest desire to intrude nothing of himself into the work, but to give to the public the words, as well as ideas, of
the real author" (4). Yet the following passage demonstrates one of his seemingly
unnecessary intrusions:

> [By degrees, Darnford entered into the particulars of his story.] In a few words,
> he informed her that he had been a thoughtless, extravagant young man; yet, as he
> described his faults, they appeared to be the generous luxuriancy of a noble mind.
> (27)

Godwin's introduction into Darnford's tale is superfluous as Wollstonecraft has handled it in her own way. Godwin's bracketed additions most often appear in *Maria* as
nuisances to the reader than as aids to understanding that particular passage.

This invasive act of editing continues today, which is why I found myself questioning my own attempt at intertextuality. A recent endeavor similar to the type of intertextuality performed by Godwin involves the work of Ralph Ellison who, when he died, left behind an incomplete manuscript, a fragment. John F. Callahan "spent more than three years wrestling with the unfinished novel's manuscripts" (Feeley 1999, 51) in order to publish "the incomplete manuscript Ellison struggled with for four decades before his death, in 1994" (50). Toni Morrison edited the manuscript left behind by Toni Cade Bambara after her death, but in a book review in the *New York Times Book Review*, Sven Birkerts recognizes a dramatic difference between the work of Morrison and Callahan:

> When Toni Cade Bambara died in 1995, she left behind a massive, nearly completed novel, which her longtime friend and editor, Toni Morrison, has now prepared for publication. Morrison's contribution, unlike that of John F. Callahan, who worked with Ralph Ellison's myriad drafts to effectively create the novel, "Juneteenth," seems to have been mainly one of editorial condensation. Bambara's manuscript, reportedly some 1,800 pages long, was shaped down to a relatively less unwieldy work in which the author's intentions are clearly on view. (2000, 17)

It seems as if Birkerts believes that Morrison's editing of Bambara's novel was less invasive and more attentive than that of Callahan's handling of Ellison's novel. Perhaps this difference is dependent on what each novelist left behind for each respective editor. However, it might be interesting to consider the dilemma that gender and race might raise here. Godwin edits the text of Wollstonecraft, a woman; Callahan is a white male delving into the text of Ellison, a black man. Morrison and Bambara are both women, and black. Since entering a text to edit it, and thus alter it, represents an endeavor that should be handled cautiously and respectfully, perhaps being of the same gender and culture removes obstacles that would preclude an editor from actively honoring a text. Here we encounter identity politics. Can only a black woman respectfully edit another black woman's text? Is it possible for a man to edit a text by a woman without seeming invasive or penetrating? Is it feasible for a white man to edit a black man's text without being construed as oppressive? My own sense is that Godwin and Callahan positioned at the privileged end of the gender and race spectrum might have ignored important parts of the texts they edited due to their misunderstanding or ignorance of the author's lived experience.

I argue, then, that there is a "negative" intertextuality and a "positive" intertextuality. These two types come under the heading of purposeful intertextuality, or active intertextuality. This is not in reference to Kristeva's, or Bakhtin's, unconscious intertextuality, where we as writers — critics, novelists, playwrights, poets — bring to our writing all the texts to which we have been exposed or with which we have been involved in one way or another. "Positive" intertextuality is the respectful use or editing of another text where the result is a mutually beneficial outcome. "Negative" intertextuality is purposeful intertextuality involving editing that is performed without care, imposes upon the text being edited, and most importantly, overrides the original work. It occurs most often when an editor does not acknowledge his bias or intrusion into the text.

In Anne K. Mellor's essay "My Hideous Progeny," Mellor identifies Percy Shelley as an intruder into his wife's *Frankenstein*, claiming that his editing of the novel altered the originally intended messages of the text. There are considered to be three texts of *Frankenstein*: the manuscript, the 1818 version, and the 1831 version. The original manuscript is available for research at the Bodleian Library, and can be distinguished from the published 1818 text as a result. Percy Shelley's editing is apparent, and quite intrusive to Mary's original work. Mellor attributes this invasion to Mary's anxiety of authorship; she "doubted the legitimacy of her own literary voice, a doubt that determined her decision to speak through three male narrators . . . the structure of her novel, and the revisions of her text" (1989, 53). This is how Mary censored her own speech, through "a series of screens around her authentic voice" (57). According to Mellor, though, the most overt censorship that took place in the creation of *Frankenstein* was Mary's request for Percy to edit the manuscript. Percy performed a rigorous revision of the novel, "which Mary almost invariably accepted" (58). Percy was lauded for his efforts by the editor, James Rieger, of the 1818 edition of *Frankenstein*. Yet Mellor claims that "Percy is clearly responsible for much of the inflated rhetoric in the text" (61), and

> on several occasions actually distorted the meaning of the text. He was not always sensitive to the complexity of the character created by the author. He tended, for instance, to see the creature as more monstrous and less human than did Mary. (62)

In her essay "Choosing a Text of *Frankenstein* to Teach," Mellor makes it clear that she is displeased with James Rieger and his contemporary editing of the 1818 *Frankenstein*:

> Even the first published text of *Frankenstein* has moved away from Mary Shelley's original style and conception [due to Percy Shelley's editing] . . . Furthermore, the account given of this manuscript by James Rieger, the editor of the only available reprint of the 1818 text of Frankenstein, is so inaccurate and so prejudiced in favor of Percy Shelley that students must be warned against its misleading combination of truths, half-truths, and unwarranted speculations. (Mellor 1996, 160–1)

Again, a woman writer's work is compromised and undermined, in this case doubly, not only by the domineering forces placed upon it, but by her inability to stand up for her text.

Another example of invasive intertextuality in the form of editing but in the guise of translation is H. M. Parshley's translation and editing of Simone de Beauvoir's *The Second Sex*. He aggressively states in the Translator's Note:

> At the publisher's request I have, as editor, occasionally added an explanatory word or two (especially in connection with existentialist terminology) and provided a few additional footnotes and bibliographic data which I thought might be to the reader's interest; and I have also done some cutting and condensation here and there with a

view to brevity, chiefly in reducing the extent of the author's illustrative material, especially in certain of her quotations from other writers. Practically all such modifications have been made with the author's express permission, passage by passage; and in no case do the changes involve anything in the nature of censorship or any intentional alteration or omission of the author's ideas. (Beauvoir 1989, xli)

This passage is problematic in that Parshley, a zoologist, adds explanations of the existentialist terminology present in Beauvoir's text. He cuts and condenses, excluding selected parts of the author's "illustrative material." He deletes quotes from some of the writers she discusses. "Practically all" is a vague term giving Parshley a large window of opportunity to insert himself into Beauvoir's text (there were many times he later claimed he could not get an adequate response from the writer, and so went ahead with his editing). At the same time, he follows this vague, and almost meaningless phrase with his contention that he has not censored or intentionally (vague and meaningless again) altered or omitted any of the author's ideas. Like Godwin, he insists that he wants to retain the ideas of the author, or as Godwin refers to Wollstonecraft, the "real" author.

Many scholars concur that Parshley's translation of *The Second Sex* exhibits egregious errors, and Toril Moi has been at the forefront of the effort to uncover Parshley's most misleading translations. For example, Parshley translates Beauvoir's "l'ensemble de la litterature feminine" (Beauvoir 1949, 30) as "books by women, on women" (Beauvoir 1989, xxxiv); Moi's literal translation reads "all of women's writing" (1999a, 4). Even I, with only an elemental understanding of the French language, can recognize Parshley's mistranslation of Beauvoir's phrase.

Both Parshley and Godwin enter a woman writer's text, and actively deny, in writing, that they are intruding any of themselves into the text. It is not even possible, or logical, to make this claim. Of course they intrude themselves into the text just as Percy Shelley did with his wife's text. These men entered the text of another with their own biases, not keeping in mind that they harbored these biases. They did not have the experiences of that writer, live that writer's life, or have that writer's mind. And, in these cases, they were men entering a woman's text, and thus came from a place of privilege that she did not know. Here again, we encounter the dilemma of identity politics. Perhaps all three men felt as if they were gracing these women writers with their more established writing skills, and thus were "validating" these texts. Is a text by a woman more valid if it has been edited by a man?

In an attempt to transcend identity politics, though, consider Toril Moi and Simone de Beauvoir. Even if Moi translates Beauvoir's *The Second Sex*, she will enter the text with a bias. Moi is a woman writing fifty years after Beauvoir; she cannot know the difficulties and obstacles that Beauvoir encountered in her lifetime, what those felt like to experience firsthand. Moi benefits from the women's movement being fifty years further along than it was when Beauvoir was writing. However, the key point to be made is that Moi's acknowledgment of her bias and limitations in entering Beauvoir's text will ensure, I believe, a more cautious and less invasive or intrusive translation of Beauvoir's text. (Recently, in 2009, Beauvoir's *The Second Sex* was finally published again in the United States as a new translation by Constance Borde and Sheila

Malovany-Chevallier, and as it reads on the inside flap of the book cover, Beauvoir's masterpiece has been "Newly translated and unabridged in English for the first time . . . Sixty years after its initial publication.")

It is important for writers to recognize their desire to fill a text. We want to fill in the spaces, or complete what has been done, or begun, by another writer. If we recognize that we are limited in our efforts, and somewhat intrusive no matter what we do, we can enter a text conscientiously and carefully. I believe that a man can responsibly edit a woman's text, and that a white man can do the same with the text of a black man, if they recognize their biases, and also their privilege. However, if we deny our entrance into a text as intrusive and interactive, whether it be as critic, editor, translator, or creative writer/adapter, no matter what our "identities" are, we then invade the text and assume possession of something that is not ours to possess.

Fragmentariness further complicates the concept of purposeful, strategic intertextuality. A text that is left behind as a fragment, unfinished by its author either because of unanticipated death or even loss of interest, can often be seen by other writers as a unique opportunity to "save the text." If a writer finishes a fragment, it is then saved. It is complete. It is whole. However, again, a writer is intruding into the text of another writer. It is intrusive and invasive; one could call it penetrating. Hans-Jost Frey, in his book *Interruptions*, implies that we are afraid of fragments, because they are not ordered. His book addresses the concerns with which fragments, or unfinished texts, leave us: "whether it is possible to define — i.e., to delimit — what constitutes a text for the purposes of literary study . . . [and] where and how a text — any text — begins and ends" (1996, vii).

Fragments make us uncomfortable. We need a beginning and an end. But, according to Frey:

> The text writes itself towards the beginning, which slips away from it more and more precisely for this reason. The more the text strives towards its goal — to be able to begin — the more it is already beyond it, past it in time and space . . . What, having begun, cannot begin, cannot end. The end would be the chance to begin, which the text endlessly misses by going on. (1996, 23)

There is no beginning and there is no end. There is the text, which starts somewhere that is not at the beginning, and ends where it really does not end. It goes on, and it has been going on before it started. But we desire order, and Frey seems to believe this limits our understanding of a text, to demand a beginning and an end. He writes:

> The fragment that has been understood is not a fragment anymore. By being ordered into a context it is done away with. Here the process of understanding is a struggle against its object. This shows that an experience of the fragmentary is already at work in the will to understand — in the urge to do away with the fragmentary. (40)

This passage is taken from a section of Frey's text entitled "Fear." Frey posits that "the will to understand is provoked by fear" (41). We want to understand something, nail it down to a conclusive meaning, master it, because then we feel in control, banishing our fear.

When I read *Maria* for the first time, I was determined to find a way to finish this unfinished text, this fragment. Perhaps its fragmentariness unnerved me. I'll admit that I felt as if I would be doing Wollstonecraft a favor, gaining her notoriety, but also myself I suppose. I would finish out her plan, she'd be redeemed, and I'd be the hero/heroine. However, as I learned more about fragments, Wollstonecraft, and the limitations of writers imposing themselves on the texts of other writers, I began to reevaluate my position. I explored my desire to fill in the fragmented sections of *Maria*. Why did I find the unfinished fragmentariness of *Maria* discomforting? Had I been trained to view texts as worthwhile literature only if they were "complete?" The more I worked on my project, the more I did not feel justified in entering into the text of another writer, and claiming to finish it for her. The more research I have done on the completion of fragments, the more questionable I have found this practice to be.

The fragmentariness of *Maria* can be seen as its most outstanding feature, but it also proves to be its most controversial feature; the fragmentariness of this novel leaves it open to disregard and neglect. The literary study of fragments often falters when they are viewed from the perspective of a close textual reading, with the expectation that the sum of the parts will add up to the whole. Frey explains what happens in trying to "understand" a fragment:

> The fragmentary text is the text from which something is missing. That something is missing from it can be seen from what is there. Incompleteness is perceived because not every element of the text that one has can be related to something else in a satisfactory manner. The unfinished text contains elements that do not signify, that do not fulfill their referential function because of the missing context. (1996, 49)

However, studying a fragmentary text can prove to be enlightening, and in fact, offer insight not only into the contents of a particular text, but into the idea of the "text" itself. Thus viewing *Maria* from a poststructuralist perspective allows its fragmentariness to enhance the interpretation of the text. New historicism and deconstruction show that *Maria*'s fragmentariness can be viewed as a reflection of the lives of women writing at the time, and of Maria herself who also writes a fragment, her memoirs, within the fragmented novel. And, the concept of the fragment opens up a subject that is often controversial. In fact, isn't all writing fragmented? Is there a definite point in time when a novel is complete? It is documented that Wollstonecraft was planning to complete *Maria* but left it unfinished when she died. Perhaps Wollstonecraft would have made a considerable amount of changes to the novel, and we would not have read it as we do now.

As I continued to analyze *Maria*, the possibility that Wollstonecraft intentionally may have left *Maria* a fragment needed to be addressed. A critic can never assume a writer's intention. Perhaps Wollstonecraft would have added more to the novel, but how much more she intended to add or would have added will never be known. This possibility evoked in me a new discomfort with the original plan of my project. What if I finished a text that was already considered finished by its author? And, wouldn't I detract from what the novel in its purest form was saying, reflecting, conveying?

Even if Wollstonecraft hadn't planned on *Maria* being a fragment, we can say that everything in life is a fragment. Is a text ever actually finished, simply because the author deems it so at some arbitrarily chosen point? At the same time, though, Frey writes: "Nothing is essentially unfinished. That which, by its essence, cannot be finished fulfills its essence by remaining unfinished and is thereby whole" (1996, 30). However, he continues this thought by differentiating the "accidental fragment. It breaks off before becoming what it was meant to be. A poem remains incomplete because the poet has died" (30). And, justly, some critics argue that a fragment is significant in and of itself and thus must remain a fragment. That is, a text should be afforded the respect of being allowed to stand for itself. In endeavoring to rewrite and "complete" *Maria*, was I, then, "penetrating" the text? I wanted to open up the text, the "sacred" text, and would I become, then, the strong, phallic, raping critic? I feared being construed as an assaulting force working against the text. How could I position myself in this type of "violence?"

In December of 2000, Julia Barrett published the third attempt at "completing" Jane Austen's last novel, *Sandition*. Barrett titled her work: *Jane Austen's "Charlotte": Her Fragment of a Last Novel, Completed.* One major criticism of this "completion" by a reviewer is that the novel is missing the character and personality of the original author. James Kincaid writes that "I have only one complaint myself: that the cruelty, the dirty-dog underhanded nastiness so characteristic of Jane Austen is nowhere to be found, here or in any other (eight!) books that I read with otherwise perfect contentment. I find something missing without the artful Austenian bile" (2000, 63). He concludes his review with a quote from the Derbyshire Writers' Guild, who have "tampered" with Austen's texts (resulting in 1,021 new texts):

> "We make no claims to be able to reach the literary heights of Miss Austen, but, because we all wish she had lived longer and written more, we feel the need to expand." I like Jane Austen too and very much wish she had lived longer and written more. I am glad for all those who feel the need to expand. I doubt that it's so much a felt need, really, as a pleasure indulged, but that's even better. (63)

I must agree with Kincaid. I think completing a fragment is more like a pleasure in which we indulge ourselves as writers. We want to rationalize it in some way, but I don't think we can. I believe an editor can enter a posthumous text and perhaps polish up the rough edges. Even then, I'm not so sure I agree with that act. Perhaps those rough edges mean something. And perhaps it is a desire for order, and the belief that order leads to meaning, that prompt us to polish the rough edges, finish the sentences, and finish the thoughts.

Another widely discussed controversy of a "writer" entering another writer's text in the guise of editing has centered around Ralph Ellison's *Juneteenth*, edited by John Callahan, previously mentioned above. Ellison had been working on his manuscript when he died, and left no instructions as to how to finish the work. Callahan, however, cut the manuscript down from Ellison's 1,500 pages and "at 354 pages, *Juneteenth* is a radically pared version of the novel Ellison was writing, its sprawling narrative winnowed to a single narrative thread" (Feeley 1999, 51). In fact, "Callahan even chose the title *Juneteenth*, which refers to June 19, 1865, the day slaves in Texas belatedly got word of the Emancipation Proclamation" (51). Reading about Callahan's "editing" of Ellison's text finalized my decision; I could not "finish" Wollstonecraft's *Maria* with a clear conscience.

Deciding to write my own novel based on and from *Maria* eased my conscience. My internal struggles with "finishing" *Maria*, though, helped to guide my own process in ways I hadn't expected it would. Working on my own novel allowed me to experience an intertextuality that involved editing or revision as an enhancement of a work, and not as an invasion or penetration. In the creation stage of my novel, I worked with novelist (and professor) Joshua Harmon, who helped me determine the organization of the novel, guide its creation, always providing me with feedback at each step, each chapter. I'd get my chapters back, written all over, with his pointed questions on the last page, gently nudging suggestions. The strategy for my novel, though, remained solely my own, and I made the decisions as to what to do with his suggestions. He never inserted himself into my work so that I had no choice, and I never allowed that to occur. Based on his expertise, and his more objective perspective, I would utilize most of his recommendations, and we would discuss those I wasn't convinced I should use. Often, our discussion more than his actual editing advice provided more insight into where I wanted to go with the creation of the novel. At this point in my project, the authority I had over my work reiterated to me that finishing *Maria* would usurp Wollstonecraft's authority over her text, and I didn't feel comfortable with acquisition of that power.

After the first draft of the novel was completed, I began working with poet and novelist (and professor) Paula Closson Buck. In the revision stage, she helped me to craft my work, urging me to move from direct realism into artistic realism. A scene should convey more than one feeling or meaning, she taught me. She encouraged me to develop the complexity of my characters, modulate the pace of the dialogue with summary and scene, and avoid repetition by cutting material and also by relying more heavily on the intertextuality of my work. However, with all the revisions we discussed, I always reserved the right to make or not make the alterations. Again, based on this experienced writer's expertise and more distanced perspective from my work than my own, I trusted her editing suggestions, and we worked on revisions together. Her minimalist approach to fiction, due to the focal point of her own work being predominantly poetry, added a unique dimension to the evolution of my novel as I worked on revision with her. However, I always played the major role in working towards the completion of my work.

But perhaps what is most pronounced about my positive editing experiences is that I didn't experience the anxiety of authorship from which women writers in the past have suffered. Sandra Gilbert and Susan Gubar discuss the "anxiety of authorship" of women writers in their text, *The Madwoman in the Attic*. They suggest that for women writers, the "anxiety of influence" described by Harold Bloom, "a model of literary history that is intensely (even exclusively) male, and necessarily patriarchal" (1984, 47), is replaced for women by an "anxiety of authorship," which is an anxiety built from complex and often only barely conscious fears of that authority which seems to the female artist to be by definition inappropriate to her sex. (51)

Whereas, according to Bloom, male writers exhibited an anxiety in their texts that reflected the influence of writers who had gone before them and their attempt to reject or redirect these influences to make their own way into the literary world, Gilbert and Gubar claim that women exhibited an anxiety in their texts that grew out of a sense of their intrusion into a world in which they were made to feel they didn't belong. That is, in merely picking up the pen, women writers of the past, my foremothers, were infringing upon a world rarely welcoming or accepting of them as writers, and it resonated in their writing.

I did not experience an anxiety of authorship as I wrote my novel. I wrote with confidence and assertiveness. I believed it needed to be written. When it came to suggestions during the creation process or revision, I insisted on authority over my own work, and was not afraid to voice my opposition to an edit when necessary. However, I agree with Gilbert and Gubar when they state:

> For if contemporary women do now attempt the pen with energy and authority, they are able to do so only because their eighteenth- and nineteenth-century foremothers struggled in isolation that felt like illness, alienation that felt like madness, obscurity that felt like paralysis to overcome the anxiety of authorship that was endemic to their literary subculture. (51)

It is because Wollstonecraft and her daughter, Mary Shelley, picked up the pen, and wrote against a current of male domination that continued to and did threaten their work. Reading how Bloom writes of the "anxiety of influence," I assume that he doesn't realize women writers do produce texts of high quality. In his foreword to Eugene O'Neill's *Long Day's Journey into Night*, Bloom provides an exhaustive list of the writers who influenced O'Neill either directly or indirectly. None of those writers are women. Bloom fails to mention that O'Neill dedicated the play to his wife and wrote:

> I give you the original script of this play of old sorrow, written in tears and in blood. A sadly inappropriate gift, it would seem, for a day celebrating happiness. But you will understand. I mean it as a tribute to your love and tenderness which gave me the faith in love that enabled me to face my dead at last and write this play . . . (O'Neill 1987, dedication)

Bloom, in his foreword, names the novelists Emile Zola and Joseph Conrad, the poets Dante Gabriel Rosetti and Algernon Charles Swinburne as O'Neill's greatest influences. He writes:

> We can recognize Hawthorne in Henry James, and Whitman (however repressed) in T.S. Eliot, while the relation of Hemingway and Faulkner to Mark Twain is just as evident as their debt to Conrad. (v)

Bloom goes on to mention Ralph Waldo Emerson, Saul Bellow, John Ashbery, Edgar

Allan Poe, Herman Melville, Nathaniel West, Thomas Pinchon, and even briefly writes of O'Neill's treatment of his country in his art as Shelleyan (Percy, of course). Again, he doesn't mention O'Neill's wife, who, gathering from the dedication, may have enabled the writing of the play. That's certainly a detail worth looking into and researching further.

Clearly, Bloom's concept of the "anxiety of influence" concerns male writers. Bloom discusses a purposeful misreading of old texts in an effort to create a new text that is truly new, and not just a replication of the old. Bloom writes:

> The strong misreading comes first; there must be a profound act of reading that is a kind of falling in love with a literary work. That reading is likely to be idiosyncratic, and it is almost certain to be ambivalent, though the ambivalence may be veiled. Without Keats's reading of Shakespeare, Milton, and Wordsworth, we could not have had Keats's odes and sonnets and two *Hyperions*. Without Tennyson's reading of Keats, we would have almost no Tennyson. (1997, xxiii)

Bloom's anxiety of influence is the anxiety experienced by a male writer when he writes and is, in effect, killing the author that has gone before him, the father. It hints of Oedipal undertones, although Bloom denies this connection in the second edition of *The Anxiety of Influence*. But it is unmistakably present in his text, and how do women writers position themselves, then, in this Oedipal "anxiety of influence?"

Perhaps most women writers appreciate our few foremothers who extended beyond themselves and the constrictions inherent within their societies to write, and this leads us not to desire to kill the mother, but to respect the mother. As I struggled with whether or not to complete *Maria*, I was tormented by the thought of killing its author, so to speak. Instead, I wanted to build upon her text, and I wanted to see it establish its place in the literary world beside mine. I did not want to usurp her recognition as *Maria*'s creator, or imply that she had written an insufficient, inadequate text.

Ultimately, the decision to write my own novel and abandon the completion of *Maria* became clear when I honestly answered the questions that the text's fragmentariness had raised for me. Entering spaces in Wollstonecraft's novel that I judged to be unfinished or in need of more work did not seem justified or warranted. I was not a woman living at the end of the eighteenth century; I did not know what Wollstonecraft intended for her novel; and, I was not Mary Wollstonecraft. She died too early, too young, and unfortunately before she finished *Maria*, but my completing *Maria* would not resurrect the author, just as Barrett's completion of *Sandition* failed to resurrect Jane Austen. Yet that was my desire, I believe, feeling frustrated by Wollstonecraft's early death and incompletion of *Maria*. Gregory Feeley, in a piece entitled "Invisible Hand" for the *New York Times Magazine*, writes of Callahan's treatment of Ellison:

> In trimming the false starts and longueurs of an unfinished manuscript, a posthumous editor inevitably makes choices that *penetrate* the sphere that remains, properly, the author's. And so we are left to struggle with the post-mortem novel, born of our desire to have more from great authors who themselves are not more. (Feeley 1999, 53, my emphasis).

Penetration is an especially charged issue from a woman's perspective. Rape is a reality in every woman's life, as a fear or an actual experience. It is fairly agreed upon that as an experience, it alters one's life, and the person one has been up to that point. Violence shatters a woman's life, and often it is the silence expected to accompany the aftermath of that violence that incurs the greatest damage. If I compared *Maria*, the text, to a woman's body, and thought of myself as the raping critic, penetrating the text, without the permission of the author, would I alter the text and distort the strategy of its author? I'd be guaranteed her silence. Thus my discomfort with entering the text, and completing it in an act of usurpation of the corpus of the text began to mount.

The dilemma I faced in completing *Maria* became exacerbated as I learned more about Mary Wollstonecraft, her life and her writing, and yearned to absorb any information about her. Although I wanted to rationalize finishing her text, and not feel as if I was "penetrating" Wollstonecraft's text, I was faltering in my aims for the project. I could claim that I was entering the text, getting inside of it, and that through me, missing, and perhaps lost, pieces of the text could be discovered and put together. I could claim my task paralleled the process of putting together a complex puzzle. Maybe the pieces wouldn't fit exactly to size when I was finished, but the end result, I thought, would be thought-provoking and purposeful, each piece playing its part in the puzzle that didn't have to be perfectly fitted, but, perhaps, artistically interwoven. However, I kept thinking of myself as raping the text. A woman who is raped, and left shattered in fragmented pieces, would not appreciate the man who raped her putting those pieces back together. He is the one who ripped her apart; how could he be so presumptuous as to then step in and put the pieces back together into a newly deformed puzzle? He causes her fragmentariness; then he wants to complete her. Was I opening up *Maria* just so I could be the one to put it back together? I began to feel like a literary criminal in my motives, and as if I was imposing myself upon a text where I had no right to be.

From the beginning of my project, though, I desired Wollstonecraft's original text to remain unscathed. I wanted to enter into her text to produce another text, but I did not want her fragment replaced on the bookshelves by my "completed" novel. I was not endeavoring to update an old model. I was instead building on an older text to create a new text. Obliterating the old text was not my design, as Bloom might infer it was. Instead of experiencing an "anxiety of influence," I felt an anxiety of usurpation, power, or even exploitation. I didn't want to misuse or misappropriate an already vulnerable text. The more I studied Wollstonecraft's *Maria*, the more resistance I encountered within myself to enter her text and complete it where I thought it needed completion. However, in my own defense, I suppose I had initially been seduced by the suggestion of what could be, as Roland Barthes describes in his *The Pleasure of the Text*:

> Is not the most erotic portion of a body where the garment gapes? In perversion (which is the realm of textual pleasure) there are no "erogenous zones" (a foolish expression, besides); it is intermittence, as psychoanalysis has so rightly stated, which is erotic: the intermittence of skin flashing between two articles of clothing (trousers and sweater), between two edges (the open-necked shirt, the glove and the sleeve); it is this flash itself which seduces (1998, 9–10).

I resisted this seduction; in finishing *Maria*, I would have to assume a power over the text that was not deserving. How could I, a woman living two hundred years after Mary Wollstonecraft, finish *Maria* and have it make sense? I did not feel comfortable continuing with my project in this way. I controlled my desires.

Instead of "completing" Wollstonecraft's *Maria*, which could have resulted in a penetrating, harmful form of purposeful intertextuality, I decided to draw from the concept of a positive yet purposeful intertextuality as a tool for my own creative work. I used *Maria* as my guide, a model for my own novel, while excerpting various passages from *Maria* that had relevance to my story. I excerpted passages cautiously, and I rewrote the endings of *Maria* through my characters. I positioned this editing within my work to develop the complexity of these characters, while also giving attention to *Maria*. The use of intertextuality in my novel has been carefully designed to be as noninvasive as possible. I've felt comfortable with this process, because I do feel a connection with Mary Wollstonecraft as my foremother, and I sense that I am drawing from a legacy she has left behind for me, and my daughter, and all women. She used her writing as a subversive act; I do the same. It is how I began writing. It is how I continue. I had to feel as if Wollstonecraft would approve of my work. And I think that, regarding my own writing and her inclusion in mine, she would have. I have battled the anxiety of usurpation of my mother's work, and I have taken her advice, instead of simply making her work my own. I developed my writing style for this novel through *Maria*, Wollstonecraft, but also many other writers and texts that have influenced me, and I believe my project has grown into an example of purposeful intertextuality that enhances both the new and the old text.

Part Two

On Literature Becoming Film

Chapter 12

My Novel as a Film

So, from what I've read about other novelists, I was fortunate. I've been slow in work-ing on my novel, for a variety of reasons, many of them to do with being a single mother and head of household. But there are other reasons as well, that have to do with the writing, and the novel, itself. I wasn't introduced to the idea of my story as a film by way of a book contract, because I haven't attempted to publish my book yet. It hap-pened in a more roundabout way, and that has made all the difference.

To go back a bit, it was the spring of 2001, and I remember tucking my elementary-school-age children into bed, imbibing in my prewriting ritual (or procrastination process), then slowly, painstakingly, making my way to my laptop. And once begun, the chapter that night would unfold, from roughly 11.00 p.m. to 3 or 4 in the morning. It was a spring of seismic proportions. The intensity of the writing had begun as winter was ending and culminated as spring began. I remember how I would lose myself in the writing as the nights would turn into morning. I remember how I would read my chapters the next day, after getting the kids off to school and sleeping for a few hours, and marvel at where these thoughts had come from, mysterious in their appearance yet not so unfamiliar at the same time. I remember how lost I felt when I'd completed the last page of the first draft. I remember how close I felt with the characters, and suddenly it was as if they'd left me, after encompassing so much of my mind for the past several months.

I let the novel be for a while. Yet as I continued my analytical work investigating the process of literary creation, the story stayed with me. I remember the moment that sparked a new way of looking at my novel. It was a rather ordinary circumstance, at my son's basketball game talking to the father of one of my son's friends. Diego was a very lively individual, the type always looking at all the possibilities in every situ-ation. He asked me, as most other parents didn't, about my graduate work. I told him I'd recently written a novel, and he asked what it was about. When I explained my novel, briefly, his immediate response was, "Well, who's going to be in the movie?" I was taken aback, although I didn't show it. I honestly hadn't even thought about my novel, my precious story, being made into a film. This story that I'd lived with and through, the characters who had at times been more real to me, and more of a comfort to me, than any people in my life at the time; I'd never thought about them coming to life in front of me on screen. How that would cheapen them, and what I'd meant for them, and to them. I couldn't give them over to someone else to recreate. Could I?

It was fun to think about, yet as Diego and I sat there, laughingly discussing who would be Annie, and who would be Seth, my protective instincts were being challenged. This was my story, my "blood, sweat, and tears" (a lot of tears), and as amusing as it was to think of it being made into a film, the reality of that possibility unnerved me. I never saw my novel the same from that moment forward.

In fact, I'd been trained by a professor and mentor who'd taught a short story seminar in my graduate program that a writer should never envision their novel as a movie. He would look at us askance if we so much as whispered that we'd seen a film without having read the book from which it was adapted. He privileged the literature. His stance didn't affect me or influence me; I was so caught up in writing my story that it was a movie in my head, but not one that I saw on a silver screen. The story detailed actual people walking around inside my head, living out their lives, as I tried to flesh them out, know them to write most accurately how they would react to certain situations that I created for them. However, I learned that Joyce Carol Oates does exactly that, envisions her story as a film as she writes it. Yet I don't know where I heard this, so I could be misinforming. She did say in an interview for *Arch Literary Journal* that when she returns, in her mind, to a place she used to live or had been in order to write about it, "the writing is just creating this vibrant dream into which you kind of step." Based on what I've read of Joyce Carol Oates and her in-depth explorations into writing, and the changes she's documented in her writing and her writing process as she's progressed in her writing career, all of it seems to indicate that she visualizes her characters and sees them in herself and her life, but not necessarily as if it were a film in her mind.

Therapists have employed a tool for trauma victims, to envision the traumatic event as if they were watching it as a movie. They then see it, while outside of it, remembering it as if it were a movie. I suspect it's meant for the survivor to revisit the event, reconstruct it, put the pieces back together, pieces that they don't remember when only thinking of one part of it or another. Then the idea is to let the memory go, allow it to lose its hold over the survivor's present. I don't know that it works for everyone. Sometimes I would think reliving the event so vividly could cause further trauma. And just as writers have their own ways of carrying out their work, their own processes, so do trauma survivors. Perhaps the movie therapy works for some survivors while it exacerbates the pain for others. Perhaps it also might work for some writers to envision their narrative as a film in their minds, and not so for others.

However, I don't think it does film justice to think of it as something one carries on in their mind as if it were the past reconstructed, or the written story reconstructed, in the medium of film, in one's mind. First, it makes film seem easy to accomplish, as if you can simply envision it, and then bring it to life. This is not the case. It also makes it seem as if film simply recreates that which has already happened, as closely to the original event as possible. Or film simply recreates a written story as it has been written. This, also, is not the case in most instances, and usually can't be. Film has its own qualities, its own elements, that are used to put together a narrative meant to have an impact, to move its audience. And it is this fact that scares most authors when their work is adapted to film. They know it will be interpreted by someone else, and the process of making their text into a film will be carried out in a way that is beyond their control, and at times beyond the control of the director as well.

In fact, many writers have expressed their concerns and fears when it comes to their novel being made into a film. Michael Cunningham's words haunt me most, taken from the brief documentary about the making of his novel *The Hours* into a film. When considering his novel for film, he states simply but firmly, "I'd rather no movie be made of *The Hours* than a bad movie." John Irving in his book *My Movie Business* writes of the exorbitant amount of time and energy it took to bring *The Cider House Rules* to film, and how delicate the process was, the screenplay — finally written by Irving himself — altered each time it was considered and worked on by four directors until the fourth pushed through the process and accomplished the product. Lit-to-film adaptation is no easy process to take on, or to complete. Granted, neither a novel nor a film separately is an easy project to take on, but a process that involves both comes with complications in itself with more just waiting to happen. And authors aren't always satisfied with the results. Cunningham was content; yet he was involved in the process at least for some of the way. Irving retained a central role in the making of *The Cider House Rules*. More recently, the author of *The Time Traveler's Wife*, Audrey Niffenegger, was quoted in *Poets & Writers Magazine* in November of 2009 as saying she wouldn't be seeing the film adaptation of her novel. Kevin Nance, the writer of the piece on Niffenegger, states:

> Six years after the book was first published, sales remain remarkably brisk; in the weeks leading up to the release of the film version in mid-August, the novel returned to the top of the trade paperback best-seller lists, and at one point was outselling all books in all categories — hardcover, paperback, fiction, nonfiction, you name it. (In September 2007, when filming for the movie adaptation began, Niffenegger had significant misgivings about the screenplay, which had at least four different authors, none of them herself. "I find it painful to be rewritten by people who don't have the same goals that I do," she said then. Nowadays she's studiously circumspect. "My official position on the movie is that I haven't seen it and I'm not planning to see it," she says tautly. "I think the movie should have its chance, and that I should not be inflicting my views on other people.") (2009, 57)

Nance goes on to report that Niffenegger received a $5 million advance for her upcoming book, *Her Fearful Symmetry*. The possibility of it becoming a movie might have something to do with that whopping advance, although the article focuses on the fact that there is "a huge audience for her work" (59).

I haven't tried getting my novel published yet. The story was not an easy one to write, nor was it easy to return to, but when I did, it was after incorporating film adaptations based on literature, a study of both the literature and the films, into the courses I taught. The question persisted in my own mind. If my novel would get published, how would I feel about a film being made out of my story? I'd explored in my analysis of literary creation the influences that had affected the invention of my novel: my imagination, my lived experiences, literary influences, critical analysis, strategy, cultural influences, the determination of my novel's organization and structure, and ultimately, and which was still ongoing, revision. The further I have gone into the exploration of film adaptation, the more of a conundrum I have found myself in, the conundrum from which this book on film adaptation has grown.

I'm not sure I will allow a film to be made out of my novel. And, if that makes it unpublishable, at least by a major publishing house, if only for that reason, then so be it. Because, after all the research I've done, of most concern to me is the marginalization of women in film, and the marginalization of women in the film industry. I must feel confident that my novel will be respected by a filmmaker in the form of a film adaptation of the novel. This of course has nothing to do with any skepticism that film can do my novel justice. I have no qualms that my novel can be adapted into a brilliant film, with the appropriate effort and suitable amount of awareness as to how carefully the project would need to be carried out. My concern is that it won't be carried out as such. And I would rather no film be made out of my novel than an irresponsible one that distorts what I've tried to accomplish with my novel. I feel the weight of too many women's actual lived stories upon me, represented by my own diligent work, to allow those stories to be misrepresented and grossly distorted in a film adaptation of my work.

As a woman considering a novel I've written about women for adaptation to film, the fact that the film industry is not a particularly welcome place for women not only astounds me in the new millennium, but concerns me. Will my work be purposefully misinterpreted and transformed into some perverse homage to violence against women that will bring out the masses ad nauseam, especially men? Manohla Dargis, a female film reviewer for the *New York Times*, wrote a piece entitled "Is There a Real Woman in This Multiplex?" heralding the summer of 2008, when *Iron Man*, *Batman*, and the "Big Angry Green Man" were due to hit the theaters. She states unequivocally at the beginning of her essay: "Hollywood has realized that the best way to deal with its female troubles is to not have any, women, that is" (2008, 1). She continues to criticize the film industry for its treatment of women, and there is a sense that she's been repressing her thoughts for a while and can no longer hold them in as she quips:

> All you have to do is look at the movies themselves — at the decorative blondes and brunettes smiling and simpering at the edge of the frame — to see just how irrelevant we have become. That's as true for the dumbest and smartest of comedies as for the most critically revered dramas, from No Country for Old Men (but especially for women) to There Will Be Blood (but no women). Welcome to the new, post-female American cinema. (1)

Her argument came as the summer's explosion of extremely male-dominated, male-oriented films were on their way. Her article was published in the *New York Times* in early May of 2008. Dargis observes: "Nowhere is our irrelevance more starkly apparent than during the summer, the ultimate boys' club." She continues to say that "the girls of summer are few in number, and real women are close to extinct" (1). Not exactly uplifting for a novelist writing about just that, "real women," and reading this article that relates the following facts, further deflating my ambitions to see significant changes in society when it comes to women:

Last year only 3 of the 20 highest-grossing releases in America were female-driven, and involve a princess (Enchanted) or pregnancy (Knocked Up and Juno). Actresses had starring roles in about a quarter of the next 80 highest-grossing titles, mostly in dopey romantic comedies and dopier thrillers . . . There may be more women working in the industry now — Amy Pascal is co-chairman of Sony Pictures Entertainment — but you wouldn't know it from what's on the screen. The reasons are complex and certainly beyond the scope of a seasonal rant like this one. Some point to the lack of female directors, whose numbers in both the mainstream and independent realms hover at around 6 percent. (2–3)

Six percent? And I'm not supposed to be a bit hesitant about my novel — about women by a woman — being made into a film? Because it's the art of it that matters? No, much more than that matters.

Certainly, I'm not giving up, but I'm also not giving in. Another article, again in the *New York Times*, about the making of the film adaptation of *Watchmen*, the well-known graphic novel, states that Zack Snyder had been working on the adaptation for more than two and a half years, and "his greatest challenge would be satisfying the desires of the book's devoted fans, who, like him, regard it as an exemplary work of postmodern storytelling" (Itzkoff 2009, 1). However, further on in the article, Snyder is quoted as saying, "I wouldn't say it's a short movie by any stretch. But it's the tightest version that I could give them and not feel like I raped it a little bit" (2). From a woman's perspective (although as an individual I'm supposed to see the metaphorical use of the term), to hear the term "raped" used in a statement made by a filmmaker about adaptation is not comforting. In fact, I want to run, holding my book close to me, sprinting somewhere away from where it could be raped. But I will persist, and perhaps I will drag this project out until I am completely satisfied by how I envision the resultant outcome. Perhaps this is the time for a woman to stand up for the women she's written, who are based on a woman from two hundred years ago and what *she* wrote; this is the time to stand up for the women she's researched who are represented, albeit fictionally, in her novel; and this is the time to stand up for her daughter, following closely in her footsteps, and her granddaughters who will soon follow. Perhaps it's "women's time," as Julia Kristeva titled one of her famous essays; perhaps it's women's time in the film industry. If it isn't, I doubt my novel will make it to the screen. I don't envision signing that contract.

That it's women's time in film couldn't be a more contradictory idea than during the winter of 2009 into the spring of 2010. The good news is that Kathryn Bigelow won Academy Awards for Best Director and Best Picture for her film *The Hurt Locker*, which won several other Academy Awards as well. However, during the months leading up the Academy Awards, hundreds of people involved in the film industry signed a petition in support of Roman Polanski's release after being arrested in an airport for a criminal charge he'd fled and outrun for thirty years. The crime he committed was statutory rape of a thirteen-year-old girl. In Hollywood, the argument that the girl looked older than thirteen years old seems to be adequate for most of the film industry. Unfortunately for them but not for thirteen-year-old girls everywhere, that reasoning is insufficient to clear Polanski. However, the hundreds who signed the petition are the concern. And how do I, the writer of a novel about a thirteen-year-old girl who is raped by her forty-something father (the age of Polanski when he had sex with the thirteen-year-old girl — who did look older than thirteen according to Angelica Huston) sign over movie rights knowing that a director such as Polanski could buy those rights and turn my story on its head? I don't. And I won't. I couldn't live with that and sleep at night. It was a surprising turn of events to watch an industry that claims to be so liberal and open-minded, come down on the side of a rapist. We can call him a statutory rapist which is accurate and uncontestable, and soften the charge? His most recent film was released in March of 2010, showing that rape hasn't precluded him from continuing on with his life, and especially, his career. Surely, a good amount of the names on that list have some monetary interest in being on that list. Anyone on that list, though, is banned from my list, not that it will ever matter perhaps to anyone but me. But to me, it does matter. I do know how rape can preclude a woman from continuing on with her life, at the simplest of levels.

Chapter 13

A Marriage of Media?

When I first began to explore lit-to-film adaptation, the studies done thus far seemed to pit the literature against the film, and vice versa. The majority of scholars writing on film adaptation studies seem to be film experts, film theorists. And the defensive language applied to these studies seems protective, overprotective, of film. Yet, here I was, a novelist, hearing and reading the words "rape," even from directors when viewing a piece of literature, and it felt as if these scholars were protecting the perpetrator. I'm not saying that's the case; I'm saying that's how I felt. And thus, to be fair to both "parties," I tried to find a way to mend the fences, and see the two mediums in a way that could bring them together, and be seen together, as equals. I started exploring the idea of lit-to-film adaptation as a marriage of media.

We join hands
in love and friendship
to become one,
promising never to forget
we are two.

These were the sentiments written on a wedding invitation I once read. And this is where I began to explore the implications of marriage in a union of literature and film into one final product. Clearly, in a lit-to-film adaptation, we never forget that literature and film are two. Yet what seems to be the most difficult hurdle to manage in a marriage between two people is not in remembering they are two, but being mindful that they are also one, a unit of sorts, especially with children involved. Two people come together to form one entity, as well as remember they are two. But can a source text and its adapted text ever truly be thought of as "one," as a unit? Is a marriage of media possible?

I chose the metaphor of marriage to discuss film adaptation for three reasons. One, the concept of film adaptation seemed to me rife with confusion and elusiveness as has always been the concept of marriage to me. We make our rules about each, then we bend or break them, and we're never quite sure for the good of whom, or what, that we do. Two, using the metaphor of marriage with reference to film adaptation required a reevaluation of the way film adaptation was viewed, and at times I felt it was viewed quite negligently. We neglect to remember that film adaptation is the combination of two mediums. Theorists seem to be mindful of the two, but don't have much time for the union, and maybe there is a reason for that, but I desired to know more. Three, as a writer of a novel (in the revision process) who had had the question put to me often as to whether I'd like to see my work adapted to film, but also as an instructor investigating the union of literature and film with my students, I'd hesitated in considering the prospect of a film adaptation of my own work. I didn't begin with this attitude of hesitancy, but I'd gained some reservations about seeing my work adapted into an audio-visual, performative representation. Film adaptation, to me, seemed to have very little to do with attempts to make a good marriage out of two separate entities but only in keeping them just that, separate, and analyzing them that way as well.

Perhaps it was the failures of marriages and relationships around me, which resulted from both a misconception of what it meant to be two when making one but also a lack of skill in making one out of two, that prompted me to fixate on the fact that film adaptation is the combination of two mediums often misjudged and misinterpreted as separate mediums, and rarely considered of any importance together. It became imperative for me to consider how, if I were to allow my novel to be made into a film, it might be a marriage of media. And, the question I posed, then, was what would make a marriage of media work? But first, what constituted a marriage of media? Or, what did I mean when I made reference to a marriage of media?

A marriage of media would be the purposeful combination of two distinct and unique mediums — in this case, a novel and a film — that can stand alone quite effectively, but that can also merge their qualities in a way that each is enhanced by the other while at the same time they form a "dyadic" union of sorts that extends its own benefits. I attempted to argue that for a marriage of media to work, the marriage needed to be considered as such, and it needed to be made with this goal in mind: to enhance the individuality of each while achieving eminence by their combination or marriage.

The marriage of a novel to a film represented a new way of looking at film adaptation, but perhaps a necessary view to take. It required that the film was as beneficial to the novel as the novel was to the film, and it required that their marriage produce an entity in itself that the media achieve in their commitment to each other. It was this factor alone that prompted my investigation of the idea of "marriage" in film adaptation. Film adaptation, as I'd studied it, seemed to follow a system or process of sorts patriarchal in nature, whereby one partner in the marriage claimed more dominance than the other. A novel, if it was adapted for film, tended to play the more submissive role to the film's dominance in this "marriage." Let me explain. The film takes from the novel and often doesn't give anything back, and in so doing, the two don't make a marriage. Film adaptation seemed like one area where two mediums came together and only separate entities were produced, the novel used up and left discarded and the film based on the novel, but no final product that visibly contained the two was accomplished by their combination. Let me also explain that I'm not in agreement with this way of viewing lit-to-film adaptation, but this is the path I took to fleshing out what actually goes on within the process of lit-to-film adaptation, and how the mediums turn back in on each other, if they in fact do.

Complicating the argument, then, the film wasn't always privileged over the novel.

It often acquired a large audience, quickly, which just as quickly dissipated. A novel could achieve a larger audience that often established itself over time. A novel often would be judged "better" than the film adapted from it — primarily by a mainstream audience but not always limited to such an audience — which also detracted from seeing film adaptation as a marriage of media. Instead, film adaptation seemed a competition between the two mediums. The question often became, who did it better? I fervently argued, and hold to this argument, that such a competition devalues the process of film adaptation, and can potentially cheapen it.

Understandably, then, I had good reason for reservations about seeing my novel adapted to film. In fact, the history behind the writing of my novel served to effect my concerns with film adaptation. The reasoning I adopted in writing my novel paralleled and even foreshadowed the struggles I was encountering as I entertained the possibility of a film being made out of my novel. I didn't like that phrasing: a film made out of my novel. When I employed the metaphor of marriage to film adaptation, which was the only way I could digest the idea of my novel and its film version, did it then follow that one partner in the marriage was formed of the other? Or, would it be that one partner was adapted into the other? In a marriage, does one partner develop out of the other, then leave that partner behind? Certainly, not in long-lasting, mutually beneficial marriages. What I was discovering was that in saying that literature is adapted to film, in that expression weren't we essentially belittling and minimizing literature? Wasn't a disservice being done not to see the combination of two powerful representations of similar material as a marriage?

The question became for me, what is film adaptation? How should we see it? Being at the literature end of a possibly upcoming marriage, I contended that literature is the inspiration for a film version of the material put forth by that literature. The literature then is the driving force behind the film. It inspires and guides the film. My next question became, what does the film do for the literature? I argued that this question had not been asked, and if it had, not nearly seriously enough. A healthy marriage requires a give-and-take arrangement between both partners. And, relying on the metaphor of marriage to view film adaptation from a more just perspective then requires the film to give back as much as it takes. Only then would the combination be fair and equal. Only then would it be a healthy exchange of ideas and thought. Only then could it be a marriage that works.

What I intended to accomplish by exploring film adaptation from outside the process as well as within the process itself was to develop a heightened perspective concerning film adaptation. I wasn't ignorant to the question looming before me as I continued and explored: is it even possible to view the joining of novel to film in a film adaptation as a marriage? However, by considering the adjoining of my own novel to its corresponding film version as a marriage, I expected to clarify the concept of film adaptation for myself, so that the process could be more effectively achieved no matter the stature of the author (or his or her presence in the process), but most importantly more adequately articulated and analyzed once the process was complete.

An Intertextual Commitment

It was ten years ago. As soon as graduate school had begun, the pressure was on to determine what would be the main focus of my years there. I was immediately attracted to the work of Frances, or Fanny, Burney. It fascinated but also angered me that Burney had destroyed the first manuscript she wrote, at fifteen years old, because she feared her stepmother would find it and warrant her unmarriageable as a result of her writing it. I envisioned the scene of young Burney throwing her manuscript into the fire while her sister looked on, crying. Burney interested me. She went on to write *Evelina*, her main character being the daughter of the girl she'd created as her main character in the destroyed novel. She wrote *Evelina*, hiding the manuscript as she went along, and published it anonymously. When it was received well, she revealed her authorship.

I'm still fascinated by Fanny Burney, and continue to teach her and enjoy the lessons her work and life offer my students. However, it was a text I read for a pre-Romantic class I was taking that changed the course of my studies, and life. Sitting at my young daughter's soccer practice, waiting for her to be finished, I read *Maria, or The Wrongs of Woman* by Mary Wollstonecraft for my class the next day. It was about a woman who was committed to a dank, dreary insane asylum at the end of the eighteenth century by her husband who was a drunk and libertine, whom she had left. She'd been abducted from her apartment, her infant daughter whom she'd been holding taken from her. I came to the following passage: "She found however that she could think of nothing else; or, if she thought of her daughter, it was to wish she had a father whom her mother could respect and love" (Wollstonecraft 1975, 23). In that moment, I found myself grappling with the fact that I didn't believe much or enough had changed in the past two hundred years.

I learned about Mary Wollstonecraft. She'd written a formidable feminist text at the incipience of the French Revolution entitled, *A Vindication of the Rights of Woman*. The text put forth an argument for equal rights of women with men at a time when women had no rights, and she did so strategically and brilliantly. We have yet to achieve Wollstonecraft's expectations of us, as women and as a society.

Wollstonecraft's personal life was riddled with obstacles as she navigated her way through her own life conflicted by society's standards for her and her standards for herself. She made mistakes, and she faltered. Her mistakes and stumbles have been unfairly criticized since this woman tried to live a life of freedom in a world that wanted to keep her in chains. Her life became an obstacle course and her difficulty to hop sprightly through it is somehow, even today, viewed as entirely her fault. However, at the end of her life, she became involved with a man who respected her work and her mind, she got pregnant, they married, and then sadly, she died ten days after giving birth to their child, Mary Wollstonecraft Godwin, who later became Mary Shelley, author of *Frankenstein, or The Modern Prometheus*.

Maria, the novel I was reading that warm autumn afternoon, was the novel Wollstonecraft left unfinished at her death. William Godwin, her husband, wrote her memoirs and edited what she'd completed of her novel, and published both. The memoirs he wrote of her were ill-received, and her reputation as a writer scarred for decades. *Maria* had only recently reemerged when I read it, and I became obsessed with the novel, and Wollstonecraft. She became a foremother for me that I hadn't known existed. And, I decided, in tribute to her, and also for my graduate work, I would "finish" her novel, and document the process of doing so.

This was easier said than done. As soon as I began the process, and discussing it with my mentors, the project became problematic. How could I, a contemporary writer and scholar, complete the work of a woman who had written two hundred years before me? How could I know what her intentions were for the completion of the novel no matter how intensely I studied her other writings, letters, and notes? How could I penetrate her text to finish it when in its current version it stood alone as a testament to what it was like to live an interrupted life as a woman writer in the late eighteenth century?

I couldn't. After grappling with the issues of finishing this text, I changed direction: I would write my own novel, a contemporary story based on the ideas and thought Wollstonecraft brought forth in *Maria*. My novel grew out of two short stories each portraying a woman as protagonist. The friendship of these two women became the driving force behind the resolution of its plot. However, the other part of this novel I planned was to intersperse my story with chapters from *Maria*, finished by me. As I continued to plan out this project, the concept itself became cumbersome, and I again changed direction. My final plan for my project became, then, to write my own novel with a contemporary setting, using excerpts from *Maria* to enhance my own writing. In using *Maria*, I also desired to bring *Maria* into fuller view of academicians and critics. However, what began as a simplistic combination of my work and Wollstonecraft's work also developed into my own quest to understand the process of creation. I intended to embark on a new way to create a novel, and in so doing, discover the many intricacies of creation. The project having been redefined, and thus begun, I continued to encounter problems and concerns as I wrote my novel.

My chief concern, the issue I struggled with most, involved my respect and devotion to Wollstonecraft. This woman, and her writing, had single-handedly altered my perspective of not only my personal life but my academic and writing life, and I would not use her work to showcase my own. I worried that my contemporary work would be privileged over her 1798 text. How could I enhance her work the way she was enhancing mine? Thus much of my attention as I wrote my novel focused on not only adapting my text out of hers, but shedding light on her work through mine, and perhaps interesting my audience in a perusal of *Maria*.

I see my novel and *Maria* as a marriage of sorts. *Maria* has its themes and meanings; the novel provides scholars with a text that informs through its literary intents and its place in history. My novel has its own set of themes that are similar in some ways to *Maria* but also different. However, the marriage of the two texts offers its own value, the most important being a study of "the wrongs of woman" two hundred years ago compared and contrasted with those of today.

Maria, or The Wrongs of Woman begins as Maria, the main character, awakens to find that she is in an insane asylum, and struggles to remember how she arrived at such a place. She describes her surroundings as the novel begins:

Abodes of horror have frequently been described, and castles, filled with spectres and chimeras, conjured up by the magic spell of genius to harrow the soul, and absorb the wondering mind. But, formed of such stuff as dreams are made of, what were they to the mansion of despair, in one corner of which Maria sat, endeavouring to recall her scattered thoughts! (Wollstonecraft 1975, 7)

Maria begins to remember the events leading to her incarceration over the following chapters. She meets Jemima, who watches over the inmates of the asylum, and although this guard is resistant at first, Maria is able to befriend her. Maria encounters Darnford, an inmate of the asylum, whom she remembers meeting before but can't recall the specifics of their meeting. The three form an alliance and begin to tell their stories. Darnford relates the libertine behavior that made him vulnerable to his being committed. Jemima tells of her unfortunate working-class background that gave her no choice but to accept the miserable job of caring for the asylum patients. Finally, Maria, who has been writing with the pen and paper Jemima agreed to allow her, gives Darnford a copy of her "memoirs," promising Jemima a perusal of them as well. At this point in the novel, Maria's memoirs begin, and she addresses them to her daughter, the infant daughter who was ripped away from her when her husband found her and had her incarcerated for leaving him. The memoirs end, the story returns to the asylum, and Darnford and Maria are released. Maria has fallen for Darnford, whom she assumes has fallen for her. However, according to the contradictory notes left for the ending Wollstonecraft didn't have the opportunity to complete (nor did she complete other fragmented sections of the novel), the reader is left unsatisfied. Does Darnford abandon Maria, who lost her child to her husband, and then Maria commits suicide? Or does Darnford abandon Maria, but instead of going through with her suicide, Maria chooses to stay alive when Jemima and her daughter come into the room? Maria could be in a dream state in this latter version of the ending, and hallucinating as she's dying from a drug overdose. Or, it could really be happening, since she throws up the drug, exclaiming that she will stay alive for her child. Perhaps it was that Wollstonecraft couldn't decide whether or not to end on a more positive note, with only a mere suggestion of hope but hope nonetheless, or on a more tragic note, and in a sense exhibiting the punishment of a woman exerting such independence as Maria does, especially with careless abandon. These endings leave the reader in a quandary not only over how the novel ends, but why Wollstonecraft seemed to have been struggling with an ending.

It wasn't difficult for me to bring this novel into a contemporary setting. As Wollstonecraft states in her introduction to *Maria*, "the sentiments I have embodied." I have embodied the sentiments, or the emotions felt by the women in my novel, but reading *Maria*, I also could relate to the frustrations and conflicts expressed by Maria in Wollstonecraft's novel. My characters, then, embody the sentiments of *Maria*, in a society where we believe we cannot fathom the significant similarities between women two hundred years ago and women today, but where in fact there are.

I wrote two short stories about two separate women struggling with trauma in their lives. When I began my project to write a novel out of *Maria*, these two women became instrumental to my plot. In my novel, Annie and Lindsay, the women from my short stories, meet in prison and the story spirals from that starting place, moving backwards and forwards, and all around, in a purposeful haphazard motion to reflect the turbulence of these women's lives. Briefly, Annie has murdered her ex-husband in an uncharacteristic explosion of rage after she discovers he's been sexually molesting one of their daughters. She has been convicted of the murder and is serving a life sentence in the same prison where Lindsay is serving a sentence for killing the man who had abducted and brutally raped her. She killed him when he fell asleep, making a plea for self-defense inadmissible. The women become friends in prison, and also befriend their guard. Annie writes the account of her life for her daughter as she sits in prison, reflecting on the circumstances that led her there. She also finds Wollstonecraft's novel, *Maria*, that she remembers from her studies as she began a PhD program, and now it has come more to life for her than it had previously. She determines that she and her daughter, Lexi, should work together to finish the novel for Wollstonecraft. The novel ends with Annie's and Lexi's versions of an ending for *Maria*, and its own ending.

While writing my novel, I couldn't shake my responsibility to the novel that had inspired me and guided me to this place where I was writing. My responsibility in this intertextual project was to remain faithful to Wollstonecraft's original message, and not to distort it for my own misuse of it. *Maria* is clearly a critique of the treatment of women in society during Wollstonecraft's time — their lack of rights, voice, and choices. I argue that an intertextual work with its roots in a previous text should honor and respect that text by remaining close to what the text conveys in its original context. This is where the concept of a marriage began to be important for me. Two texts should not come together if they are incompatible. One should not disregard the "feelings" of the other, the convictions of the other, or the concerns of the other. Doing so would make for a difficult marriage, for one or both partners. I argued that treating adaptation in this same manner makes for a difficult, and problematic, adaptation.

Yet, I wondered, perhaps the word "adaptation" was the problem in itself. Adaptation describes the process of changing to fit new circumstances or conditions. Something has been modified for a purpose. Some synonyms are version, edition, altered copy, reworked copy. Brian McFarlane, in his essay "Reading Film and Literature," uses the first of those terms when referring to a novel adapted to film as he writes: "The 1992 *version* of Howards End . . . needs to be considered not just as a *version* of E.M. Forster's novel but also as a Merchant Ivory production and as an example of 1990s British 'heritage cinema' [my emphasis]" (2007, 27). McFarlane seems more concerned with the film being given the credit it's due as a text than the novel given the respect it deserves as the only version of itself, since he in very simplified terms refers to the film as a "version" of Forster's novel. My text, my contemporary novel, is not a "version" of Wollstonecraft's text. However, I did "adapt" her text to form my text. And I discuss my process and project at such length because if we consider a film as a text, which we do, and we should, then according to the concept of adaptation, a film based on a literary work is a reworked copy, or version, of the original text. But I can't agree with this perception of film adaptation. It isn't fair to the literary work, and it isn't fair to the film.

McFarlane, who contradicts himself throughout his essay and especially at the end, describes one way in which the relationship between novel and film "might be seen, if not as siblings, at least as first cousins, sometimes bickering but at heart having a good deal of common heritage" (28). Now, a sibling is not a version of another sibling, at least not in the midst of a healthy family dynamic. Nor is a first cousin a version of another. However, I do applaud McFarlane's attempt at mending the fence where he firmly resides between novel and film (although his feet seem clearly implanted on the film side of the fence for the most part), but I see a deeper relationship that must be made between the two. Thus perhaps they must marry if they want to form a mutually beneficial relationship where one isn't martyred for the other's cause, or too blended into the other to be seen as separate. It is a give-and-take relationship, or it should be.

It was my own experience working with a few writers on a possible screenplay of my novel that challenged the possibility of viewing lit-to-film adaptation as a marriage of media. First of all, to refer to a marriage of mediums is different than referring to a marriage of actual texts in the case of lit-to-film adaptation. Literature and film can be married to produce a film with the literature embedded within it. However, the actual marrying of a source text with an adapted text can't really happen. They can be married when viewing them from an analytical perspective, seeing their relationship with each other. But one can't be married to the other as the process ensues. The source text, the literary text, is reconceived to become the adapted text, or the film text. One is reworked and transformed to become the other. This is not a marriage. It is not two siblings or first cousins. The analogy doesn't work. Two partners when marrying come from different sources and merge to become one. This is not the case with lit-to-film adaptation. Siblings come from the same source yet the younger sibling is inevitably different from the older sibling. The literary text and the film text of an adaptation do not come from the same source.

The most viable way of viewing lit-to-film adaptation from an analogical perspective would be to see it as parent and child, not that I don't realize this relationship has been considered many times before. However, viewing the parent as the source text, and the child as the adapted text, makes the most sense to me. It also lends much more freedom to the adapted text than if considered a partner in the relationship. A child must move beyond its parent, grow out of and possibly even subvert its parent. Yet it is without a doubt that the child has as its source that parent. A child is based on the parent. I think what can also be evaluated is whether or not an adaptation is more a father–child relationship or a mother–child relationship, and a consideration of the gender of the child could lead to a fascinating study. Reproductive cloning could lead as well to an interesting connection to lit-to-film adaptation. I for one, and perhaps this is surprising coming from a novelist, am adverse to the idea of cloning in lit-to-film adaptation (as I am against the technology of human cloning as well). However, the parent–child relationship if used to understand and explain the complexities and vicissitudes of lit-to-film adaptation is worth exploring in more detail.

Chapter 14

Attempts at a Screenplay

So, when I began to explore the concept of the marriage of media, I had no idea what challenges I would encounter along the way. I began with the following proposition: What if a budding novelist and a newbie screenwriter combined their talents and purposefully partnered a novel with a film? What if the adaptation was occurring as the novel was in its revision stages? What if the goal was to produce a novel and a film that could be marketed together? Maybe film adaptation defies limits and must do its own share of adapting as popular culture evolves and changes. I argued that a literary novel and a film adaptation of this novel in its earliest drafts could be designed as companion pieces yet partnered in ways that would not compromise the individuality of either text or their abilities to function as separate entities. The novel and film adaptation of *The Hours* provided me with an example of companion pieces that were not designed to be so. Teaching the novel *The Hours* with the film adaptation had proven to enhance my students' experiences of both texts. In addition, the film *Memento* offered another example of companion pieces since the film was adapted from a short story, and the story was written by one of the two brothers who put together the film. I knew it was possible to create companion pieces of literature and film, and it was possible to work on the two simultaneously. I began to explore these possibilities — the problematic aspects of such a project and the advantages of its success.

That question, who would be in the movie, kept coming, again and again. I would joke around about it to people, and even to my students. I said to some film students, "Hey, someday you can make my novel into a film." Then I challenged one of my students to take it seriously, and he did. He seemed up to the challenge. While others would go along with the joke, and we'd enjoy a moment of a dream that we knew probably wouldn't come true, the dream seemed palpable when both Dan and I began more serious discussions on the topic. So we began, and as we did, I began to document our travels. We were only beginning on the road, and perhaps because I invested so much of myself, my time, and my vision of society into my novel, I was invested in seeing a film version of my work do all of that effort justice, as I've made clear.

Dan was young, and inexperienced, yet had he been older with more experience, he would have been dangerous to my work. When we decided to work on the project — our plan to work together as I revised my novel and he wrote the screenplay, so that in the process of adaptation we would collude and benefit from each other to produce the film adaptation — things went awry quickly. I found myself increasingly anxious about adapting my novel to film. I discovered it was Dan working on it that unnerved me more than the possibility of seeing the novel adapted to film. Dan wanted to design the film to be from the point of view of the men in the novel. He never read the novel, but simply went on my summary of it, and my explanations of how it had come to me, the research I'd done, and what I wanted to accomplish with the novel. He harped on about the entertainment value of the film, and that the audience for film had to be satisfied, so the film needed to focus on the men in the novel. The novel is not about the men. The novel is about the women — women as mothers, daughters, sisters, friends — the focus is women. There is one male character who works with the women, and is a part of their "circle," so to speak. Dan focused in on that character, but the novel is appropriated from a novel written and left unfinished two hundred years ago by a woman about women. To focus in on Grey would be to do a disservice to the character himself (that I'd created). Dan was soon out, and I was on my own.

I thought I'd write the screenplay myself. I'm still not adverse to this prospect, although based on John Irving's description of writing a screenplay in his *My Movie Business*, it does not seem very appealing:

> There is no language in a screenplay. (For me, dialogue doesn't count as language.) What passes for language in a screenplay is rudimentary, like the directions for assembling a complicated children's toy. The only aesthetic is to be clear. Even the act of reading a screenplay is incomplete. A screenplay, as a piece of writing, is merely the scaffolding for a building someone else is going to build. (1999b, 153)

Irving in no way discounts the importance of the screenplay here, but he does elucidate the resistance a novelist might have to writing one. Still, I thought to continue my project of working on the novel while working on the screenplay to see if a mutually beneficial relationship could be developed, I would write the screenplay. Then a young woman whom I respected as a writer and friend asked if she could read the novel. And, she read it! She read it in a weekend while alone in a new apartment, with no furniture, and only my novel to read, in its still-to-be-revised form. She loved it, and asked if she could work on a screenplay for it. She began to do that, and we talked about the issues in the novel. She knew how important the issues in the novel were to me, but she also had her own vision of how she'd like to see those issues conveyed on screen. And we began to learn from each other as we went along. Although my first experience with a screenwriter was horrifying, it led to the beginning of a positive experience, affirming to me that this project might be able to be done without the subject of my novel being grossly compromised.

However, then Lauren began to work on her own book, and had to heavily invest herself in her own project. I was working on this book, besides our plan to work on the novel and screenplay together. I quickly learned that we were both in over our heads. Her personal life also veered her in a direction away from the material that I thought would compromise her original plans for the screenplay. Whether we care to admit it or not, in the midst of life experiences that directly go against what we're writing about, we can't help but come out sounding disingenuous. Or so that was my fear. Although

Mary Wollstonecraft is rigorously castigated for not living the life a feminist today approves of, and being too hard on other women of her time especially, the writer did attempt to live out her own ideas, even though it resulted in temporary bouts of emotional instability and ultimately near ruin, until she determined to get her life together. I've observed that when we live against what we write, and then are essentially writing against the way we live, both our writing and our life suffer immense consequences. I didn't want that to happen with Lauren. So, our working relationship ended.

I called on the talents of another young woman who'd read my novel and had helped me with some revision suggestions. She'd written a screenplay before, for an amateur film she'd put together. She tried her hand at a scene adapted from the novel. However, at this point, I'd become disillusioned by the entire project, and was not quite sure where to go from there. I'd abandoned the idea of the marriage of media, mostly in favor of the more accurate parent–child relationship between source text and adapted text. I now plan to revise my novel to where I feel it to be finished, and look into getting it published. Movie rights will be an issue, and self-publishing is an option I have not ruled out, and might even be leaning towards.

My views have changed considerably. After having worked with three different screenwriters, and based on the information compiled to write this book, I must assert that the literary text being considered for adaptation needs to be complete, by the author's standards. In Wollstonecraft's case, this couldn't be achieved due to her untimely death. But when at all possible, the text in question should be considered completed by its author. In that way, the story that the author intended has been recorded, and doesn't become muddled with an adapter's sense of it. Although I began with the idealistic view that a screenwriter/filmmaker could add clarity to a novelist's work as she was writing it, I have discovered that this practice doesn't bode well for novel or film. The novel should be complete, only open to interpretation, but not revision or changes to its content.

It might not have been the screenwriters and their work on the novel that was insufficient in any way. Looking at the work they did, they all brought to the table some talented and innovative ways of looking at the novel. Yet, due to its unfinished state, I've discovered, I'm defensive against any intrusion. I need to finish my vision for the novel, before I can discuss and hear out another's vision for an adaptation of the novel. I need to know my work is complete, and my intentions — both conscious and unconscious — for it solidified, recorded, and set in stone so to speak. Then I can feel freer to consider the opinions of others. I'm open to an experimental take on my novel. It was experimental in itself. But I need to know that my job is done first. So perhaps I don't believe in a marriage of media. A parent–child relationship seems more in line with my own sense of lit-to-film adaptation. The best parent is the one who knows whom she/he is before bringing another being into the world. A parent might discover things about herself that a child can bring out, but the child will need guidance and then freedom to use that guidance in what the parent hopes will be a positive way, in a way that's a positive contribution to society. A parent must be confident of whom she is before she can help another being become who they desire to be.

Part Three

The Creation and Study of Film

Chapter 15

My History with, and an Abbreviated History of, Film

It's only fair that I write of my own history of film. It is not vast, nor is it intense. Film is not my passion, as creative writing and literature are. Yet, the more I learn about film, the more I've come to appreciate it as an art and a medium for disseminating meaning and significance. I must begin at the beginning, so to speak. I suppose as any individual experiences, I had my share of rebellion against my parents. However, mine may have included a rejection of film as art. Not that I didn't see film as art; I did, secretly. The problem was that my parents *only* saw film as art! My father was so entranced with the "great" films, he'd watch *Casablanca* on television any time it appeared on a random Saturday afternoon. He'd have me sit there with him and watch it, and I'd have to stay until the end when Humphrey Bogart and Claude Rains think they might be beginning a beautiful friendship.

There is also the infamous family scene when my sister and her fiancé were sitting at my parents' kitchen table, and the discussion was *The English Patient*. My sister's fiancé hadn't liked the film, to my father's horror, or irritation. Regardless, my sister's fiancé said, nonchalantly, "I go to the movies to be entertained." My father responded, chuckling, "Spoken like a true idiot." (This kind young man did go on to marry my sister, and they now have four sons.)

I was horrified by my father's reaction, and embarrassed. I was angry that I couldn't talk to my father about action movies, or dare I say it, entertaining movies. He didn't find them worthy of discussion. Up until only a few years ago, I'd held true to the conviction that my favorite film was *Speed*. (I have to admit that this honor has since been bestowed upon *The Hours* and *Children of Men*, most likely a sign of my late-in-life maturity.) Part of *Speed* being my number one for several years was of course thumbing my nose at my father. Part of it was that I loved the story and found that the concept of a bus that would blow up if its "speed" went under 50 miles per hour created an aura of suspense in the viewer incomparable at the time. The film world has since surpassed that film in suspense quality: *Transformers*, *The Dark Knight*, the *Bourne* films, and so forth. However, *Speed* will always hold a special place in my filmic heart.

As we all do, I grew up. I got over my intense rebelliousness. It wasn't due to a mellowing or maturing, though, as much as to the fact that I started teaching film. Actually,

I started teaching film adaptation. I began to see certain films over and over again, and although repetition is not something I take kindly to, I grew to know these films and appreciate them in a way with which I had formally been unfamiliar. And, although I began to find film adaptation problematic in that it didn't seem to have adequate critical methodologies for teaching analysis of it to students, especially introductory students, film itself began to garner my interest. Learning how film works has been fascinating, eye-opening, and necessary of course to my work with film adaptations. It's important to begin with the basics, and the place to start is when and how film came to be, and how it continued to be. It's good to know film's history, but I will keep it brief and rather simplistic.

Film history at its earliest beginnings, near the end of the nineteenth century, is focused on four major areas. Film history begins with the technological development of the equipment that allows film to be made. It then moves into filmmakers becoming more adept at using this equipment. Once filmmaking begins to develop and grow, it also begins to become an industry with concerns about how to produce film, distribute it, and present it. As the industry expands, the response and receptivity of film's audience changes, growing more sophisticated as film simultaneously becomes more complex, often in its attempt to meet the demands of its audience, and also to challenge its audience (Desmond and Hawkes 2006, 7).

The timeline below follows the history of film, and it can be seen how these four areas overlap at the beginning, and continue to overlap as film as a medium matures with time. The following information is taken from Tim Dirks's website, www.filmsite. org. He created this website in 1996 to address the dearth of information about classic American films on the web at that time. His website is educationally oriented, and has expanded beyond his expectations, he writes. It has tens of thousands of viewers daily and is linked to film studies courses for high school, undergraduate, and graduate students (www.rottentomatoes.com). Thus Dirks has compiled a comprehensive website, and it includes the major milestones in film history. The following information is taken from the section of his website labeled "Timeline of Influential Milestones and Important Turning Points in Film History." For more in-depth information and a more thorough treatment of the history of film, consult Dirks's website.

The History of Film

Pre-1900s

- 300s BC — Aristotle observes a light after-effect: a persistent image after gazing at the sun then looking away.
- 65 BC — Titus Lucretius Carus describes the *persistence of vision* as "the optical effect of continuous motion produced when a series of sequential images were displayed, with each image lasting only momentarily" (Dirks 2010).
- 1820s — Peter Mark Roget rediscovers the *persistence of vision* principle.
- 1882 — Etienne Jules Marey develops a chronophotographic camera, shaped like a gun and referred to as a "shotgun" camera; it could take twelve successive pictures or images per second.

- 1886 — William Friese-Greene develops one of the earliest motion-picture cameras and projectors, a Biophantascope, for which he receives a patent (1890), which can take up to ten photographs per second, using perforated celluloid film — he became the first man to witness moving pictures on a screen.
- 1888 — George Eastman introduces the lightweight, inexpensive Kodak camera, using paper photographic film wound on rollers.
- 1890 — William K. L. Dickson, commissioned by Thomas Edison, builds the first modern motion-picture camera and names it the Kinetograph. The first motion picture ever produced on photographic film in the United States is filmed, *Monkeyshines No. 1*.
- 1891 — Edison and Dickson invent the Kinetoscope, a single-viewer peep-show device in which film was passed over a light.
- 1893 — Edison builds the world's first motion-picture studio in New Jersey, a Kinetograph production center called the Black Maria.
- 1894 — The first hand-tinted films are publicly released featuring the dancing of vaudeville-music hall performer, Annabelle Whitford Moore. Her routines are filmed at Edison's studio in New Jersey. Male audiences are enthralled watching these depictions of a clothed female dancer on a Kinetoscope — an early peep-show device for projecting short films.
- 14 April 1894 — The Holland Brothers' Kinetoscope Parlor opens for business in New York City. The mostly male audience is entertained by a single-loop reel depicting clothed female dancers, sparring boxers, and body builders, animal acts, and everyday scenes.
- 20 May 1895 — Premier of a four-minute black-and-white silent film of a boxing match filmed a few weeks before, making it the first motion picture to be screened before a paying audience.
- 28 December 1895 — The Cinematographe is patented, invented by two brothers in France, Auguste and Louis Lumiere. "It was combination hand-held movie camera and projector, capable of showing an image that could be viewed by a large audience. They held their first public screening . . . often considered 'the birth of film' or 'the First Cinema' — when they projected a motion picture onto a screen for the first time . . ." (Dirks 2010) The ten short films were depictions of everyday life, and the audience was not a sophisticated one by any means.
- 1895 — *The Execution of Mary Queen of Scots* uses the first special effect (in-camera).
- 23 April 1896 — The Edison Company purchases the Vitascope, the first commercially successful celluloid motion-picture projector in the United States.
- 1896 — Alice Guy-Blaché, considered now to be the world's first female director, contributes to the development of narrative filmmaking with her first film, the one-minute fictional film *La Fee aux Choux* (*The Cabbage Fairy*). "Some historians consider it to be the first ever narrative fiction film" (Dirks 2010).
- 1899 — French magician Georges Melies becomes the film industry's first filmmaker to use artificially arranged scenes to construct and tell a narrative story. The first known Shakespearean film, an adaptation of the play, is made in the UK, *King John*.

The 1900s

- 1902 — The first movie house for showing motion pictures is built in Los Angeles, and is a precursor to the nickelodeons that opened in 1905.
- 1903 — Hollywood is officially incorporated as a municipality.
- 1904 — Narrative film begins to become the dominant form.
- 1905 — Harry and John Davis open their first movie theater, calling it a nickelodeon. Its opening feature is *The Great Train Robbery*. The cost of admission is a nickel, hence its name.
- 1906 — J. Stuart Blackton makes the earliest surviving example of an animated film.
- 1907 — The first filmmakers arrive in LA. They realize LA is an area good for filming due to its clement weather and variety of natural scenery. (Previously, movies had been filmed in NYC and Fort Lee, New Jersey.)
- 1908 — Nine leading film producers set up the Motion Pictures Patents Company (MPPC) in an attempt to monopolize production in the rapidly expanding film industry. The first horror film premiers in Chicago, William Selig's sixteen-minute *Dr. Jekyll and Mr. Hyde*.
- 1909 — The *New York Times* publishes its first movie review. The first independent film is released, not affiliated with MPPC. An American court rules that unauthorized films infringe on copyrights, and as a result, film companies begin buying rights to books and plays.

The 1910s

- 1910 — Film companies begin to move to Hollywood, and the first film made in Hollywood is released. Hollywood purchases rights to adapt a novel for the first time. They buy Helen Hunt Jackson's *Ramona* from Little, Brown, and Company for a D. W. Griffith film. The first Frankenstein film in the United States is made, a sixteen-minute (one-reel) version made by the Edison Motion Picture Studios: "The monster appeared misshapen and pathetic rather than horrifying in this first film adaptation of Mary Shelley's novel. In this early version, the Monster was created in a cauldron of chemicals" (Dirks 2010). Vaudeville press agent William Foster launches his Foster Photoplay Company, the first African-American film production company. Max Factor creates the first makeup for use in film. The MPCC tries to monopolize film distribution and absorb independent distributors by setting up the General Film Company. Independent William Fox responds by making his own films.
- 1911 — Pennsylvania becomes the first state to pass a film censorship law. The Nestor Company builds the first full-time studio in Hollywood, now a district of LA.
- 1912 — Fifteen film companies are now operating in Hollywood.
- 1912 — William Fox establishes The Fox Film Foundation, which soon becomes one of Hollywood's leading studios.
- 1912–1913 — Motion pictures move out of nickelodeons and into real theaters. The first movie palaces begin to appear in 1913. "Motion picture acting gained respect

and was no longer looked upon as degrading, due in part to greater attendance from the American middle class" (Dirks 2010).

- 1913 — American director D. W. Griffith, director of hundreds of short films, is credited with defining the art of motion pictures. His techniques are still used today. The first animated cartoon is made in the United States.
- 1914 — World War I interrupts European motion-picture production and eventually it comes to a temporary halt, never to regain its dominance in the marketplace. Lois Weber becomes the first woman to direct a feature film in the US. Charlie Chaplin's first film, *Making a Living*, is released. Paramount Pictures is founded.
- 1915 — D. W. Griffith's three-hour Civil War epic, *The Birth of a Nation*, premiers with a ticket price of $2, previously unheard of. It is based on the novel *The Clansman*, by Thomas Dixon. This film introduces the historical epic and period piece, and defines the language of film. Producer/director Thomas H. Ince introduces a factory system to mass-produce films. The Supreme Court rules that states may censor films, encouraging scrutiny of movies during future decades. The Technicolor Motion Picture Corporation is founded in Boston, and pioneers the development of color film processes known as Technicolor.
- 1916 — The first film to feature an African-American actor is the short comedy film *A Natural Born Gambler*.
- 1917 — The first African-American studio, the Lincoln Motion Picture Company, is founded.
- 1918 — The four Warner brothers — Jack, Albert, Harry, and Samuel, open their first West Coast studio. The US Supreme Court orders the MPPC, known as the "Edison Trust," to disband.
- 1919 — The German film *Different From the Others*, by director Richard Oswald, is reportedly the first representation of male homosexuality in a feature-length film.
- 1921 — D. W. Griffith's film *Dream Street*, with experimental sound, is considered to be the first feature film to use sound.
- 1922 — Russion filmmaker Lev Kuleshov experiments with montage, a new editing technique pioneered by Russian filmmakers. Hollywood censors itself by creating the Motion Picture Producers and Distributors of America (MPPDA). The first Walt Disney cartoon is *Little Red Riding Hood*.
- 1923 — The Hollywood sign is built for $21,000.
- 1924 — Erich von Stroheim directs the film *Greed*, a ten-hour epic based on the novel *McTeague*, by Frank Norris. The movie is edited down to two hours before release, and exemplifies one of the first directorial versus studio conflicts.
- 1926 — Warner Brothers debuts *Don Juan*, the first Vitaphone film and first publically shown "talkie" with synchronized sound effects and music, but no dialogue.
- 1927 — Fox releases *They're Coming to Get Me*, a five-minute black and white short film, the first "talkie" using the Movietone system.
- 1927 — The effective end of the silent era of films comes when Warner Brothers produces and debuts *The Jazz Singer*, the first widely screened feature-length talkie with dialogue. Fox's Movietone newsreel, the first sound news film, is produced. The Academy of Motion Picture Arts and Sciences (AMPAS) is founded. The first awards ceremony is held in 1929 to honor films made in 1927 and 1928.

- 15 May 1928 — The first Mickey Mouse film, *Plane Crazy*, debuts. Walt Disney also introduces the first popular animated cartoons with synchronized sound.
- 1928 — Warner Brothers releases the gangster melodrama, *The Lights of New York*, as the first 100 percent all-talking feature film. Paramount becomes the first studio to announce it will only produce "talkies."
- 1929 — The first Academy Awards ceremony is held, with Paramount's *Wings* winning Best Picture, the only silent film to win an Oscar for Best Picture. Hollywood releases its first original musical, and the first full-length talkie to be filmed outdoors is released as well. Walt Disney Productions is formed. Alfred Hitchcock's first sound film is released with his earliest cameo appearances.
- By the end of this decade, the careers of many silent film stars were destroyed by their inability to change over to sound. Either their voices were unsuitable and or didn't fit their silent film image. Other actors did adapt well to sound, however.

The 1930s

The 1930s and the 1940s "are referred to as 'The Golden Age of Hollywood' by film critics and historians, and considered the apex of film history . . . The 'Golden Age' came to a close with the breakup of the studios and declining attendance from challenges brought by shopping centers and television" (Dirks 2010).

- 1930 — Public pressure mounts, and further censorship guidelines are applied to films — what is acceptable and what is unacceptable. Concerns about premarital sex, alcoholism, immoral and criminal activity, among other such subjects, lead to the establishment and adoption of the Motion Picture Production Code. As head of the MPPDA, William Hays establishes this new code of decency, and this code becomes known as the Production Code, or Hays Code.
- 1930 — The movie industry begins to dub in dialogue to export to foreign markets.
- 1931 — The first of Universal's series of classic horror films are released: *Dracula* with Bela Lugosi and *Frankenstein* with Boris Karloff. African-American filmmaker Oscar Micheaux's *The Exile* is released, the first feature-length sound film from a black director. *M*, by a German director, is released, being the first talkie to effectively use sound, and the first serious psychological crime film about a serial killer.
- 1932 — Victor Halperin's independent, low-budget *White Zombie* is the first zombie film, starring Bela Lugosi.
- 1933 — *King Kong* is released, with stop-motion special effects animation from Willis O'Brien, ending with the image of King Kong on top of the Empire State Building. It's one of the first films to have an animated central character and to be advertised on the radio. The Payne Fund study, *Our Movie-Made Children*, argues that films shape children's behavior. The Screen Writers Guild is established. The first drive-in movie theater opens in Pennsauken, New Jersey. *Deluge* is the first "end of the world" disaster/science fiction film in the sound era, featuring revolutionary sound effects.

- 1934 — An amendment to the Production Code establishes the Production Code Administration (PCA), requiring all films to acquire a certificate of approval before release or be charged with a hefty fine.
- 1935 — Century Pictures and Fox Film merge to form 20th Century Fox.
- 1938 — A group of movie stars organize the Motion Picture Democratic Committee, to support a political party. This is a first. African-American leaders publicly call on the Hays Office to make roles other than doormen, maids, and porters available to blacks. The first prototype of Bugs Bunny appears. The California Child Actor's Bill is passed to protect the earnings of child actors.
- 1939 — "This year has been called the 'greatest year in film history' by film buffs, movie historians, and critics, chiefly due to the inordinate number of classic films. Some of the greatest films ever made were released in 1939, including *Gone With the Wind*, *The Hunchback of Notre Dame*, *Mr. Smith Goes to Washington*, *Ninotchka*, *Stagecoach*, *The Wizard of Oz*, and *Wuthering Heights . . .*" (Dirks 2010).
- 1939 — Television is formally introduced at the New York World's Fair in Queens. The Radio Corporation of America (RCA) displays its first TV sets for sale to the American public.

The 1940s

- 1940 — The first agents begin to assemble creative talent and stories in exchange for a percentage of the film's profits.
- 1941 — Orson Welles, at 24 years old, directs and acts in *Citizen Kane*, a movie about a powerful newspaper publisher named Charles Foster Kane, modeled after William Randolph Hearst. It's been the most highly regarded film in cinematic history. A Senate subcommittee launches an investigation into whether Hollywood is producing films designed to involve the United States in World War II. It dissolves shortly after the attack on Pearl Harbor in 1941. The first film noir is released, John Huston's debut film, *The Maltese Falcon*. The Society of Independent Motion Picture Producers is founded by a group of film people, from actors to producers to directors. The Society aims to protect the rights of independent producers in an industry controlled by studios.
- 1942 — Best Picture-winning *Casablanca*, based on the play "Everybody Comes to Rick's," premiers in New York.
- 1942–1943 — "The war years had a distinct influence on Hollywood. The Office of War Information (OWI) stated that filmmakers should consider seven questions before producing a movie, including this one: 'Will this picture help to win the war?'" (Dirks 2010).
- 1942 — Lena Horne signs a long-term contract with a major studio (MGM), a first for an African-American woman, as a specialty performer. This means she is initially cast in parts and subplots that can be edited out for showings in Southern theaters.
- 1943 — Columbia Pictures releases its first Technicolor film, a western. Influential Russian filmmaker Sergei Eisenstein publishes *The Film Sense*, a film theory book that takes a critical look at film and its impact.

- 1944 — The first Golden Globe awards ceremony takes place at 20th Century Fox Studios. Billy Wilder's *Double Indemnity* is adapted from a James M. Cain novel, and represents the peak of film noir. The first TV ad for a film is broadcast by Paramount at one of its TV stations.
- 1945 — When the war ends, the federal government ends restrictions on the allocation of raw film stock, midnight curfews, and bans on outdoor lighting displays, as well as censorship of export/import of films.
- 1945 — "The House Un-American Activities Committee (HUAC), an organization created in 1938 with the goal of domestically stopping subversive activities, un-Americanism and communism, was made into a permanent standing committee under Congressman John Rankin (of Mississippi). By 1947, the Hollywood motion picture industry became one of its main targets when the committee initiated an investigation of Communist influence there" (Dirks 2010).
- 1946 — The Cannes Film Festival debuts in France.
- 1947 — "In Washington, D. C., the HUAC . . . subpoenaed 41 witnesses, its first wave of witnesses in an investigation of alleged communist influence in the Hollywood move industry. Witnesses included the 'unfriendly' 'Hollywood 19' (13 of the 19 were writers). In 1948, the 'Hollywood 10' . . . were charged with contempt of Congress and jailed for refusing to cooperate with its inquiries and answer the question, 'Are you now or have you ever been a member of the Communist Party?' 84 of 204 supporters of the Hollywood 19 or 10 who signed an amici curiae Supreme Court brief were blacklisted. Many promising and established careers were destroyed by anti-Communist blacklisting — reflected in the growth of sci-fi films showing paranoia of aliens and anything foreign in the 50s decade" (Dirks 2010).
- 1948 — The Supreme Court rules that the major movie studios are guilty and had to end their monopolization of the industry. This marks the beginning of the end of the studio system.

The 1950s

- Early 1950s — Film theater attendance declines due to the rise of television.
- 1951 — Legendary film critic and theorist Andre Bazin establishes the *Cahiers du Cinéma* ("cinema notebooks"), considered the most influential film magazine in film history. HUAC opens a second round of hearings in Hollywood to investigate communism in the film industry, leading to the blacklisting of 212 individuals actively working in Hollywood at this time. Marking the decline of the previous studio system, the Best Picture Oscar is given to the film's producers rather than to the studio that released the film.
- 1952 — To avoid losing the battle with television, Hollywood comes out with 3D films.
- 1953 — The Academy Awards are televised for the first time. Actress Ida Lupino, one of the few female directors of her time, directs the thrilling, noirish film, *The Hitch-Hiker*. The film *From Here to Eternity* is released, based on the 859-page novel by James Jones.
- 1954 — Paramount Studio releases its first VistaVision widescreen production.

Dorothy Dandrige is nominated for an Academy Award for Best Actress, the first African-American ever nominated. The American Releasing Company is founded and begins to produce films marketed towards teenagers.

- 1954, 1956 — Two film adaptations of author George Orwell's cautionary novels are altered. The message in both films is softened and modified, revealed in the 1990s by the CIA, the reasoning being to make the tone of each film more anti-communist.
- 1955 — Disneyland opens its first theme park in Anaheim, California, at a cost of $17 million.
- 1956 — The film industry forbids racial epithets in films but begins to allow references to abortion, drugs, kidnapping, and prostitution. *The Wizard of Oz* (1939) is televised on CBS TV, an event that becomes an annual holiday event. With Hollywood studios struggling financially, Warner Brothers agrees to sell film rights to 800 feature films and 1800 shorts to the Lansing Foundation.
- 1958 — The number of drive-in theaters peaks at about 5,000.

The 1960s

- 1960 — Alfred Hitchcock terrifies audiences with his psychological horror-thriller, *Psycho*. Talented scriptwriter Dalton Trumbo, one of the Hollywood Ten, receives full credit for writing the screenplays for Preminger's *Exodus* and Kubrick's *Spartacus*, becoming the first blacklisted writer to receive screen credit. Smell-O-Vision is developed, piping odors and scents to each seat in a theater auditorium. *Scent of Mystery* is the only film made in Smell-O-Vision.
- 1961 — The 1957 Broadway hit *West Side Story* is adapted to film.
- 1962 — The first James Bond film, *Dr. No*, is released, based on the novels of Ian Fleming.
- 1962 — "The controversial production of Lolita, the first of Kubrick's films produced independently in England, was marked by a long casting search for the proper 'Lolita', the appointment of Vladimir Nabokov to write the screenplay for his own lengthy novel, Kubrick's rewriting (with co-producer James B. Harris) of Nabokov's unacceptable versions of the script, and the threat of censorship and denial of a Seal of Approval from the film industry's production code" (Dirks 2010).
- 1963 — Sidney Poitier wins the Best Actor Academy Award, becoming the first African-American to win this award, and the only instance in the twentieth century.
- 1964 — Mockumentary *A Hard Day's Night*, the first Beatles film, premieres.
- 1965 — Director John Lamb's nudist film, *The Raw Ones*, is the first to show genitalia, now permitted after a 1963 legal decision. "This was an essential linkpin between the non-genital 'nudie-cutie' films of the late 50s, and the hard-core porn of the 70s" (Dirks 2010).
- 1966 — Sweeping revisions are made in the Hays Code with reference to standards of decency, suggesting restraint rather than forbidding. It permits films to be labeled "recommended for mature audiences."
- 1967 — New Line Cinema is formed.

- 1968 — A new voluntary ratings system is developed and put into effect by the MPAA: G for general audiences, M for mature audiences, R for no one under 16 admitted without an adult guardian, and X for no one under 17 admitted. Stanley Kubrick's *2001: A Space Odyssey* reinvents the science fiction genre.
- 1969 — Sony introduces the videocassette recorder (VCR) for home use. A new wave of independent filmmaking in Hollywood (called "The New Hollywood") begins with Dennis Hopper's anti-establishment release of the low-budget *Easy Rider*. Its success shook up the major Hollywood studios.

The 1970s

- Early 1970s — The New Hollywood movement of unconventional auteur directors brings in innovative thinking on film based on their new ideas and personal visions.
- 1970 — Disaster films become popular, beginning with *Airport*. *The Poseidon Adventure* spearheads the trend in 1972.
- 1971 — The blaxploitation film genre, with anti-Hollywood films aimed at a primarily African-American audience, is born with Melvin Van Peebles's *Sweet Sweetback's Baadasssss Song!* — the first commercially successful black-themed film. Kubrick's *A Clockwork Orange* and Sam Peckinpah's *Straw Dogs* both raise controversy over violence in films.
- 1972 — HBO transmitted its first cable television programming. Francis Ford Coppola's *The Godfather* is released.
- 1973 — To maximize profits, the industry decides to release films on Fridays. Also, George Lucas accepts a lesser fee for directing *Star Wars* to have more rights of the merchandising for the film. It ends up to be a wise and lucrative decision.
- 1974 — The slasher film *The Texas Chainsaw Massacre* is released. *Earthquake* is released in Sensurround, which uses large speakers to create synchronized vibrations in theaters.
- 1975 — Steven Spielberg's *Jaws* becomes the first modern "blockbuster" film, topping the $100 million record in box office business in North America.
- 1976 — The Steadicam is used for the first time in *Rocky* and then put to full use in *The Shining*. *A Star Is Born* is released with a Dolby Stereo soundtrack.
- 1977 — *Star Wars* is nominated for ten Academy Awards, *Saturday Night Fever* starts a disco craze, *Close Encounters of the Third Kind* represents aliens as kind, and Woody Allen's *Annie Hall* creates a fashion craze.
- 1977 — "Respected 43-year-old Polish director Roman Polanski had sex with a 13-year-old girl . . . following champagne . . . in actor Jack Nicholson's hot tub. Known for directing *Rosemary's Baby* (1968) (his debut Hollywood film) and the highly acclaimed *Chinatown* (1974) which revitalized the film noir genre, and for being the widower of the brutally murdered Manson victim and 26-year-old pregnant wife Sharon Tate in August, 1969. Polanski pleaded guilty to a single count of unlawful sexual intercourse with the minor but fled to France in 1978 before his sentencing. In exile, he went on to direct *Tess* (1980), *Frantic* (1988) . . . the erotic

thriller *Bitter Moon* (1992), and *The Pianist* (2002), which was nominated for Best Picture and won three Oscars . . ." (Dirks 2010).

- 1978 — *Grease* is released to considerable success, Orion Pictures is formed out of a disagreement between two other production companies, Vietnam films begin to appear, the *Halloween* series of horror films begins, and *Animal House* is released and very successful.
- 1979 — Miramax Films begins as a small production company to experience considerable growth under the leadership of the Weinsteins.
- End of the 1970s — Movie channels, through cable television, begin to appear and compete with each other.

The 1980s

- 1980 — Sherry Lansing becomes the first woman to head a major studio as president of 20th Century Fox. *Heaven's Gate* failure marks the beginning of the end of the American auteur period that developed in the 1970s.
- 1981 — MTV, the music video channel on cable, is launched 24/7. Steven Spielberg releases *Raiders of the Lost Ark*.
- 1982 — Spielberg's *ET: The Extra Terrestrial* is released. Coca Cola Company buys Columbia Pictures in a $750 million transaction.
- 1983 — George Lucas develops his THX sound technology to recreate film sound in film theaters exactly as the filmmaker intended it. The first THX film is *Return of the Jedi*.
- 1984 — The US Supreme Court rules that home videotaping or recording for home use doesn't violate copyright laws. The PG-13 rating is introduced.
- 1985 — Robert Redford establishes the Sundance Film Festival to encourage independent and documentary filmmaking. The first Blockbuster store opens in Dallas, Texas. John Hughes's *Breakfast Club* is hugely successful. Rock Hudson, a closet homosexual, dies of AIDS; he's the first celebrity to announce publicly that he had AIDS.
- 1986 — Pixar Animation Studios, part of Lucasfilm, is purchased by Apple Computer's Steve Jobs. Adaptation *A Room With a View* represents the work of Merchant Ivory film production.
- 1987–1988 — *Fatal Attraction*, *Three Men and a Baby*, *Who Framed Roger Rabbit* (blended animated imagery and live-action human characters), *Rain Man*, *Die Hard* are released during this time. Penny Marshall's *Big* becomes the first film of a female director to gross over $100 million.
- 1988 — This is the year of one of the longest halts in filmmaking due to the WGA (Writers Guild of America) strike.
- 1989 — The Sony Corporation of America purchases Columbia Pictures Entertainment, Inc. and TriStar Pictures from Coca-Cola for $3.4 billion. Warner Communications merges with Time, Inc. to become the largest media company in the world. Spike Lee's *Do the Right Thing* brings him an Academy Award nomination for Best Original Screenplay. Disney's *The Little Mermaid* earns $74 million. *When Harry Met Sally* reestablishes the potential success of romantic comedies.

The 1990s

- 1990 — The rating of X is changed to NC-17 (not for children 17 or under) to differentiate between "adult-oriented" films and hardcore pornographic movies. *Pretty Woman* is an unexpected blockbuster, Johnny Depp breaks out in *Edward Scissorhands*, Kevin Costner's *Dances with Wolves* is an unexpected success, Rob Reiner's *Misery* garners an Academy Award that a horror film hadn't achieved since 1932, and Warren Beatty's *Dick Tracy* is the first 35 mm feature film made with a digital soundtrack.
- 1991 — Disney's *Beauty and the Beast* is the first animated film to be nominated for Best Picture by the Academy of Motion Pictures Arts and Sciences, and Jonathan Demme's horror film, *The Silence of the Lambs*, unexpectedly wins Best Picture and Best Director awards.
- 1993 — Steven Spielberg's *Jurassic Park* is released, with its full-motion, computer generated (CGI) dinosaurs. DTS Digital Sound also makes its theatrical debut in the film. Spielberg's *Schindler's List* wins Best Picture and Best Director in 1994, while Tom Hanks receives Best Actor for Jonathan Demme's *Philadelphia*.
- 1994 — Spielberg, Disney executive Jeffrey Katzenberg, and music industry mogul David Geffen form the film studio DreamWorks SKG. It's the first new major studio in more than fifty years.
- 1994 — Best Picture winner *Forrest Gump* uses revolutionary digital photo tricks to place the film's main character into archival historical footage. Oliver Stone's *Natural Born Killers* is criticized for its graphic violence, even though the aim of the film is to show the media's exploitative preoccupation with violence.
- 1995 — IMAX 3D is introduced.
- 1996 — Kenneth Branagh's *Hamlet* set in nineteenth-century England is the first unabridged cinematic version in film history of Shakespeare's play. It is one of the few films in history to exceed a four-hour running time. *Twister* is the first Hollywood feature film to be released on DVD. *Dragonheart* uses CARIcature software to create the very complex CGI or digital film character of a talking dragon with realistic facial animation and expressions.
- 1997 — James Cameron's *Titanic* is the most expensive film at the time of its release, but also becomes the highest grossing and most successful film of all-time in Hollywood history. It's the first film with a budget of $200 million, and it's the first movie to gross $1 billion. When adjusted for inflation, though, *Cleopatra* (1963) had the highest budget, and *Gone with the Wind* (1939) was the highest grossing.

The 2000s

- The 2000s — The Hollywood studio system is dominated by six global entertainment companies: Time Warner, Viacom, Fox, Sony, NBC Universal, and Disney. These companies farm out the production of their films to dozens of other independents and subsidiaries.
- 2000 — Julia Roberts wins a Best Actress Oscar for her role in *Erin Brockovich*. Christopher Nolan's time-shifting, episodic, neo-noir independent film *Memento* is

a huge success. The Coen Brothers' *O Brother, Where Art Thou?* is entirely color-corrected by digital means.

- 2001 — The first film to be adapted from the popular *Harry Potter* book series is released, as is the first installment of the J. R. R. Tolkien *The Lord of the Rings* book series by director Peter Jackson. DVD sales revenues first exceed VHS sales revenues. *Not Another Teen Movie* is released. African-Americans win in both Best Actor and Best Actress Oscar categories: Denzel Washington for *Training Day*, and Halle Berry in *Monster's Ball*. Paramount releases *Lara Croft: Tomb Raider*, becoming the most successful movie adapted from a video game.
- 2002 — *My Big Fat Greek Wedding*, Polanski's *The Pianist*, Eminem's *8 Mile*, and the first Bourne film, *The Bourne Identity*, adapted from a spy novel, are released this year. Michael Moore's *Bowling for Columbine* wins several awards.
- 2002 — In the second part of the trilogy, *The Lord of the Rings: Two Towers*, CGI imagery is combined with motion capturing to produce the character of Gollum.
- 2003 — Film studio revenues from home entertainment surpass theatrical box office returns. DVD rental sales top those of VHS videotape rental revenues. Sofia Coppola is nominated for Best Director for *Lost in Translation*, becoming the first American woman nominated and only the third woman ever to be nominated. Disney announces that it will no longer produce traditionally hand-drawn animated feature films, and that it will switch to the 3D, full-CGI style of Pixar.
- 2000–2005 — Most of the films of this part of the decade that were moneymakers are comic-book related, serials, animated films, or based on children's fantasy stories.
- 2004 — Michael Moore's *Fahrenheit 9/11* wins awards and is successful at the box office as well. A Harvard School of Public Health Study finds that more sexual and violent scenes are being allowed in films rated G, PG, PG-13, and R than eleven years before when the study had previously been conducted (1994).
- 2005 — The Family Entertainment and Copyright Act of 2005 is introduced to Congress, designed to make technology available to parents that will help shield their children from unwanted violence, sex, and profanity in movies. The year ends with studio executives concerned about the overall slump in the film industry. Independent films that are made outside the Hollywood system face a struggle since all of the successful films came from a major studio this year. Horror films become one of the most lucrative genre franchises; they're cheaply made and bring in a large audience.
- 2006 — The first 9/11-related feature film is released, *United 93*. *Brokeback Mountain* (2005) becomes the most honored movie in cinematic history. It's a story about two gay cowboys, and raises consciousness about gay rights, and sparks controversy as well. Al Gore's *An Inconvenient Truth* achieves success at the box office. The first YouTube video is uploaded in late April of 2005, and the website is launched in November. By mid-2006, millions of videos are viewed daily on the site.
- 2007 — Robert Zemeckis's *Beowulf* uses the advanced motion-capture technology to transform live action into digital animation used by Peter Jackson for the character of Gollum in his *The Lord of the Rings* trilogy.

- 2007–2008 — The Writers Guild of America goes on strike in early November 2007, and the strike lasts for three months.
- 2008 — Female director Catherine Hardwicke's *Twilight* is a box office success, and is adapted from the *Twilight* series of books written by Stephenie Meyer. The majority of the film's audience are female, and half are under 25.
- 2009 — The R-rated comedy, *The Hangover*, is an unexpected success. Hollywood studios realize that they can use the popularity of social networking sites to plug their films. *Paranormal Activity*, a low budget film, is released in select locations, especially college towns. It gets big after the use of a highly effective internet marketing strategy. Zack Snyder's *Watchmen*, adapted from Alan Moore's graphic novel, is released. *The Twilight Saga: New Moon* is also released to huge success. The AMPAS (the Academy) decides to expand the Best Picture nominees to ten films. The last time this happened was in 1943. This decision brings in an increase in viewers of the Award ceremony.
- 2010 — Kathryn Bigelow wins the Best Director Oscar for her film, *The Hurt Locker*. The film also wins Best Picture. Bigelow is the first woman to win the Best Director Award.

Although this information may not seem helpful as you're studying film, it will be. When reading about film and a film is referred to, even if it's not mentioned in this timeline of film history, you can match that film's release date to the timeline to see where it fits into the course of film history. Often, my students are frustrated when they read film essays because they don't recognize the films mentioned. It's not possible to view every film mentioned, but each film can be researched, and one place to start is where and how the film is located in the history of film.

Chapter 16

Film Production

Despite film's humble beginnings, filmmaking has grown into an industry, a multi-billion dollar industry. Making a film is a commercial enterprise and the means of production fall under two systems: the studio system and the independent system. The studio system emerged at the beginning of the twentieth century. Before that, as can be seen in the film history milestones, one person or a few people would complete all the necessary tasks required to make a film. However, the studio system gave rise to parceling out these tasks, making them into specialties or subspecialties. Linda Costanzo Cahir explains in her *Literature Into Film: Theory and Practical Approaches* that these "specialists" were "people hired to do one thing, to learn it well, and to expand upon that knowledge over time and through repeated practice" (2006, 73). So, with the studio system came the roles of "scriptwriters, producers, directors, editors, cameramen, and actors cultivated as experts in their trade" (73).

Once the studio system was firmly in place, the goal became mass production of film. And six major studios emerged: Paramount, MGM, 20th Century Fox, United Artists, Warner Bros., and Columbia Pictures. The studios had their own collection of actors, or as Cahir refers to it, their own "stable of stars" (73). In the studio, the producer was the most crucial component of the system, "shaping the artistic values and moral precepts of a given film" (74). He had control over every aspect that went into making any film within his domain.

Things have changed. Today, these studios are part of larger conglomerates, or holding companies, and they are mostly run by business people who specialize in business practices, that all hinge on making a profit. Cahir notes: "The distinct standards, styles, and artistic bearing that once distinguished one film studio from another are lost in a milieu of an ever-shifting corporate ownership that has little knowledge of and appreciation for filmmaking" (75). A good film for business people is one that makes a lot of money, and "yields power and glamour for its executives" (75).

Independent films are a bit different. They aren't made by a studio, so tend to be allowed more artistic freedom. Yet they have their limitations as well. For one, the producers of indies (as independent films are referred to) must find a way to secure the necessary finances to make the film in question. They also must find a distributor. Distributors take care of the cost of the film print — the final copy or version of the film, the cost of circulating the prints, and the advertising and marketing of the film.

Thus, an indie might end up with a studio as its distributor. So, between the producer's need to acquire the necessary funds, and the need for a distributor that can cover the other expenses, even an indie film can end up giving into quite a few compromises, to appease those providing any of the funding, expecting a return on their investment with the marketability of the film. Making the film more marketable, then, is where the compromises crop up.

Regardless of whether a film is studio-produced or independently produced, film-making is irrefutably collaborative. So much goes into making a film, it's difficult to keep track of all the different forces and individuals bearing down on it. The collaborative process begins with development of the idea, and evaluating its viability as a worthwhile project. Although this step and any step of the filmmaking process has no set way of happening, there are general rules for the way it most often occurs. In the development stages, the film begins with a story treatment. The treatment is "a brief explanation of the salient properties of the idea: the basic story, as well as clear descriptions of setting, characters, and, at times, casting requirements" (Cahir 2006, 80). This is usually the writer's only chance to put forth their idea and see if it takes, so it needs to be effective and convincing. If the story treatment passes muster, the idea will be turned into a screenplay. Cahir explains: "A general rule for a screenwriter to follow is that one page in the script is equal to approximately one minute of screen time" (81). Not all ideas come about in this manner. Sometimes an individual in the business has an idea and has the experience and connections, and even the company, to push it through. However it happens, if the script garners the appropriate attention, it will proceed through a series of rewrites until it is considered acceptable. The final stage of development is a tentative shooting schedule. This is important in budgeting for the film: how long will it take?

Once the development step is complete (and successful), pre-production begins. This step involves all the work necessary prior to the actual filming. A production team is assembled along with the cast and crew. Locations and usage permits are secured. A set design is considered, and rehearsals if time allows. The sound designer puts forth his plan, as do the production designer and cinematographer. Finally, a storyboard is drawn up:

> A storyboard is the blueprint or visual depiction, frequently via simple cartoons, of how the camera is to render each shot: what the essential framing strategies should be, where the camera is to be placed, and how it is to move. (Cahir 2006, 82)

When the storyboard is complete, production can begin.

Production is, of course, the filming of the movie. The shooting schedules are finalized, and daily call sheets let the cast and crew know what will be happening day to day. Sets are constructed; lighting is tested; makeup, hair and costuming are determined; and the camera work is decided. The screening of the dailies are done on an everyday basis to ascertain which scenes need to be redone or what needs to be changed or added. The editors begin their work as well, although this will continue into the next step.

Post-production involves extensive amounts of editing. The editing determines whether additional footage is necessary. Special effects can be added in, as other elements can be as well. The titles and credits are added. All of this leads to the answer print, or "the prototype of the film" (83). The answer print is examined as intensively as it can be, so that any incongruities can be caught and revised.

The marketing of the film remains as the final step in the filmmaking process, and possibly the most important, if the film desires an audience, which all films do. Marketing suggests the film to its potential audience with the aim of making this audience clamor to see it. The film is advertised in a myriad of ways with, most recently, social networking on the internet becoming an ingenious way of reaching an audience, especially a teenage audience. The marketing of the film takes care of publicity, the film prints and whom they're distributed to, arrangements with movie theaters, and the terms of sale and rental for the DVD versions.

Thus it can be seen how collaborative a process filmmaking is. Although I disagree with Cahir's simplistic reduction of a writer's role in creating a literary work, I do agree that filmmaking is irrefutably dependent upon a countless number of individuals performing their tasks as impeccably as possible. Cahir contrasts filmmaking with literary writing, or literature-making:

> Movie-making is a big business. It is expensive, arguably the most expensive art form. In contrast, literature is, arguably, the least expensive art form. All that is needed to create a literary work is a pen and paper. Literature can be, and normally is, produced by a single writer, who needs to secure no approval outside of his or her own. (72)

Although Cahir is right in saying that a writer only needs their own approval to sit with a pen and paper and write something, that is far too simplistic a view, if you are that writer. First of all, it's interesting that she uses the term "single." Because being single, with no family, no kids, and no outside obligations, would be ideal. Yet most writers are not single, nor do they have the luxury of a room of their own and a stipend to spend as much time in it as they need. Most writers, to develop their skill, must acquire the appropriate training, which isn't cheap, or even possible, on some salaries. Once "literature" is written, at least from the writer's perspective, it does require the approval of an agent and finally a publisher to acquire the privilege of being read by a wide audience. So although Cahir makes it seem like being a writer is a piece of cake, it's not. No, it's not nearly as collaborative as making a film is, but it has its own share of obstacles and disappointments. Just as there are many film ideas that could have been great films if they'd been able to be brought to fruition, so are there as many novels and short stories, if not more, that also never made it to fruition due to extenuating circumstances.

But undoubtedly and irrefutably, filmmaking is an extensively collaborative process that as a writer/novelist studying it, I find both exhaustive in its demands and exhausting to think about carrying out. However, some key individuals do make the process move forward more smoothly if they do their job well. And, Cahir compares these individuals to their parallel in literature-making, which is interesting.

The producer of a film pitches the initial idea to the potential financiers. This needs to be done strategically, keeping in mind the market for the film. The "creative executive" to whom the producer pitches the idea assesses the viable worth of the project. Cahir writes:

> The process is not so very different in book publishing, where the writer (often oper-
> ating through an agent) must determine which publisher is most suited to the type
> of book being written. Once the appropriate publisher has been targeted, the writer
> will submit ("pitch") a book proposal (similar to a movie treatment) to an acquisi-
> tions editor (similar to the creative executive), who will assess its merits, perhaps
> suggest changes, and, when and if appropriate, recommend its publication to upper
> management. (84)

So, here, Cahir compares the role of the producer in pitching a film with the role of the agent in pitching a book. This argument does seem to contradict her view of the single writer with pen and paper, and how easy it is to write a novel, but it is an engaging, and accurate, comparison.

If the initial idea is approved, then a screenplay needs to be written. Screenwriting is accomplished in a myriad of ways, from one person working on it, to a composite of writers working on it. Cahir explains the screenplay and how it develops, especially from a literary source:

> Screenplays have their origin in either original material or source material (examples
> include news events, biographies, or literature). A screenplay based on a literary
> source, invariably, cannot include all the details of the literature or the film would be
> prohibitively long. The screenwriter must make decisions regarding what should be
> included and omitted from the source literature. Each inclusion and each deletion is
> an act of interpretation, as the writer, in small and large ways, is determining what
> he or she sees as the essential worth intrinsic to the literary text. (85)

When Cahir is referring to the screenwriter, she moves away from comparing the film-making process to writing, and publishing, literature. (She returns to the comparison when she broaches the role of the director.) If the producer is seen as the agent or the writer of a book pitching their idea to a publisher, the screenwriter could be seen as the writer of the book taking all of the inspiration, the research, the outside influences, interpreting all that is in front of them and around them, reining it in, and writing an outline of the book, how it will be organized, and how it will be realized. The screen-writer organizes the story and puts it down on paper for it to be brought to life as scenes and moments that together will create a text that can be interpreted in many different ways. One interpretation, as an author's interpretation of the world in their novel, leads to many that an audience or readers bring to the text upon experiencing it.

Once the screenplay has been written and approved, the producer hires the director. The director becomes in charge of the filmmaking process, everyone involved with that process, and everything that needs to occur within that process. The director is usually considered the creative force behind a film while those who work under him or her are assistants to the director. This idea of the director exerting his or her control over the making of the film is the argument behind "auteur theory," which will be discussed later. The director is the auteur, French for author, of the film. Cahir states that the auteur

> of a film may be the producer or the actor . . . but, most frequently, it is the director. The director, functioning as author, integrates all the elements into one composite design, much as the author of a book may integrate the ideas or actual work of others into his [or her] overall composition. (86)

So, the director takes the screenplay as does an author with a story, and brings it to life using the elements of film at his or her disposal, drawing on what works and scrapping what doesn't. The author of a novel takes their outline of the story, even if it is merely an organization in their head or scratch notes on index cards, and brings their ideas to life, using the elements of fiction at his or her disposal, drawing on what works and scrapping what doesn't. Both director and author decide whether the story will be plot-driven or character-driven, for example. Both decide whether they will load it up with description and a lot of background information or keep it sparing and minimalist. The similarities between director and author, and filmmaking and literature-making, are more than we think.

The difference between the director of a film and the author of a book always returns to film's highly collaborative nature. The director must rely on those working with the making of the film to help her bring out what her goals are for the film. The writer primarily relies on herself. The director can't make a film without two key people, and those who work under each of these people. The cinematographer, or director of photography (DP), is in charge of everything to do with the camera work. Since the DP is "responsible for achieving the look of the film that the director wants, the DP's choice of lighting, lenses, film stock, filters, colors, camera settings, motion, angles, and even processing" (91) needs to produce this desired effect.

The director of photography needs to combine efforts with the production designer, or the art director, who is responsible for creating the look on the set that the director wants. This includes the designing and building of the sets, providing the necessary props, costuming, and anything else that helps to create the visual effects that the director has communicated and is expecting. The final stage of filmmaking is coordinating the soundtrack with the visual aspects of the film, and this process is dependent on the type of film and again, the effects the director is anticipating. Whereas an author of a book gets to decide where her book is going, and how she will bring out the different aspects she needs to in order to achieve the desired effect she's going for, a director must rely on various assistants to achieve her desired effects. As burdensome as this might seem for a director, it also allows for less to be riding on the director's shoulders. A writer sits alone, working out the details of her project, perhaps turning to a few colleagues for feedback, but the process is almost entirely riding on her shoulders alone. There are advantages and disadvantages to each situation, at least from my perspective as a writer.

Chapter 17

The Elements of Film

To study film in any capacity, and here it is in conjunction with film adaptation of literature, one must have a basic understanding of how film works, and the elements that can or do make up a film. The elements of film can be broken down into four divisions: mise-en-scène, cinematography or camera-work, editing, and sound. It's not possible to learn all that goes into making a film and the minutiae and vagaries of the process and product, especially in one sitting or even during one semester, but an understanding of the basics is manageable, and necessary to be able to look at film from an analytical perspective beyond personal preference and a purely entertainment perspective.

Mise-en-scène

Mise-en-scène is a term that comes from the theater referring to all that appears on stage. In film, it's most often used to represent all that appears in one frame of a film, or in one scene. In other words, it refers to all the components placed in front of the camera, and includes sets, lighting, costuming, makeup, props, placement of objects, and people, and the actors' gestures and movements.

Sets can be those on location, or those artificially constructed, but they encompass the physical space that the camera shows and in which the actors move. Sets on location are those that are found in the world and not constructed in a studio. Studying and exploring the set represented in a film can help detect any special significance the setting has for the film, especially how the props are used in relation to the background, and the specific arrangement of the props and characters.

Lighting in a film helps to establish the mood and focuses attention on the details of the film. The cinematographer decides on artificial or natural light, the direction it should take, and its intensity. The system of three-point lighting is most often used and describes three sources of light: a key light, a fill light, and a backlight. This allows for balance in any given shot. The key light provides the primary light source. The fill light fills in the shadows thrown by the key light. The backlight comes from behind the subject, separating the subject from the background. Some basic lighting effects that are used in films, operating under the three-point system, include high-key lighting, which means the scene is brightly lit, minimizing shadows. A scene with low-key lighting is dimly lit and there is a lot of shadow. High-key lighting creates a brighter and more joyful mood, while low-key lighting creates a harsher and more somber mood. Obviously, there are many others. It's important to identify the mood that is being created by the lighting, not only through the entire film, but also from scene to scene.

Costuming involves the clothes that the characters wear, varying from realistic dress to extravagant costumes. Costuming is important in that it creates the time period in which the scene is occurring, and provides insight into the characters. Hair styling must coordinate with the costuming. And, makeup, although not always noticeable, is recognized as an art by the film world, since it receives an Academy Award and has since 1965. Cosmetics can enhance or change an actor's natural appearance that works with the role they're playing in the film. Makeup becomes crucial especially in science fiction, fantasy, and horror films.

Props are considered any objects or items used on a set or in a scene. The props used and their arrangement can add realism or authenticity to the scene. However, it can also create the effect of irony, something out of place, or not what the viewer would expect. For example, in the futuristic film, *Children of Men*, viewers are expecting, when they read that the story is taking place in 2027, that it will be a futuristic setting of progress. Yet the first scene follows the main character out of a crowded coffee shop onto a dirty street littered with garbage, a hovering fog of air pollution, and vehicles that in their design show a regression rather than a progression, all of this effected quite purposefully.

Finally, in a mise-en-scène analysis, one would study the actors and their gestures and movements, or their figure behavior. The acting style, or how an actor plays a part, differs obviously from one film to the next, and from one decade to the next. Actors are cast based on all different kinds of reasoning, and based on various needs depending on the film and its desired effect. To study figure behavior is to study the movements and actions of the actors or other figures (animals, monsters, animated things, robots, aliens) in a scene or given shot of a film. This allows for a deeper look into what the film is attempting to do and how it does it.

Cinematography or Camera Work

The shot is the basic unit of film. It's the single image that is seen on the screen before the film cuts to the next image. But unlike a photograph, a single shot includes a lot of variety and movement. It's a single, continuous view of the scene that documents uninterrupted action. And, the frame of the movie image forms its border and contains all that is occurring in the scene, or its mise-en-scène.

The three most basic shots are as follows: the long shot, the medium shot, and the close-up. The long shot (LS) shows the full human figure of a character or characters, and often the figures are dwarfed by the background. An extreme long shot (ELS) is one in which the human figure can barely be distinguished. The medium shot (MS) is one in which we see the human figure from the waist up. The medium long shot (MLS) frames the human from the knees up, and the medium close-up (MCU) allows the viewer to move in closer and see the human from the chest up. The close-up (CU) focuses in on a specific part of the human, most often the face. The extreme close-up (ECU) focuses in on a portion of the face. All of these different types of shots describe the distance away from the human body, using the human body as the focal point of reference. One can study in a certain frame the distance from the subject that is maintained and consider why and how this distance is in fact maintained. What does it add to the scene? Why has it been filmed this way?

The camera angle is the camera's position as it's focusing in on the subject. The camera might look down on the subject, from a high angle position. Or it might look at the subject straight-on or at eye level. The low angle is when the camera is looking up at the subject. Camera angles add meaning to the subject being filmed. One can study the angle at which the camera frame represents the action and the significance of that angle. Why is it filmed in this way? The height of the frame can be a factor in determining an aspect of the scene, in that the placement of the camera determines how the viewer sees the subject or subjects in the scene. Why has it been done the way it has?

Camera movement refers to any position the camera takes when viewing the subject that changes the perspective on its subject. A tilt shot involves the camera moving up and down, so that the frame of the scene moves up and down. It may be following the point of view of the character, or giving the viewer a perspective of what is around the character, both high and low. A pan shot moves left or right, scanning the scene horizontally while staying in the same place. A tracking shot moves forward, backward, or laterally, while moving toward, away, with, or around the subject. That is, the camera isn't stationary but follows or intrudes on the action with the movement of its own position. A crane shot is a high, overhead shot that looks down on the action and implicates a dramatic change in perspective. The handheld shot is one in which the camera is carried by the camera operator.

Film speed is another consideration to take note of when studying a shot. The rate at which the film is shot is most apparent in instances of slow or fast motion. Slow motion can be used to indicate a dream while fast motion can be used to enhance the comical nature of a scene. The tone of a shot is important to note as well. Tone refers to the range and texture of colors in a film image. One can study why certain colors or tones might be used and how they relate to the themes of the film.

Editing

Editing is the linking together of one shot to the next, and usually follows a logical connection between the two. Very few films contain only one shot, and thus most join many shots together. Editing is also choosing the best camera shots taken and putting them together in a way to build a scene, a sequence, and finally, a completed film.

When considering editing as the joining of shots together, there are several types of edits. The most common is the cut; the first shot ends where the second begins. The shots are spliced together. A dissolve joins two shots together by blending them; the beginning of the second shot is briefly superimposed on the end of the first shot. The fade-in means the beginning of the shot gradually goes from dark to light. Conversely, the fade-out means the end of the shot goes from light to dark. The wipe is when a line moves across an image to gradually clear one shot and introduce another. This tends to show a connection between the scene ending and the one beginning. A jump cut is one in which a continuous shot is suddenly broken in that one shot is abruptly replaced by another that is mismatched, calling attention to the cut and disconcerting the viewer. The iris edit is the new image opening as an expanding circle in the old image (iris-in) or the old image closing as a contracting circle disappearing into the new image (iris-out).

Looking at the film from a less specific and more global perspective, continuity editing is editing the viewer doesn't notice. This editing style is referred to as invisible editing because the filmmaker doesn't want the editing to distract from the story, so avoids cuts and transitions between images. Continuity editing relies on shots called establishing shots. An establishing shot is one that begins a scene or sequence by clearly locating it in a specific place so that the shots that follow are part of that scene or sequence but as more detailed shots. Crosscutting uses alternating shots of at least two sequences of action happening in different places at the same time. The shot/reverse shot is an exchange between two characters that goes back and forth between the two characters as they speak to or look purposefully at the other character. An eyeline match means that the next shot shows the viewer what the character in the previous shot sees. A match on action follows a character's action into a new space, from a different focal point.

Disjunctive editing is continuity editing's opposite in that it emphasizes the cut from one shot to another, making it clear that the scene has changed. The term montage takes disjunctive editing further by calling attention to the discontinuity of shots. The montage technique is the juxtaposition of dissimilar shots, designed to incite the viewer to make conscious connections between the shots.

Sound

The four types of sound that are heard and can be analyzed in films are speech, music, sound effects, and silence. Speech is dialogue, spoken by the actors onscreen. Music refers to the score that establishes patterns throughout a scene, a sequence, or the entire film. Music is also used to evoke emotional reactions in the audience. Sound effects are noises made by people and objects in each scene shown. The absence of sound in a scene is called a dead track and often surprises the audience.

To analyze sound in a particular film, one must listen closely to how sound is being used in the film. There are terms that help in analyzing the use of sound in a film. Ambient sound is background noise or music that surrounds the main action and dialogue. Overlapping dialogue is the mixing and overlapping of the speech of the characters. Voice-off is the speech of a character who is not yet seen on the screen or who was seen on the screen but who is not on the screen at the time their voice can be heard. Voice-over is the voice of a narrator who is not a part of the story and cannot be heard by the other characters. Narrative cueing is the use of a sound or pattern of music that correlates to a moment or motif in the story. When these cues are sudden, they're called stingers.

Issues that can be addressed when analyzing sound in a film include determining the relation of the sound to the image in a specific scene. The sound might be used to link images, or become more important than the image being shown. The musical numbers might have a special relation to the narrative structure. Dialogue might be difficult to discern purposefully. Silence might play a role in a scene or the movie as a whole. The rhythm of the sound might be parallel to the rhythm of the editing. These are all issues that can be addressed when analyzing the sound sequences and patterns in a film, in order to identify the significance of the use of sound in that film.

These are some very basic elements of film. The four headings could be developed in much more detail, but for our purposes here, and as an introduction to film, these will suffice so as not to overwhelm the viewer. Film studies is a course of study in academia, and that's where the idea of film and the endless array of filmmaking techniques are studied in great depth. The next section will briefly introduce film theory and film analysis, in a way to get your feet wet, but not so that you'll feel like you're drowning. I recognize that it's difficult to go from viewing film simply as entertainment to viewing film as texts worthy of and requiring exploration and analysis, but there is a way to balance both, without having to give up one or the other. I think students need to understand this so that they don't feel resistant when learning how to analyze and delve deeper into the meanings and intricacies of film in general, and specific films.

Chapter 18

Film Analysis

Before moving into a discussion of film analysis, it's important to understand the different types of writing and analyses of film that can be carried out. Timothy Corrigan in his *A Short Guide to Writing About Film* explains four different ways of exploring a film: a screening report, a movie review, a theoretical essay, and a critical essay (2010, 8).

Corrigan describes a screening report as "a short piece of writing that acts as a preparation for class discussions and examinations . . . a descriptive assignment that organizes notes on a film . . . [and] should contain about three or four paragraphs (about one to two pages) focused on two to four main points" (9). The assignment might need to be related to the specific topics of the course, or the instructor might provide a list of prompts or questions to address.

The movie review can be read in a newspaper or magazine about a film. Although it is a type of film analysis, its target audience is broad and the writer most often assumes his or her reader has little or no knowledge of the inner workings of film. The function of a movie review is to recommend the film if the reviewer finds it of high quality or discourage viewers from seeing it if it's found to be below par.

The theoretical essay is at the other end of the spectrum, Corrigan explains. It is an essay that assumes its audience knows quite a bit about film, including specific films, film history, and other writings about film. Its audience usually includes advanced students or people who teach film studies, and it aims "to explain some of the larger and more complex structures of the cinema and how we understand them" (11). As an introductory student in film or film adaptation, you might read such essays, but you wouldn't be expected to write such an essay.

The critical essay is the type of essay you would be expected to be able to write. Corrigan states that the "writer of this kind of essay presumes his or her reader has seen or is at least familiar with the film under discussion" and is the type of essay you would write as a student in a film course or film adaptation course. Corrigan explains that the "focus of the essay is far more specific than that of a review because the writer hopes to reveal subtleties or complexities that may have escaped viewers on the first or even the second viewing" (11).

So, let's assume the critical essay is the type of essay you will be expected to write about a film or film adaptation. When analyzing a film, it is crucial to view it more than once. The first time, you should record your initial reaction to the film, even your emotional response. However, viewing it the second time, you should take notes, and apply some of your knowledge of the elements of film to your second viewing. What do you notice? What intricacies of the film bring out what you consider to be its themes or the messages it's conveying?

Corrigan provides questions to ask of the film as you're viewing it. The viewing should be at least the second time you're experiencing the film. He recommends that "an analytical spectator must develop the habit of looking for key moments, patterns, or images within the film" (25). He encourages such a viewer to "note which elements of the movie strike you as unfamiliar or perplexing . . . [and] which elements are repeated to emphasize a point or a perception" (25). Some specific questions he gives for approaching your viewing of a film include (and I've chosen the ones I feel will be most useful):

- What does the title mean in relation to the story?
- Why does the movie start the way it does?
- Why does the film conclude with the image it does?
- How is this movie similar to or different from the Hollywood movies you have seen recently or from those of an older generation?
- Is there a pattern of striking camera movements, perhaps long shots or dissolves or abrupt transitions?
- Which three or four sequences are the most important? (25)

Consider these questions as you approach the film a second or optimally a third time, and take notes that will help you provide answers once you've finished watching the film.

Now you want to move beyond these early observations of the film, and think more deeply into the themes of the film. What is it trying to say? How does it try to say it? Corrigan offers some questions that might be helpful in determining what you feel the theme or themes of the film to be (again I've chosen ones I feel will be most helpful):

- Who are the central characters?
- What do they represent in themselves and in relation to each other? The importance of individuality or society? Human strength or compassion?
- How do their actions create a story with a meaning or constellation of meanings?
- Does the story emphasize the benefits of change or endurance?
- What kind of life or what actions does the film wish you to value or criticize and why? (39)

Some other guidelines that are helpful involve moving beyond the viewing of the film itself to do more research on the making of the film. For example, researching the director of a film, its title, and the film's release date is a good first step. Although film is a collaborative enterprise, sometimes the director of one film has much more of a role in the filmmaking process than the director of another, which makes a difference when studying a film. Sometimes the title of a film is a simple matter, but in other cases, it can be more complex, and telling. The release date is when the film was first shown publicly to a paying audience, which is not necessarily when the film was made, and this could be important, depending on what aspects of the film are being explored and studied.

The script and the source of the film must be identified. Bruce Kawin, in *How Movies Work*, states that this is where a film would be found to be a film adaptation, "an adaptation of a pre-existing work" (1992, 13). It is important to identify who has written the screenplay. Sometimes the director writes the screenplay. For the film of *The Cider House Rules*, the author of the novel from which the film was adapted, John Irving, wrote the screenplay. For the film *Children of Men*, based on P. D. James's novel of the same name, the screenplay is credited to five writers, one of them being Alfonso Cuarón, also consequently the director of the film. However, for *The Hours*, the screenwriter is David Hare, who has no previous relationship with the novel of that name, nor a subsequent relationship with the film. Kawin states: "It is the screenplay that provides the underlying structure for the majority of films, and so it is very important to identify the writer" (14). We have seen in the previous chapters the importance of the screenplay; it's what allows all of those working on the film to bring the story to life, the backbone or initial outline of the process. Thus it's important to know more about the screenwriter(s).

Another aspect of analyzing a film involves a study of who is in front of the camera, and who is behind it, or performing a mise-en-scène analysis. It's important to study the actors and why they were chosen, and how they carry out their roles in the film. It's also essential to identify the cinematographer and his contribution to the film, and also the production designer. And the "reader" of the film must research the producer and studio. "The producer is the one who raises the money to make a picture and who decides how it will be spent" (15). Sometimes the director will also be the producer, which allows him/her more freedom in their spending plans, but often the director "must be prepared to have their more expensive ideas rejected or modified" (15). Kawin in *How Movies Work* points out that "the important issue is not really how much money was available, but how well it was spent. As the person in charge of those decisions, the producer plays a crucial creative role in the filmmaking process" (15). It's also valuable to know the studio that made the picture, as different studios are known for different types of films. Perhaps a studio has decided to try something very different for them; this is worth noting, especially if it succeeded.

It can be helpful in analyzing a film to note its running time. Kawin explains: "Because films are sometimes recut after first release, perhaps to attract a wider audience or to merit a different rating, different versions usually have different running times" (18). That said, the film editor is also important to identify since this is the person who ultimately determines the rhythm of the film, depending on what they choose to cut or keep.

The sound and the music of the film are essential elements of the film, affecting the tone and other aspects of the film. It's particularly important to identify the sound recordist who captures the texture of the environment in a film. The sound editor edits and mixes a soundtrack and this work can be as demanding as a picture track.

Soundtracks have become increasingly crucial to a film, and are often available separately from the film. In fact, a song heard in the film can be "googled" and found on iTunes within moments after viewing the film (or while viewing the film these days). Despite the obvious marketability of the soundtrack, the ability to gain access to the soundtrack allows for study of the soundtrack's influence on the film, and the film's influence on how the choices in music were made. A recent film adaptation, *Crazy Heart*, adapted from the novel of the same name, tells the story of a washed-up country singer. Songs were written for the film, and are available on a soundtrack, with Jeff Bridges and Colin Farrell singing a good amount of the songs. This soundtrack could provide material for an interesting study of the novel, which cannot make the music referred to in it audible, and the film, which is able to bring that music to the viewer. The study might focus on how the novel has been interpreted and how that interpretation has affected the composition of the music heard in the film.

These are some of the background elements of a film to consider, either before or after applying the more specific elements of a film (discussed in the previous chapter) to a closer reading of the film, remembering to use the questions (provided by Corrigan) above. As I've stated, during the second and third viewing is when the film can be examined as to its organization and why it was shot as it was.

Once the film has been examined, a methodology or critical approach can be used to ask certain questions of the film, or text. Critical perspectives applied to film are many and growing. Some examples include auteur criticism, production analysis, semiotic analysis or semiotics, formalism and neo-formalism, realism, impressionism and surrealism, psychoanalysis, poststructuralism and deconstruction, political and Marxist (or ideological) criticism, feminist criticism, gay and lesbian criticism, historical and cultural criticism, reception criticism, and more. Many of these approaches have been explained in the literary analysis section, and can now be applied to a film text rather than a literary text. The tenets of each approach do not change, but how they are used might change in some ways. However, though, some of these critical approaches are specific to film. Several of these approaches, both those more generally applied to texts and those more specific to film, are explored below.

Auteur criticism can be used to analyze a film when much is known about the director and he or she has played a sizable role in producing the film. Kawin states that "auteur criticism posits that a significant film has an author or a guiding creative intelligence. That person, usually the director, becomes the offscreen site or implicit source of coherence" (1992, 25). The auteur movement, or the focus on an individual artist behind a film, grew out of theoretical arguments of art put forth in the 1960s. Auteur theory, according to Richard Dyer, "made the case for taking film seriously by seeking to show that a film could be just as profound, beautiful, or important as any other kind of art, provided . . . it was demonstrably the work of a highly individual artist" (2000, 3). Although film analysis has since extended far beyond this limited approach to a film, it can be quite useful for analyzing certain films, if much is known about the director and his work on a particular film, or the analysis itself is focused on this director and his or her work.

Another approach that can be used to analyze a film is production analysis. "This is a matter of finding out just what happened, both on the set and in the front office, when a particular picture was being planned and made, and then applying that information when examining the finished product" (Kawin 2000, 27). For example, perhaps in analyzing the film from this approach, one discovers that the filmmaker ran out of money or the film was taken out of the director's hands for some reason or another. The question would be asked of the film, then, as to how it reflects these changes that were made, if at all. Such a question might lead to an interesting discussion of the film. Even minor details of how the film was being made can help in forming a fuller understanding of the film. In *The Hours*, Meryl Streep, playing Clarissa Vaughn, is acting an emotionally charged scene with Jeff Daniels, playing Louis Waters, who has returned to New York after many years of being away. Clarissa is visibly shaken by his presence. In one part of the scene, she walks over to the spigot to turn it on, and the spigot explosively spurts out unexpectedly. It is this that leads to her "unraveling." In a short documentary about the making of the film, the director explains that the spigot wasn't supposed to do that, it was an accident, but Streep played off of it and the editors and director chose to keep it in the scene. Such information about a film can bring it to life, and provide a background of how the actors work and how they flesh out the characters they are playing. Streep's experience here reflects the way this particular director, Stephen Daldry, works, which appears to be more relaxed and thoughtful in comparison to some other directors.

This incident with Streep in *The Hours* could also be used in a mise-en-scène analysis, mentioned above, depending on the purpose of the analysis. Mise-en-scène analysis is "the study of the 'look' of a film, the selection and organization of the elements of the image. A movie can be full of meanings that are almost entirely visual" (28). It's important when analyzing a film from this perspective to "pay attention to the layout of the visual field" (28). What is the camera doing while the characters go about their business? How are the actors arranged and where do they move? What does the set look like, what props are visible, the lighting, the shadows, the color scheme? What recurring images or compositions are present and what do they contribute to the overall project of the film?

What can also be analyzed in a film is the story and how it's told, or the lack of a definitive storyline and how that's handled. Kawin states that "narrative structure can be studied in many kinds of films, not only in those that tell stories. To narrate is to tell, to present something to the audience and often to color that presentation with a particular point of view or way of seeing the subject" (28). Point of view is an important aspect of a film to consider. It refers to the position from which something is seen and how that affects the way that something is seen. In film, though, as Timothy Corrigan explains, "we can talk about the point of view that the camera has in relationship to a person or action or even the point of view that a narrative directs at its subject" (2010, 49). Most films rely on an objective point of view, yet many break away from this point of view in interesting ways. In the film *Children of Men*, the director desired a documentary-style effect in a fictional film, and much of the film can be seen as if the camera is following the main character, Theo. In fact, there is not a scene in the film that does not include Theo, so the viewer knows what Theo knows, no more and not much less with regard to the narrative of the story. In the film *Vantage Point*, not a lit-to-film adaptation, the action in the film is played out from the point of view of several different characters successively, until the full narrative of the story has been revealed. Point of view is a significant technique that a filmmaker has to work with, and thus it's a crucial consideration for an analysis of a film. Corrigan recommends that when performing an analysis of a film, one should "observe how and when the camera creates the point of view of a character" (49). Second, one should "notice if the story is told mostly from an objective point of view or from the subjective perspective of one person" (49). Once these identifications have been made, one needs to consider how the point of view affects what the viewer sees, and how it limits and controls what is seen. Also, why might the narrative of the film have been told, or shown, from this particular perspective, or combination of perspectives? These are important distinctions to make in approaching a film.

Genre analysis is another way of studying a film, and this type of analysis "takes for its point of departure what kind of film a film is" (Kawin 2000, 29). For example, a narrative film might be grouped under one of the following genres: the Western, the mystery, the romantic melodrama, the science fiction film, the horror film, the dystopian film, to name merely a few. To identify a film by its genre is to make a statement about the film's narrative project, and allows for a study of what the picture has set out to do, and how it has accomplished that objective. As Kawin points out, though, it is important to watch for departures from the genre that a film seems to have set itself out to be:

> Some pictures follow generic formulas closely and try to live up to them, but it is just as common for a picture to *play* with generic expectations and even to work against them. And there are many films that cannot be neatly pigeonholed into particular genres or that set out to work in terms of several genres at once. (29)

Those films that "play" with the genres they seem to set out to establish themselves as can be illuminating texts to analyze. Often, several critical approaches can be used in combination to discern what the film is trying to relay to the viewer in its departure from a particular genre or its intermixing of genres in one text.

Political criticism, although not a specific approach for viewing and analyzing film, allows for an in-depth look at a film based on the political and ideological arguments it makes. A Marxist critique of a film can be included within this category of critical approaches. Questions that can be asked of a film, then, include what the political ramifications of the relationships between characters might be. What role does the film itself play in creating and/or reinforcing a set of political attitudes? Often, a film will challenge the dominant ideology of society in some way. Kawin states:

> The members of a society tend to accept the dominant ideology of society and to ignore it, so that the filter it imposes on their perception of unsocialized reality becomes familiar, automatic, and finally invisible. A good deal of political criticism is concerned with identifying and analyzing the ideological content of specific films and even of certain aspects of filmmaking practices. (30)

Thus political criticism is most often combined with one or more of the approaches used to illuminate a film's codes or system of communicating meaning, and view them in the light of their political connotations. As Kawin states, and I agree: "Texts have real power in a culture, they also express power and may reinforce power relationships" (31). A film can be one such text, and political criticism allows for a study of how a film exerts its power or expresses and/or reinforces power.

Feminist criticism of film delves further and more specifically into how power is reflected on screen, and examines the gender dynamics inherent within and visible in certain events, situations, and relationships. Kawin poses that a concern of feminist criticism is the way women are portrayed in a film, or the film's "images of women." Feminist criticism encapsulates far more than how women are "displayed" on screen. Historically, yes, "the image of women has been used, among other things, as a spectacle. She compels the gaze" (34). But feminist criticism extends far beyond this limited analysis of film into much greater issues that concern not only the representation of women on screen, but the representation of gender on screen, and the existence of sexism not only in film, but in the subject of a particular film. Feminist criticism can be applied to films that turn violence against women on its head but also to films that almost seem to celebrate or relish violence directed at women. Feminist criticism allows for analysis of films that take on issues of feminism and also of films that demean women, films that generate once again the objectification of women and films that reinforce the subjugation of women to men.

Kawin addresses a crucial concern of feminist criticism that resonates with my own work, and my resistance to seeing my novel, my story about women, made into a film, a concern that is different from the concerns of other writers (except perhaps Michael Cunningham of *The Hours* or anyone who defies the current organization of our society into its nice, neat hierarchal partitions that refuse to acknowledge individuality as if to do so would result in anarchy and chaos):

> . . . it remains well within the realm of possibility, and has given rise to much valuable debate, that the cinema of a patriarchal or male-dominated culture may be determined by a patriarchal structure of discourse (a patriarchal society or, more precisely, the terms in which that society prefers things to be phrased, which determines the terms and the structure of communication and of self-definition within that society, which itself can be seen as a structure of interlocking texts). There may be a "male camera" and an implicit male viewer to whom the spectacle of woman is presented, and the female viewer may be prompted to identify with the implicit power of that gaze. Or the camera may be neutral (making all of this a matter of projection, the viewer's reading-in), or neutral only when a woman is not onscreen, and the female viewer may have any of a variety of responses to the spectacle and to the camera. (34–5)

What Kawin writes here is cause for alarm with regard to my own creative work. Film intensely reflects, perhaps more than other art forms, the patriarchal organization of our culture. And, the fact that we live in a society with a preexistent patriarchal code governing it, even if that code is considered less restrictive to oppressed populations than it's ever been (I'm not sure I agree), provides me with great pause. The purpose of my novel, from its mere beginnings, was to challenge the patriarchal structure of our society, by first acknowledging that not enough has changed in the two hundred years since Mary Wollstonecraft wrote her novel, and by showing how the rigid definitions of roles within our culture predetermine failure of drastic proportions in far too many families. I feel as if literature has thrown wide the doors to accept writings that challenge the preexisting order of gender in our society, but film has not done the same as readily, by any means. Film seems as entrenched in the concept of the old boy network as the country club golf scene. How Kathryn Bigelow made it in this year, to win an Academy Award, or two to be exact, for her film, is surprising to many of us. That we are surprised is a concern. Yet the film was primarily about men. I'm not inferring here that Bigelow chose such a film because she knew it would be accepted. However, films about women's issues, and about women, and that also showcase a female director, haven't fared quite as well, at least not yet. Would Bigelow have won if it had been as equally an effective and poignant film, but about women? I'd like to think so, but my doubt outweighs my desire.

Sexual politics is one area of feminist criticism that dominates in analysis of film from a feminist perspective. Feminist criticism has taken on the politicized nature of sex in films, and not merely the portrayal of sexual activity but more interestingly, "*the* sex of a character or the power-and-role dynamics of encounters between men and women, mothers and daughters, etc." (Kawin 2000, 35). Feminist criticism is multi-faceted and burgeoning as it relates to film study, and it has its work cut out for it. The fact that so much work needs to be done on analyzing film from a feminist perspective, but more invaluably, in seeing films made from a feminist perspective, prompts me to hold back in my own endeavors. I hold my characters — Annie, her daughter Lexi, her friend Lindsay, even her enlightened male friend/love interest Grey — close, and I wonder if I should protect them from the male-dominated culture of film. They mean more to me than a multi-million-dollar enterprise by far.

Kawin raises the following questions in analyzing a film from a feminist perspective, and they are questions that are encouraging:

> In all the films made by men, how has the reality of women's experience been expressed? Is the story told differently when it is told by women, and is there an emerging gynocentric discourse that may find its own expressive terms and cinematic codes? How would a cinema made by and for women proceed, and what might it accomplish? (2000, 36)

Although these questions are important, I do resist the idea of women's films talking to women, which is what Kawin proceeds to suggest. My novel is a story about women, but it is not a story only to be told to women, and I am wary of any further marginalization of women's issues. The "women's issues" I put forth in my novel are as much men's issues as women's issues, and they are of concern to us all, or if not, I emphatically implore they should be. However, the existence of feminist criticism, its insistence on becoming more firmly established, and its growth as an approach to film, does offer me some comfort.

Finally, I want to mention a few critical approaches that can be applied to a film that requires a more in-depth study. Although surrealism and impressionism are important to the study of film, these concepts are key when studying the history of film studies and how these studies developed. The same is true of semiotic analyses of film, which helped to establish film not only as an art but as a text as well, and as a text with its own discernible use of (a) language. One critical approach that is useful to the analysis of a film, and in many ways can be seen as the basis to critical approaches that have been discussed above, is psychoanalytic criticism. Barbara Creed explains in her essay, "Film and Psychoanalysis," that:

> Psychoanalysis and the cinema were born at the end of the nineteenth century. They share a common historical, social, and cultural background shaped by the forces of modernity. Theorists commonly explore how psychoanalysis, with its emphasis on the importance of desire in the life of the individual, has influenced the cinema. (2000, 75)

Many of the aspects of psychoanalytic criticism discussed in the literary analysis section of this book have been applied to film as well. For example, many of Freud's theories have been used in film theory, as well as Lacan's interpretations and extensions of Freud's theories. Christian Metz's *Psychoanalysis and Cinema: The Imaginary Signifier* (1975) was "the first book-length attempt to apply psychoanalytic theory to the cinema" (Creed 2000, 78). Psychoanalytic film theory continues to expand and evolve both inside and outside of the academy today. Many scholars "draw on aspects of psychoanalytical theory to illuminate areas of their own special study" (85). Such areas include cultural theory, and also the newer areas of postcolonial studies and queer theory.

Queer theory comprises studies of sexuality and sexual orientation in texts, and society in general. According to Alexander Doty, "queer theory shares with feminism an interest in non-normative expressions of gender and with lesbian, gay, and bisexual studies a concern with non-straight expressions of sexuality and gender" (2000, 146). Critical approaches that fall under this category of theory can be applied to film. Gay and lesbian criticism allows for an approach to film that examines how gender is delineated in the narrative of a film, or how images and representations of homosexuality are portrayed. How sexual identity is constructed in a film, particularly if it's the focus of the film or a crucial aspect of the film, can provide material for a study of that construction and the thinking behind it, as well as the reception of the audience to it.

Audience reception is another area of criticism that has been developed and is related to its literary predecessor, reader response criticism. The response of an audience to a film can be studied as well as how an audience might be predicted to respond. Expanding upon the latter concept, it can be studied how a film might have been made or changed to appease or appeal to its audience, most often assumed to be a mass audience. Audience reception, though, can also be approached from a more individualistic perspective, much like reader response criticism. This approach might more aptly be termed "viewer response criticism." A viewer of a film brings to the film their own experiences and influences and this shapes their response. However, in a subsequent viewing, the same viewer might have a different response to the film, since their context will have changed since their previous viewing. Such a critique of a film text can be carried out similarly to a reader-response critique of a literary text.

And, cultural and historical critical approaches have been very useful in analyzing film. Cultural criticism can be used to approach a film from a myriad of perspectives. It can approach the film from the perspective of its place in popular culture. However, it can also be applied to the film in ways that examine the racial and ethnic aspects of the film. Historical approaches to a film can also include a variety of perspectives from which to view a film. Analyzing a film from a historical perspective might focus on an examination of the history of the film itself, or the representation of history in the film, or the cultural and historical influences that are reflected in the film, among other approaches and any combination of these approaches.

As a literary person, learning the techniques of film, I do not see film as different from literature as much as similar to it, in the way it's analyzed as a text. The process is similar and begins with a close reading and an understanding of the elements of film that are used to make the film what it is. Then an analysis progresses with an interpretation of why exactly those elements were used the way they were, for what purpose. An argument is made about the whole, and observations about the parts of the whole are used to support what is being conveyed by the whole, as the critic or viewer sees it. A novel has its readers, but also its close readers who become its experienced critics. A film has its viewers, but also its close viewers who become its experienced critics. Also, a critical approach or combination of approaches can be applied to a film much as they can be applied to works of literature.

Film scholars disagree and contest each other's views on the art of film just as literary scholars do the same with respect to literature, and in so doing, they propel film studies forward in multifarious and complex directions. Arguments persist among film experts much as they do among literary experts. It has been argued that the fact that film is not like reality justifies it as an art. Rudolf Arnheim "made the case that because the frame cannot include the whole visual world and is limited by a black rectangle, the border can be used as a structuring principle, like the frame of a painting" (Kawin 2000, 52). Other film theorists argue "that film is justified by its resemblance to the physical world and that its ideal is realism" (52). Siegfried Kracauer and Andre Bazin are two such theorists. However, as Anthony Easthope writes in his essay "Classic Film Theory and Semiotics," of the opposed perspectives of Arnheim and Bazin, there is a common thread to both of their arguments:

> Formalist theory (Arnheim) and realist theory (Bazin) appear to oppose each other. But what is crucial, and what marks off classic film theory, is the assumption they share ... Both positions suppose that cinema, based as it is in the photographic process, must be assessed as in part a mechanical reproduction, whether feeble or convincing. (2000, 50)

This supposition was eventually overthrown in film theory, yet it shows how film theorists have been arguing and the theory evolving as they argue.

Film can be seen, perhaps, as the art of the real. To understand film, according to Kawin, it's necessary to have an understanding of both of the arguments above, since they are the basis of film theory, and since, as Kawin states, both are true. He explains: "Film gives us a picture that is both like and unlike the world. It works, most often, with the materials of audible and visible reality, and it both transforms those materials and arranges them" (2000, 52–3). Film seems to have the unique capability of navigating the tension between the actual and the fantastic. This to me seems quite simplistic, and I've seen literature navigate this same tension, with the application of different techniques and through the manipulation of different receptors of its audience. Yet maybe it is this simple. And maybe it is just as simple, but true, to state that literature and film might use different techniques and encourage different elemental responses in those who experience each medium, but the creative process is essentially the same. Certain techniques are employed that are specific to that medium (although some not always only specific to that medium) to achieve a desired effect, one that proves to be successful, and possibly brilliant.

And thus, exploring and even developing critical approaches for analyzing, more specifically, lit-to-film adaptations does not seem so overwhelming or elusive. It's a matter of moving beyond the quagmire of "adaptation," what it is, what it isn't, how it's done, how it's not, and choosing a focus. I'm choosing to focus on lit-to-film adaptation, and primarily novels to film. And perhaps honing in on this specific area of adaptation can allow for a broadening of the critical analyses that can be applied to lit-to-film adaptations. We can analyze novels, we can analyze film, and we need to be able to analyze, with more available instruction, lit-to-film adaptations. Because, for one, it's fascinating. Secondly, I won't allow my novel to be made into a film until I know someone who approaches it as a contemplative viewer possesses the tools to analyze the adaptation of my novel to its corresponding film in a way that's intelligent and intellectually insightful. And if my novel never comes to be a film, I still want other lit-to-film adaptation analyses to be possible. I certainly intend on analyzing film adaptations myself. And I've been teaching lit-to-film adaptations, and now have begun teaching lit-to-film adaptation analysis. Student reception has grown as my instruction has developed and evolved in conjunction with my work in lit-to-film adaptation analysis. I plan to continue my work and my teaching.

Part Four

———

The Literature-to-Film
Adaptation Conundrum

Chapter 19

Approaching Literature-to-Film Adaptation

Thus far, we've seen that to perform literary analyses, we have at our disposal a plethora of critical approaches to borrow from, and apply to texts, resulting in a depth of exploration that yields countless benefits, both for the critic and the text. The benefits are mainly that the critic expands and enlightens his or her understanding of a text from the perspective of the approaches used, and the text is opened up to further discourse beyond this analysis, which is a good thing for any text. In the same way, we've seen that to perform film analyses, various critical approaches are at our disposal as well, and analyzing a film as a text allows for an understanding of that text that is also beneficial to both critic and text, just as analysis is useful for the literary text.

Although these critical approaches, and many overlap for studying both literature and film, since they are textual-based critical approaches and both literature and film produce texts, help in exploring the text and seeing it from a different and often fascinating perspective, these approaches also examine the elements of a text and their usefulness and effectiveness. These approaches require a text to be of quality or at least of some use in offering enlightenment about something. It seems dull to some to have guidelines to follow when analyzing a text, but to do so not only provides the opportunity to venture into territory previously uncharted when analyzing a text. It also holds a text accountable for being complex enough and interesting enough to warrant examination and investigation. And such approaches put at least some pressure on an artist, a creator, even an industry, to adhere to certain standards in order to be considered of the quality deserving and capable of withstanding rigorous critique.

When I'd completed the first draft of my novel, and in discussing it with friends and especially students, the question of making it into a movie would continually come up in the conversation. The concept of film adaptation then began to interest me as a writer with a novel in the works. The story was complete; the novel needed to be crafted and revised and made into a piece of art that I could feel satisfied with and proud of. The story interested people, and immediately seemed to bring to mind what kind of film it would turn out to be. I'd spent so much time with this novel, this story, even before I'd written it, which I discovered as I was writing it. This was my "baby." What if someone else didn't see it the way I did? What if someone destroyed all my hard work by making a bad movie out of it? A Lifetime Original, which — nothing against Lifetime — I didn't want to see my novel become.

My reasoning behind this aversion to a Lifetime film paralleled Mary Wollstonecraft's challenge to the gothic novels of her time, implied in the way she wrote *Maria, or The Wrongs of Woman*. Her novel begins with a gothic scene, yet soon the reader discovers that Maria's reality is much darker and more sinister than any gothic scenario Wollstonecraft could have created. Instead, Wollstonecraft chose to impress upon her reader that women's reality is at least as harmful and victimizing as any story concocted in a gothic novel. When I explain my novel, I usually abbreviate it considerably, saying it's about a woman who kills her ex-husband because she finds out he's sexually abusing their daughter. That's my stock synopsis, still to this day. Perfect fodder for a Lifetime Original. Yet it's not. I tried to write it as a sensational story, which we are accustomed to seeing in a Lifetime Original, but I formed it in a way that made it realistic. I researched news stories to be sure that what I wrote had all occurred in one capacity or another, that the sentences delivered to the "perpetrators" were accurate and possible sentences, that the crimes committed were credible. And in fact, some of the crimes in the novel were inspired by stories I read and knew before I sat down to begin writing or even planning the writing of it. Some of the incidents in my novel grew out of stories that women had shared with me over many years.

My concern for an adaptation of my novel led me to studying film adaptation, and teaching it. The fascination students had with my novel being made into a film led me to devise a first-year writing course that incorporated the study of adaptation into it. I was an adjunct professor at the time, and working at different colleges, yet all three schools approved of my idea. Although I began with a focus on specific adaptations, I soon learned that adaptation could be studied as both a process and a product. The process of carrying out a lit-to-film adaptation involved the study of the myriad, and infinite ways of doing it, but also for a specific adaptation, how it had been done. Adaptation also comprised examining the product, or the net result of the adaptation process.

When I began teaching film adaptation, I hadn't quite gotten the hang of it, and fell right into the trap of fidelity criticism. Without any guidance or knowledge of books that addressed the subject of film adaptation, I turned to what comes most naturally to adaptation studies. As I tried to veer the students away from developing personal preferences about the novel/short story and film, I encouraged them to notice what was different or similar about the story in each medium. I noticed an especially difficult problem with students attached to the book and unwilling to give the film a chance. However, my choices of literature and films helped to reduce this problem. The most glaring problem I had was that the class was terribly boring. It lacked purpose and it wasn't as interesting to the students as I thought it would be. Even I was bored. I thought, what am I doing wrong?

My next step was to look for supplemental materials. I'd simply been using my extensive background in analyzing literature and my limited background in analyzing film to introduce first-year students to lit-to-film adaptation, thinking they'd love writing about adaptation, the mixing of media, and so forth. But we were all bored. My search for supplemental materials turned up helpful materials for me in understanding that adaptation studies had been written about, and was widely argued. I learned more about lit-to-film adaptation, and mostly the attitudes of all those involved in establishing it as a worthy discipline of study. However, I didn't find much that helped me in teaching it. And I found very few essays or books that I could use with my introductory students. Even the essays I introduced to them elicited responses like, this hurt my head, or, I had to look up almost every other word in the dictionary. Not that this was a bad thing, for they obviously were being challenged. Yet I didn't want to scare them away from film adaptation or frustrate them with it. I'd already done my share of boring them with it.

I persevered, but I kept falling back on comparison/contrast, where inevitably in their papers, they'd slip into which version of the story they liked better. And the analyses were fully based in fidelity, what was different, what was the same. I couldn't get myself out of this rut. My vested interest in and concern with my own novel being adapted to film merged into my fascination with a way to teach lit-to-film adaptation without putting us all to sleep or slipping into purely opinion and personal preferences (which by the way, offered nothing in class discussions since it's difficult to argue with someone's personal preferences — a 'I feel what I feel' sort of deal). Yet I needed to reach the students on their level and raise them to a higher level without making them feel as if they weren't smart enough to get what they were reading or making them lose interest.

I tried an essay by Thomas Leitch entitled "Twelve Fallacies in Contemporary Adaptation Theory," which is challenging for introductory students, but mostly over their heads and offers nothing in the way of how to analyze lit-to-film adaptations. It does address some issues about lit-to-film adaptation that we were able to discuss in class. I then used an essay by Brian McFarlane entitled "Reading Film and Literature," which is a bit more manageable than Leitch's essay for introductory students, reiterating some of what Leitch discusses in his essay, but also providing more insight into the dynamics of lit-to-film adaptation (since Leitch's piece is primarily focused on his list of twelve fallacies). Yet, although McFarlane's essay states that it's about reading film and literature in the title, it's primarily a defense of the film part of that relationship, and since it is only an essay, it's limited in how much guidance it can give. It discusses the dynamics of analyzing lit-to-film adaptations but doesn't instruct on how to analyze lit-to-film adaptations. I next tried Timothy Corrigan's "Literature On Screen, A History: In the Gap," which offers a wealth of information in a short piece, but also fails to instruct on how to carry out an analysis of lit-to-film adaptation, or offer any hint of suggestions.

This isn't to say I didn't try to find some books on the subject. However, many of them were focused on the theory of adaptation studies, and not with how to analyze lit-to-film adaptations from an instructional perspective. Many books I found were primarily comprised of case studies, but I already had my repertoire of literature and films I intended to pull from. I needed some guidance on how to teach it. Most of my selections were more contemporary, which worked with my own studies and the accessibility of the material for the students. I did use excerpts from Linda Costanza Cahir's book, *Literature Into Film: Theory and Practical Approaches*. I discussed with the students the idea of translation to describe the process of adaptation (which I find limiting and ineffective, and will explain later), which Cahir uses in her book. She also writes an informational section on the business of filmmaking, which helped the students see film from a more enlightened perspective, than simply from the consumptive perspective. I also used excerpts from John Desmond and Peter Hawkes's book *Adaptation: Studying Film and Literature*, but it proved confusing for the students to be introduced to an entirely different terminology for addressing lit-to-film adaptations. Both Cahir and Desmond/Hawkes rely on comparison for analysis, and Cahir refers to literal, traditional, and radical translation, while Desmond/Hawkes refer to close, intermediate, and loose adaptations.

And, although I learned a lot from Robert Stam, mostly that I wasn't too thrilled about poststructuralism being applied so openly, as is typical of poststructuralism, to lit-to-film adaptation in the manner in which he suggested, I couldn't even begin to use his work for introductory students. Although he had impressive and lofty points to make, even he seemed to become confused by them.

I was left in a conundrum once again. How could I teach lit-to-film adaptation, and lit-to-film adaptation analysis, to my students? How could I make lit-to-film adaptation more interesting since they were determined to talk about the books they read that had been made into films? The material was accessible for them, and they were more than willing to approach it. Yet how could I lead them to explore it in more depth? How could I get them to move beyond their personal preferences and enter the fray with critical minds and thought at work?

Thus I began to explore and develop ways to make the study of lit-to-film adaptation more interesting and more provocative. I devised five analytical methods that students could use to approach lit-to-film while also incorporating critical approaches already used for both literature and film. I've been working at these methods, through my own writing efforts and in my teaching, with my students. My students are becoming increasingly more engaged as my evolution continues.

Although this project began as a means by which an adaptation of my own work could be challenged and criticized by a set of established standards in place, through the use of effective tools, the focus of my project expanded to include devising a way to teach critical thinking skills to introductory students. In doing so, I've discovered that these particular critical thinking skills could help them challenge a world of various media bombarding them, instead of blindly welcoming and embracing all the intrusions, and only responding to those for which they develop a personal preference, not even understanding why. The discussion should never end there. And it hasn't.

Chapter 20

The Conundrum in Practice

Why would anyone want to adapt a novel for film? I mean, really. What is the fascination? They must know they're up against quite a jury of immense proportions, of all different types of people with different interests judging the "success" of the adaptation. In fact, the only individuals on the adapter's side, it seems, are the scholars who fight tooth and nail for respect of the film that comes out of the adaptation process. Linda Hutcheon in *A Theory of Adaptation* states that as important as it is to determine who the adapter is, in conceptual terms, it's also important "to find out why anyone would agree to adapt a work, knowing their efforts would likely be scorned as secondary or inferior to the adapted text or to the audience's own imagined versions" (2006, xv).

For, despite the fact that adaptations are often considered inferior or secondary offshoots of their source texts, Hutcheon explains that the prevalence of such adaptations are increasing in numbers, and asks: "Why, even according to 1992 statistics, are 85 percent of all Oscar-winning Best Pictures adaptations?" (4). Dudley Andrew, in his essay "Adaptation," published in 1981, states that the "making of film out of an earlier text is virtually as old as the machinery of film itself. Well over half of all commercial films have come from literary originals . . ." (1999, 263–4). So, why?

Besides the argument that audiences tend to flock to lit-to-film adaptations, at least those adaptations affiliated with well-known texts, and thus such films have the potential to be big moneymakers, there is more to it than that. If one has the connections in the film industry, and the ability to get a treatment and budget approved and financed, combined with the talent and experience to carry through a lit-to-film adaptation, I would think such a film project presents an exciting challenge to a filmmaker. Filmmakers themselves, just as everyday readers do, fall in love with a story they've read and want to see it brought to life in the medium that they excel in creating within, while at the same time they have the opportunity to bring the story to life for a large audience. (Filmmakers can do with a novel what everyday readers can only wonder what they'd do with it if they created a film from it.) If all goes well, in many ways it can be a win-win situation, despite the criticisms of the mainstream audience. Even if the viewers are not completely satisfied with the adaptation, they'll pay to see it. They'll recognize the association and that will bring them to the theaters. They might have their disgruntled responses, but the movie will most likely fare well at the box office regardless. Yet I do think it's often more for the director and those involved with the film a desire to see a story they've enjoyed reading either for a long time or fairly recently come to the screen in a way that they've imagined for it. That creative process is unique and extraordinarily difficult, taking into account all the obstacles that must be navigated.

The process begins with the screenwriter, who can be the director, but usually is an individual who is known as being particularly adept at screenwriting. Sometimes the author of the novel writes the screenplay, as John Irving did for the adaptation of his novel, *The Cider House Rules*. But often, it is a screenwriter who is asked to adapt a novel into a screenplay. Horton Foote, in "Writing for Film," explains the difficulty inherent in screenwriting, especially in writing screenplays based on novels and short stories. Foote recalls a time when films were silent, and remembers the first talking picture he saw: "I remember my father cried all the way through it and said afterwards that there ought to be a law against making people cry like that" (1988, 5). Foote at that time wasn't interested in silent or talking films, but wanted to be an actor. Instead, he ended up in New York City writing plays, which led to writing early television plays, then films.

Foote describes his second Hollywood writing assignment — he considers this one "of importance here" (5) — for Warner Brothers, when writers punched a clock and basically worked a desk job writing a script that might never be used. This particular assignment was to adapt a novel by Erskine Caldwell. The assignment didn't pan out well for Foote. He and several other writers wrote a screenplay draft for a film, his was reworked by a producer who brought on several other writers, and then it was passed on to another producer who, going through all the other screenplays as well, decided on Foote's. Foote writes of the producer: "He said that he had, based on mine, a final version, which he would like to send to me and that he would like to put me back on salary to do some final polishing" (6). Since Foote himself couldn't recognize the screenplay as his own when he read through it, he "politely" declined the offer. He thought that was the end of his Hollywood career.

However, a year later, he was asked to write the screenplay for *To Kill a Mockingbird*. He was told that "Harper Lee did not want to dramatize the novel and that I was the choice of all of them to do it. I read it and liked it, and I consented to the task" (7). He records it as an experience that changed his view of writers of films. His adaptation of the novel was used for the film, and the film won an Academy Award for Best Screenplay, among other awards. Yet, Foote's experience with the screenplay offers insight into how difficult an adaptation of someone else's work can be:

> Adapting my own plays presents certain problems, certainly, but adapting the work of other writers is in some ways for me the most difficult and painful process imaginable. And I do anything I can to avoid it. You see, when you're dealing with your own work, you're inhabiting a familiar world, and you can move around with confidence and freedom. But when you try to get inside the world of another writer, you're under constant tension not to violate this person's vision. (7)

Foote went on to adapt the work of others, despite how painful he found it to be. He writes that to be good at adapting the work of someone else, "one must like the original work" (7). He doesn't think you have to understand it necessarily but like it and be willing to come to an understanding of it, going through "the painful process of entering someone else's creative world." And each time, he says, he finds "that entrance into that world is different" (8).

Foote goes into intimate detail about adapting William Faulkner's short story "Tomorrow." He provides a plot summary of the story, chronologically, explaining that Faulkner didn't write it chronologically or "in this straightforward manner" (11). When asked by an interviewer if there was anything different about working on an adaptation as opposed to an original screenplay, this was part of Foote's response:

> When you're working on something of your own, you call upon a lot of unconscious things that you have been storing up and thinking about . . . [With someone else's work,] a great deal more is conscious, and you have to approach consciously what must have been an unconscious process for the original writer. (11)

In Faulkner's "Tomorrow," Foote became engrossed in the character of a woman on whom Faulkner spent only a few paragraphs in his story. Foote writes that Faulkner in his short story "told me enough about her so that my imagination went to work, and she became somebody I knew" (11). In his screenplay, Foote developed this woman's character and her connection to a more complex character in the story. He describes his writing of this aspect of the screenplay: "I worked on it that night and finished it early the next morning. And from that time . . . I have never changed it. It seemed to me moving, but I realized that what I had written was monstrously out of proportion to the rest of the story" (14). However, it so moved him that he decided to keep what he'd changed and rearrange the rest of Faulkner's story to fit, centering the rest of his version around the story of the two people he'd developed beyond Faulkner's story.

And, perhaps that's what the fascination is, at any given point in adaptation: the desire to move oneself and others. Foote begins his essay with his first experience of a talking film, witnessing his father crying due to how deeply the film moved him. Foote remembers his father's reaction to the film, and desires to move those who witness his own material brought to film. We are fascinated by what moves us, and we tend to be fascinated by how what moves us can move others, especially as creators, if we recreate it or remake it, the way we see it. And, there are those of us who are fascinated by what moves creators and how they transform what moves them into something that moves us, and the product of that transformation.

However, as I began my exploration into lit-to-film adaptation for my own benefit in understanding the dynamics of it and also for teaching it, I became frustrated by the number of theorists and scholars who have spent a plethora of time and energy on the subject of adaptation, yet in doing so have left me with very little I can extend to my students in helping them analyze lit-to-film adaptations. These individuals either become overly involved in the misconceptions they feel abound on the subject of adaptation theory, especially lit-to-film adaptation; and/or, they discuss adaptation in a language that is simply too lofty and complex, and thus inaccessible, for introductory students to grasp; and, overall there is a lack of an agreed-upon, consistent way of referring to adaptation practices. All of this results in confusion for students. Scholars not only use different terminology amongst themselves to refer to the same practice and subject, but also contradict themselves trying to navigate their way to a means for analyzing lit-to-film adaptations. Some don't even try to navigate to a means for actively analyzing lit-to-film adaptations. They postulate about why it hasn't yet been done in a way that's consistent or adequate, or they theorize and use case studies to show how to analyze adaptations. Unfortunately, unless the students reading or the teachers teaching are familiar with the texts (the literature and films) being analyzed, it's difficult to connect the methodology used with a more generalized methodology that can be used for other lit-to-film adaptations, or maybe even, any lit-to-film adaptation.

In the next section, I provide a reading guide of sorts to the essays I've used with my students. It might be helpful in understanding the conflicts and tension that seem not only to emanate from discussions of adaptation studies but also seem to inhibit adaptation studies from moving forward, a movement that all of the scholars writing on the subject acknowledge and agree is necessary for it to do.

"Twelve Fallacies of Contemporary Adaptation Theory" — Thomas Leitch, 2003

What I do here is, instead of listing Leitch's twelve fallacies, I explain what he is actually stating to be true. I also argue against some of his points since I'm not always in agreement with them. The issues he raises in this essay continue to be raised (as you will see in the following essays), and I'm trying to extend beyond these issues to come to new ones that are interesting to students, and in which they can also become fully engaged.

1. Contemporary adaptation theory still today isn't well-developed nor has it adequately addressed the questions it prompts. For example, "is adaptation . . . collaborative, or is it the work of a single agent — the screenwriter or director — with the cast and crew behaving the same way as if the film were based on an original screenplay? . . . [and] how is a film's relation to its literary source different from its relation to its screenplay?" Such questions, Leitch contends, "have remain unasked, let alone unanswered" (2003, 1).

2. Differences between literary and cinematic texts are not as rooted in essential properties of their respective media as we've been led to believe. Literary and cinematic texts can often achieve similar effects drawing from their medium specific techniques, depending on the effect desired. Even though a frequent topic of discussion has been "what novels can do that films can't, and vice versa" (2), what novels and films can do at any given moment depends more on the techniques being developed or used within their respective medium at the time they're being created, and their reaction against or embracing of what's current, than on the distinction between it being a novel or a film.

3. Literary texts are verbal for the most part, and films are audiovisual, but there can

be crossover and overlap. Leitch states that "instead of saying that literary texts are verbal and movies aren't, it would be more accurate to say that movies depend on prescribed, unalterable visual and verbal performances and literary texts don't" (4). However, in response to Leitch here, we writers do have our characters perform and "show" in our stories in ways that convey visual and verbal "performances" to the reader rather than put forth a simple journalistic recounting of our characters' movements. Readers can see the characters performing the movements suggested by an author by imagining them. Leitch needs to follow through here on refuting the differences between novels and films, like he does in #2.

4. Novels are not better than films. The basis of comparison that ends in favor of the novel in adaptation most often relies upon reasoning that is not sound, only impossible to refute, Leitch argues. I add here that neither are films better than novels in lit-to-film adaptation, nor should they be given special preference by those who feel that film is the underdog as their perceived privileging of the novel runs rampant. However, although this unjust privileging of the novel seems to come up in every discussion of film adaptation, amongst many scholars, there are no statistics to back it, and yet this claim is also impossible to refute.

5. Both novels and films deal in both concepts (ideas or thoughts) and percepts (recognizable sensations or impressions received by the mind through the senses), just as any relational or performative art form does. Also, seeing both as texts should encourage a reading and rereading/viewing or reviewing of them, allowing for a conversion of percepts into concepts not only in novels but in films as well. I agree with Leitch here; we need to analyze both novels and films to interpret the conceptual messages they are conveying.

6. Both novels and films allow access and invite readers/viewers into the psychological states of characters in a myriad of ways, with some crossover in technique, depending again on the desired effect in the particular medium.

7. The reader's/viewer's imagination is evoked by both novels and films through different techniques (again, there is crossover here), and especially through the use of different storytelling devices. In fact, differences in how the imagination is evoked occurs more in each medium, comparing film to film, or novel to novel, than across mediums, comparing novel to film, or at least as frequently (or so we hope as frequently, I must add here, rather than being subjected to the same type of text every time we read or view).

8. The fidelity of adaptations to their source text is "a hopelessly fallacious measure of a given adaptation's value" (8). Fidelity evaluations, according to Leitch and many other scholars, will always privilege the source text in such analyses. With fidelity as the criterion for evaluating lit-to-film adaptations, adaptation studies will never move away from "evaluation as a critical project" into "analytical and theoretical problems" (8). I disagree with Leitch here, as I develop later. I contend the problem isn't fidelity criticism, but its use in *evaluation* of the product. Evaluation of the product does not constitute an analysis or exploration of the product, much less the process. The evaluation should only occur as the analysis proceeds in that: can the adaptation be analyzed intelligently? Is the adaptation complex enough to warrant interesting and engaging study?

9. Source texts are considered more original than adaptations. Leitch draws from a poststructuralist argument in his claim that all texts are intertexts, and consist of texts that have gone before them, and texts around them. A source text, then, is an intertext and thus not original, as is its adaptation. However, Leitch here doesn't distinguish between an inevitable intertextuality that occurs naturally as creation embodies a myriad of influences bearing down on it, and a purposeful intertextuality where a filmmaker determines to adapt a particular text, directly, into film. The distinction needs to be made between inevitable and purposeful intertextuality. To not do so borders on plagiarism, and perhaps a discussion of plagiarism needs to be addressed, from a poststructuralist perspective? Poststructuralism should not be employed to encourage plagiarism, since we could confuse our students unnecessarily. Adaptations are purposeful intertextual endeavors, when referring to the source text; this source text is not inevitably or unconsciously included in the adapted text. In fact, adaptations represent a purposeful intertextuality that embeds unconscious intertextual movement within the source text that will inform in many ways the adapted text. The adapted text then is a combination of conscious (purposeful) and unconscious (inevitable) intertextualities.

10. Adaptations, novel to film, adapt more than simply the novel. They derive their creation/production from many "precursor" texts, not only from the source text. The author himself/herself — their work, their life — could be a precursor text to the adaptation. Leitch draws from Mikhail Bakhtin, and his thought on the novel, implying that Bakhtin's argument that the "real task of stylistic analysis consists in uncovering all the available orchestrating languages in the composition of the novel" (10) should be applied to adapted texts as well, or lit-to-film adaptations. However, what he doesn't offer is a way to do this, and we need to move beyond detection of the problem to solution of the problem. This is a common problem I have found in reading many of these scholars. They have detected the so-called problems but have offered very little in the way of solutions, which makes the problems they've detected suspect. Are the problems they've uncovered really problems?

11. Adaptations and their source texts are all intertexts. They all borrow from other texts. When studying or discussing a lit-to-film adaptation, critics and analysts often focus too much of their attention on the source text and the influence of the source text on the adaptation, or the adaptation's response to the source text. Leitch views these critics as assuming "an intertextual responsibility to its source novel" (11). He states:

> Although it is certainly true that adaptations are intertexts, it is equally true that their precursors are intertexts, because every text is an intertext that depends for its interpretation on shared assumptions about language, culture, narrative, and other presentational conventions. (11)

So, Leitch reiterates that every text is an intertext. He ends this section quoting Deborah Cartmell on looking at adaptations "for their generation of a plurality of meanings. Thus the intertextuality of the adaptation is our primary concern" (11).

Based on this line of inquiry and approach to film adaptations, I argue that it needs to be determined if the critic/scholar in question is analyzing the process or the product of the lit-to-film adaptation, or both. That makes a difference in the focus of their analysis; the source text is paramount in a study of the adaptation process. And, I ask here: isn't any text once established as such expected or even required to generate a plurality of meanings?

12. Adaptation study is currently a marginal enterprise that does not need to be. Leitch explains that twenty years ago, Dudley Andrew called for a broad generalization of adaptation study that would encompass all its intricacies, but this hasn't happened. Instead, notions of essentialism, originality, and cinematic equivalents to literary techniques still dominate the field. Leitch argues here, and reveals the crux of his essay, that adaptation study has fought for its own place in the academy for all the wrong reasons and that really the academy must change to make a suitable space for it in a new discipline called textual studies. He concludes by suggesting good questions adaptation study asks, and that these are the questions that would be "at the very center of intertextual — that is, of textual — studies" (12).

In Leitch's essay, his references to business and institutions comes across as especially problematic as his own agenda seems to find its way into the argument. But, in fact, textual studies can be and are managed within the current organization of the academy. How have we not been conducting textual studies? Media studies seems the more appropriate change to be advocating, or media/textual studies. Leitch in this essay has an acerbic tone when discussing the ways he believes adaptations previously have been approached. However, there is a long line of scholars voicing quite similar complaints, very few of whom offer any solutions. In fact, no one seems poised to push forward to a way to treat adaptation study with the respect it warrants and requires, which includes a respect for both the source text and the adapted text, and not a privileging of either.

As helpful as the poststructural movement has been in opening up possibilities for uncovering, and exploiting to some degree, meanings in texts, it has many of us desiring to cover ourselves and the texts we respect (and those we write as well) with a protective cloak for fear that "meaning" found within a text, in the form of many meanings derived from a plethora of various approaches (not all of them skillfully applied or carefully monitored), will become so diluted as to render the text "meaning-less."

"Reading Film and Literature" — Brian McFarlane, 2007

Much of what McFarlane writes in this essay is similar to Leitch's "Twelve Fallacies." Thus to read in conjunction with each other would result in reading reiterative arguments and not competing arguments.

Similarly to Leitch, although not the entire focus of his essay, McFarlane disposes of some of the preconceived notions of lit-to-film adaptation study. He claims that it shouldn't be necessary to focus on fidelity to the original text, and goes on to point out that many writers on lit-to-film adaptation agree that fidelity as a criterion is insufficient in addressing and discussing lit-to-film adaptations. He states that it always comes down to, "It wasn't like that in the book" (16). I must suggest here (and will develop later) that this constant refutation of fidelity as criterion might need to be reexamined. Perhaps this is our natural response to adaptation, at least when we view those films we know to be adaptations and have read their source texts. It seems likely that if we've viewed one and read the other, we're inevitably going to compare and contrast. Perhaps we must find a way to utilize and delve deeper into this response when analyzing lit-to-film adaptation.

McFarlane addresses another common misconception about lit-to-film, that "film makes fewer demands on the imagination than a book does" (16). McFarlane refutes what he considers to be the common belief that reading a continuous narrative with a set of characters operating over a period of time requires greater effort than viewing a film based on that story. Yet, rather than even the playing field, he tries to one-up the novel, by stating that maybe "in coming to serious terms with a film, much more is being required of us" (16) than a novel requires of us. And, the competition begins, with film, in McFarlane's (and Leitch's) hands, pulling out in front.

According to McFarlane, "there has been a pervasive suggestion that some sorts of literature are more susceptible to screen adaptations than others" (16). He mentions a novelist who doesn't understand how a film can "find its *own* voice through its own means" (17) when adapting the voice of the novel. I agree with McFarlane when he counters: "Complex and difficult novels and plays are not unamenable to film adaptation, but require the most intelligent and resourceful talents to address the task" (17). This is true, and what can be fascinating about lit-to-film adaptation is studying such a complex and rigorous process.

McFarlane continues, emphasizing that those who are adept at analyzing novels do not necessarily have the experience or training to analyze film, and this causes difficulty in adaptation analysis. I agree that along with literary training, a requirement for studying lit-to-film adaptation is also at the least a basic understanding of how film works, and not only how film works, but how filmmaking happens. I do agree with his criticism of his colleague with a literary background. She critiques a film adaptation, deciding it not as subtle or complex as the novel from which it was adapted. McFarlane states that "the colleague's literary training had equipped her to recognize subtlety and complexity in the verbal medium but not in the film" (18). A knowledge of film would certainly result in his colleague's critique being deemed more thoughtful and credible, because with more knowledge of film her critique undoubtedly would be more thoughtful. However, it is the next anecdote he uses that I find problematic.

McFarlane discusses another woman, this one not pleased that her grandchildren had seen films of the stories she'd brought to read to them. He states:

> The source of her disappointment seemed to lie in the ingrained notion that the written word not merely preceded but (invariably) outranked the audiovisual moving image. Was she really expecting these small children to respond to the quality of the prose and, if so, is there never an occasion when the images on the screen might be just as effective? (18)

Although he uses a very clever argument here, I'm not sure it's one that is very effective. Study after study has determined that it's important for children to have books read to them, to develop an association between words on a page and words spoken. I'll admit that I used to sit my young children in front of a video of a film to have them settle down for a few hours in the afternoon when they'd given up their naps. Yet they weren't quite ready to be taught how to analyze a film, or even be asked too many questions about a film. They saw film as entertainment. And to sit with your child while you're watching a film is not as interactional an experience as reading to them. When children are being read to, they love to ask questions, or point out pictures, and the adult can say, "Yes, that's a lion, you're right." And then maybe they tell you a long, albeit garbled imaginary story about a lion. But my children never said much beyond "That's a lion," when they watched *The Lion King*. The film had its value, but saying that film may one day replace books and reading is not a legitimate argument. We're not nearly ready for an entirely image-based and voice-recognition-based society, and I hope we never are.

McFarlane goes on to argue that those filmmakers fascinated by adapting film from literature "are, more often than not, more deferential in their attitude to the works they are adapting than the critics are in appraising the filmed results" (18–19). He doesn't provide support for this argument, but it does bring him around to suggest that it might be "more helpful to consider what film and literature have in common than either to require film to 'reproduce' the experience of the book . . . or to insist simply on the autonomy of the film" (19). Novels, he says, are the most commonly adapted form of literature. McFarlane then broaches the subject of researching the frequency with which novels are adapted to film. It's a difficult number to discern, he asserts, due to all the ways it could be evaluated, but the figures that he does relate, "rough as they may well be, serve to confirm one's impression that it is the novel above all which has absorbed filmmakers' attention among possible literary sources" (19).

McFarlane contends that the compatibility between novel and film implied by the frequency in which the novel is adapted to film has to do with the compatibility of the systems of language in which they operate:

> In semiotic terms, it is perhaps true to say that, in the novel and immeasurably more so in the film, the gap between the signifier and the signified is narrower than it is in drama and poetry . . . In both cases the imagination is kept active in creating this world, whether by a conceptualizing based on the words given on the page or by a conceptualizing based on the diverse perceptual information taken in while watching the screen and listening to the soundtrack. (20)

This makes sense in that when either reading a novel or watching a film, you enter into a different world, an alternate universe. You forget your own life for a while, and escape to immerse yourself in the lives of others. In this way, novels and films are very similar, especially for their audiences. Of course, McFarlane then has to differentiate film from the novel insisting that film

> has its own codes: we are required to distinguish lengths of shot, distance of action from the camera, angles from which the action is viewed, the kinds of editing employed . . . These all signify differently; [so that] . . . it is hard to maintain that

accessing the information of film narration is a pushover compared to the serious reading of a literary text. (20–1)

Although I agree with him here, is the defensive tone really that necessary? I've found that my students are more than willing to see film more analytically, based on its own codes. They simply haven't been taught to do so with any attention to detail or development.

McFarlane continues to distinguish between novels and film based on the ways in which they go about rendering time and place. He feels that they can similarly depict place, but when it comes to duration of time, and the tense of the story, they differ in how they denote time. He states that "novels are characteristically, but by no means exclusively, narrated in the past tense" . . . and that film "is always happening in the present tense" (21). I disagree with this distinction, as does Robert Stam. I teach my students to write about both literature and film as if it is happening right now, because really, the story is always happening. It never becomes the past. Stam comments in his *Literature and Film: A Guide to the Theory and Practice of Film Adaptation* on "the issue of 'tense' in the cinema, about which a good deal of nonsense has been uttered. A common idea . . . is that the cinema has only a single tense — the present — since in a film everything unrolls before our eyes, in the present." (Stam and Raengo 2005, 20) Stam goes on to argue, though, that "on a phenomenological level, the same point could be made about reading novels: the action, even in an historical novel set in the distant past, always unrolls in the virtual present of our reading." (20) I don't always agree with Stam, as will be apparent later, but on this point I concur.

McFarlane continues to compare and contrast novels and film, and their specificities — what they do and how they do it, especially differently — and finally seems to come to the crux of his argument: "Those who repudiate the notion of 'fidelity' as an evaluative criterion when talking about the relations between film and literature can bolster their case by invoking the far more productive notion of intertextuality." (2007, 26) And, once again, the concept of intertextuality enters the scene. Yet he doesn't only refer to the intertexts within a text (as is Leitch's primary focus of intertextuality), he also refers to the texts we bring with us when we read or view a text, although he localizes his focus to film: "The way we respond to any film will be in part the result of those other texts and influences we inescapably bring to bear on our viewing." (26) This is true, except here he is pointing out that not only the text the film was adapted from comes with us in our viewing of the film, but other texts as well. He argues that:

> When we turn to a film adapted from literature, or in some other way connected to a literary text or texts, we need to realize and allow for the fact that the anterior novel or play or poem is only one element of the film's intertextuality, an element of varying importance to viewers depending on how well or little they know or care about the precursor text. (26–7)

I understand what he's saying here, but as a novelist, it is discomfiting that the novel I've obsessed over and given so much of my life to for many years becomes used as the basis for a film, and subsequently gets reduced merely to "one element" of the film's intertextuality. He also blurs the line here, much as Leitch does in his essay, between inevitable intertextuality, what the audience unconsciously brings with them into the theater, and purposeful intertextuality, that the filmmaker has consciously chosen to fashion his film from a source text which is usually of the same title.

He does go on to state that reading a novel after seeing the film version of it can allow for an enhanced reading of that text, even if one has read it before. In a recent class, my students divulged to me that there have been times when seeing a film of a literary text has motivated them to read the text. A few of the students ended up reading *Push* after viewing its film adaptation, *Precious*. They didn't realize the book existed until they saw the film. So, films can encourage the reading of the literary text, which is a positive experience for students, and a comforting byproduct of film adaptation for the novelist (or at least I think so). And, of course, it would be helpful then to have a ready means for students to analyze and discuss their experience.

McFarlane concludes by addressing the problem of personal preference and opinions being declared after the viewing of a film that has been read in its literary version. He states that opinions ". . . are private reactions that don't necessarily forward the discourse about film and literature" (2007, 27). Although I acknowledge the problem with personal preferences being expressed, I have to say that I have students who when assigned a novel that is highly thought of and rife with meaning, exclaim that they hate it; either they've read it before and still hate it, or they hate it when they read it for me. I politely ask their reasoning, and often it can get to the root of their dissension, the aspects of the novel that disconcerted them. Usually I simply hear them out, and then let them know that I expect them to step back from their opinions and preferences, and focus on what the book is saying, whether they like what it's saying or how it says it or not. Personal preference is much easier to interject into a discussion than critical thinking about what one has read or viewed that leads to a more in-depth analysis. My favorite question and my students' most dreaded question that I ask them is "why?" Why didn't you like it? Most often, they don't have a very good answer. Why did you like one more than the other? Again, usually not a good answer. I ask of myself and anyone involved in lit-to-film adaptation studies, how do we get students to look further, more deeply, and in some capacity enjoy doing so, or at least benefit intellectually from doing so?

I must make one last point about McFarlane. He finishes his essay by saying that literature and film "might be seen, if not as siblings, at least as first cousins, sometimes bickering but at heart have a good deal of common heritage" (28). What irritates me about McFarlane's statement here is that he puts literature and film side by side as equals, yet spends almost his entire essay privileging the film aspect of that supposedly equal relationship, and doesn't address that in many ways, one could see the literature as parent to the film. I don't see what would be so horrific about that, yet the "anxiety of influence" will be addressed further in this chapter and the next, along with the "death of the author." Father-son issues have so long dominated anxiety amongst writers that it's carried over into a time when it's become antiquated in practice.

I do see parent–child as an accurate metaphor for lit-to-film adaptation, at least one worth considering, or reconsidering. I am a parent with older children, not fully grown, but they are based on me in some ways, and then they have their own individual qualities. When they go out in the world, some people will know them without ever knowing me, and some people will meet me and see the connection between them and me. Either way they are still that film, out there to stand for themselves, but also reflecting their source, whether it's known or not. In my case, as a single mother, head of household, with not much presence on their father's part, I've played a large role in whom my children have become. For all children, it's very different. Some children transcend bad parents. Some children shame good parents. Intertextuality seems in keeping with humanness. We are all influenced by what's around us, including other humans, and a very human-made world, taught by humans as we learn to grow into the world around us. If texts are intertextual, then humans are interhuman-al. Yet there are certain humans who exert more of an influence on our coming-to-be than others. My parents exerted the greatest influence on me, but at the same time, my children are the second greatest influence on whom I've become as a human. Again, as I've stated before, I think parent–child, mother–child, father–child are worthwhile metaphorical relationships that could afford exploration in understanding literature to film adaptation and intertextuality.

"Literature On Screen, A History: In the Gap" — Timothy Corrigan, 2007

Corrigan takes a more historical approach to lit-to-film adaptation in this essay, with also a focus on its establishment as a discipline in the academy. He begins by explaining that since the beginning of film, there have been film adaptations. And they've been greeted with both scorn and admiration. He also starts the essay by stating that before film came along, there existed a bias against it, since "critical voices worried about how photography had already encroached on traditional aesthetic terrains and disciplines, recuperating and presumably demeaning pictorial or dramatic subjects by adapting them as mechanical reproductions" (29). But once film began to develop, filmmakers quickly began to use adaptations to attract audiences, as early as *Cinderella* in 1900 and *Gulliver's Travels* in 1902.

Corrigan explores the relationship between "adaptation" and "discipline" in this essay and his argument is as follows:

> On the one hand, adaptation, in its specific and more general sense, suggests alterations, adjustments, and intertextual exchanges, while on the other, discipline denotes and connotes rules, boundaries, and textual restrictions. The changing relationships between literature and film and how viewers and scholars have understood that relationship can, I want to argue, be mapped across this gap between film as an adaptive process and film as a discipline. The many textual, cultural, and industrial territories inhabiting this gap become the prominent fields where the cinema's textual integrity, its cultural status, and its scholarly and academic boundaries are often hotly contested. (30)

Corrigan makes it clear his focus is on the film aspect of the literature and film connection in adaptation, and begins his discussion with a study of specificity and fidelity.

Specificity, he states, "assumes that different representational practices, such as literature and film, have individual material and formal structures that distinguish and differentiate them from other practices" (31). Each medium uses different techniques and form to bring across their desired effects. Fidelity, on the other hand, is "a differential notion that purportedly measures the extent to which a work of literature has been accurately recreated (or not) as a movie." (31) This, of course, has been addressed in both of the previous essays discussed, and as can be seen, is a quite present dilemma amongst those who write on adaptation studies. What's most noticeable is that although these writers express dissatisfaction with the fidelity criterion used for "evaluating" film adaptations, and fidelity criticism for analyzing film adaptations, they themselves get entrenched within comparison studies of literature and film throughout their essays. Corrigan puts forth his own reasoning why fidelity discussions about lit-to-film adaptations are inadequate and inaccurate: the specificity of literature and film "implies a translation between 'languages' that will always be only approximate or, at best, capture the 'spirit' of the original text" (31). He continues to insist how different literature and film are, and for this reason, they can never be the same, so why try to judge them by how similar they are when it's impossible to achieve that "sameness." Corrigan states: "To the degree that a film is faithful or not to the textual specificity of a literary work . . . or to the 'spirit' of the original, cinematic adaptations will always measure . . . the power of film — to assimilate, to transform, to distort, or to overcome — the specifics of that source material" (31–2). Yet, my question here is, how do critics measure or discuss the effectiveness, quality, or analyze the meaning(s) of the cinematic adaptation based on the source text? And I haven't found my answer in these essays, or in most of the books I've researched, although I've come up with some ideas of my own, based on my research.

Corrigan mentions the "casual responses" to lit-to-film adaptations that are based on the notions of specificity and fidelity, but explains that "the most important film scholars and critics of the twentieth century have also taken strong positions around these terms, frequently as a way of defending the power and art of cinema" (32). At least he admits that there is often a privileging of film in these discussions, as he then goes on to add to the many who defend film in the literature-and-film intertextual connection.

Corrigan lists the three most important forces used to control and guide lit-to-film adaptations: cultural status, economic power, and legal rights. And, these three social forces "identify, in turn, perspectives on cinematic adaptations in terms of three critical categories: cinematic texts, genres, and authors" (33). Then he launches into a history of film adaptation that is helpful to know and understand. He begins at 1895 to the turn of the twentieth century, with the earliest films, and how debates about those films arose as to whether or not they should be considered a science or an entertainment. Should the advancements in science that led to film determine its identity, or what the machinery produced? The first film adaptations began to appear at this time, and by 1903, movies were establishing themselves as an entertainment industry. The movies of the early twentieth century identified with working class and immigrant audiences but then movies began "to adapt literary subjects to suggest and promote a kind of cultural uplift that would presumably curb many of the social and moral suspicions about their power over children, women, and the putatively educated" (34). Literature, then, in a sense "saved" film, and began to raise it to a higher level in our culture. In fact, the increasing use of narrative literature to create films led to a standardization of film narrative. D. W. Griffiths's *Birth of a Nation* (1915) was adapted from the novel and play *The Clansman* (1905), setting a new cultural standard for film narrative and more intricately designed films. The movie business went from nickelodeons (for the price of a nickel, hence the name) to $2 for admission to the *Birth of a Nation*, leading the way to movie palaces.

In 1907, the first copyright lawsuit drew attention to the drawbacks of the commercial and cultural gains in adapting literature. Soon after, the scriptwriter emerged, "and the necessity of scripts and screenplays as key components in the production of films" (35). However, this emergence also added to the economic costs of making film and led to more control over the film process. In the late 1920s and 1930s, adaptations of contemporary literature became more popular than ever before, primarily due to the introduction of sound in film, or talkies, in 1927. Talkies allowed for more complexity in film. Also, the Motion Picture Producers and Distributors of America (MPPDA) "and its censorious arm, Will Hays's Production Code, watched carefully to be sure that sensational literature did not cross over into the more popular realm of film" (35). During this time, prestige films began to be developed and evolved. They were based on classical literature, which helped them make it through the Hays Office more easily since they were based on "stories whose canonical status could protect them from too close scrutiny by the censors" (36).

One of the initial claims for cinematic authorship came in the early 1930s with "the celebrated confrontation . . . between Bertolt Brecht and German filmmaker G. W. Pabst over the adaptation of Brecht's *Threepenny Opera* where . . . both the legal and artistic rights of the filmic author superseded those of the literary author once a work had been sold to a filmmaker" (37). This conflict and the result foreshadowed the era of the auteur. In the 1950s and 1960s, there was a rebellion against "A Tradition of Quality" that was built around adaptations of classical literature. This rebellion became the French New Wave — this was the period in film history when films were considered texts that had an author, or auteur, who was the director: the film camera, especially with the development of new technologies, was "comparable to the writer's pen" (37). The filmmaker as author now became "the measure of cinematic distinction, cultural specificity, and quality" (37) while fidelity in adaptation became a function of "authorial expression and authenticity" (37). Thus, that two critical models commonly opposed, film genre (industrial) and film auteurs (individual expression), built "their foundations in the cultural positioning of film/literature exchange reminds us of the fluid dynamic that binds the categories" (37).

Corrigan now moves into film adaptation's finding a place in academia. He states:

> Paralleling the changing cultural positions of film adaptation and its primary con-
> figurations as specific texts, genres, and auteurs, a century of scholarly debates has
> both reflected and challenged the many different aesthetic and social relationships
> between film and literature. (38)

And I'd like to point out here that although scholars insist that literature has had more time to become established as a discipline than film, English became a discipline in the late nineteenth century, and intense focus on critical analysis of literature didn't get into full swing until further into the twentieth century. So, although writing has enjoyed a much longer tradition than film, the studying of literature didn't become institution-alized and taken on with any kind of fervor until the twentieth century. It's not that far ahead of film when it comes to acceptance into the academy. Thus it's interesting that Corrigan explains that since the early 1920s, film gradually and perhaps painfully gained a foothold in the academy, trying to get out from under the shadow of literature and literary studies, "and establish its formal and intellectual independence" (39). Yet the discipline of English, or the study of literature, had only been established towards the end of the previous decade, and literary theory and literary analysis began to bur-geon in the 1920s as well.

From 1927 to 1933, there was *Close Up*, "The Only Magazine Devoted to Film as an Art," and in the 1940s in France, the filmology movement developed, "an intellectual field devoted to the study of film in society" (39). The "insistence on the singular-ity of film practice as a discipline" continued through the 1950s into the 1960s when experimental filmmakers tried to break with the narrative traditions that had developed in filmmaking, and film ventured out to stand on its own elements and qualities. One experimental filmmaker, Maya Deren, declared that the integrity of film "required a complete divorce from its former literary partners" (39).

Film studies began to enter college and universities in full force, and began to articu-late itself "more consciously as a scholarly discipline developing out of the humanities" (39). Film form came to be seen as a language, and film scholarship used literary and linguistic models to discuss film, while at the same time film studies moved to estab-lish itself as a discipline within academia through an emerging canon of films and their respective auteurs. In the 1970s and 1980s, film studies shifted in two principal directions, neither of which was particularly helpful for adaptation studies. The one direction it took went towards medium-specific, neo-formalist studies, which cham-pioned the distinctive difference of film from literature. The second direction it took was towards ideological studies, which embraced "broader conceptual grounds for film based in poststructuralism, psychoanalysis, and contemporary ideological models" (40). However, both were attempts to define film as a discipline.

In all of this, adaptation studies of a more conventional kind flourished, according to Corrigan, but "almost as a third and separate field on the fringes of the emerging discipline of film studies" (40). The early association of film with language and lit-erature departments could be sensed in the questions and terms used to address film adaptations. The pervasive question unable to be shrugged off was still "How does the film compare with the book?" with the answer being "The book is better" (40). What transpired were "dull close readings of literature adapted as film" (41). Corrigan states that in the 1990s, however, new scholarship began to emerge "opening the questions informing the relations of literature and film in larger, less predictable, and more con-crete ways" (41). But, still the discipline needs to develop a "poetics of adaptation" as Robert Ray called for in 2000, and Corrigan is optimistic that the discipline is headed in such a direction as he concludes his essay by stating:

Between disciplinarity and adaptation, between literature and film, adaptation studies provide, I am convinced, especially ambiguous, risky, unstable, and enormously interesting opportunities today. When opened out beyond questions of specificity and fidelity, adaptation studies necessarily and productively trouble and open disciplinary boundaries (both those of literary studies and film studies). It is in the gap that many of the most compelling ideas appear. (42)

I also argue that adaptation studies could become very interesting if opened out not only beyond questions of specificity and fidelity but within questions of fidelity and specificity. We need to encourage those who study lit-to-film adaptations to first of all become more knowledgeable and experienced at analyzing film, much as they are introduced to analyzing literature. Then we need to address lit-to-film adaptations. One method may be to examine what changes have been made from one medium to another, then explore why these changes might have been made, and what these changes reflect not only about the source text, but about both mediums and the time in which they were both produced. The possibilities become endless, building from the natural inclination to compare and contrast a familiar story in two different mediums.

Books

I tried using excerpts from two books that seemed more accessible to undergraduate students than others that I considered using. I used some selections from chapters of Linda Costanza Cahir's *Literature Into Film: Theory and Practical Approaches*, and one section of a chapter from John Desmond and Peter Hawkes's *Adaptation: Studying Film and Literature*. The main problem with using these selections together is that the books employ different terms for looking at and considering lit-to-film adaptations. Both books do rely on fidelity and comparison as a means to discuss lit-to-film adaptations. Desmond and Hawkes explain their terminology and how they use it:

> [W]e use fidelity not as an evaluative term that measures the merit of films, but as a descriptive term that allows discussion of the relationship between two companion works. To begin the description of the relationship between and film, we ask you to compare the two in detail and then to classify the adaptation as a close, loose, or intermediate interpretation. (2006, 3)

They go into more detail to define each term — close, loose, and intermediate — and how these terms can be applied to specific lit-to-film adaptations. Although this terminology can be easily understood by undergraduate students, it doesn't allow for very engaging discussion or writing. A film adaptation is a close adaptation because the "narrative elements in the literary text are kept in the film, few elements are dropped, and not many elements are added" (44). Details can be given concerning the literary text and the film to prove that an adaptation is a close one, yet it doesn't allow for an understanding of the complexities inherent in both versions, or in the adaptation of one to the other. It somehow falls flat.

The aspect of this book, though, that is helpful is Desmond and Hawkes's discussion of film. Cahir, in her book, also does a fine job of explaining film, and especially the film industry. It proved useful information for students, and they were surprised to discover all that goes into making a film, particularly from the business end of things. However, Cahir's reference to film adaptation as film translation becomes troublesome. First of all, Cahir's "translation" diverges from Desmond and Hawkes's use of the term "interpretation." But also, I don't view lit-to-film adaptation as translation, as if it were simply reinventing a story written in one language into the same story written in another language. Lit-to-film adaptation is more complex than that. I'm more in agreement with Desmond and Hawkes. Lit-to-film adaptation is an interpretation or reading of the source text, in some capacity, that is then reimagined for film and in the medium of film.

Using my own novel as an example, I don't see my novel as needing to be translated in order for it to be understood by film viewers. It needs to be interpreted intelligently, with a certain amount of respect for the author and her efforts and commitment to her project, and then reconceived, re-envisioned to be portrayed in a different medium, the medium of film. Seeing lit-to-film adaptation as a translation of sorts seems to inhibit the sense of play in reimagining or re-envisioning the source text for film. It also seems limiting. Cahir states that the "first step in exploring the merits of literature-based films is to see them as translations of the source material and to understand the difference between 'adaptation' and 'translation'" (2006, 14). She explains the more scientific meaning of adaptation, and this definition of placing the same entity into a new environment does require the entity to be adapted to that new environment. However, scientifically, that entity most often adapts itself to that new environment. The adaptation happens within the entity, and of its own accord. Adaptation in textual studies does not so easily coincide with its scientific definition, as can be seen here. Thus Cahir turns to translation to describe adaptation, meaning to move a text from one language to another, requiring action to be taken, from the outside, so that the text can be understood in another language. To explain adaptation she uses the concept of an entity, and to explain translation she uses the concept of a text. Although Cahir's argument is interesting, it's convoluted and must be contorted to fit her agenda.

Yet it is her explanation of the three different types of translations that occur with adaptation, based on John Dryden's three types of translations, that is very similar to what Desmond and Hawkes present in their book. Desmond and Hawkes simply use different terminology and a different basis for using their terminology, although with not nearly as thorough a foundation given for its use as Cahir provides. Yet I prefer their use of "interpretation" rather than "translation" to describe the act of adaptation.

Cahir explains the three different types of "translations" that occur in literature-based adaptations:

1. Literal translation: which reproduces the plot and all its attending details as closely as possible to the letter of the book.
2. Traditional translation: which maintains the overall traits of the book (its plot, settings, and stylistic conventions) but revamps particular details in those particular ways that the filmmakers see as necessary and fitting.
3. Radical translation: which reshapes the book in extreme and revolutionary ways

both as a means of interpreting literature and of making the film a more fully independent work. (16–17)

After perusing some of her case studies, I found them somewhat dull. Cahir focuses
on the quality of the adaptations, their successes and failures, and I argue for looking
beyond quality and which is better due to which type of translation was used and how
well. In fact, I believe even an adaptation considered of very little merit can reflect
something of interest to its viewer, and critic, beyond its quality and "success."

Despite some of the problems I encountered using these books for instructional
purposes, I was able to use them with relative success, supplementing the readings
with my own guidance. Several of the other books on lit-to-film adaptation were not
helpful because they were comprised of an introduction to a handful of case studies.
I wasn't teaching the adaptations being studied, so these books weren't useful to me.
One I feel it necessary to mention was different in its purpose than Cahir and Desmond/
Hawkes. Christine Geraghty in *Now a Major Motion Picture: Film Adaptations of
Literature and Drama* insists that her book "does not argue 'from page to screen,'
and my emphasis is not on the process of adaptation" (2008, 4). She continues by
explaining: "The judgments I make about individual films or television programs are
not based on how they work as adaptations but rather on how they work in themselves
. . ." (7). She works at avoiding comparison, she declares repetitively, but can't avoid
it. She contests "the relationship with an original source as the main criterion for judging adaptations, [but still wants] to explore the particular ways in which adaptations
make their own meanings" (4). In many ways, Geraghty seems to have misled her
reader if they're expecting to learn more about film adaptation and how it can be analyzed as both a process and product. Geraghty's focus is on the product of adaptation,
which doesn't help undergraduate students channel their natural bent towards fidelity criterion into something interesting and engaging. Geraghty wants nothing to do
with any of that, or so she says. However, then I don't see the usefulness of this book
in teaching both the literature and the film of lit-to-film adaptation since Geraghty's
focus is on the product of the adaptation, and viewing it as a film that stands on its own
as such.

This leads me to the books that I found inaccessible for most undergraduate and/
or introductory students, however helpful they were for me as a writer on the subject.
Before I launch into Robert Stam, who is entirely inaccessible to introductory students,
I want to explain why I didn't find Kamilla Elliott's book *Rethinking the Novel/Film
Debate* very useful for my purposes. It's a wonderfully written and beautifully arranged
book, yet it is beyond the comprehension of my students. It also is more specific to
older adaptations, when my focus is primarily on more contemporary adaptations. I
feel the need here to explain not only my students, but the students towards whom I
am writing this book. Very few of them are English or film majors. I am simply fortunate to have such majors enter my classroom. Most of my students are in the sciences,
especially nursing, and they are taking my course to satisfy a requirement. However,
I am also writing this book to students at a community college, students interested in
lit-to-film adaptations but with no interest in pursuing it in any way as a career, and
high school students (juniors and seniors), and even laypeople interested in moving

beyond personal preferences in discussing lit-to-film adaptations. With regards to high school students, I've found a potential learning experience being lost as students watch the film of the classic book they've recently read, but the teacher leads no discussion about the film and the adaptation of the book. I've discussed such issues with high school teachers, and they say they haven't had any training or found useful resources to be able to do so.

Moving into the next section, Robert Stam would not be able to offer such a resource. And that's okay, but we need one.

Literature and Film: A Guide to the Theory and Practice of Film Adaptation — Robert Stam and Alessandro Raengo, eds., 2005

Robert Stam is probably the most quoted and referenced author/authority on not only film adaptation but film in general. However, his writing on film adaptation is primarily theoretical and inaccessible to introductory students. At the same time, he brings forth intense and complex thought on film adaptation, but also falls into the pattern of other writers on film adaptation, fiercely defending film in this literature and film connection and debunking fidelity criticism as a way of looking at film adaptations. In addressing some of Stam's thought on lit-to-film adaptation, I hope to help students navigate through his writing on adaptation to more fully understand his perspective, while I also broach the core of his work and some of its problematic areas for me, and others. The introduction to his and Raengo's *Guide*, entitled "Introduction: The Theory and Practice of Adaptation," is quite extensive in both its scope and length, and will be the focus of my discussion here. Much of what he writes in this introduction he has addressed and put forth in other publications.

Stam begins his introduction by discussing the film *Adaptation. Adaptation* is a film about adapting a book (*The Orchid Thief* by Susan Orleans) for film, and is a creative yet peculiar film that raises the issues that surface with the making of a lit-to-film adaptation. Stam states that the film "foregrounds the process of writing" (1) as the character of Susan Orlean is seen with books strewn around her as she writes, and Charlie Kaufman the adapter is seen sweating through writer's block at his computer. Stam declares, as he will continue to show throughout his introduction: "Film, we are reminded, is a form of writing that borrows from other forms of writing" (1).

"The Roots of a Prejudice"

Stam then moves into a critique of the terminology that is used to refer to adaptations, and believes that terms such as infidelity, betrayal, and violation come across as "profoundly moralistic . . . [and] imply that the cinema has somehow been done a disservice to literature" (3). Violation, he even says, "calls to mind sexual violence" (3). The terminology exemplifies the root of the problem: that there exists an inherent prejudice against the filmic adaptation of novels. Stam lists and elaborates on eight such hostilities or prejudices:

1. The assumption is "that older arts are necessarily better arts" and that "the arts

accrue prestige over time. The venerable art of literature, within this logic, is seen as inherently superior to the younger art of cinema . . ." (4). However, I will counter Stam here, arguing, as I've said before, that literature was not studied as a discipline, which prompted more intense study of literature and how to approach it, until shortly before the development of film. In addition, novels are a younger art within literature, and short stories even younger, only coming into full swing around the time film was as well. So, although this argument of literature being assumed superior to film is relied upon heavily to defend the downtrodden medium of film, it seems as if it might be time to dispose of it once and for all.

2. "A second source of hostility to adaptation derives from the dichotomous thinking that presumes a bitter rivalry between film and literature" (4). Stam feels that the writer and filmmaker often are seen as one trying to outdo the other. In fact, he goes so far as to state that "film is perceived as the upstart enemy storming the ramparts of literature" (4). Perhaps there are those who feel that because filmmakers began to adapt novels in order for film to garner more respect in the world, it should be eternally prostrate to literature for that. Yet we're moving beyond this way of thinking, especially as film becomes more respected as an art. And this is happening, and has been happening, despite the quite visible defensive stance that many writers on adaptation feel the need to take when it comes to film. In addition, film is becoming more technologically advanced, increasingly polished, and impressively diverse in all that it can accomplish as a medium.

3. "A third source of hostility to adaptation is iconophobia" (5), Stam says, or that for a long time now, the visual arts have been held suspect for corrupting the minds of their audience with "dangerous" fictions. Yet, Stam states that the concern is that film "and other visual media seem to threaten the collapse of the symbolic order, the erosion of the powers of the literary fathers, patriarchal narrators, and consecrated arts" (5). To be clear, film is an overwhelmingly male-dominated industry, especially in terms of who has the most control. Many of us don't have a problem with the order being challenged along with the literary fathers and patriarchal narrators. What we do have a problem with is how accurately (or inaccurately) literary mothers and multicultural narrators are being adapted and represented in a white male-dominated industry that controls in so many ways to what degree the symbolic order is supposedly challenged. Even Linda Hutcheon in her book, *The Theory of Adaptation*, seems to challenge Stam's problem with this hierarchy he believes alienates the field of adaptation studies as she says that "what he calls iconophobia (a suspicion of the visual) and logophilia (love of the words as sacred)" (2006, 4) might not be a root cause of the negative view of adaptation at all. According to Hutcheon, it "might simply be the product of thwarted expectations on the part of a fan desiring fidelity to a beloved adapted text or on the part of someone teaching literature . . . needing proximity to the text and perhaps some entertainment value to do so" (4), which in many ways is something that can't be controlled.

4. The fourth source of hostility "to film and adaptation" (Stam adds "film" here when he's previously used only "adaptation") is the privileging of the written word as the basis of communication, or as Stam calls it, "the valorization of the verbal"

(Stam and Raengo 2005a, 6). He sees the written word as the most exalted form of communication across disciplines, but he doesn't take into account the "people" and students as well. The growth of multimedia communication is expanding exponentially and rapidly becoming more intricate and complex as well, eliciting not only a countless number of users but also enthusiasts. In fact, the modes of communication are uproariously expanding and changing as I write these words. This fourth source of hostility, if it isn't already, will soon be obsolete, even in academia.

5. Stam's fifth source of hostility to film and adaptation focuses on film's representation of reality: "its incarnated, fleshly, enacted characters, its real locales and palpable props, its carnality and visceral shocks to the nervous system" (6). Stam even relates how Virginia Woolf in an essay on the cinema "describes spectators, in terms that borrow from racist discourse, as twentieth-century 'savages,' whose eyes mindlessly 'lick up' the screen" (6). Woolf was writing quite a long time ago, and the demographics of film audiences has gone through many changes since Woolf's time. A literate and more educated audience views film today. Stam seems to say that novels are considered more cerebral and on a higher level than films because "novels are absorbed through the mind's eye during reading, films directly engage the various senses" (6).

6. He goes on to relate that a "sixth source of hostility to adaptation is what I would call the myth of facility, the completely uninformed and somewhat puritanical notion that films are suspectly easy to make and suspectly pleasurable to watch" (7). Although I agree that this can be an assumption made quickly without the proper information, it's rather simple to correct. I've found students to be very receptive to the correct information about film and its inner workings and complexities, and a follow-up discussion proves fascinating in addressing this particular hostility so familiar to our students. I agree with Stam when he writes (and encourage my students to see film this way): "Like novels of any complexity, films too bear 'rereading,' precisely because so much can be missed in a single viewing" (7).

7. "A seventh source of the hostility to the cinema and adaptation is a subliminal form of class prejudice, a socialized form of guilt by association . . ." (7). Stam feels that since the film audience is a more popular, mass audience, this automatically is seen as degrading film and the respect it warrants. Literature gets that reverence due to its very nature and tradition, according to Stam. And so, adaptations then "are the inevitably 'dumbed down' versions of their source novels, designed to gratify an audience . . . which prefers the cotton candy of entertainment to the gourmet delights of literature" (7). Sometimes, adaptations *are* "dumbed-down" versions of their source texts, and seeking primarily a sizable profit. However, many adaptations are brilliant. So, how do we keep the dumbed-down adaptations in check and demand better? Certainly supporting all of them, or defending their "honor" so to speak as Stam seems to do is not the answer. We need to know how to address discussions of adaptations, so to elevate the desires of filmmakers to do more than simply make a lot of money from an adaptation based on its association with a popular novel or series, but spark intelligent and even intellectual discussions. Many filmmakers are in the business more for that reason than to make

money. Yet money is necessary for them to stay in the business and make films. I get that.

8. Finally, the last source of hostility that Stam addresses is that of parasitism: "Adaptations are seen as parasitical on literature; they burrow into the body of the source text and steal its vitality. How often have journalistic reviews claimed that an adaptation has 'drained the life out' of the original?" (7). Perhaps for some this is the view, but for others adaptations offer a unique interpretation of a text that they've read, that they can discuss and that might even invite them to reexamine their previous reading of the source text (or read a source text for the first time after having seen its film adaptation).

These roots of prejudices on which Stam elaborates are fairly generalized reactions against and attitudes towards lit-to-film adaptations. Yet, when individuals and students are given the proper training to approach such adaptations, and unfortunately even simple guidelines (or especially simple guidelines) on how to do so prove scarce, these preconceived notions of adaptations are easily dispelled and a fruitful study of adaptations can commence.

"The Impact of the Posts"

Due principally to poststructuralist thought that came into its own in the 1970s, the concept of what is "original" has been challenged, and Stam uses this challenge to further his own thought on lit-to-film adaptation. I must state my doubt that the post-structuralist challenge to what is "original" was meant to be applied to a direct and purposeful intertextual connection between two texts. However, Stam thinks so. I've explained before that Jacques Derrida put forth the idea that a text has no center, and therefore no one unified meaning, and is never "original." Texts always come from somewhere else. Stam writes:

> Although intertextuality theory certainly shaped adaptation studies, other aspects of poststructuralism have yet been marshaled in the rethinking of the status and practice of adaptation . . . A film adaptation as "copy," . . . is not necessarily inferior to the novel as "original." The Derridean critique of origins is literally true in relation to adaptation. The "original" always turns out to be partially 'copied' from something earlier . . . (8)

Stam goes on to write that the "poststructuralist interrogation of the unified subject . . . fissured the author as point of origin of art . . . [and that] authors are fissured, fragmented, multi-discursive, hardly 'present' even to themselves" (9). Perhaps this is true, but even so a story that comes from such an author still develops out of that author's experience, research, and their intertextual explorations, both conscious and unconscious. The adapter of such a story or narrative, created by that first author, is interpreting and then re-envisioning the story for film. The adapter then is creating his or her own "original" version of that story, but their work is a purposeful offshoot of a source text, or another creator's "original" material. And, although Roland Barthes caused quite a stir with his well-known and well-used essay, "Death of the Author," Peter Brooker states in his essay on postmodern adaptation that "almost fifty years after Barthes's essay, . . . in the world of everyday reading, book reviews, as well as much academic criticism, the author is as strong a presence as ever" (2007, 107). I think he's got a point.

Although much of my literary training was focused on the poststructuralist approach to literature, my experience with writing a novel from my own observations, life occurrences, research, and unconscious response to that to which I've been exposed combined with my novel's possible adaptation by someone else, I recognize that poststructuralism and its opening up of texts could threaten to degrade their value to some extent, and it could also potentially undermine my position as the author of my own work, as if I wrote it as randomly as it might be analyzed. My own narrative didn't simply channel itself through me unconsciously, leaving me the conduit and nothing more.

Stam champions the minimization of the concept of originality with his own agenda in mind as he explains that "if 'originality' in literature is downplayed, the 'offense' in 'betraying' that originality, for example through an 'unfaithful' adaptation, is that much less grave" (Stam and Raengo 2005a, 9). To simply discount originality altogether seems counterproductive, especially in academia, where you have to prove your thought is original just to be able to present it at a conference as a paper or presentation.

Poststructuralism should not be used as a means to justify a practice that in many ways simply needs to be better understood so that more individuals are equipped with the tools both to carry out an adaptation and to approach an adaptation from an analytical perspective in a way that is engaging and explorative. Poststructuralism, at least as I view it, was never meant to be disrespectful to or dismissive of the author. Nor was it meant to encourage the dilution of meaning in a text. It was meant to encourage a heightened respect for the text by focusing in on the text itself, and exploring its cavernous and multiplicitous meanings, which in turn does respect the author and the author's effort. However, poststructuralism also was never meant to open a text so wide that it could be made to fit into whatever the reader/analyst/adapter wants it to be, whether it can be justified as that or not. Poststructuralism was meant to give the text, and a limitless number of texts beyond the narrow constraints of the canon at the time, more significance, not less.

Christine Geraghty, in the introduction to her book *Now A Major Motion Picture: Film Adaptations of Literature and Drama*, discusses Stam's intense focus on intertextuality in his work on adaptation. This focus leads him "to suggest that adaptations are merely examples of what is at play in any kind of text" (2008, 3). She contends, and I agree with her, that:

> The openness of Stam's approach is indeed productive, but it might lead to textual accounts that deliberately seek to escape the interpretative and social processes that work to pin down meaning at a particular point. This not only makes analysis almost impossible, given the number and fleetingness of possible associations and connections between texts, but also does not necessarily help our study of adaptations. (4)

Geraghty goes on to say that she doesn't agree with focusing on the original source and its relationship with the adaptation based on it as "the main criterion for judging adaptations" (4), she contends that she wants to investigate how adaptations "make their own meanings" (4). Thus Stam's seemingly over-reliance on poststructuralism to open up a film adaptation and view it as an unconscious conglomeration of many texts, only one being its source text and that one not being any more important to it than the others, allowing the text meanings so multiplicitous to be infinite and vast, unnerves Geraghty to an extent.

Stam takes this approach even further when he discusses the idea of adaptation in "the post-celluloid world of the new media: the Internet, electronic games, CD Roms, DVDs, virtual environments and interactive installations" (Stam and Raengo 2005a, 11). Now that we have all of these multifarious forms of digital media that "incorporate all previous media into a vast cyber archive" (12), intertextuality seems for him to have multiplied exponentially so that it is impossible to distinguish one lone text from another lone text without taking into account all the other texts that are a part of those two lone texts as well. He claims, then, that: "Novels, films, and adaptations take their place alongside one another as relative co-equal neighbors rather than as father and son or master and slave" (12). This conclusion comes across as reductive thinking on lit-to-film adaptation, an opening up that astounds by its reduction. I still maintain that the most appropriate analogy to describe the dynamics of a lit-to-film adaptation is parent–child, although father–son is delimiting since it's been so overused and overdone in literature, yet the mother–child relationship might be the most interesting to develop and apply to lit-to-film adaptation. Certainly, the master–slave relationship is an exaggerated over-dramatic analogy to apply to lit-to-film adaptation, and completely inappropriate.

"The Aporias of 'Fidelity'"

Stam argues, as most of the other writers on adaptation theory and study concur, that "it is most important to move beyond the moralistic and judgmental ideal of 'fidelity'" (Stam and Raengo 2005a, 14). He refers to the discussion surrounding this ideal as fidelity criticism and argues that it is insufficient and ineffective in evaluating and judging adaptations. For me, the problem is in the evaluating and the judging. Stam queries:

> . . . is one to be faithful to the author's intentions? But what might they be, and how are they to be determined? In cases where an author . . . writes a screenplay for his own novel, should the filmmaker be faithful to the novel or the screenplay? What about cases where a novelist/filmmaker . . . is 'unfaithful' to his own novel? (15)

These are fascinating explorations on which to embark, and I think the question of whether the filmmaker should be "faithful" to the novelist's novel or their screenplay suggests that perhaps the filmmaker should simply be faithful to what he or she sees, from an informed and thoughtful perspective, as the author's vision, as Foote refers to it. How can the film best represent the vision of the book, and more specifically, the way the filmmaker perceives that vision?

Stam complicates the argument of fidelity when he says that "while filmic rewritings of novels are judged in terms of fidelity, literary rewritings of classical texts such as Coetzee's rewriting of *Robinson Crusoe* are not so judged — change is presumed to be the point!" (15–16). Yes, why would we need an exact written copy of something already written? The point would be to change it or not to bother "re"-writing it. It's the same medium; the only way to make it interesting is to alter it, and often that's accomplished by bringing it into contemporary society. It's most likely going to be a text from another time period, because why would anyone rewrite a text written a year ago (or be legally allowed to do so)? However, the narrative of a novel re-envisioned for film, a different medium with a different set of techniques to consider as tools for telling the story, requires an alternate approach that's not necessarily about judging the outcome but analyzing what has been produced.

Fidelity as an evaluative criterion for a lit-to-film adaptation is insufficient. However, one argument supporting this claim that seems to be glossed over is: a judgment should never be made that praises a lit-to-film adaptation simply because it is faithful to the source text. Such faithfulness might make for a horrible film and thus adaptation. Likewise, a faithful rendering of a source text in film could make for a beautiful film as well. It needs to be remembered that not everyone who views a lit-to-film adaptation has read the book, so the quality of the film needs to be considered. Fidelity as a way to judge a film is insufficient because it doesn't allow for true judgment of the film itself. However, fidelity, and infidelity, as analytical tools to examine and explore not only the product of adaptation but the process can prove to be an engaging study.

Stam relates: "If one has nothing new to say about a novel, Orson Welles once suggested, why adapt it at all?" (16). I say that to adapt a novel is to say something new about it, regardless of whether or not the adapter aspired to say something new or not; it is a new perspective on an original idea developed and created by someone else. To adapt a novel is to accomplish something new and innovative, perhaps not necessarily well or brilliantly, but maybe quite so. Stam also relates: "Simply adapting a novel without changing it, suggested Alan Resnais, is like reheating a meal" (16). I disagree with this statement although I don't argue against changing a novel. An adaptation can be faithful to a novel and be a new "meal" in a new medium, but I also think change, even drastic change, is welcome as well, if done thoughtfully, respectfully, intelligently. But I will contend, from an author's perspective of course, that "respectfully" must be demanded in a world full of profit seekers. Recklessness with an adaptation is not welcomed by any writer, and that can happen with a filmmaker who simply wants to make a lot of money. Whether or not it will be acknowledged from the ivory tower, this does happen in the film industry, and it is probably just about every author's nightmare, especially today.

"The Automatic Difference"

Stam reiterates the point I make above when he writes in this section that a "filmic adaptation is automatically different and original due to the change of medium" (17). However, it is an original perspective of the source text due to its being re-envisioned in a new medium, and that needs to be clarified. The film is another way of looking at the story, in that the story wasn't planned or written in its original form to be a film. How the filmmaker puts together the various elements of the story is "original," but not the story itself. The filmmaker is not the mastermind behind the subject of the film but the mastermind behind how that subject is conveyed in a new, different medium.

In this section, Stam dismisses not only the time and energy it takes to write a novel, but the artistic talent and even training it requires. To write a novel might not require as much money as making a film, but it's not free. And a sentence published in a novel might seem effortless, but Anne Lamott explains in her book *Bird by Bird: Some Instructions on Writing and Life*, that a writer can write ten pages and end up with one sentence they can use from those ten pages, that sentence encompassing maybe a day or week of a writer's time. And it might be that very sentence that Stam insists cost "almost nothing" to write while it will cost a filmmaker "substantial sums" to stage. Stam has an accomplished understanding of what goes into making a film, yet he doesn't seem to understand what goes into making a novel, which might help him understand the defensiveness of writers and literary people. It might not be the great tradition of literature that makes the literary folks defend their place in lit-to-film adaptation, but perhaps the disregard for what exactly goes into making a novel, in favor of how extraordinarily difficult and painstaking it is to make a film.

"Specificity and the Multiplicity of Registers"

This section is a defense of the medium of film and all it has to offer, which has been handled in this book already in the film section and also discussed in the summaries of previous essays about lit-to-film adaptation above. Stam's main point in this section is that "adaptation criticism has tended to emphasize the cinema's impairments and disabilities vis-à-vis the novel" (20). He defends filmmaking and its specific difficulties when he makes the statement that the "absence of actors brings enormous advantages to the novelist" (22) and then goes on to say how fortunate novelists are that they don't have to worry about temper tantrums, pregnancies and deaths of the actors. However, and adamantly I counter, novelists still do have to deal with chance in other ways. Here it seems pretty convenient for Stam's arguments that writers work in the dark, while actors' and filmmakers' lives are out in the light where everyone can see, and much is visible and known. Novelists run into problems with their characters, too, like when the character begins to change as the writing of the book evolves, and the writer has to take a hiatus to clear her head and figure out the character. Or money runs out and you have to get a job to pay the bills, and the character and the novel must wait, and quite possibly, the time elapsed will result in the character's change, perhaps not for the better. Regardless, it will be a different novel, much as chance will change the course of a film and its outcome.

Stam's arguments seem so contrived in this section that I have to wonder why he finds it necessary to fight like the dickens for the dignity of film. As a novelist, it puts me on the defensive, and it doesn't comfort me in the least to think about my novel being adapted to film amongst all its argued vicissitudes.

"From Infidelity to Intertextuality"

Stam insists in this section that it's time to move beyond fidelity criticism to "a new language and a new set of tropes for speaking about adaptation . . . Instead of denigrating terms for adaptation, such as 'betrayal' and 'infidelity,' one might speak of a 'Pygmalion' model, where the adaptation brings the novel 'to life,'" (Stam and Raengo 2005a, 24).

Interestingly, Mary Wollstonecraft herself, the writer behind the source text from which my novel is derived, challenges the concept of a Pygmalion model through her character Maria in the following passage from her novel:

> Having had to struggle incessantly with the vices of mankind, Maria's imagination found repose in pourtraying the possible virtues the world might contain. Pygmalion formed an ivory maid, and longed for an informing soul. She [Maria], on the contrary, combined all the qualities of a hero's mind, and fate presented a statue in which she might enshrine them. (1975, 33)

The concept of the Pygmalion model can then, according to Wollstonecraft herself, go very wrong. Maria is an example of a woman who does not have the education or the experience necessary to make sound judgments on the ways of the world, Wollstonecraft is showing here, and she is a fictional portrayal of the women about which Wollstonecraft speaks and remonstrates in her *A Vindication of the Rights of Woman*. During her time, the women to whom she refers in *Vindication* are the overwhelming majority, and she is arguing for their release from subjugation and for them to be allowed an education and tools to guide their own lives. Wollstonecraft insists allowing this for women of her time would make them better mothers and managers of households. But if women don't have the wherewithal to process the world, they like Maria will misuse their imagination, think solely of what they want from the world, and mold what's in front of them into looking like what they want it to in their minds. This is self-betrayal. And, in film adaptation, seeing what one wants to see in the novel, to turn it into a film, more for profit rather than quality, can occur. How do we challenge that practice? Where are our tools? We can speak of adaptation, but how do we critique a specific adaptation, and analyze it? Stam doesn't offer any solutions, really. He speaks of adaptation, and about adaptation, and what needs to be changed in how we approach adaptation analytically, but he doesn't give us any guidelines on how to do that.

"Bakhtin, Genette, and Transtextuality"

In this last section of Stam's introduction that I will address concerns Stam's attempt to explain the concept of intertextuality to the extent where he is not only confusing to the reader, but quite possibly to himself. I argue that intertextuality, to be understood, does not need to be explained and expanded in such a complex manner. It can be understood, at least in its simplest of meanings, by even a layperson, and definitely an introductory student. However, Stam begins by introducing Mikhail Bakhtin's concept of intertextuality. One of my problems with Stam in much of his theoretical workings is that he makes the assumption that these concepts that have been developed primarily in relation to literature can be applied directly and unequivocally to film. A novel is a text, it is made up of intertexts, and is thus intertextual. A film is a text, it is made up of intertexts, and is thus intertextual. And, Stam states: "Virtually all of the theory and literary analysis directly or indirectly related to 'intertextuality' . . . bear relevance to film and adaptation" (Stam and Raengo 2005a, 26). He doesn't justify why this might be true. He goes on to focus on Mikhail Bakhtin and reiterates: "Many of Bakhtin's conceptual categories, although developed in relation to the novel, are equally germane to film and adaptation" (26). Stam doesn't explain why or how, but simply pushes through to use these theoretical frameworks to discuss film and adaptation. He places emphasis on Girard Genette's expansion of intertextuality into a much more complex and broadened view of textualities. As Stam explains, "Genette posits five types of transtextual relation, all of which are suggestive for the theory and analysis of adaptation" (27).

So, Stam moves from a discussion of intertextuality and its importance to film adaptation, to its categorization within the broader category of transtextualities. Again, he states that these "five types" are useful in the understanding of adaptation but fails to explain why or how. Stam then begins to list and describe Genette's five types of transtextualities. The first transtextuality, he says, is intertextuality. The second kind of transtextuality is paratextuality. However, then Stam states that the third type of intertextuality, when he means transtextuality, is metatextuality. Metatextuality he explains as being most useful for application to the analysis of film adaptation. He explains the fourth kind of intertextuality, and again he means transtextuality, is architextuality. (Here is where the reader, especially an introductory student, would be entirely confused.) And, finally, "Genette's fifth type, 'hypertextuality,' is perhaps the type most clearly relevant to adaptation" (31). Even Stam might have to admit there is an easier way to explain intertextuality to introductory students so that they can apply the concept of intertextuality to lit-to-film adaptation, because he himself becomes confused trying to explain Genette's many and difficult textualities. Genette's textualities are difficult to process but when they become muddled by the writer explaining them, they become almost impossible to understand.

Like I've said, there has to be an easier way to understand all of this, and apply it to an analysis of a lit-to-film adaptation. And, there is. In the next chapter, I offer some strategies that I've used with my students for approaching lit-to-film adaptations. I've only begun to use them in practice, but I'm finding students to be genuinely intrigued by the idea of exploring a new area of analysis, in which introductory students, students just beginning to analyze in an academic fashion, haven't been encouraged to engage. The theory and practice of lit-to-film adaptation analysis hasn't been nearly as accessible to introductory students as it would need to be as they're starting out in their academic careers. However, the area of lit-to-film adaptation is rife with possibilities for them to utilize their blossoming analytical skills and focus them in an area with which they are familiar, very familiar. The generation I'm working with for the most part witnessed the *Harry Potter* phenomenon as first a widely popular book series, before the film sequence was a thought in anyone's mind. My now 16-year-old son brought the third *Harry Potter* book to his first-grade reading picnic, an event for children to share their favorite book with their parents. The films didn't appear until much later, but with such fame and success attached to them, that this generation learned quickly the hovering presence of film adaptation as they read, and that what they read could easily be seen later in the medium of film. I don't see this as a bad thing, but when it's not used to teach critical thinking to engaged minds, minds already open to the concept of books being made into films, I see it as a wasted opportunity. This is not the generation on which we can afford to fritter away such an opportunity.

A Maternal Metaphor Instead

Before I formally began this project, this exploration, I'd set out to establish lit-to-film adaptation as a marriage of media. It was admittedly self-motivated since I wanted to assure myself that a film adaptation based on my own novel would result in a partnership between my novel and the film. However, as I became more entrenched in this exploration, the idea of seeing lit-to-film as a partnership began to fall flat. Yes, there are certain lit-to-film adaptations that are seemingly in a partnership sort of relationship. And this is good. Yet there are many lit-to-film adaptations that in no way resemble a partnership. A lit-to-film adaptation will always share a connection, but how deep that connection is, and how close, is dependent upon not only the adaptation itself, but the nature of the book as well. And it's not always about how accomplished the film adaptation turns out to be. I stay away from faithfulness here, because faithfulness is not a measure of how accomplished and effective an adaptation is representing its own medium, nor a unique interpretation of the book it has adapted.

However, I do want to introduce a way to view adaptations in a metaphorical sense that will help those who approach lit-to-film adaptations to understand the nature of the connection between the source text and its resultant adaptation. What I do here is combine my experiences as an author, a woman, and a mother not only to challenge the patriarchal metaphors so deeply ingrained in literature and thus film, and now being easily and thoughtlessly applied to lit-to-film adaptation, but to suggest a new way of viewing the creation of art and the intertextuality embedded in how the traditions get passed along.

As soon as I came to lit-to-film adaptation from the perspective of an author, Roland Barthes's "Death of the Author" took on new meaning for me. I appreciate the idea of the essay, that the text is limitless in the meanings it holds, and keeping the text closely conjoined with its author compromises how limitless those meanings can be. Barthes places the emphasis on the reader of the text rather than the author. In some ways, I see Barthes's essay as saying that without a reader, there isn't a text. Without the presence of an audience, a text doesn't really exist. The author isn't as crucial to the text as the reader is, according to Barthes. And I understand he was trying to rid the author of his/her godlike status, so that a text could be read without the author's shadow hovering above it. The text needed to stand for itself. However, I do believe that it's important to remember that without either author or reader, the text wouldn't exist. The author's work wouldn't have made it to textual status without the author, while at the same time a work can't be seen as a text unless it has a reader, a reader upon which to impress its meanings. Barthes believes "a text's unity lies not in its origin but in its destination" (1977, 148) and I believe a text's unity lies in both its origin and its destination.

Barthes writes that the

> removal of the Author . . . is not merely an historical fact or an act of writing; it utterly transforms the modern text . . . The temporality is different. The Author, when believed in, is always conceived of as the past of his own book: book and author stand automatically on a single line divided into a *before* and an *after*. The Author is thought to *nourish* the book, which is to say that he exists before it, thinks, suffers, lives for it, is in the same relation of antecedence to his work as a father to his child. In complete contrast, the modern scriptor is born simultaneously with the text, is in no way equipped with a being preceding or exceeding the writing, is not the subject with the book as predicate; there is no other time than that of the enunciation and every text is eternally written *here and now*. (145)

In this passage, a rejection of the relationship between the author and the text as one of a father to his child can be noted. Barthes propels away from this metaphorical relationship by saying the father is born with the child, and the focus is on the child which is the here and now. Thus, the author and the text are not like father and child at all. The child is one with the father, who is born when the child is born. In many ways, this essay by Barthes appears to be an example of the son trying to break away from the father, a quite common theme raised by many (male) theorists.

Decades before Barthes encouraged killing the author (so to speak), T. S . Eliot insisted that authors and artists could not escape their fathers, the authors and artists who'd gone before them. In his essay "Tradition and the Individual Talent," Eliot argues that "no poet, no artist of any art, has his complete meaning alone. His significance, his appreciation is the appreciation of his relation to the dead poets and artists. You cannot value him alone; you must set him, for contrast and comparison, among the dead" (2000, 91). In comparison to Barthes, Eliot is saying here that an author/poet is influenced, whether he recognizes it or not, by those who have gone before him, his fathers. He maintains that a new work of art grows out of the works of art that have preceded it, while at the same time this new work of art invites a revisitation and a new way of looking at the art that has gone before. Eliot goes on to say that: "the past should be altered by the present as much as the present is directed by the past. And the poet who is aware of this will be aware of the difficulties and responsibilities" (92). He has an inevitable obligation and responsibility to what has gone before, and as Eliot states, he will be "judged by the standards of the past . . . not judged to be as good as, or worse or better than, the dead . . . a judgment, a comparison, in which two things are measured by each other" (92). Previous texts then, according to Eliot, are altered by what is new and present. Eliot explains why this is true: ". . . the difference between the present and the past is that the conscious present is an awareness of the past in a way and to an extent which the past's awareness of itself cannot show" (93). The poet in the present provides a new way of looking at texts of the past, telling us things about the past texts that the past texts couldn't. The present hadn't occurred yet to illuminate that past when that past was the present.

Eliot relays the role of the poet or author in creating a text as one of surrender of himself and in many ways to that which has gone before him:

> What is to be insisted upon is that the poet must develop or procure the consciousness of the past and that he should continue to develop this consciousness throughout his career . . . What happens is a continual surrender of himself as he is at the moment to something which is much more valuable. The progress of an artist is a continual self-sacrifice, a continual extinction of personality. (93)

To relate Eliot to Barthes then, Barthes believes the author and the text are born when the text comes into being while Eliot believes the author must surrender himself to the text, lose himself to bring the text into being, and in so doing, he becomes one with the text but cannot be seen in the text. The text is separate from him. However, the text will inevitably reflect the father, his fathers of the past. He cannot escape the father. While Barthes tries to relieve his text of the father's, or the actual author's, influence, Eliot insists that the text is influenced by the fathers of the past through the poet or author of the present anyway. Thus the "father" is inescapable.

Harold Bloom tries to decipher the influence of the father or precursor (as Bloom refers to him) on a poet or author in his book *The Anxiety of Influence*. He explains this influence in his "Synopsis: Six Revisionary Ratios" (1997, 14):

1. "A poet swerves away from his precursor, by so reading his precursor's poem as to execute . . . a corrective movement in his own poem, which implies that the precursor poem went accurately up to a certain point, but then should have swerved, precisely in the direction that the new poem moves."
2. "A poet . . . 'completes' his precursor, by so reading the parent-poem as to retain its terms but to mean them in another sense, as though the precursor had failed to go far enough."
3. This is the "movement towards discontinuity with the precursor . . . The later poet, apparently emptying himself of his own . . . imaginative godhood, seems to humble himself as though he were ceasing to be a poet . . .," but this is temporary.
4. "The later poet opens himself to what he believes to be a power in the parent-poem that does not belong to the parent proper [the precursor poet], but to a range of being just beyond that precursor. He does this, in his poem, . . . as he [generalizes] away the uniqueness of the earlier work."
5. "The later poet . . . . yields up part of his own human and imaginative endowment, so as to separate himself from others, including the precursor, and he does this in his poem . . ." as well.
6. This is the "return of the dead . . . The later poet, in his final phase . . . holds his own poem so open again to the precursor's work that at first we might believe the wheel has come full circle . . . But the poem is now *held* open to the precursor, where once it *was* open, and the uncanny effect is that the new poem's achievement makes it seem to us, not as though the precursor were writing it, but as though the later poet himself had written the precursor's characteristic work." (14–16).

Now let me be clear that viewing writing, the author's influence on the text, and the influences on the author of the text, have for the most part been seen through the eyes of men, and described and explained in terms of men and male writers. The above examples are only a few of many. My hesitation with Stam being allowed to simply apply literature-based theories directly to the practice of lit-to-film adaptation lies in what I consider to be the inability to simply apply the theory behind the influences on the author and on the text that has been based on men, male authors, and an indefatigable male tradition to the theory behind female authors, their influences and their anxieties. A theorist writing on adaptation should know that to apply already established theories based on one particular textual medium will need to be adapted, convincingly, for another medium, not merely carried over.

Sandra Gilbert and Susan Gubar offer a new perspective on literary influence and anxiety when they broach the subject from the perspective of women writers, and with women writers as their central focus. It's fascinating what they uncover, and illuminating for how we must begin, and still haven't, to redesign how we think of textual creation and its metaphors. Gilbert and Gubar begin their book *The Madwoman in the Attic*, first published in 1979 and only one volume of two that focuses on women writing in the nineteenth and twentieth centuries, with a very direct question: "Is a pen a metaphorical penis?" (Gilbert and Gubar 1984, 3). In many ways, this was believed to be the case. Women were biological reproducers. Men were cultural reproducers. The womb was the woman's tool. The pen was the man's tool. "Male sexuality . . . is not just analogically but actually the essence of literary power. The poet's pen is in some sense (even more than figuratively) a penis" (4). Thus man gives birth to literature. He is its father. Gilbert and Gubar state that "the patriarchal notion that the writer 'fathers' his text just as God fathered the world is and has been all-pervasive in Western literary civilization" (4). They state further that "the text's author is a father, a progenitor, a procreator, an aesthetic patriarch whose pen is an instrument of generative power like his penis" (4). The text is a man's creation, his child, and interestingly, a man views his text much as he views his children in the eighteenth and nineteenth century, as his possessions. He is not the nurturer of his child, or text; he is the owner and ruler of that text. This is an important distinction to make as one attempts to understand the difficulties women writers encountered in trying to pick up the pen, or penis. Women did not try to own or rule their texts; they yearned to write. They yearned to pick up the pen, and for those who actually did pick up the pen, their yearning had grown to a point where they could not hold themselves back from writing.

Yet, where did thinking of texts as possessions and their authors as fathers leave women? Gilbert and Gubar ask, "Where does such an implicitly or explicitly patriarchal theory of literature leave literary women? If the pen is a metaphorical penis, with what organ can females generate texts?" (7). Their womb was the woman's organ for creating life, the future, and not for texts. In fact, all of women's reproductive organs were representative of this purpose of giving life as well. Thus women were mothers of children, but certainly not of texts. The widely-held belief that men were the fathers of texts inhibited many women from picking up the pen. In this context, women's use of the pen was seen as threatening to men, in a castrating manner. Women writers were considered thieves, robbing men of their right to culturally reproduce unchallenged. Gilbert and Gubar state that "the pen has been defined as not just accidentally but essentially a male 'tool,' and therefore not only inappropriate but actually alien to women" (8).

Criticism was heaped on women for picking up the pen. They were thought to be going against nature. As Gilbert and Gubar state, "not only is 'a woman that attempts the pen' an intrusive and 'presumptuous creature,' she is absolutely unredeeemable: no virtue can outweigh the 'fault' of her presumption because she has grotesquely crossed boundaries dictated by Nature" (8). Women were to remain in their domain of domesticity, giving birth to children, not texts. Most women adhered to these implicit instructions, but some did not. The women who did not, however, often apologized for functioning within a sphere they knew they were not welcome in. In the majority of female texts that were published from the seventeenth into the nineteenth centuries, the introductions by the authors include some form of apology, or explanation for why the female author is writing. Women writers had learned from the women who wrote before them. Gilbert and Gubar state:

> When seventeenth- and eighteenth-century women writers — and even some nineteenth-century literary women — did not confess that they thought it might actually be mad of them to want to attempt the pen, they did usually indicate that they felt in some sense apologetic about such a "presumptuous" pastime. (61)

Anne Finch and Anne Bradstreet are two such women. Finch admitted in her writing that she feared it was a fault within her character that she desired to write. Bradstreet admitted in her writing that no matter how well she wrote she would never be given credit for her work. If it was good, she implied, she would be accused of plagiarizing; but if it was at all possible to do so, if it didn't measure up in any way, her work would simply be scorned, because it was that of a woman. Anne Killigrew refused to apologize for her writing, and was attacked for plagiarism, a punishment for her refusal to be modest and self-deprecating. Other seventeenth- and eighteenth-century women who did not apologize for writing, such as Margaret Cavendish, the Duchess of Newcastle, and Aphra Behn, the first professional writer, were thought to be monstrous and freakish. Behn was considered an outcast in society, thought to be promiscuous and self-indulgent. She did not apologize for writing; she wrote in spite of what others thought. Her reputation suffered. Women writers after her knew this. Unfortunately, this was the legacy Behn left for future women writers, which unfortunately held more sway in their minds than her writing accomplishments.

It wasn't only the view of who should author texts, but it was also the content of male texts that inhibited women from writing. Male texts portrayed women in submissive roles, with no power, and often worse, as angels if submissive, or monsters if they had any kind of power. Women were imprisoned in male texts as objects. As Gilbert and Gubar state, "since both patriarchy and its texts subordinate and imprison women, before women can even attempt that pen which is so rigorously kept from them they must escape those male texts which . . . deny them the autonomy to formulate alternatives to the authority that has imprisoned them and kept them from attempting the pen" (13). Women writers had to fight against their portrayal in male texts that did not allow room for women to act as writers, a powerful role. If they wrote, they were powerful, and thus monsters. Women did not want to be thought of as monsters. This would ostracize them from society. Women feared picking up the pen, as it could literally destroy their lives.

According to Harold Bloom, as I've shown above, male authors had to contend with the anxiety of influence. According to Gilbert and Gubar, female authors, not sure which of their predecessors they should emulate, had to contend with the anxiety of authorship. "Thus the 'anxiety of influence' that a male poet experiences is felt by a female poet as an even more primary 'anxiety of authorship' — a radical fear that she cannot create, that because she can never become a 'precursor' the act of writing will isolate or destroy her" (49). Gilbert and Gubar explain this "anxiety of authorship" as "an anxiety built from complex and often barely conscious fears of that authority which seems to the female artist to be by definition inappropriate to her sex" (51). Some women writers tried to resolve this anxiety of authorship by impersonating a man. Although this allowed these writers more freedom to express themselves, they encountered the problem of how to write as women if they were impersonating men. "For a woman artist is, after all, a woman — that is her 'problem' — and if she denies her own gender she inevitably confronts an identity crisis as severe as the anxiety of authorship she is trying to surmount" (66). How can she write woman? This, inevitably, becomes the dilemma. Yet, despite the controversy surrounding their act of picking up the pen, women found a way to reveal themselves in their texts. The first step was picking up the pen, and using it. This act was the most difficult. The obstacles must have at times seemed insurmountable. However, we have certainly begun to see that women writers left a legacy for us to carry on; we just have to be willing to see beyond the biases we have developed as participants in our own patriarchal system. The first step towards understanding ourselves as modern women writers is looking at what made women write despite all the obstacles they encountered in how they were received as writers.

Women found pleasure in writing. What did it provide for them? It allowed for the release of their emotions, the expression of their thoughts, the healing of their pain, and it allowed them hope for the future, hope in the form of reform and change perhaps even through their own writing. Women's reasons for writing were different than those for men, and the conditions under which they wrote were different as well. Picking up the pen provided women with a purpose beyond how they could make themselves more beautiful to men, and more pleasing to men and their children and their parents in everything they did. Women writers rebelled against what they were supposed to be as women, even if their readers did not perceive their writing as rebellion. Just that they wrote was an act of rebellion.

Mary Wollstonecraft became one of the first women writers to show that "a literary woman must shatter the mirror that has so long reflected what every woman was supposed to be" (76). She attempted to shatter this mirror in *A Vindication of the Rights of Woman*. Her text presents itself as a revolutionary text, both at the time it was written, and in some ways, still so today. *Vindication* is a carefully composed rallying cry for women to be taught through education and experience to use reason to guide their own lives. And this is where my project that led to here began. I started with my fascination with Mary Wollstonecraft and her courage to be true to herself in a society that didn't allow even education for women let alone their ability to be who they wanted to be. It grew into a reverence for my foremother and an indebtedness towards her for picking up the pen so that I, and women writers today, have for the most part been freed of the anxiety of authorship, and don't have to think twice before picking up the pen. I have an idea, I run for my computer, and I know that for the most part, how I develop that idea will have as good a chance if it's written well to be published as any man's writing.

However, lit-to-film adaptation studies and theory concerns me. Here we are in the new millennium relying on the old ways of viewing texts, from a rather patriarchal perspective, rooted in literary and film traditions that have been male-dominated for over a century in the academy, and several centuries in literature. Still, we rely on the subtle metaphorical depiction of author to text, or past author to present author, as a father to son relationship of some sort. If it isn't being used to describe the relationship, it's being used to reject the relationship.

So here I go. For me, lit-to-film adaptation didn't fit with a partnership of sorts, or a marriage of media or texts, to describe the relationship between literature and film. I haven't been satisfied with other descriptions of this relationship. However, I know of one that I think works quite well, and it's worthy of consideration and has been so for centuries, but more appropriately in the last few centuries since women (from our foremothers to our mothers) began writing, too.

One of the most influential critical essays in my development as a scholar has been "Women's Time" by Julia Kristeva. In it, Kristeva contends that women's time can be thought of as different from the time frame or structure of history, or linear time. Toril Moi explains in her preface to Kristeva's essay that Kristeva believes "female subjectivity would seem to be linked to *cyclical* time (repetition) and to *monumental* time (eternity), at least in so far as both are ways of conceptualizing time from the perspective of motherhood and reproduction" (Moi 1986, 187). In her piece, Kristeva focuses intensively on motherhood, and subtly relates it to literary creation. She states that "the majority of women today see the possibility for fulfillment, if not entirely at least to a large degree, in bringing a child into the world. What does this desire for motherhood correspond to?" (206). Kristeva believes this is one of the new questions for the new generation, at the time she was writing (in the late 1970s). She explores the concept of pregnancy and what it can be seen as, when she writes:

> Pregnancy seems to be experienced as the radical ordeal of the splitting of the subject: redoubling up of the body, separation and coexistence of the self and of an other, of nature and consciousness, of physiology and speech . . . The arrival of the child, on the other hand, leads the mother into labyrinths of an experience that, without the child, she would only rarely encounter: love for an other . . . the slow, difficult and delightful apprenticeship in attentiveness, gentleness, forgetting oneself . . . It then becomes a creation in the strong sense of the term. For this moment, utopian? (206)

Kristeva immediately and almost abruptly counters this discussion of pregnancy, saying, "On the other hand, it is in the aspiration towards artistic and, in particular, literary creation that woman's desire for affirmation now manifests itself" (207). She connects pregnancy and women's desire for a child with the desire to affirm one's identity through artistic expression, especially through writing. And thus artistic creation can be seen as a mother–child relationship, with the creation developing inside the creator, gestating, and then arriving.

With reference to another essay that Kristeva published two years previous to "Women's Time," Moi, in her preface to this essay "Stabat Mater" (the mother stood), explains that Kristeva questions in this essay why "the feminist critique of the traditional representation of motherhood still has not produced a new understanding of women's continued desire to have children" (160). Kristeva, Moi says, answers her own question by pointing to "the need for a new understanding of the mother's body . . . Kristeva herself has not really followed up her own 'programme' for research into maternity" (161). Perhaps if she had we'd have more evidence for using the metaphor of mother and child for artistic creation of any kind. "Stabat Mater" itself is an experimental exploration into the doubling that comes with pregnancy and giving birth. Structurally, Kristeva organizes the essay with sections of prose typical of any critical essay, but then that divides rather abruptly at times into two columns, almost to reflect the doubling that occurs with motherhood, the doubling and then the going back to being one, but never really being one again. She writes in one of these columns about her connection to her child even after she has given birth:

> My body is no longer mine, it doubles up, suffers, bleeds, catches colds . . . the pain, its pain — it comes from inside, never remains apart, other, it inflames me at once, with a second's respite. As if that was what I had given birth to and, not willing to part from me, insisted on coming back, dwelled in me permanently. One does not give birth in pain, one gives birth to pain: the child represents it and henceforth it settles in, it is continuous. (167)

This relationship as it is described here can be applied to an author and her text. However, it can also be applied to lit-to-film adaptation, the adapting of a text into another text, the creation of a text out of a source text. The source text is pregnant with possibilities — what can it bring forth? The adapter gestates his/her adaptation within the body of the source text, then the adapted text is released into the world. Kristeva writes: "The calm of another life, the life of that other who wends his way while I remain henceforth like a framework. Still life. There is him, however, his own flesh, which was mine yesterday. Death, then, how could I yield to it?" (169).

The child will stand for itself, as it will also reflect the mother and how it was formed inside of her, and formed of her. At the same time, the child as Kristeva explains it, will also always be inside the mother. The connection will always be there, while both can stand on their own, and perhaps be known without being visibly connected to each other. In much the same way, the adapted text is a creation that grows out of the mother, who was also a creation that grew out of a maternal presence and body. Just as with a film adaptation, when you see the credits go across the screen that this film was based on a novel or short story, it is clear that this film has a source text. It has experienced a different creation process than a film that has come from an original screenplay, a screenplay that delineates a story idea directly for film, not one that adapts a story previously told in another medium. The film adaptation has gestated inside another body or text, and then is ready for its arrival as a fully formed individual text.

This is one way of looking at lit-to-film adaptation, from a feminist perspective I suppose, although Hélène Cixous says it quite well, allowing for perhaps a more "equal" view of the mother–child metaphor by expanding it to parent–child in her essay "The Laugh of the Medusa":

> It will be up to man and woman to render obsolete the former relationship and all its consequences, to consider the launching of a brand-new subject, alive, with defamiliialization. Let us demater-paternalize rather than deny woman, in an effort to avoid the cooptation of procreation, a thrilling era of the body. Let us defetishize. Let's get away from the dialectic which has it that the only good father is a dead one, or that the child is the death of his parents. The child is the other, but the other without the violence, bypassing loss, struggle. (1997, 359)

Cixous argues against the death of the author here, and interestingly offers an apt metaphor for artistic creation in that the child is the other, the creation from the parents, without the violence, the loss, the death of those who have given it life. Cixous goes on to write that "there are thousands of ways of living one's pregnancy: to have or not to have with that still invisible other a relationship of another intensity" (359). Here she is addressing women, saying that becoming pregnant with a child is only one way of "living one's pregnancy" and that there are many ways to have such a connection in life, leaving the idea open for artistic creation fulfilling the desire to live one's pregnancy. And so this isn't relegated to only women. And I know that men have the desire that can be metaphorically described as yearning to give birth to something, something to which they can develop an intense relationship with, and nurture and guide to fruition. Women have been fitting themselves into the metaphors created by a male-dominated world that often only sees the varieties of life through the male experience. However, often women's experience will suffice quite fittingly to describe and represent conditions and desires in life as well. "Bring the other to life" (359), Cixous declares. She continues: "Women know how to live detachment; giving birth is neither losing nor increasing. It's adding to life an other" (359). And, perhaps that is exactly what a literary text offers when it is adapted or created into another rendering of itself; it is adding to life an other, or another, yet an entity that can also stand on its own and for itself.

My middle child graduated from high school last year. At one of his friend's graduation parties, I sat with the mother of one of his other friends. I asked her if she was ready to let her son go, and how she was doing with it. (That's pretty much what mothers discuss at graduation parties.) She said, very matter-of-factly, that she wouldn't have done her job as a mother, as a parent, successfully if her son wasn't prepared to head out into the "real world." She went on to say that this is what we prepare them for, and she was proud of herself and him that he was ready to be out in the world on his own. She was confident he'd do well, and that was most important to her. I thought of my own son as we sat talking, and watched him playing volleyball with his buddies. He'd become his own person, and would now stand on his own. I am his source text, from where he has come, his beginning and essence have come from me, but what he does with what goes with him will be ultimately that which defines him as an entity, separate from me.

Personally (obviously) but also intellectually, I find motherhood to be an apt metaphor for any act of creation, and its many intricacies from the process to the product, and any stage along the way. I would like to see it explored much further, and by greater minds than mine.

Chapter 21

Twelve Observations about Literature-to-Film Adaptation Studies: A Disgruntled Novelist's Perspective

1. It's not true that literature has been studied as a discipline for thousands of years, while film has only been more recently explored. English literature as a discipline didn't take hold until the late nineteenth century, and focused critical study of English literature didn't really begin until the early twentieth century. Film began to be studied at about this same time, albeit with much less rigor and fervor at first. Yet, although film is a bit behind, it's not as behind as film theorists like to imply to their readers.

2. Novels are older than film, but not by very much. And, they had to wait a long time to garner respect as art, much like film. Short fiction, on the other hand, is not much older than film; in fact, short fiction and film are roughly about the same age.

3. Novels aren't considered higher art than film by everyone, and intelligent, informed individuals do exist outside the walls of academia who appreciate film as a text as much as they do a novel. In fact, some individuals within the walls of academia privilege film while they dismiss or overlook novels, especially more contemporary novels.

4. Even if it is assumed that film studies is still trying to find its place in the academy (of which I'm not convinced), all of the liberal arts and humanities are struggling in the academy right now. Film probably has more of a chance of survival since the academy is consumer-driven, and also driven by how much money one can make or the lucrative job one can procure when leaving the university. The film industry is burgeoning, as is mass media and communication studies, and jobs are certainly available in the occupations associated with these areas.

5. Writers can't just pick up the pen and start writing, while filmmakers require phe-nomenal amounts of financial support to complete a film. Writers need training, money, and a room of their own (Virginia Woolf advocated this for women in the

1920s, but now it can be used to justify that all writers have such needs) to write a novel and actively pitch it to get it published. They need time, too, and lots of it. Time to be creative, and time to pound the pavement so to speak, trying to "sell their wares." The rarity of a J. K. Rowling, a struggling single mother picking up a pen to write blockbuster novels that subsequently turn into films, is about as common for novelists as the exceedingly low-budget films like *The Blair Witch Project* or *Paranormal Activity* making it big are to budding filmmakers.

6. Similarly, money is an issue for novelists, as it is for filmmakers. Obviously, money is not as much of an issue for novelists, but often filmmakers have more of it than novelists do; thus in some ways, it evens out (or doesn't). A novelist can't devote the time they need to produce a worthwhile work if they have to punch a clock and feed their family. If theorists want to assume best-case scenario for a novelist writing a book, then they need to be fair and assume best-case scenario for a filmmaker as well. That's only just. Instead scholars explain how easy it is to write a novel and how difficult to make a film. Linda Costanza Cahir states: "Movie-making is big business. It is expensive, arguably the most expensive art form. In contrast, literature is, arguably, the least expensive art form. All that is needed to create a literary work is a pen and paper" (2006, 72). Is it that easy to write a novel that resonates with readers, and sells? That hasn't been my experience nor that of most — no, all — of my writer friends and colleagues.

7. The author in most or at least many lit-to-film adaptations is not (at least literally) dead. In fact, many authors work on the film adaptation of their own work: Michael Cunningham, Cormac McCarthy, John Irving, Dennis Lehane. In the adaptations I've studied of women's novels, I don't know of any of these writers having helped to work on the adaptation of their work. However, I won't sign off on mine unless I can be a part of it. I'm certainly as deserving of doing so, if the occasion should arise, as the male authors cited above.

8. Obviously, there are more metaphors to be created for creation beyond "fathers" and "sons." Why mothers and children haven't been considered as a more apt metaphor I have no idea, besides the fact that the tradition of a male-dominated society still ties us to old ways of thinking, and being. Women, as potential mothers, hold the potential for giving life to something new inside of them, whether they choose to or not, or whether — should they choose to — that life turns out okay, or healthy, or extraordinary, and the anxiety associated with that. How rife motherhood, pregnancy and childbirth are with metaphorical significance in relating to creation, and especially, lit-to-film adaptation.

9. Adaptation studies often is (and shouldn't be) used as a guise to teach film. Adaptation studies should focus on the intertextual relationship between the source text and the film adaptation text, and the process of reaching the product.

10. Adaptation studies as discussed among scholars could be construed as condoning plagiarism to undergraduate students. Unfortunately, students are not allowed a Derridean argument when they deny the idea of originality in the paper they've written that borrows from others in an intertextual manner, which is consequently unacceptable in the academic community.

11. In his book *From Where You Dream: The Process of Writing Fiction*, Robert Olen

Butler explains how closely related fiction techniques and film techniques are. In his chapter "Cinema of the Mind," he makes it clear that he's not talking "about how to translate a book to the screen or how a film could be transformed into a novel, but about deep and essential common ground" (2005, 63). He's addressing fiction writers specifically when he writes: "All of the techniques that filmmakers employ . . . have direct analogies in fiction. And because fiction writers are the writer-directors of inner consciousness, you will need to develop the techniques of film as well" (64). Butler sees a relationship between writing fiction and making films that should be encouraging to both novelists and filmmakers as they combine efforts in whatever way it happens to coordinate a lit-to-film adaptation.

12. Using this chapter from Butler's book with students helps them in understanding how closely related the processes of creating literary narratives and film narratives really are, and in doing so, demands at the same time a better understanding of both, and a respect for both as texts, and art.

Chapter 22

Literature-to-Film Adaptation Analysis: Charting Some New Territory

So, how does one teach students to analyze lit-to-film adaptations? It's important to me that there are some mechanisms in place to rely on for analyzing lit-to-film adaptations. If my novel were made into a film, I would want to know that critical approaches are in place that can be applied specifically to lit-to-film adaptation, not only as a product but also as a process. For one thing, it's necessary for an adapter to know that he or she is going to be held accountable for the outcome of the adaptation, but I think it's also essential that an adapter expect their work and the result of that work to be intelligently and extensively discussed, if it is in fact worthy of such discussion. And, perhaps if such discussions became more commonplace, adapters would be more concerned with the intellectual quality of their work and less with the amount of money they make. Perhaps they'd be more encouraged to fulfill their intellectual obligations to the literary text. I'm aware that brilliant adaptations have been achieved, but at the same time I'm also aware of the adaptations that have been more focused on profit than the art of the process or product. My experience with screenwriters, albeit amateurs, resulted in one horrific experience that opened my eyes to how vulnerable to the adapter an author's work can be, and how utterly dependent. As I mentioned in an earlier chapter, one potential adapter of my work wanted to change the focus of the story (a story primarily focused on women's lives and experiences) from the female characters to the male characters, because he felt the film wasn't going to make any kind of worthwhile profit unless it brought men into the theaters. The only way to do that, he believed, was to make the film from the male perspective.

So, although I try to view lit-to-film adaptation from the perspective of a critic, a scholar, desiring to analyze lit-to-film adaptations, and consequently, teach my students how to conduct such analyses, it's my always-present perspective of a novelist that fuels my concern. Admittedly, my perspective as that of neurotic novelist panicking over seeing my creation made into some sort of monster I wouldn't have approved of had I been able needs to be quelled at times to focus on the work of analyzing lit-to-film adaptations that I study, and teach to my students. When researching film adaptation theory and scholarly discussions concerning how to analyze adaptations, I purposefully limited my focus to lit-to-film adaptation even though some of the most illuminating and thought-provoking discussions of adaptation focus on adaptation processes of varying kinds. For my work, especially with students, I remained focused on lit-to-film connections, thus the most useful research for me focused on literature and film.

What I found in my research was somewhat problematic. First of all, film adaptation scholars are discontented with comparison studies of literature to film. This is clear, and from one scholar to the next, they adamantly disapprove of any comparison or fidelity studies, claiming that the hierarchy that is inherent in that comparison is unfair to film. However, in discussions by most scholars, the central focus of most of them seems to be fidelity criticism, debunking it but also getting caught up in it themselves in spite of how reductive and limiting they argue that it is. And I don't entirely disagree that fidelity criticism is limiting. It's not only potentially limiting, but it can be dreadfully dull.

What I also found increasingly troubling in my research was the defensive tone in all of this writing, depending on which side of the fence each scholar preferred to stand, so to speak. And, it did seem that the majority of the more experienced scholars on adaptation studies, the ones who'd been writing about it most extensively, had both feet firmly planted on the film side of that fence. Regardless, though, the problem I encountered that seemed at the heart of the disenchantment with comparative studies was that it didn't seem to be as much a problem of comparative studies as it was a problem of competition studies that concerned them. Yet there at the heart of it, I had to wonder if they were fueling the fire rather than providing another way of looking at lit-to-film adaptation. The question these scholars abhorred was that infamous one, did you like the book or the movie better? And their discontent was rooted in the most frequent answer being a personal preference for the book. This was mentioned in one way or another in every scholar's discussion of lit-to-film adaptation. And as I was reading, I felt like I was in the middle of a battlefield — the literary enthusiasts (I heard from these folks more than read them) on one side proclaiming it impossible to adapt a novel of intense rigor and rife with meaning into a film, particularly a commercial film (my god!) — and the film scholars on the other side, claiming how well a film can translate a novel, of any quality, especially those of the best quality, into an artistic masterpiece. It was as if I needed to put my hands up and say, okay, okay, I get it.

The literary types (and often literary-trained) are suspicious of film's take on their favorite novels, the ones they've been teaching, and even the ones they've escaped to when summer comes and they can read what they like. The film people are insistent upon the ability of a film to take a remarkable story, written fastidiously and brilliantly, and bring it to "life" in a thoughtful, interesting way, designed equally as brilliantly. And, these folks are vociferously adamant that the film *should not* have to be prostrate in any way to its source text. Could there be some sort of compromise? Because what I discovered was not much lit-to-film adaptation analysis going on, while literary analysis and film analysis continued to thrive and evolve and engage. And what I didn't find was much pleasure emanating from any of this quiet ongoing battle.

For scholars, there is a pleasure in exploring texts. Or there should be. The fun factor (and I say this from the perspective of a scholar who loves to think and ponder and ruminate and argue and challenge) in lit-to-film adaptation studies is missing. It's not there. The love of film adaptations is not jumping off the page. I sense tension and tight-lipped scowls and defensive posturing, shoulders stiff and fists positioned for battle.

I'm going to go out there on a very fragile limb, or so it seems after all the research I've done, and say that I do not have a problem with comparative studies being the basis for lit-to-film adaptation analysis. It makes sense. Any of us who have read a book and seen a film of that book naturally compare and contrast the two. It's what we do in life with just about everything, and so it's what we do with texts, especially two texts that have similarities and differences. What's more interesting and funny than looking for what's the same and what's different? *Sesame Street* used to have an exercise for children (and maybe it still does) that would appear a few times in the hour of each show, asking the young viewers to find what doesn't belong, or what is different from the rest. Similarly, in a restaurant, an exercise on the placemat might include seem-ingly two of the same picture side by side. The instructions tell the diner something is minutely different about them and the diner, while waiting for their food, must exam-ine the pictures closely to detect that tiny difference. Our minds work that way, and doing so challenges our minds.

Noticing difference and defining our lives and experiences in terms of difference is almost a way of life. We have been taught to think of difference as a way to raise ourselves up above others, if we fall into that trap, and I think we all have at one time or another. I would assume we've all felt somehow "less" in some identification of ourselves as different. But difference can be celebrated, and we can learn from dif-ference. We can also learn that things we thought were so different from one another can be strikingly similar in other ways. Determining these differences and similarities, where they come from, what they mean, how they can be detected, are interesting and represent a powerful tool to teach and exercise critical thinking skills.

That being said, I honestly couldn't find a way around comparative studies when trying to come up with a way to critically analyze lit-to-film adaptations. What we need to do is to get rid of the competition inherent in comparative studies of literature and film. We need to allow for pleasure in adaptation studies, which are, whether we like it or not, comparative studies. I don't think scholars will find comparative studies so dis-tasteful if we view adaptation studies as interesting, fascinating, instead of a privileging of one of the texts involved in the study. Julie Sanders in *Adaptation and Appropriation* embraces the idea of pleasure as necessary in looking at adaptation:

> [I]t is the very endurance and survival of the source text that enables the ongoing process of juxtaposed readings that are crucial to the cultural operations of adapta-tion, and the ongoing experiences of pleasure for the reader or spectator in tracing the intertextual relationships. It is this inherent sense of play, produced in part by the activation of our informed sense of similarity and difference between the texts being invoked, and the connected interplay of expectation and surprise, that for me lies at the heart of the experience of adaptation and appropriation. (2006, 25)

Sanders introduces in this passage the nature of the comparative analysis that really can't help but be applied to adaptations. Adaptation studies must be viewed as an intertextual comparison. Intertextuality is not easy to define, and the concept is often misused in certain instances, but in the case of adaptation, intertextuality unmistakably is involved. Sanders makes it clear that as she treats them in her book, at a theoretical level, "the processes of adaptation and appropriation . . . are in many respects a sub-section of the over-arching practice of intertextuality" (17). Lit-to-film adaptation falls within the confines of the subject of her book, and is indeed a matter of intertextuality.

The concept of intertextuality was first proposed by Julia Kristeva and her development of this concept grew out of her study of Mikhail Bakhtin's work on dialogism. Bakhtin in his *The Dialogic Imagination* defines dialogism as the following:

> Everything means, is understood, as a part of a greater whole — there is a constant interaction between meanings, all of which have the potential of conditioning others. Which will affect the other, how it will do so and in what degree is what is actually settled at the moment of utterance. (1981, 426)

Kristeva grounded this idea of the interaction between meanings, on meanings in texts. She defines intertextuality in the following passage from her book, *Revolution in Poetic Language*:

> The term intertextuality denotes this transposition of one (or several) sign-system(s) into another . . . If one grants that every signifying practice is a field of transpositions of various signifying systems (an intertextuality), one then understands that its 'place' of enunciation and its denoted 'object' are never single, complete and identical to themselves, but always plural, shattered, capable of being tabulated. (1986a, 111)

Thus a text is not a self-contained, individually authored whole, but the absorption and transformation of other texts. But in applying intertextuality to adaptation, as I myself did when adapting my novel from another novel, intertextuality, or the relationship between texts, texts that always contain intertexts, certain distinctions need to be investigated. What I discovered was that intertextuality can refer to its more rigid definition, that all texts are made of other texts, and all texts then have relationships with other texts. When I was writing my novel, I was influenced by other texts without being aware that I was. My text holds in it other texts. This is inevitable, and an inescapable intertextuality that occurs. However, there is a purposeful intertextuality that also occurs when writing. And this can happen by different degrees. When I was doing research for my novel, I chose those texts to inform my own text. It was a purposeful choice on my part as the author. Editing the work of another and also adapting the work of another, or using direct passages from another text, are extreme examples of purposeful intertextuality. An editing of a manuscript by someone other than the author is an intertextual endeavor in that it is taking the work of another and adding to it and deleting from it words, bits of text, to alter the text. It is adding text by someone who is not the author of the text to an already existing text by that author. Adapting someone else's text into another text is also an example of purposeful intertextuality.

And using text — words, passages, direct quotes — from another text for one's own text is purposeful intertextuality.

The reasoning behind making these distinctions is twofold. For one thing, purposeful intertextuality has the potential to be carried out irresponsibly, and therefore requires a means to hold the intertextual undertakings accountable. At the same time, a purposeful undertaking carried out responsibly, thoughtfully, and intelligently, can produce not only a brilliant text, it can also offer itself up as engaging material for analysis and for attempts at understanding its inner workings, not only as a text itself, but as the product of an intertextual project.

This all being stipulated as the basis for the critical approaches I put forth here, I find the idea of *intertextual comparison* most applicable to lit-to-film adaptation studies so that intellectual pleasure can be achieved through such analysis. When Linda Hutcheon refers to adaptation in her *The Theory of Adaptation* as "an extended intertextual engagement with the adapted work" (2006, 8) or source text, I see this engagement as being of great interest when analyzing both the process and product of a lit-to-film adaptation. Hutcheon also explains the "doubled definition of adaptation" (22) as a product and as a process, and that using such a definition is "one way to address the various dimensions of the broader phenomenon of adaptation" (22).

In the next section, I describe five different critical approaches under the umbrella of intertextual comparison that can be seen as specific to lit-to-film adaptations. I've labeled them as the following: adaptability analysis, adaptation process analysis, fidelity/infidelity analysis, specificity analysis, and audience reception anxiety analysis. To help to see them put into practice, I will draw from lit-to-film adaptations that I've used with my students. I do not offer case studies as I don't find them helpful in other books if I'm not teaching those adaptations. Most often, I hadn't read the source text or viewed the film in the books I'd researched, and thus the case studies weren't able to provide me with much enlightenment as a result. What I do here is offer some suggestions for using the books and films I rely on as examples. This way, students can approach these lit-to-film connections with some basic guidelines, while they can veer off on their own tangents, perhaps finding something in the book and film that fascinates them. Also, if they don't know the book or film, they can at least see how one could approach a lit-to-film adaptation through application of the critical approach in question. The rest of the section discusses the adaptation of short story to film, and also mentions the use of previously established critical perspectives that could be aptly applied to lit-to-film adaptations.

Note: Before engaging in any of these analytical approaches to a specific lit-to-film adaptation, I strongly recommend a close textual reading of both the literature and the film. A close textual reading will most often, if carried out for its optimal use in this analysis, require a second reading/viewing of each text, even if that second look is to focus on the details of each text. This will not only be helpful in applying an analytical approach to the lit-to-film adaptation, but it will also help in choosing which approach would work best for one's purposes and what one has discovered by performing a close textual analysis of each piece.

Adaptability Analysis

Hutcheon asks: "Are some kinds of stories and their worlds more easily adaptable than others?" (2006, 15). She goes on to say that linear realist novels are more adaptable to the screen than experimental novels. However, is this necessarily the case? Adaptability analysis is the study of such concerns. Such an analysis allows for a study of the source text and its adaptability. Obviously, since the source text has been made into a film, it is "adaptable," but perhaps the source text is experimental in nature and not seemingly adaptable. Or, perhaps it could be seen as easily adaptable as a linearly structured film, but the film isn't made that way. Adaptability analysis of film adaptation allows for a study of how the literature is reconceived for a film, looking at both the book and the film, and studying the adaptability of the book, and then how that adaptability pans out in the film. This approach encourages a particularly close textual reading of the book, but also of the film adaptation as well. This analysis might look at the book and the film from a broader perspective or focus in on smaller points and finer details of both texts.

This approach seems to me particularly important since my own novel is experimental in nature, yet I don't see this as compromising its adaptability. In fact, my stance is that any text is adaptable. However, the success of that adaptation is firmly rooted in how well the adapter has identified the limitations of the text but also the opportunities of the text. In an adaptation analysis of the source text, these limitations and opportunities could be identified and explored, and then the film could be studied as to how attentive the adapter was to them.

Frankenstein might just rank as the most elusive text to adapt. It would not appear so, due to the countless number of plays and films, and various other types of adaptations that have been based on Mary Shelley's novel. However, I contend that it could indeed be its elusive nature that attracts these adaptations, and as yet, not one has captured the intensity of this text. Perhaps it is not meant to be "captured." An adaptability analysis of *Frankenstein* would focus on the text and its textualities. Its adaptability to film would be explored, and the techniques that the medium of film could offer the text. The types of difficulties that are encountered when approaching the text to adapt it might be explored. The advantage of this approach is learning how to think like an adapter.

Some questions that might be asked of *Frankenstein* and either its 1931 film adaptation or its 1994 film adaptation, in conjunction with the novel's adaptability, are as follows:

1. Is *Frankenstein*, the novel, adaptable? What are its complexities? What are the difficult aspects of the novel to adapt? For example, Mary Shelley herself does not provide the actual details of the scientific experiment that leads to the creation of the creature, and she is altogether vague concerning Victor's discovery of how to animate life. How might this experiment then be adapted to film? (How has the experiment been adapted in both the 1931 and the 1994 films?)
2. How many adaptations have been made of *Frankenstein*? Research the adaptations that try to follow the book closely, and those that veer away from the novel.
3. *Frankenstein* of 1931 was one of the first horror films, and was actually based

on the play by Peggy Webling, which was an adaptation of the novel. The 1931 monster doesn't speak, and his actions are not motivated by revenge, but are portrayed as disastrous bumblings of a dumb brute. How does Webling's play adapt the novel and how does it influence the adaptation of the 1931 film?

4. *Mary Shelley's Frankenstein*, released in 1994, was an attempt to adapt the novel more faithfully, as the creature is smart and speaks, but the father/son showdown near the end of the novel veers from the novel, reflecting more modern day concerns. Yet, how does this film show the difficulties in adapting *Frankenstein* more faithfully? What obstacles does the film seem to have encountered in adapting the novel?

5. *Rowing in the Wind*, released in 1989, focused on Shelley's writing of the novel. Since we know so much information about the circumstances surrounding the writing of *Frankenstein*, this film proves insightful in showing how a writer's creation is influenced by her life and at the same time influences her life. What statements might this film be making about the adaptability of *Frankenstein*?

6. What might be an example of an adaptation idea for *Frankenstein* that incorporates one of the many fascinating interpretations of the text that have yet to be broached by film?

Adaptation Process Analysis

Adaptation process analysis looks closely at the process by which the novel was adapted and the film made. Hutcheon explains that

> an emphasis on process allows us to expand the traditional focus of adaptation studies on medium-specificity and individual comparative case studies in order to consider as well relations among the major modes of engagement: that is, it permits us to think about how adaptations allow people to tell, show, or interact with stories. (2006, 22)

This analysis of the process is usually dependent upon access to "behind the scenes" information. However, with the incipience of DVDs that often include behind-the-scenes mini-documentaries, and almost always provide the option of commentary from the filmmaker and actors, access to this information has become more readily available, and an adaptation process analysis is more possible now for many adaptations. Also, novelists, screenwriters, and directors seem more willing in recent years to reveal their processes. For example, at least two books are available that discuss the making of *Memento*, one book including the short story written by one of the Nolan brothers, which both brothers used for adapting the film. John Irving wrote a spry memoir, *My Movie Business*, which documents the making of the film from his novel of the same name, *The Cider House Rules*, for which he wrote the screenplay and to which four directors were attached until one finally managed to get the film made.

I do want to address an issue with Robert Stam that exemplifies the need to theorize while an opportunity to engage in an understanding of lit-to-film adaptation and specific lit-to-film adaptations is being ignored or completely missed. Stam states, in his insistence to downplay the literary text as the "original" source:

How, then, might the new technologies facilitate new approaches to adaptation and to adaptation studies? . . . Laser disks and DVDs which include sequences cut from released versions of films implicitly cast doubt on the idea of the 'original' or definitive text, revealing its status as the arbitrary result of constantly changing decisions about inclusion and exclusion. (Stam and Raengo 2005a, 13)

Or, the new technologies might facilitate a new way of analyzing lit-to-film adaptations by investigating the process by which the adaptation was carried out. What's more, these technologies provide more information about the film aspect of lit-to-film adaptation than we've ever had access to previously. Thus what Stam misses about these DVDs is that we're given information about the process that helps us to understand and analyze the product in a way never imaginable. We actually get to watch the process in action, or at least some of it. We can analyze the scenes that were deleted and try to figure out why. Bottom line, these DVDs are of great value in analyses of lit-to-film adaptations.

If one were to approach the film *The Hours* from an adaptation process perspective, the DVD provides valuable features to examine. One special feature, "The Lives of Mrs. Dalloway," interviews the novelist Michael Cunningham, the screenwriter David Hare, and the director Stephen Daldry. The interviews are done separately, but are joined together in the order that they each affected the outcome of the product, in order then of their parts in the process. All three men offer insightful commentary to how *The Hours* came to be from each of their different vantage points. The personality of each individual is captured particularly well. Another special feature is a group interview of the women of *The Hours*, Meryl Streep who played Clarissa Vaughn, Nicole Kidman who played Virginia Woolf, and Julianne Moore who played Laura Brown. It offers some behind-the-scenes footage, and the actors discuss what it was like to play these parts as they laugh together about the long hours on the set of *The Hours*. A biographical background documentary of Virginia Woolf is provided on the DVD, which is especially helpful in understanding the character in the film and the portrayal of the character. (This documentary is very helpful for teaching *The Hours*. Very few students, it seems, are familiar with Virginia Woolf.) Questions that might be asked of this material are as follows.

1. How do the contributions of the novelist, the screenwriter, and the director affect the outcome of this film?
2. What are some of the constraints the actors face, and also the director, and how do they work around them in a way that seems fitting for the work of an adaptation?
3. How does the background information on Virginia Woolf help frame a better understanding of the character's portrayal in the film?
4. How does this information provided on the DVD allow for a more in-depth understanding of the film, and its adaptation of the book?
5. How does this information reveal and explain the intricacies involved in making this novel into a film?
6. Finally, what aspects or elements of the product reflect the vicissitudes and intricacies of the process?

Thus adaptation process analysis focuses on what went into making the film adaptation and requires availability of information that often can be found on the DVD, and also information that can be found on www.imdb.com, www.metacritic.com, and in articles, interviews, and reviews that can be researched. As I've said, many of the well-known and more recent films are associated with books detailing the making of that particular film; screenplays can be found on the Internet and often screenplays of more major films can be bought in book form.

Fidelity/Infidelity Analysis

Although fidelity criticism has been treated as a heinous crime consistently committed against film adaptations among film adaptation theorists and scholars, I insist on retaining it as a valuable means to analyze film adaptation. Admittedly, when used simply to point out the similarities and differences between the two texts, or what was not included or what was replaced, it can result in a dreadfully dull analysis. However, I've coined a different phrase: fidelity/infidelity analysis. Fidelity criticism or as I prefer, fidelity/infidelity analysis, can be applied to lit-to-film adaptation analysis to explore an understanding of why the film was made the way it was, and why the filmmaker adapted the novel the way they did, and what about the novel was used to formulate the film. This type of analysis is not to be used to say the film did this as well as the book, or the film didn't achieve the adaptation as it should or could have. This analysis is not meant for evaluative or judgment purposes or in any way to encourage the competition studies that seem a staple of this discipline. Instead, fidelity/infidelity analysis can illuminate why certain scenes might have been used in the film, but weren't in the book, or why certain scenes were retained in the film and some almost "as is." When an important scene in the book is dropped, it's valuable to consider, based on an understanding one has come to about both the book and the film, what the reasoning might be behind losing the scene as well as why one might be added, or kept.

This analysis can be applied to the film *Children of Men*, adapted from P. D. James's *The Children of Men*. The film drastically reinvents the book in filmic form, yet both build from the basic premise of a future plagued by, among other disasters, universal infertility. The film is so different from the book that an analysis could be quite extensive (see Appendix C). Some questions that could be asked of this film adaptation are as follows.

1. How does Alfonso Cuarón, the director, and those who work with him create the documentary effect, and why? What does this style bring to the film?
2. How does Cuarón's style as director compare/contrast with James's style as author?
3. The screenwriter made drastic changes to the plot and the characters. What was the effect the screenwriters (supposedly five in this case) were going for? Why might those changes have been made taking into account the main thrust of the film, in comparison to the main thrust of the book?
4. There are two scenes, one in the book and one in the movie, that both depict a chaotic attack on the main characters. The scene in the book is towards the end, while

the scene in the film is more towards the beginning, and in each scene a major but different character dies. How does the choice of the character who dies in the film reflect the choice of the character who dies in the book?

5. Why might Cuarón have chosen to use long scenes with continuous shooting? How does this affect the feel of the movie, while challenge the feel of the book?

Fidelity/infidelity analysis is the rare occasion where neither fidelity nor infidelity is necessarily a good thing or a bad thing. It depends on how the degree of fidelity or infidelity influences the outcome of the film and in what ways and why. This is the question that predominates: why? This analysis involves an examination of why the filmmaker chose to make the changes that were made, or why very few changes were made, or for what greater overarching purpose and effect either changes or no changes were made. The crux of this analysis is to determine whether the fidelity or infidelity accomplishes a certain goal or feel in the film, and whether or not that might have or might not have been the desired goal.

Specificity Analysis

Specificity analysis can be an intriguing way to look at each text in its respective medium and how each medium is used to bring out the story it does. This study can focus on the techniques specific to each medium, and explore why certain techniques were used in each medium. It can be interesting to see how one technique in the book brings out the same effect in the film but through a different technique. Perhaps a tone is created in the book due to the minimalist format of the text, and its sparseness. It might give the characters a simplistic feel. However, in the film, this same effect is brought out through the types of props used, or the costuming of the characters, even their hair and makeup. However, different techniques can be used to purposefully effect different results, and this can be examined as well. It can usually be assumed that the director planned for the effect that has been achieved, but the viewer might see something in the film that the director didn't plan for a viewer to see, much like a novelist can't possibly know the myriad of ways their novel will be interpreted. So the questions for specificity analysis concern what techniques were used in the novel to bring out certain aspects of the narrative or story, and what techniques were used in the film to bring out certain aspects of the story. Such questioning could lead to a discussion of different techniques used in each medium to achieve similar effects, and different techniques used to achieve purposefully different effects. It might also involve a discussion of similar techniques used in both the novel and the film — such as point of view, or the plot structure, among others.

The specificity approach can be used to analyze *The Constant Gardener* in a very focused manner. In John Le Carré's spy novel, chapters 11 though 14 are various intertexts of emails, news articles, letters, excerpts from books, documents, police files, transcripts, and one very nasty note that indicates to Justin Quayle that his wife had been threatened before she was killed. Justin tells the boy working on Tessa's computer: "Whatever she was working on, I want to follow her footsteps and read whatever's in there" (2001, 251). This is a rather experimental format for a spy novel, and cannot be treated in the film as it's presented in the book; it would be too dull. Thus these documents and emails and correspondences are revealed in different ways, although some can be seen on the computer although not read. The information must be provided to the film audience in different ways, resulting in changes made and various techniques used in the film that the book doesn't, or couldn't, use. Questions that might be asked of this examination include:

1. What information do the intertexts of chapters 11 through 14 of *The Constant Gardener* provide to the reader of the book and why are they important?
2. How is this information revealed in the film, and what techniques are employed to do so? How much of this information is revealed in the film? What is excluded?
3. How important is this information to the film in contrast to the book? That is, what is the main thrust of the film in comparison to the book, and how does the information fit into what each text is trying to convey to the reader/viewer?
4. In what ways does Ralph Fiennes as Justin Quayle have to incorporate the discovery of this information into his character, especially how this information must transform Justin's demeanor in ways the viewer might not expect?
5. On another note, how does the film bring out the setting of Africa using different techniques from the book? Africa seems a more dominating presence in the film than in the book. Why might this effect have been a goal of the filmmaker?

Specificity analysis is a useful type of analysis for helping students become more accustomed to applying the tools they've learned about film to an analysis of the lit-to-film adaptation. It can lead to an important study of the adaptation of one medium into another, and how this is achieved.

Audience Reception Anxiety Analysis

Audience reception anxiety can influence the filmmaker in both positive and negative ways. Such an analysis would require research about the audience's expected reception of the film. What was predicted about how the audience might respond? How well-known is the film? Is there a particular group that might have an expectant concern about the outcome of the adaptation? Thus this type of analysis might explore the anxiety the filmmaker might feel in reaching the audience. This anxiety might affect the feel of the film, the way the film was made, and how the book was interpreted. The anxiety could be attributed to the subject matter of the book, the popularity of the book or its popularity among a certain population or group, the notoriety of the author, or even the author's biographical background. For example, Zack Snyder was interviewed for an article about his making of *Watchmen*, the film adaptation of the graphic novel. He expressed in the article his concern for appeasing the avid followers of the graphic novel. And, in fact, he stayed very faithful to the novel, which may have been due to the anxiety produced by the expectant readership. Also, another factor that may have led to some anxiety on Snyder's part could have been caused by Allan Moore's refusal to be named in the credits as author of his novel. In the article, it claimed that Moore had been so disenchanted with previous film adaptations of his work that he refused to have his name put to this one, even as author of the source text, or in this case, graphic novel (Itzkoff 2009, 1).

This type of analysis could be applied to the lit-to-film adaptation of *The Lovely Bones*. Peter Jackson directed the film, and many of the changes made in the film draw more attention to the victim than the book does. Alice Sebold is the author of the book, and is also the author of a memoir, its focus on her being raped when she was in college, and the devastating aftermath that followed. Jackson's focus on the victim in his film might have been in some ways influenced by his knowledge of the author's background. Some questions to ask of the lit-to-film adaptation to explore this idea might be:

1. Why did Peter Jackson change the character of Holly and how she died?
2. In what ways does the book *The Lovely Bones* seem to focus less intensely on the victim than the film does? In what ways does it focus more on the family's reaction to Susie's murder?
3. Why might Jackson have chosen to thematically structure the film around the victim and all that she lost when she was killed? Could he have been concerned with the author of the book and her background? Has he combined some of the elements of her first book, *Lucky*, with her novel? Was Jackson concerned that the following for both of Sebold's books would be the audience he'd most need to satisfy?

Although this type of analysis might seem to rely on speculation, research and background information on the film, interviews with Jackson, and clues within the texts of Sebold's texts and the screenplay used for the film could provide more than enough to support such an argument. It's an important consideration to address, since filmmakers must at times feel burdened by their need not only to satisfy the audience, but lure them to the theater at all.

Short Story to Film

In analyzing short story to film adaptations, the methods above can be applied and can be especially useful in the classroom due to the length of the literature. It also can be a good place to start teaching lit-to-film adaptation. For the students, short story to film doesn't seem as overwhelming as analyzing both a novel and a film. Also, short story to film adaptation in a teaching scenario with a restricted time allowance can often work better if the instructor wants to encourage reading/viewing the texts more than once.

A list of short stories that have been made into film more recently and have been useful with my students include the following.

1. The film *Million Dollar Baby* is based on three short stories by F. X. Toole. I use all three short stories, and also an autobiographical essay by Toole (not his real name) since he himself got into boxing, and later in his life, much like Maggie Fitzgerald in the film and story, but even later in his life than she did. She began in her thirties, he in his forties, after a heart attack. The interesting aspect of this film adaptation is the way in which these short stories and F. X. Toole's experiences are melded together for a film that focuses on a female boxer while the stories of

the characters around her reflect the characters in the other short stories. These characters are separated by the short stories while the film brings them together and has them interact with one another. The film, despite its dark subject, is beautifully wrought.

2. *In the Bedroom* is a film adaptation of Andre Dubus's short story, "Killings." Dubus has a magically understated way of telling a story, even about a subject as tragic as the one portrayed in both the story and the film. This lit-to-film adaptation shows how a fidelity/infidelity analysis can focus on the reasons why certain elements and scenes of the story were included or not included in the film. The film focuses on grief, and it is clear that the scenes chosen from the story were done so to bring out this theme, effecting a poignant and thoughtful film.

3. The film *Brokeback Mountain*, based on the short story of the same name, is rife with material to analyze, from the adaptability of the story not only structurally but topically to audience reception anxiety, but also taking into account critical approaches that have already been established for both literature and film. The film's setting is breathtaking, the landscape open and wild, while at the same time it can be held in contrast to the closed-off nature of the people living in this expansive environment. The story uses other means of conveying a similar theme.

4. *The Curious Case of Benjamin Button*, the film, can be difficult to use in class due to its length, but that being said, the film along with the short story make for an engaging analysis, and one quite accessible to students. (Admittedly, Brad Pitt is helpful.) What's interesting about this film is that the short story is not considered one of F. Scott Fitzgerald's best, and in fact, became hidden behind his more visible accomplishments. There are some who still don't find this story of quality, but I find it very moving, albeit allegorical, and quite useful with students today. The focus of the film is interesting to analyze with regard to how the filmmaker interpreted the story. The focus of the story seems to be about an individual struggling with being different from everyone for his entire life, and the inability of others to accept this difference. The film focuses more on the concept of time, timing, age, and aging.

5. *Away from Her* is a film based on Alice Munro's short story, "The Bear Came Over the Mountain," both texts focusing on a couple in their seventies facing the wife's encroaching illness. I've taught this lit-to-film adaptation for several different groups of students, and it continues to be a challenge for them. What most amazes me about the students is their resistance to the title of the story, and pondering more deeply its significance. However, it helps me to understand why Sarah Polley, the director and writer of the adapted screenplay, chose not to use the title of the story for the film. The film allows for a study of the closeness of the film to the story in some ways, of deviations from the story in other ways, and a clear distinction between the focus in each text, although this distinction is seemingly slight so that some students miss it. Therefore, this lit-to-film adaptation proves to be a valuable teaching tool since it requires guidance, but gently given, the students can be led to think "out of the box" so to speak. (Assignments that I use for this lit-to-film adaptation are provided in Appendix A.)

Already Established Critical Approaches

Critical approaches that have already been established for literature and for film, as have been mentioned and discussed in this book previously, can be applied to lit-to-film adaptations. It's necessary to be sure that the approaches can be applied to literature as well as to film. For example, returning to Robert Stam's extensive discussion of Gerard Genette's five types of transtextuality and applying these types to film adaptation, he doesn't explain his justification for applying Genette's theory to the text of film. Peter Brooker, in his essay, "Postmodern Adaptation: Pastiche, Intertextuality, and Re-functioning," responds to Stam's use of Genette's theories when he states: "If Genette helps us to distinguish the kinds of transtextualities necessary to systematic poetics, his terms do not in themselves help us understand the important 'process' of adaptation" (2007, 113). Thus, although certain approaches and theories are useful for analyzing in one medium, it doesn't necessarily follow that these same approaches can be applied to another medium. For example, auteur criticism would not be useful in applying to literature, although biographical criticism might be considered the parallel approach in addressing literature from a similar perspective. However, an interesting analysis of a lit-to-film adaptation might include a biographical approach to the literature and a critical approach to the film that focuses on the director or the auteur of the film. Comparing the author and the director and their previous works, along with the texts in question that form the lit-to-film adaptation, could make for an engaging discussion.

Lit-to-film adaptations can be approached in a myriad of ways. The example above shows that two different critical approaches can be used for each text, the source text and the film. Yet the same critical approach can also be applied to both texts in an inter-textual comparison study. And various critical approaches can be used in conjunction with each other and applied to both texts. As Robert Stam makes clear in the conclusion to his thorough introduction to *Literature and Film: A Guide to the Theory and Practice of Film Adaptation*, lit-to-film adaptation is rife with material to analyze, in so many ways. He states:

> The source novel . . . can be seen as a situated utterance, produced in one medium and in one historical and social context, and later transformed into another, equally situated utterance, produced in a different context and relayed through a different medium. The source text forms a dense informational network, a series of verbal cues which the adapting film text can then selectively take up, amplify, ignore, subvert, or transform . . . The filmic adaptation of a novel performs these transformations according to the protocols of a distinct medium, absorbing and altering the available genres and intertexts through the grids of ambient discourses and ideologies, and as mediated by a series of filters; studio style, ideological fashion, political and economical constraints, auteurist predilections, charismatic stars, cultural values, and so forth . . . Adaptations redistribute energies and intensities, provide flows and displacements; the linguistic energy of literary writing turns into the visual-kinetic-performative energy of the adaptation, in an amorous exchange of textual fluids. (Stam and Raengo 2005a, 45–6)

Thus the complexity and intricacies of both the source text and the film adaptation that occurs in a lit-to-film adaptation process to product offers a wealth of subjects and material upon which to base extensive analyses. Critical approaches can be applied to such analyses, depending on a plethora of factors to be considered. Lit-to-film adaptations can be an absorbing exploration into the application of various criticisms, in ways that previously haven't been attempted. And, lit-to-film adaptations can most assuredly be a valuable tool in the classroom, for assisting students in developing their critical thinking skills while they approach an adaptation from a critical perspective or combination of critical perspectives, having been taught these perspectives and how they can be used. The desire to examine lit-to-film adaptations is proven. Their popularity is evident. People go to the movies to see adaptations of their favorite literature. Now it's time to help them understand how adaptation works, and how to analyze not only the product, but the process. Now it's time to encourage students to move beyond their personal preferences and limited views to broaden their horizons by expanding their understanding of both literature and film, and how the elements of each can be used to bring out meaning in a text of each medium. Lit-to-film adaptation analysis is not only for those who are experts in either field, literature or film, or only for those studying to become experts. It can be a study that undergraduates, introductory students (first-year college students), high school students, and even laypeople can engage in and draw from it valuable skills and knowledge.

One example of using lit-to-film adaptation to construct a course is provided in Appendix B. Soon I will be teaching a course devoted entirely to lit-to-film adaptation. Up to this point, I have included lit-to-film adaptation in my first year writing course and my literary analysis course. I've also introduced it in what might seem unlikely courses to include lit-to-film adaptation, such as Science Writing and British Romantic Writers. However, no matter the course, the students respond positively to the inclusion.

I was asked by the chair of my department at the college where I'm employed to devise a course that would focus on lit-to-film adaptation, and the role of women in both literature and film and the process/product of lit-to-film adaptation. I've titled the course Lit, Flicks, and Chicks. The course will primarily focus on a feminist approach to lit-to-film adaptation, but from the broader perspective of gender and sexuality in the texts I'll be using. Although such a course will be an engaging experience, I plan to devise and teach a course that will allow me to explore, and also help and observe students explore, the many ways a lit-to-film adaptation can be approached. My preference for a course would be to open it up to the study of lit-to-film adaptation from a variety of perspectives, not in any way limited by the course itself. That, to me, would be the most appealing course I could teach. I plan to get that chance, and many more chances to follow.

Analysis of Book Cover Images — Before the Movie and After the Movie Is Released

One final note involves the ways that the designs of book covers can be analyzed, the cover designed before the film was conceived, and after the film is released. Such an analysis can lead to important discoveries and interesting explorations. Consider the before-movie book cover of *The Lovely Bones*, and the cover used after the release of the film, *The Lovely Bones*.

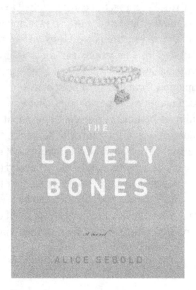

Figure 1   Figure 2

What's interesting about the original design of the book cover is that it's an inaccurate depiction of the charm bracelet in the book. Mr. Harvey takes the bracelet from the main character after he murders her. Yet it is described in the following way:

> On the way back to the wagon Mr. Harvey put his hands in his pockets. There was my silver charm bracelet. He couldn't remember taking it off my wrist. Had no memory of thrusting it into the pocket of his clean pants. He fingered it, the fleshy pad of his index finger finding the smooth gold metal of the Pennsylvania keystone, the back of the ballet slipper, the tiny hole of the miniscule thimble, and the spokes of the bicycle with wheels that worked. (Sebold 2002, 53)

Mr. Harvey stores keepsakes from each of his murders of girls and women, and he chooses the Pennsylvania keystone from Susie's murder: "He liked the Pennsylvania keystone, which my father had graved with my initials — my favorite was the tiny bike — and he pulled it off and placed it in his pocket." (54) The charm on the cover of the book is not mentioned, but it does represent the simple suburban life of which Susie had been a child in the '70s. This charm of the house, however, becomes the charm that is central to the murder in the film. The keystone, central to the book, isn't used in the film. The focus of the cover after the release of the film is on the murderer and his victim. The book cover before the film was made allows for a representation of the murder, while the movie tie-in edition more literally represents the characters involved in the plot of the story.

The original design of the book cover for the novel *The Hours* portrays the

Figure 3

importance of flowers in the novel, which symbolize the different types of relation-ships being explored. Yellow flowers are discussed at length in the novel, yet in the image are dulled a bit by their depiction in black and white. Examining this depiction might prove to be an interesting exploration for students. Flowers frame the novel in that each of the first three chapters, focusing on each of the three women of the book, begins as such:

Mrs. Dalloway: "There are still the flowers to buy." (Cunningham 1998, 9)

Mrs. Woolf: "Mrs. Dalloway said something (what?), and got the flowers herself." (29)

Mrs. Brown: "*Mrs. Dalloway said she would buy the flowers herself.*" [Laura Brown is reading the first sentence of Virginia Woolf's *Mrs. Dalloway*.] (37)

The movie tie-in cover (not shown) hones in on the three women of *The Hours*, repre-sented by Meryl Streep as Clarissa Vaughn, Julianne Moore as Laura Brown, and Nicole Kidman as Virginia Woolf. Clarissa Vaughn, the modern-day Clarissa Dalloway, is holding the flowers in her arms. Students should be encouraged to examine images and explore how each of the images represents the changes made in moving from novel to film.

The original design of the cover for the novel *The Constant Gardener* depicts bees, which implies the House of Three Bees, the chemical corporation at the heart of the conspiracy that resulted in Tessa Quayle's death, which begins the novel. Christine Rodin provided the design for the cover, and when asked how she came up with the idea for the image, her response was as follows:

Figure 4

To tell you the truth, the art director told me exactly what to shoot. He said something about Napoleon having bees as his "thing", they were embroidered onto his robes, but for the life of me I don't know what that has to do with anything. I shot the bees and flowers separately and he put them together in photoshop. I shot a few shots of bees at different angles to have more than one. It was a real, dead bee. I don't always get to read the book and lately they have the concepts already on their minds. That is why so many book covers are not so hot, many people in publishing take the stories too literally. This cover was done long ago and I think it is good because it is suggestive instead of literal. (Email, April 14, 2010)

A movie poster of the film *The Constant Gardener* was used as the book cover (not shown) once the film was released. Ralph Fiennes is front and center, playing Justin Quayle, who is a main character in the novel as well. There is the shot of Justin and Tessa (played by Rachel Weisz) and a white-out silhouette of Justin Quayle, pointing a gun. Both in the film and in the book, Justin is a gentle, peaceful man stirred to react to his wife's untimely death (murder). He never quite fits comfortably into the role of the avenger, purposefully so, yet this isn't portrayed on the movie tie-in cover.

Investigating the book cover designs of pre-release versions of a book and its movie tie-in version can allow for interesting observations and analyses to be made. Also, doing so encourages students to look beyond the images to which they are being exposed and make connections between the images and their meanings that might, or might not, be representative of the book or film.

Chapter 23

Why Teach Literature-to-Film Adaptation Analysis? Why Learn It?

I chose to narrow the domain of adaptation to literature-to-film since I view this area as particularly rife with pedagogical means for teaching students critical thinking skills that will benefit them in any field for which they choose to become prepared. And, lit-to-film adaptation has been a steadily increasing practice yet is becoming even more prevalent as film also becomes a more insistent presence in all of our lives. To teach lit-to-film adaptation, and to be a student of lit-to-film adaptation, requires a defined set of standards, with of course room for play and discourse. Lit-to-film adaptation seems to be held back in some ways by what I see as a contradictorily limiting sense of freedom of expression. In lit-to-film adaptation, just as in literature and in film, quality has to have measurements. And, creators who want to produce "quality" work need to feel the presence of what it will "cost" them, what it will require of them to do so. Standards and measures of complexity need to be hovering about those who take on a lit-to-film project, and it is not a project to be taken on lightly. I learned this in my own project of adapting a previously-written novel into a contemporary novel. The project becomes more engaging the more the source text is afforded the respect and reverence it warrants. The source text at the least must be respected as someone else's work, someone else's idea. Plagiarism is a hot topic in high schools and universities; it is not something we should displace or ignore when it comes to lit-to-film adaptation.

Film adaptation studies are intriguing. Many advances in thought have been introduced and developed. However, as I've discussed in this book, such studies are most often elevated beyond the understanding and accessibility of introductory students. Other concerns for teaching lit-to-film adaptations are the contradictions and repetition in such studies. Many studies discuss other approaches that are being practiced, which is common for a newer field, and lit-to-film adaptation is a relatively young field. However, teaching lit-to-film adaptation analysis left me in a quandary not only as to what text or texts to use, but as to what terminology to use. Scholars discussing the same precepts use different terms to refer to them. I found it confusing to study and the information difficult to draw from for teaching. The information is invaluable in what it addresses, but delinquent in its accessibility to introductory students, many of whom are coming of age in a cultural environment where they tend to believe it is only a matter of time before a book they read and become excited about as a collective will become a film. As I write this, the young adult novel *The Hunger Games* is popular among my children and their cousins. My brother, the father of twin twelve-year-old girls and a nine-year-old boy, bought *The Hunger Games* and *Catching Fire* for my parents, so they could stay in touch with their grandchildren. My sister's son and I talk about Katniss and Gale, and he says to me at dinner at my mom's, excitedly, "I like Cato! And Thresh, too!" In the next breath, he says to me, with his ten-year-old I-kind-of-know-everything voice, "You know, they're making a movie out of *The Hunger Games*. Isn't that cool?"

Is it? Only if we teach this generation how to think critically about the films that are being made out of the literature they're reading. Many of my students, most of whom are 18 to 22, say they prefer the book to any film. Some do say they like the film better. When I probe further, it's apparent their preference is based primarily on personal desires, what they enjoy more. Usually, the readers like the book better, and the film enthusiasts like the film better. However, once we explore both literature and film, they develop a more informed and advanced analysis. I understand why most students initially prefer the book to the film. Reading a book is a private, almost intimate experience. Viewing a film is seen by students as a more public experience. We as humans tend to defend what is private and intimate, and stand up for that. It's very personal and we protect what is personal. I don't want to discourage students from doing that. It's more important now to defend what is private and intimate in our society than it's ever been before. Yet, as I teach students literature and we share in the reading of literature and compare our perspectives and views, students come to see reading and understanding literature as less of a private experience and more of a public one. Likewise, as I encourage students to argue their position on a film and what it's conveying and how it does so, film becomes less of a public experience to students and a more private one. They realize how they view a film can be at least somewhat personal, or individualistic.

Thus, since students need to be encouraged to see reading as a less private experience and film as a less public experience than they currently do, I see analysis of both as the cure. Analysis of literature forces students to acknowledge other perspectives about what they're reading. Analysis of film forces students to define to others their private reception of the film they've viewed. Lit-to-film adaptation is the connecting force that aligns both the literature and the film, and extends beyond each medium to how they can overlap. It's a way for students to understand how both reading and viewing a film can be both private, thus individual, and public, thus collective. Lit-to-film adaptation studies encourages students to critically think through their previously held notions about both literature and film. It makes an experience they've taken for granted as purely entertaining and personal, and moves it into the realm of a learning experience. Students are encouraged beyond merely discussing with their friends with little or no basis except personal preference why they like the book better, or in some cases, the film better, in a lit-to-film adaptation. Instead, through lit-to-film adaptation analysis, students are encouraged to look at how a particular adaptation was done, and ask why. Why was it done this way? What is the book conveying to them, its reader, and how? What is the film conveying to them, the viewer, and how? Why was the lit-to-film adaptation carried out the way it was? In many cases, how it was carried out is information that is readily available.

Lit-to-film adaptation is an up-and-coming means to teaching students how to analyze and think critically, through their reading of a text, through their viewing of a text, and through their comparison/contrast of the one entity used to make another, and the influences that can bear down on each medium. What was needed was a way to organize the teaching and learning of lit-to-film adaptation analysis so that it could best be taught and learned. That organization can then allow for further variations on this elemental foundation for both instructors and students, but it needs to begin simply and accessibly, and that is what I've tried to do here. This is only a beginning, requiring further and extensive work of my own, and the same of others.

Lit-to-film adaptation analysis is a valuable tool for not only teaching but reaching students today. Since all of us are being bombarded every day by verbal, audiovisual, auditory, and visual messages, it's important to help students learn to critically think their way through the overabundance of messages they're receiving at any given moment. Lit-to-film adaptation analysis can assist students in learning to explore the messages and meanings in not only literature and verbal texts, but in auditory, visual, and audiovisual texts as well. Everywhere there are screens blasting all kinds of messages to those growing into our society of today. To learn that one can analyze such screen representations is a crucial aspect that education today must incorporate into its curriculum. I don't know which umbrella it can fall under, but it needs to fall somewhere. And, it needs to develop and evolve because screen representations are only going to multiply exponentially in use. Most of us carry a screen with us everywhere we go, now that cell phones have enhanced their screens, or visual capabilities. I can read the news on my cell phone. I can watch a film on my cell phone. So can those of us who haven't learned how to process all this information quite yet. It's time to figure out a way to encourage those growing into this world to do so, because process they must; critically think through what they're being exposed to they must; and, have control over their reactions and responses to what is being aimed at them they must.

Appendix AI

"The Bear Came Over the Mountain": Formalist Questions for a Close Textual Reading of the Story

Respond to these questions as thoroughly as you can. This assignment is due on
_____.

1. Make a list of the characters and describe them, from their physical attributes to how they're portrayed (based on the information you're given in the text).
2. Describe the setting, giving as many details as you can.
3. Outline the plot, and how events unfold. Be very specific. Then attempt to arrange the plot sequence into Freytag's Pyramid — beginning with the exposition to the denouement. This story does jump around quite a bit, but identifying the main turns in the plot will be helpful to your understanding of the story. How does the structure of the plot, especially its jumping around, affect your reading of the story?
4. What is the point of view in the story? That is, who narrates the story, and from what perspective? How does the point of view affect your reading of the story?
5. How does the title relate to the story?
6. How is symbolism used in the story?
7. What is the theme of the story? Explain it in a single sentence.
8. Now, go back through the first six questions, and show how each of the fictional techniques used in the text as you've described above helps to bring out this theme.
9. Provide five passages from the story and explain their significance to the meaning or theme of the story.
10. Finally, after having carried out these analytical tasks, write a brief paragraph of what this story means, and which fictional techniques used are most important to bringing out that meaning. (Consider this an introductory paragraph to a paper that would then develop the ideas put forth in this introduction.)

Appendix A2

Questions to Ask of Film
— *Away from Her*

1. What does the title mean in relation to the story?
2. Why does the movie start the way it does?
3. Why does the film conclude with the image it does?
4. How is this movie similar to or different from the Hollywood movies you have seen recently or from those of an older generation?
5. Is there a pattern of striking camera movements, perhaps long shots or dissolves or abrupt transitions?
6. Which three or four sequences are the most important?
7. Who are the central characters?
8. What do they represent in themselves and in relation to each other? The importance of individuality or society? Human strength or compassion?
9. How do their actions create a story with a meaning or constellation of meanings?
10. Does the story emphasize the benefits of change or endurance?
11. What kind of life or what actions does the film wish you to value or criticize and why?

Appendix A3

Questions of *Away from Her* (and its source text) — To Discuss in Class

1. What was your initial response to the film?
2. Based on the aspects of the film you were to be looking for as you began watching the film, what most stood out to you as you viewed the film?
3. What scenes in the film stood out to you, affected you, and made the most impression on your reception of the film? Which were most touching or poignant?
4. What is the theme of the film? What is the message being conveyed? How does this differ from your interpretation of the story?
5. What is the setting of the film?
6. How are the characters used to bring out the messages of the film? What did you think of Fiona, Grant, Marian, Kristy, Aubrey in comparison to in the story?
7. How is the plot structured? Why the jumping around do you think? Is it similar to the story? Hard to follow? Why do you think they organized the film in the seemingly haphazard manner that they did, although it had its own organization to it? The story of Grant going to talk to Marian is linear if you follow it on its own. The story of Grant and Fiona is the part of the plot that jumps around a lot. Why might they have done it that way? This will be important to think about when rereading the story.
8. What similarities stand out to you when comparing the story and the film?
9. Differences?
10. What is your perspective on the fidelity of the film to the story? Infidelity? Why the similarities, differences, do you think?
11. What techniques are most relied upon in the film to bring out the message(s)? (Fiona reading about Alzheimer's disease, camera work in focusing in on the characters' facial expressions.)
12. What techniques are most relied upon in the story to bring out the message(s)?
13. What are your criticisms of the film?
14. How is the quality of acting? Casting?
15. How is the camera work used to bring out the tone and meaning of the film?

16. How is music applied to the film in a way that also brings out the tone and meaning of the film?
17. Any other comments or observations to add that haven't been asked above?

Appendix A4

Intertextual Comparison of a Literature-to-Film Adaptation

This writing assignment will involve the analysis of a film adaptation. We will be studying both the short story, "The Bear Came Over the Mountain," and the film adapted from the story, *Away from Her*. Such an analysis will require an intertextual comparison of the story and the film. Julie Sanders in her book, *Adaptation and Appropriation*, refers to the connection between the source text and the adapted text as intertextual as she states:

> [I]t is the very endurance and survival of the source text that enables the ongoing process of juxtaposed readings that are crucial to the cultural operations of adaptation, and the ongoing experiences of pleasure for the reader and spectator in tracing the intertextual relationships. It is this inherent sense of play, produced in part by the activation of our informed sense of similarity and difference between the texts being invoked, and the connected interplay of expectation and surprise, that for me lies at the heart of the experience of adaptation . . . (2006, 25)

Sanders argues that analyzing the similarities and differences between the texts involved, in this case a short story and a film, is the central focus of adaptation studies. What she refers to can be called, then, intertextual comparison. We're going to be examining the similarities and differences between the story and the film, and discussing the intertextual play between the story and the film. Then you'll be able to choose one aspect of the adaptation that stands out to you, and that you want to develop in your paper.

For this paper, I want you to consider four methodologies that you can apply to your analysis of the intertextual comparison of "A Bear Came Over the Mountain" and *Away from Her*. I recommend that you focus on one of these methodologies and develop your analysis of the story and the film using that methodology. There can be some overlap, however, when using these tools; so if you feel comfortable applying more than one of the methodologies to your work, you certainly can do so.

The four methodologies you can draw from are those that we discussed in class before watching the film, and they are as follows.

1. *Adaptation process analysis* — This type of analysis can be used if you can find information about the making of the film. Perhaps the director, who also wrote the screenplay, has written about her strategy in making the film, or has been interviewed. The DVD itself does have deleted scenes, but doesn't offer much insight into the making of the film. Still, if you can research the process by which the film was made, through research of the film, then you can use this analysis, and discuss the film adaptation from the perspective of how the adaptation process was carried out.

2. *Adaptability analysis* — This methodology allows for a discussion of the literature and whether or not "A Bear Came Over the Mountain" can be viewed in its literary form as "adaptable" to film. Does the plot structure seem as if it can lend itself to the medium of film? What problems do you think might be encountered in adapting the story to film? In what ways is the story highly adaptable to film? What elements of the story seem a better fit for film than other elements? You can look at the story and the film from a broad perspective or focus in on smaller points and finer details of both.

3. *Fidelity/infidelity analysis* — This methodology has always been a popular way of viewing film adaptation, but I want you to take it further than simply comparing how closely, loosely, or experimentally the film was adapted from the story. I want you to explore why the filmmaker might have chosen to include certain scenes from the story and not others, and why the filmmaker might have added scenes to the film that were not in the story. It will be important to determine the message you feel the filmmaker is trying to bring out in the film, especially if you find it quite different from the message of the story. You can focus in on a few scenes and discuss how they were similar to the story, different from the story, or not in the story. Be sure to include why as your overarching purpose to your paper.

4. *Specificity analysis* — This methodology allows for an examination of each medium, literature and film, and how the elements of each were used to achieve the effect you feel each has achieved. You can explore why certain techniques were used in each medium, and how they not only might have achieved the same effect in each, but purposefully different effects. Assume that the director of the film has planned for the effect that has been achieved, that it has been carefully thought out, and the film in its final form is the product of that planning and thought. This type of analysis allows for an examination of why each medium relied on certain techniques to bring out the message you see in each.

These are the critical approaches I want you to use to analyze this intertextual comparison between "A Bear Came Over the Mountain" and *Away from Her*. It will be important to have thought through in some depth what you believe the theme of each, the story and the film, to be, and then choose an approach to the intertextual comparison that explores aspects of the adaptation process, or focuses on a textual analysis of the story and its adaptability to film, or examines how the story and the film bring out the meanings you've identified using similar/different details and/or techniques. Draw from the prep work — relating to the story, the film, and the litfilm comparison — that you've done and that we've discussed in class.

This paper is required to be four pages in length. If you use outside sources, you must use proper in-text citation and include a works cited page. We will have a freewriting session on _____. A thesis statement and outline will be due _____. The first draft will be due _____. The final draft will be due _____. I will let you know what will need to be included with the final draft as the due date approaches.

Appendix A5

Grade Sheet for Intertextual Comparison Paper

CONTENT = ____/50
____ Satisfies assignment (10)
____ Thesis statement (10)
____ Introductory paragraph (10)
____ Development of intertextual comparison — relevant, concise, fluid, effective (20)

STYLE/FORM = ____/20
____ Clarity (10)
____ Organization of essay (10)

WRITING = ____/10
____ Grammar (5)
____ Punctuation/mechanics (5)

SPECIFIC TO THIS PAPER = ____/20
____ Use of both film and story to support argument (10)
____ Overall presentation of intertextual comparison analysis (10)

Paper   =   ____/100
Prewriting   =   ____/10
First draft   =   ____/20
Peer review   =   ____/20
Total Grade   =   ____/150

Appendix A6

Sample Paper One

Olga Roque

Scene Selection: A Vital Part of the Adaptation Process

The adaptation process from novel to film is one that encompasses much thought with regard to details. Throughout the process, the filmmaker is faced with numerous decisions that have to be made in order to address the details of the movie. One such vital decision is the matter of whether or not the message of the novel will be carried into the film. The message that the director employs is of importance because the details that will be used to explore the message have to be considered. One particular detail that coincides with the message is the use of scenes. The omission or addition of scenes from the novel is a tool that the director uses for the benefit of the audience. The process of scene selection is evident when looking at *Away from Her* and the short story from which it is adapted, "The Bear Came Over the Mountain" by Alice Munro. It is clear that the scene choices that have been made for the film are due to the precise intentions in the mind of the director, Sarah Polley, taking into account that she also wrote the screenplay.

Soon after the reader watches the movie, it is evident that there are similar scenes in the two mediums. One reason for this might be that the director decided to maintain the same message for the film as is conveyed by the short story. For both, the message relates to how hard it is to manage one's life when his or her loved one is not "there"; that is, the loved one is not mentally there. To make sure that the message stays close to the short story, then, the director retains many of the same scenes. One scene that is clearly the same as in the short story concerns Grant's return to Meadowlake to see Fiona for the first time after her initial thirty days in the home. The scene itself demonstrates an important moment for both Grant and the audience. Beforehand, Grant, steeped in denial, had not taken Fiona's brain deterioration seriously. However, the moment when Fiona begins to talk to him as if he were a new patient at Meadowlake serves as a realization point for Grant. With the scene the same as in the short story, the audience is aware of how insignificant Grant all of a sudden feels because of Fiona not remembering him. The sense of his heart breaking can be noted and allows the audience to empathize with Grant. The scenes that are taken directly from the short

277

story are scenes that offer a view into the minds of the characters, which in turn helps to explain and depict the situation more effectively for the audience.

Essential observations that the audience can make occur when significant emotions are shared between the characters. In *Away from Her* the director makes sure that the emotions between characters are evident to the audience through the use of the same scenes. One such scene that demonstrates the emotional connection between the characters to the audience is the very last scene in both the movie and short story. Fiona suddenly remembers Grant and that he has not "forsaken" her. She doesn't recall her interactions with Aubrey, her new friend at Meadowlake. The scene is a powerful moment for both Grant and Fiona. By using this scene as it is in the story, it can be noted that the director wants to ensure the power of this moment is transferred to the movie. It is important for the audience to witness this shift in the relationship between the two main characters. In the short story, the dramatic shift in the relationship is evident because of this last scene. The director wants to make certain the same power is captured on film. There are numerous scenes that Polley keeps the same since they provide what she feels is necessary for the film. However, as with any adaptation, there are new scenes that the film introduces that are crucial to the overall quality of the film.

Since in the short story, an indirect approach is taken to reach the reader, the readers are left to decipher why certain things are said and done and to conclude what they may. This is not the case with the film. In other words, short story or any written work for that matter has the opportunity to state what is going on in the minds of the characters and in the environment around the characters. *Away from Her* takes more of a direct approach by filling in the holes that the author leaves with what the director wants the audience to see. One obvious scene added to the film involves Marian and Grant making love. The short story never addresses how close of a relationship Grant and Marian develop over time. The scene that Polley includes is something that she must have felt necessary because it adds a different element to the situation with all the characters. Specifically, it adds the element of loneliness that the two are feeling in their separate situations. During the scene, the two are seen lying in bed and laughing about how they have just made love. The audience can gather that the two are surprised at how their actions have led to them making love and having a connection. It is almost as if the two do not realize the extent of their loneliness until they are together. The scene is added to convey this loneliness that the director felt was necessary.

The addition of scenes also can serve as a unique tool for the director. The director's goal is not only to add her own perspective to the overall story, but also to add dimension to the characters themselves. For instance, the short story views the entire situation mostly through Grant's eyes. Fiona's role in the story is basically as the wife of Grant and the person that requires him to go through the hardship. For the film, it is as if the director wants to add more depth to Fiona's character and allow her perspective to be more evident in the film. The director shows more of Fiona and Grant as a couple and also Fiona as the individual who is dealing with brain deterioration. For instance, in one scene, Fiona goes for a skiing adventure by herself and ends up getting lost. Fiona finally takes the skis off and just throws them to the ground and plops herself on the ground, on her back, with her arms stretched out. With this scene, the audience gets a feel for what Fiona must be going through. The whole action of throwing everything down and her collapsing onto the ground demonstrates her frustration with the disease, almost as if she is giving into the disease. This scene then offers her outlook on the situation, and not just Grant's. By adding this scene, the director is consequently demonstrating that she felt it necessary to include Fiona's take on the disease.

The idea of keeping the message relatively the same in both mediums also correlates to the reasoning behind scenes added to the movie. The author uses symbolism to help emphasize the meaning of the short story. Some of the symbolism from the short story, however, cannot be adapted to film. Since the symbolism cannot be transferred in the way the author wrote it, the director employs a different method of providing the same symbolism. To do this, new scenes are added. For instance, one scene that is not in the short story involves Fiona's return to Grant's and her house after being at Meadowlake. In the scene, it is clear that she becomes aware that the environment does have importance, but cannot pinpoint why it does. She then becomes uncomfortable and wants to leave. The house helps to symbolize the couple's love and the comfort of their relationship, what it used to be. When Fiona is unable to remember Grant's and her relationship, it signifies their loss of what they once had. To provide the strong sense of their relationship and how it has been lost to the disease, the director adds this particular scene.

All scenes, whether or not they are from the original medium, serve a purpose in the adapted medium. Scenes work towards creating the message for which the director is aiming. When the director's goals vary from the intent of the author, it can be assumed that the director will add different scenes to demonstrate a new perspective, her own perspective. Yet the desire to reflect the same message in the film as in the literature can be a reason why new scenes are added to the film. If scenes in the literature are not easily adaptable to screen and the director wants to convey the same message, the director will figure out other means for conveying that same idea.

Appendix A7

Sample Paper Two

Marital Infidelity and Modes of Forgiveness in a Literature-to-Film Adaptation

Alice Munro's short story, "The Bear Came over the Mountain," and Sarah Polley's adapted film, *Away from Her*, both share a similar message using different ways of conveying it. Both renditions have different tones but share the same plot: a husband who regrets many previous adulterous, extramarital relationships. In the short story, the husband remains remorseful for his adultery as his wife develops Alzheimer's disease and then cannot provide forgiveness. The film version is similar in that the husband is on a quest for redemption with the exception that his wife has already verbalized her forgiveness for his infidelity. When Grant's wife, Fiona, has to enter Meadowlake, a home for the elderly, Grant has to learn to cope with the changes in her. The underlying message in both versions of this story is forgiveness. However, in the short story Grant tries to attain his wife's forgiveness, and in the film Grant is searching to forgive himself. Interestingly, both the story and the film must depict the past of the main character, Grant, through different techniques specific to each medium.

The short story makes use of flashbacks that are very vague in terms of the material they contain. The flashbacks are usually little more than a description of a scene and the idea that Grant is with another woman. These flashbacks are used to imply infidelity without giving any intimate details as to the nature of his relationships, their quantity, or length. The flashbacks are used because they are impartial and allow the reader to form their own opinions of Grant's infidelity. The little that can be taken from the flashbacks is that Grant was involved in many extramarital relationships. In retrospect, Grant thinks to himself: "And of deceiving Fiona — as of course he has deceived her — but would it have been better if he had done as others had done with their wives and left her?" (Munro 2002, 286). Here Grant admits his infidelity but does not imply any particular attachments; this is left to the reader to discern, although it seems by the tone of the confession that Grant remained in love with Fiona during his infidelity because he chose to stay with her. The author allows readers to form their own opinions, because rather than being told in the first person, the story is told by a

281

third-person narrator. This allows the reader further ranging and more interpretations of Grant's personal feelings and attachments. In this way, then, the story is not about judging Grant for his past mistakes but watching him make up for them. Grant does this by supporting Fiona in her relationship with another man, while she does not remember being married to Grant. Since Fiona cannot voice her forgiveness to Grant for his past adulteries, which unlike Fiona he was very conscious of, Grant feels that by helping Fiona in her relationship he can gain her forgiveness in a sort of karmic way. Grant's inner questioning reminds the reader that now that his wife has Alzheimer's, she can never answer the question that Grant is posing to himself. That is why Grant supports Fiona's "adultery," almost as a way to redeem himself in his wife's eyes by stepping aside and giving in to her relationship with another resident at the home.

In the film, the past is explored as Grant reminiscences in Marian's kitchen. Marian is the wife of Fiona's elderly "lover." Grant goes to Marian to convince her to put her husband, Fiona's new friend, into Meadowlake permanently. Grant is trying to make Fiona happy. The film is framed by the scene in Marian's kitchen. Grant is sitting in the kitchen and while he tries to convince Marion to return her husband to Meadowlake, he reminisces about the last year during which his wife has been at the Meadowlake facility. The use of this frame offers a more sympathetic view of Grant than in the story, since it appears all his thoughts are about his wife. Therefore, the film is primarily in first person as the majority of it can be assumed to take place in Grant's memory. Also, many of the camera shots tend to be angled from over his shoulder in scenes when he is in conversation, implying that the viewer is looking from Grant's side and through his eyes at the scene.

Inside this frame and in one of his memories, much of Grant's adulterous relationship is revealed as he talks to Kristy, the head nurse at Meadowlake and Grant's friend. Grant tells Kristy that she must resent the elderly of Meadowlake because they have lived such "easy" lives and have only been faced with real hardship at the end while their loved ones are deteriorating. Kristy responds by objecting to this, because she does not wish to be judged, and gives Grant some perspective in this scene. Kristy says, "In my experience, at the end of things, it's almost always the men that think not too much went wrong. I wonder if your wife feels the same way." Kristy implies here she has some knowledge that Grant was in an adulterous affair. She wants him to know that his wife may have different thoughts from Grant on the success of their marriage. This line visibly affects Grant as the camera focuses in on him for some time after Kristy leaves. Kristy recognizes Grant's internal struggle with his infidelity and makes it clear that it is not something he can simply write off by saying he's had an easy life and an easy marriage. Grant is not shown talking to Kristy again until he brings his wife's new friend, Aubrey, to Meadowlake, which is his way of redeeming himself in his own eyes. Grant overcomes his personal jealousy for his wife's happiness, allowing the viewer to sympathize with a downtrodden Grant who has learned to sacrifice his own happiness for that of his wife.

Surprisingly, much of the dialogue of the original short story is used in the film but is enhanced for the film. For example, sometimes what is revealed through the narrator, through Grant's eyes, in the short story must be relayed through another character in the film. For example, when Grant thinks in the short story, ". . . would it have been better if he had done as others had done with their wives and left her?" (286), this is synonymous with Fiona in the film telling Grant on the ride to Meadowlake, "I think you did alright. Compared to your colleagues. The ones who left their wives." The difference in delivery is due to the difference in point of view. In the short story Grant is questioning himself. The question Grant is asking is rhetorical because neither Grant's thoughts nor his emotions are vocalized here. In fact, a narrator is providing his thoughts and emotions for the reader. Therefore the question is posed to the reader and allows them to form their own opinions about Grant's morality. In the film when Fiona openly approaches Grant in the car about his infidelity, that is her way of forgiving him outright. Grant does not respond to Fiona's monologue and he shuts down about his infidelity. The rest of the film shows Grant trying to forgive himself.

When Grant brings Fiona's Aubrey back to Meadowlake, Kristy smiles at Grant because she knows that Grant has sacrificed his pride to provide for his wife, who does not recognize him from other men, and her happiness. This scene indicates that Grant has forgiven himself for his adulteries because he is secure enough to allow Fiona to be happy in any way she can while she suffers from Alzheimer's. It even means forgoing his own level of comfort as he encourages her to be with another man who appears to make her happy, as her disease prevents her from knowing she is doing any wrong. In this scene, there is no question that Grant is trying to redeem himself and is at heart of good character even if he participated in adulteries in the past.

In the short story, Grant's infidelity can be taken as part of the past, possibly that his wife did not know about, and he seeks her forgiveness. When Fiona brings up Grant's infidelity directly in the film, Grant's weakness is exposed; the viewer can sympathize with this exposure because it is implied Fiona has forgiven him and made the infidelity part of the past. In the film Grant must forgive himself; this is evident in the confidence he shares with Kristy about his guilt. While the short story is about Grant's quest for being forgiven by his wife, the movie is more concerned with Grant forgiving himself. In both versions, Grant must learn to accept his changing wife and he does this by learning to forgive their past.

Appendix B

ENG 260: Lit, Flicks, and Chicks

Cedar Crest College
Fall 2010
Saturdays 9:00 a.m. to 3:00 p.m.

Texts

Cartmell, Deborah and Imelda Whelehan. 2007. *The Cambridge Companion to Literature on Screen*. New York: Cambridge University Press.
Cunningham, Michael. 2000. *The Hours*. New York: Picador.
James, P. D. 2006. *The Children of Men*. New York: Vintage.
LeCarre, John. 2005. *The Constant Gardener*. New York: Scribner.
Sebold, Alice. 2007. *The Lovely Bones*. New York: Back Bay Books.
Shelley, Mary. 1995. *Frankenstein, or The Modern Prometheus*. New York: Norton.
Handouts.

Course Description

This course will focus on literary narratives (novels and short stories) and their film adaptations. Through the use of textual and intertextual analysis, we will be exploring literature, film, and film adaptation — how they function separately and in connection with each other (or intertextually). The use and practice of literary and film criticism will be emphasized as a means to explore the complexities inherent in an intertextual endeavor. In the case of film adaptation, both the process of adaptation and the product of that process will be examined. Gender criticism will be practiced most often when viewing the literature-to-film adaptation process/product: What part do women play in adaptation, whether as their roles as writers of the literature, or their portrayal in both the literature and the film? The most important goal of this course is for students to achieve an understanding of how to approach lit-to-film adaptations from more than simply a personal preference type of response but with the tools to analyze and critique from a place of substantial and informed authority.

Course Objectives and Outcomes

Upon successful completion of this course, the student will demonstrate competence in the following:

- an understanding of literary and film theory, with a special emphasis on gender criticism
- an understanding of how to put such theory and critical tools into practice when analyzing literature, film, and literature-to-film adaptations
- an understanding of the intertextual process that leads to a film adaptation
- an understanding of how to critically analyze lit-to-film adaptation(s), and express that analysis in their speech and through writing
- an ability to detect and evaluate the role/portrayal of women and gender in lit-to-film adaptation, and explore how this representation of gender reflects larger issues in the world (outside literature and film)
- an ability to critically analyze the influence of various media on an individual's belief system (whether reinforcing it or challenging it), and more broadly, the effects of media influence on societal norms and expectations.

Assessment of Course Outcomes

Assessment of the student's performance will be based on five shorter papers that will assess the student's ability to analyze the intertextual process/product of literature-to-film adaptations assigned for and experienced in class. Students will demonstrate their awareness of the interpretive possibilities for literature-to-film adaptations through participation in class discussions as well. Finally, students will demonstrate their understanding of what they have learned throughout the course through a final project that will include a multimedia presentation and a related written analysis of a literature-to-film adaptation process and/or product. This project will be shared with the class as a presentation, in an effort to expose the entire class to film adaptations beyond those taught during the course of the semester.

Grading

Your work will be evaluated as follows.

Five writing assignments (3–5 pages) — 50% (10% each)
Final project — 30%
Participation — 20%

Assignments: These will be smaller yet formal assignments. You will be given detailed instructions to follow and these assignments must be typewritten and double-spaced. The assignments will require:

- **Close textual analysis** — Whenever you make a claim about any text or texts, you must support it with textual evidence. In addition, your analysis should be precise. Furthermore, you should be attentive to the complexities and ambiguities of the text you're analyzing.

- **Cohesion** — Your papers should not be collections of random ideas that barely relate to each other. These assignments should progress logically and build toward conclusions. You should take your reader step by step through your argument.
- **Clarity** — Your reader should not have to read the assignment twice to comprehend your argument, nor should she be confused about your position on an issue you're discussing.

All assignments must be **typed, stapled, and double-spaced**.

Final Project: This project will include a presentation and bring into it all that has been discussed throughout the course in some capacity. It will be evaluated based on its satisfaction of the assignment parameters, its development of the topic chosen, how well the project is put together, and the creativity with which it's presented.

Participation: You will be required to participate in class, and be respectful and open-minded with others, including myself. I will be calling on students during discussions, so be prepared. In addition, this grade will reflect attendance, which represents your contribution to the intellectual environment of the class, requiring you be here to contribute. The following rubric for your participation grade will apply:

A Regularly demonstrates excellent preparation: has clearly read the assigned material and thoughtfully considered any suggested questions, etc. Brings original thought and perspective to discussion, making significant contributions that expand and extend our collective understanding and appreciation of the written work. Listens attentively to other class members and instructor and responds constructively. Maintains active involvement throughout the semester.

B Regularly contributes to class discussions and has clearly read the assigned material, considering any suggested questions, etc. Brings original thought and perspective to discussion. Listens attentively to other class members and instructor. Maintains consistent ongoing involvement throughout the semester.

C Contributions to discussion show that the assigned materials have been read. Listens attentively to other class members and instructor. Level of involvement variable, but can contribute when called upon.

D Doesn't often contribute without being called upon. Completion of assigned reading sometimes in doubt. Level of involvement consistently unsatisfactory.

F Does not contribute to discussion unless called upon. Contributions when called upon indicate that assigned materials have not been read.

Appendix C

Sample Academic Essay: A Study in Intertextual Comparison

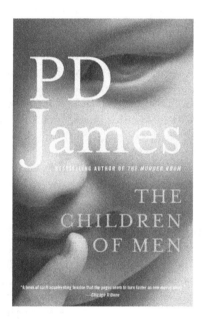

Figure 5

(The) *Children of Men*, and Two Visions of One Premise: What Would our World be Without Hope?

Friday 1 January 2021
Early this morning, 1 January 2021, three minutes after midnight, the last human being to be born on earth was killed in a pub brawl in a suburb of Buenos Aires, aged twenty-five years, two months and twelve days . . . I had settled down to begin this diary of the last half of my life when I noticed the time and thought I might as well catch the headlines to the nine o'clock bulletin.

(James 1992, 3)

The world is bleak. Everyone's turned to stone. Children have disappeared from the surface of Earth, which has exacerbated the corrosion of its inner spirit. We see all of this through the eyes and sometimes the journal of one man, Theodore Faron, "Doctor of Philosophy, Fellow of Merton College in the University of Oxford, historian of the Victorian age, divorced, childless, solitary . . . cousin to Xan Lyppiatt, the dictator and Warden of England" (James 1992, 4). Theo reveals that he never was adept at emotion or connection with other human beings, and as he turns fifty years old, the world has also adopted his apathy. Dolls, kittens, basically a novelistic shop of horrors dash in front of Theo's eyes while he observes as merely a witness, and recorder of sorts. Even so, his observations uncover tiny elements of humanity fighting to remain, almost bursting through the seams, as the end of humanity threatens to draw near and close in around what's left.

Enter a bright young woman with a "pre-Raphaelite face" and a deformed left hand (James 1992, 39), well into Book One of the grim novel, *The Children of Men*. Theo sees her at a church service, remembering her from a class he taught. She approaches him, asking, "Could I please speak to you? It's important." (39) Theo's connection to the leader of the country, his cousin, has brought her to him. It is this new connection, however, that changes the course of his life, and his manner of dealing with life for fifty years. Julian, with four other misfit souls, totaling the Five Fishes, wants to change (what's left of) the world: end the mass murdering of the old, reinstate the rights of immigrants used and abused as slaves, reconfigure the penal system, and end reproductive testing. The Five Fishes ask Theo for help due to his family ties with the dictator, and he agrees. However, at the end of the first book, identifying feelings for Julian that are foreign and frightening to him, he decides to make his escape and travel, while he still can, to visit places that soon may not be accessible. He writes in his journal:

> I am fifty years old and I have never known what it is to love . . . Fifty is not an age to invite the turbulence of love, particularly not on this doomed and joyless planet when man goes to his last rest and all desire fades . . . I shall tear this page from my journal. Writing these words was an indulgence; to let them stand would be folly. And I shall try to forget this morning's promise. It was made in a moment of madness. I don't suppose she will take it up. If she does, she will find this house empty. (James 1992, 133–4)

Theo has abandoned all hope, and to do so is repetition of what he's always done. One can't be disappointed bitterly if one doesn't believe hope can exist. One can't be held accountable if one doesn't take control of any situation, including one's own.

Enter this woman again in Book Two, when Theo has returned from his attempt to escape his own feelings of humanity. Miriam of the Five Fishes has shown up on his doorstep to take him to Julian. She tells Theo that Julian needs him, and when Theo hesitates, she reminds him, "You told Julian you'd come if she wanted you. She wants you now." As they drive in his car to where Julian is hiding from the "law," Miriam reveals the significance of the situation at hand: "Julian is pregnant. That's why she needs you. She's going to have a child" (James 1992, 148). Theo doesn't believe her, but Miriam says he will see for himself. In his disbelief, Theo probes for more information from Miriam, who reminds him quickly that she's a midwife. She's confirmed the pregnancy, she tells Theo, and has "had time to get used to the glory of it" (148). She reminisces to the time many years ago when she knew something was wrong:

> I was twenty-seven at Omega and working in the maternity department of the John Radcliffe. I was doing a stint in the antenatal clinic at the time. I remember booking a patient for her next appointment and suddenly noticing that the page seven months ahead was blank. Not a single name. Women usually booked in by the time they'd missed their second period, some as soon as they'd missed one. Not a single name. I thought, what's happening to the men in this city? Then I rang a friend who was working at Queen Charlotte's. She said the same. She said she'd telephone someone she knew at the Rosie Maternity Hospital in Cambridge. She rang me back twenty minutes later. It was the same there. It was then I knew, I must have been one of the first to know. I was there at the end. Now I shall be there at the beginning. (James 1992, 148–9)

Theo, then, has been backed into a corner by a miracle of sizable proportions. Even he, a cynical academic who has found a way to rationalize and reason away any tiny emotion he might chance to experience, can't turn away from this. Julian is miraculously pregnant, however not by her husband Rolf, one of the Five Fishes, but by another Fish, the priest, Luke. Luke dies a violent death. Rolf discovers the truth, flagellates himself, and eventually runs off to betray his wife. Over Luke's dead body, Theo asks if Julian loved Luke. Miriam tells him: "I think she was sorry for him. I don't think she loved either of them, neither Rolf nor Luke. She's beginning to love you, whatever that means, but I think you know that. If you hadn't known it, or hoped for it, you wouldn't be here" (James 1992, 187).

After Luke's death and the subsequent discovery, Theo talks to Julian. They share their thoughts on love. When Julian asks him if he loved his wife, Theo sums up his portrait of marriage, using his own as a model:

> I convinced myself I did when I married. I willed myself into the appropriate feelings without knowing what the appropriate feelings were. I endowed her with qualities she didn't have and then despised her for not having them. Afterwards I might have learned to love her if I had thought more of her needs and less of my own. (James 1992, 189)

Julian's experience with Rolf had been similar. Her affair with Luke, she admits shamefully, had been her use of his intense love for her. If she'd loved Luke, she believes it would have been less sinful. Theo challenges that by saying, cynically, ". . . love justifies everything, excuses everything?" Julian retorts, "No, but it's natural, it's human." She says she used Luke, and knowingly hurt him, because she could no longer love. Does Theo understand? He does (James 1992, 189).

When they bury Luke, Julian asks that Theo say the burial service for him. With Julian on his left, Miriam on his right, and Rolf (who hasn't left yet) at the foot of the grave, Theo reads the psalm. At first it sounds "strange to his own ears," but then he seems to know the words by heart:

> Lord, thou hast been our refuge: from one generation to another. Before the mountains were brought forth, or ever the earth and the world were made: thou art God from everlasting, and world without end. Thou turnest man to destruction: again thou sayest, Come again, ye children of men. For a thousand years in thy sight are but as yesterday: seeing that is past as a watch in the night (James 1992, 194).

After Rolf abandons Julian, Theo becomes sole proprietor of the future of the child. The rest of the story revolves around what must be done to ensure the entrance of this child into the world, the only chance of saving humanity. Thus, Theo, rather late in life, learns the art of sacrifice for the sake of love and new life. He stands up to his egomaniacal cousin, ruler of the kingdom. He conquers this incumbent ruler, with a bullet through the heart, saves the first child born on the planet in twenty-five years, and puts on the ring of power:

> Theo thought: It begins again, with jealousy, with treachery, with violence, with murder, with this ring on his finger. He looked down at the great sapphire in its glitter of diamonds, at the ruby cross, twisting the ring, aware of its weight. Placing it on his hand had been instinctive and yet deliberate, a gesture to assert authority and ensure protection. (James 1992, 240)

Theo observes that after childbirth Julian seems vulnerable for the first time since he's come to know her. She sees the ring on his finger, and states simply, "That wasn't made for your finger." He's irritated, and tells her it's useful for the present. Her continued idealism, while he's had to face the reality of the situation, and what went into saving this child, erects a slight but definite wall between them. He baptizes the child, a boy, Luke Faron: "It was with a thumb wet with his own tears and stained with her blood that he made on the child's forehead the sign of the cross" (241). The reader is left to wonder at this "beginning." Is it a beginning, or merely a resumption?

This plot structure is P. D. James's vision of a future void of children, developed in her 1992 novel, which she aptly titled, *The Children of Men*. James is a female British novelist best known for her adeptness with the mystery genre, many of her novels in this genre following the leads of Adam Dalgliesh, a seasoned police officer, to the solving of a particular crime. Ms. James has in fact been coined the Queen of Crime by some, and is considered one of the best mystery novelists writing today by a host of various reviewers of her many crime novels. However, she takes a different turn with *The Children of Men*, writing of a crime committed against humanity by humanity, a mystery never to be solved — women cannot get pregnant, sperm is ineffectual. After years of research and testing, and the promise of great reward to whoever can uncover the cause of this universal infertility, nobody — and no company or research organization — has achieved success. Similarly, the fact that one woman (considered a defect and thus disqualified for reproductive testing) miraculously becomes pregnant, is never explained by James either. Perhaps with this novel, she'd tired temporarily of life always having answers, and crimes having solutions.

In certain chapters the novel's focus on Theo's journal, and thus his inner thoughts, and the action of the novel seen only through his eyes by a third person narrator in alternating chapters, allow for a penetrating view from an individual perspective as the world deteriorates with no future in sight. Theo takes the reader into this world, and we can experience it as if we are Theo, or walking beside him. We see the women bereft, childless, clinging to kittens and china dolls as substitutes for the children missing from their lives. We see the horrific acts leveled against individuals around Theo, now that such actions can be rationalized away so easily. The old are clogging up the remaining reserves and need to be exterminated. The immigrants are being used to do the dirty work; when they are no longer useful, they're shipped back to their respective countries to die. A world that has lost generations for which to leave anything behind is a world that is pointless and lacking any kind of meaning. We see this through the eyes of a historian, whose only livelihood — if it can be called that — was studying the past from his place in the future. There will be no place in the future from which to study this past. We feel the mind-numbing torture of this predicament.

Although P. D. James has always been interested in evil, one interviewer writes, she's approached its complexities while writing within the genre of crime novels. James states in this interview:

> [I]n an age when murder is so often random, the crime novel is a comforting form — it reassures us of the sanctity of life (if you get violently killed, someone will care) and of the fact that we live in a comprehensible, rational world, a world in which human authority, and human skill and integrity . . . can put things to rights. (Dalley 1992, 2)

However, James changes course with *The Children of Men*. There are no answers, the world is not a rational place, and human authority loses all meaning when the world as we know it threatens to end with a finality that is slow and tortuous. James claims the idea for *The Children of Men* "'. . . came to me so strongly, I had to write it straight away.' Its genesis was a newspaper article which reported human fertility in the West had fallen dramatically in the last 20 years . . . shortly afterwards, she read that the majority of life forms that have existed on the planet have died out" (Dalley 1992, 2). This knowledge prompts her to imagine a world with no future, where in one year — 1995 — the last of the humans are born. It raises questions to her such as: "What would it mean for the way people lived, their motivation? It is almost unimaginable, what it might do to human beings" (2).

Several reviews of *The Children of Men* speculate that in the novel, James is expressing dissatisfaction with the time in history in which she was writing the story — the nineties, nearing the end of a century and a millennium — and lamenting how the world as we'd known it until then was changing drastically. James Sallis writes in his review of the novel:

> Since useful works of art rarely are about what they seem to be about, then we must wonder, finally, whether *The Children of Men* may not be at its deepest level a kind of

eulogy for Britain and for a way of life James recognizes is gone. Her metaphor of a world from which the life force has departed, her portrait of a final, declining generation, even the novel's polite, dissembling language, suggests this. (Sallis 1993, 2)

However, it must be noted that the novel does end with at least some semblance of hope, and perhaps a question put forth by Ms. James herself: If we have one chance to restructure the way things have been done, to build a future that we didn't think we'd have, will we do it differently? Or will we simply revert back to the way we've done things before, and end up here all over again in another century or two? It's a valid question that she leaves us with, one that has far-reaching significance beyond the fictive world she's created in her novel.

Alfonso Cuarón's film, based on James's novel, also represents a vision of a future with no children in it, caused by universal infertility. His film originates out of a period of time known as post-9/11 that we all have become accustomed to hearing, yet we still grapple with understanding its implications for our lives and our society. So, while James might have been expressing a longing for a way of life that no longer existed as we were moving towards the new millennium, Cuarón presents a critique of where and how that past has led us to the current state of society — a state that visibly reflects violence and pollution, amidst a myriad of other issues. Cuarón explains his interest in making the film, *Children of Men*, in an interview: "It was when I realized that the premise of the book, the premise of infertility and humanity, could serve as a metaphor for the fading sense of hope that I feel humanity has [today]. It was an amazing opportunity" (Guerrasio 2006, 2). He tells another interviewer that even though he'd never had an interest in doing a science fiction film, "the premise kept haunting me . . . I realized the premise of the film . . . could be a point of departure for an exploration into the state of things that we're living in now, the things that are shaping this very first part of the 21st century" (Voynar 2006, 2).

Cuarón's film begins with a black screen, as the voices of two British newscasters — one male and one female — introduce the news report:

> "Day 1000 of the Siege of Seattle" (male) . . . "The Muslim community demands an end to the army's occupation of mosques" (female) . . . "The Homeland Security bill is ratified. After eight years British borders will remain closed. The deportation of illegal immigrants will continue . . . Good morning, our lead story" (male) . . . "The world was stunned today by the death of Diego Ricardo, the youngest person on the planet" (female) . . . (*Children of Men*)

The black screen is suddenly replaced by a view of the inside of a café. People are staring at a television above and behind the camera's view, captivated by the news that has just been reported. The female newscaster continues: "Baby Diego was killed in a bar fight in Buenos Aires after refusing to sign an autograph" (*Children of Men*). A man enters the coffee shop, nudging past the other customers glued to the television, to get a coffee. The male newscaster then continues: "Witnesses at the scene say that Diego spat in the face of a fan who asked for an autograph. He was killed in an ensuing brawl. The fan was later beaten to death by the angry crowd" (*Children of Men*). The news report gives biographical information about Baby Diego, a celebrity due to being the youngest person on earth. He was born in 2009, and at his death was "18 years, 4 months, 20 days, 16 hours, and 8 minutes old" (*Children of Men*). As all of this is being revealed, the man orders his coffee, briefly glances at the television above him, receives his coffee, and nonplussed by the weeping and sniffling that has begun, heads out of the café. Superimposed on the screen is the lettering: "London, 16th November 2027" (*Children of Men*). The man looks to be about fiftyish, in a dingy trench coat, with sallow skin and an apathetic air about him. He turns left onto the street and puts down his coffee on a newspaper vending machine to administer cream and sugar. The atmosphere is drab and grimy, stone gray. Dilapidated cars and motor scooters drive by, seemingly emitting diesel fumes. Everything appears small, dusty, merely functional, and maybe barely so. No one notices each other amidst the honking and noisiness. Although it's 2027, society hasn't progressed, but visibly regressed.

Suddenly, the coffee shop explodes, and the man is propelled 10 feet backwards away from his coffee. One lone survivor of the blast stumbles out of the café, holding one of her arms in her other hand, crying and moaning unintelligibly. The scene ends, and the screen announces in bold white letters against stark black: CHILDREN OF MEN.

We then follow Theo, the man who only lost his coffee during the blast (not his life or his arm), to work, where his officemates are crying over Baby Diego's death. Theo feigns grief to his boss and heads home with a flask of what looks like whiskey or scotch, tucked inside his trench coat in a pocket made for such a purpose. The next day, his miserable existence (except for the warmth he shares with his good friend, Jasper, who Theo appears to visit on a regular basis) is interrupted by his abduction by the Fishes. They take him to Julian — their leader and his past. She needs his help to transit papers from his cousin, Nigel, who has access to such papers since the government funds his "Arc of the Arts," as Julian refers to it. She needs the papers for a girl, a fugee, to get her past checkpoints and to the coast. Theo gets the papers from Nigel but must accompany the girl, since he tells Nigel the papers are for someone he's seeing. This particular fugee (the word itself a reference to refugees) is a young black woman named Kee.

Theo joins Julian, Luke, Miriam, and Kee in a car that will take them to where Kee, Theo and Miriam can be transported to the coast. At the beginning of the journey, Julian is shot and killed in an intense and long scene that takes place inside their small car. At a "safe" house the remaining travelers drive to after burying Julian, Kee reveals her pregnancy to Theo. Theo also discovers that Luke, Julian's henchman, ordered the hit on Julian so that he could begin a violent uprising against the government. Julian had believed peaceful maneuvers would work — clearly, Luke believes in violence. Yet, amidst the global state of universal infertility and massive societal destruction, with very few people making any sort of sense at this point, by some miracle Kee is pregnant with a child.

Kee tells Theo that Julian had told her to trust only him. "I don't know why she said that," Theo responds, his hesitance to get involved still intact (*Children of Men*). But when he discovers that Luke planned the hit on Julian, he's in it for good, and he assumes control for getting the child born safely. He takes Kee and Miriam, her midwife, to the only safe place he knows — Jasper's country hovel, hidden out in the middle of nowhere. Or so it seems. The action slows for a while, allowing a respite for both the characters and the viewers, and Theo finds a pair of shoes to wear: flip-flops. While Jasper has gone to find a way for them to get to the coast and Miriam is doing her exercising, Kee tells Theo how she discovered she was pregnant, and that she's not sure who the father is. She wants to call the baby Froley. Jasper returns triumphant, with his plan. As Theo comes in to the house after hiding the car they arrived in, he hears Jasper talking about faith and chance, then telling Kee and Miriam about Julian and Theo, and the child they lost — a boy, Dylan.

Jasper's plan to get them to the coast and meet up with the Human Project must begin earlier than they'd thought. As they're sleeping, the alarm sounds; the Fishes have found them. Theo watches Jasper get killed from a safe place above the house where he has taken Miriam and Kee while Jasper was to distract the Fishes. Jasper knew he was going to die. Theo, distraught due to his helplessness and the loss of his only friend, gets Kee and Miriam away.

Jasper's plan is followed. They are to "break in" to a refugee camp. They wait for Jasper's connection, Syd, at an unused dilapidated elementary school, with graffiti along the walls showing stick figures of children in what appears to be chalk, but must be pastel-colored paint. Windows are broken, and a deer trotting through the school startles Theo as he's going to retrieve Kee and Miriam when it's time to leave.

Kee is out on the school's swingset and Miriam is waiting in what used to be a classroom. As Theo enters the room, watching Kee outside, Miriam pensively shares with him her witnessing of what happened to the world:

> I was 31, midwife at the John Radcliffe. I was doing a stint in the antenatal clinic. Three of my patients miscarried in one week. Others were in their fifth and sixth months. I managed to save two of the poor babies. The next week five more miscarried. Then the miscarriages started happening earlier. I remember booking a woman in for her next appointment and noticing that the page for seven months ahead was completely blank. Not a single name. I rang a friend who was working at Queen Charlotte's and she had no new pregnancies either. She then rang her sister in Sydney, it was the same thing there . . . As the sounds of the playground faded, the despair set in. Very odd. What happens in a world without children's voices. I was there at the end. (*Children of Men*)

She has walked over to where Theo is by the window, and as she pauses, and sighs, Theo says, "Now you're going to be there at the beginning." Her voice sounds grateful as she replies, "Yeah. I'll be there at the beginning," and after she takes a deep breath, she continues, "Thank you" (*Children of Men*).

Syd, an officer of the refugee camp who Jasper supplied with marijuana, operates under the pretense that Theo, Kee, and Miriam are refugees he's bringing to the camp. Once in the refugee camp, Miriam sacrifices herself to deflect the attention away from Kee's labor pains. Theo delivers Kee's baby once they are in a room of a rundown house that has been secured for them through Marichka (pronounced Mareeka), a gypsy woman who doesn't speak English. The baby is a girl. After a grueling battle due to the commencement of the uprising, they make it to the buoy in a small row-boat. This is where they are to be met by the boat, *Tomorrow*, their connection to the Human Project. As they wait by the buoy, Kee realizes Theo has been shot. Theo tells Kee, "Whatever happens, whatever they say, you keep her close. It's going to be okay." As he's dying, Kee tells him she's naming her baby Dylan. "It's a girl's name, too," she says. Theo faintly smiles, then gently slumps over, as Kee calls out his name. Moments later *Tomorrow* appears. Kee says, "Theo, the boat. It's okay. We're safe now. We're safe," and begins to sing softly to the baby. The camera moves out, and then the screen once again goes black, as bold white letters proclaim CHILDREN OF MEN, and children's voices are heard. John Lennon begins singing "Free the people now." (*Children of Men*)

The novel *The Children of Men* portrays the feelings and actions of human beings when they expect the race to end as its primary focus. The film *Children of Men* moves further back, to examine a more societal view of humanity coming to an end. Yet this view doesn't seem so removed from the world in which we currently live. A review of the film states: "Although it's set in the London of 2027, Cuarón's film isn't some high-tech futuristic fantasy. It takes place in a grimly familiar location: the hell we are currently making for ourselves" (Stevens 2006, 1). This reviewer also comments on the textual clues in the film that reveal the numerous devastating events — besides the condition of universal infertility — that have brought the world to this point: "Nearly every frame is a palimpsest of visual information, from TV screens to graffiti-covered walls to the newspaper headlines and propaganda posters plastered everywhere in the gray and squalid London of Cuaron's imagination" (2). Jasper himself has covered his home from top to bottom with news articles and headlines, featuring his own work he published as a cartoonist, and the captivating headline of his wife, a photojournalist, having been tortured — the same woman who is now catatonic and must be fed and groomed, and who only responds with eerie silence and blank eyes. A striking photograph resounds from Jasper's wall of pictures and articles: Theo and Julian, holding their baby, Dylan.

Cuarón also employs the use of long shots and a fluid camera that moves with the actors and action. Cuarón's goal for the film was to emulate documentary-style camera work, and he explains his decision to do so in an interview: ". . . a character has the same weight as the social environment. In other words you don't use close-ups because you would be giving more weight to the character instead of the environment. Everything is kind of loose and distant trying to absorb real time and trying to minimize editing and montage" (Guerassio 2006, 2). Thus, Cuarón's response to the premise of universal infertility was to show a futureless world unfold more from a distance, rather than up close — the way James chose to portray it in her novel, through Theo and especially his journal.

In fact, Cuarón didn't read James's novel, a purposeful choice on his part. He explains in an interview:

Once we decided to do this exploration on the state of things — and you don't have to go very far to realize that the environment and immigration are pretty much on the top of the list — then we had to craft a story. I had the story I wanted to tell so clear in my head that I was very afraid of reading the book and getting completely confused. I read an abridged version of the book, and Timothy J. Sexton, my writing partner, read the [entire] book. But our whole idea was let's find out what elements are relevant to what we're doing and let's disregard what we think is irrelevant. (Guerrasio 2006, 2)

Interestingly, on perusal of the screenplay written by Cuarón and Sexton, several deviations are quite noticeable when comparing the screenplay to the film. These distinctions most likely can be made due to Clive Owen, the actor who portrays Theo, coming on board. According to Cuarón, Owen "got involved in this project with Tim and myself, we locked ourselves in a hotel room, and first we went over his character. And he had so much insight that we decided, Tim and myself, that Clive should be involved with the rest of the writing process, even if it was not about his character" (Guerrasio 2006, 2). Cuarón continues to credit Owen as a co-filmmaker as well, since "he was not only performing for the film I was doing, he was trying to achieve from a filmmaker's standpoint, not just an actor" (2).

The collaborative efforts of those working on the film, and these efforts having grown out of a post-9/11 awareness of the state of society, reflect the different concerns that we have today with the world today than we had in the nineties. James brings to light concerns such as how human beings behave if the end of the world is imminent, and just how selfish they will allow themselves to become. In post-9/11, Cuarón brings to light more far-reaching concerns, and he does so without taking much of a leap beyond the state of our society today. Cuarón references James's novel when he discusses making the film relevant to today:

I really wanted to make a film that would speak to the 21st century. And the specific dynamics that the 21st century has taken as opposed to the 20th century. I think it's important to separate those elements out, because, I think, there's a certain nostalgia for the 20th century that I don't know is healthy. There's this whole idea of tyranny created by a single figure, a dictator. In the book, there actually is a dictator of Great Britain . . . this notion of a Big Brother, a dictator. And we wanted to make this world, this universe, a democracy. Britain is a democracy. But, by the way, being a democracy doesn't mean people are choosing the right things or what is just. (Voynar 2006, 6)

Cuarón challenges the fairness that is supposed to be inherent in any democracy, and does so through the images presented in his film. He states that he is "against the blind faith that is put in democracy," and that in the 21st century, we are doing exactly that. However, he claims, "any tyranny now can have the makeup of a democracy, and then in a way, you can start to justify all the elements of the tyranny" (Voynar 2006, 6).

So, while James was castigating a society that would accept a dictator, and assuming a vulnerable society would end up with a dictator, Cuarón puts forth that a vulnerable society just as easily can become corrupted by a democratic system. And Cuarón has us as viewers questioning whether in fact this might be happening all around us, right now. We read James's novel, and we can see ourselves reacting similarly in many ways to the characters in her book if no children were left on the planet and we were left to die in a futureless world. We view Cuarón's film in the dark of the theater, the grayness of the film not lighting our way out of that darkness. And, when we walk outside, much of that grayness does not dissipate. He has reminded us that the world he imagines, and the world imagined before him by James, is entirely plausible. Both creators have made their dystopian visions easy to imagine for everyone, despite their differences in approach and the time periods in which they've formulated their visions. Indeed, they have both offered us some inspiration for reform, now, before it's too late.

Bibliography

Adaptation. 2003. Dir. Spike Jonze. Perf. Nicolas Cage, Tilda Swinton, Meryl Streep, and Chris Cooper. DVD. Columbia Pictures.

Allen, Graham. 2000. *Intertextuality.* New York: Routledge.

Althusser, Louis. 1971. "Ideology and the Ideological State Apparatuses" in *Lenin and Philosophy and Other Essays.* New York: Monthly Review Press, 127–86.

Andrew, Dudley. 1981. "Adaptation" in *Film and Literature: An Introduction and Reader.* Timothy Corrigan. Upper Saddle River, NJ: Prentice-Hall, 1999.

Armstrong, Isobel. 1995. "The Gush of the Feminine: How Can We Read Women's Poetry of the Romantic Period?" in *Romantic Women Writers: Voices and Countervoices.* Paula R. Feldman and Theresa M. Kelley (eds.). Hanover, NH: University of New England, 13–32.

Arnheim, Rudolf. 1957. *Film As Art.* Berkeley and Los Angeles, CA: University of California.

Atonement. 2008. Dir. Joe Wright. Perf. Keira Knightly, James McAvoy, and Saoirse Ronan. DVD. Universal Studies.

Away from Her. 2007. Dir. Sarah Polley. Perf. Julie Christie, Gordon Pinsent, and Olympia Dukakis. Lions Gate.

Axelrod, Mark. 2007. *I Read It at the Movies: The Follies and Foibles of Screen Adaptation.* Portsmouth, NH: Heinnmann.

Aycock, Wendell, and Michael Schoenecke, eds. 1988. *Film And Literature: A Comparative Approach to Adaptation.* Lubbock, Texas: Texas Tech University Press.

Badmington, Neil and Julia Thomas, eds. 2008. *The Routledge Critical and Cultural Theory Reader.* New York: Routledge.

Bakhtin, M. M. 1981. *The Dialogic Imagination.* Austin, Texas: University of Texas Press.

Barry, Peter. 2009. *Beginning Theory: An Introduction to Literary and Cultural Theory.* 3rd ed. New York: Manchester University Press.

Barthes, Roland. 1968. "The Death of the Author" in *Image, Music, Text.* Trans. Stephen Heath. New York: Hill and Wang, 1977.

Barthes, Roland. 1971. "From Work to Text" in *Image, Music, Text*. Trans. Stephen Heath. New York: Hill and Wang, 1977.

Barthes, Roland. 1974. *S/Z*. Trans. Richard Miller. New York: Hill and Wang, 1974.

Barthes, Roland. 1975. *The Pleasure of the Text*. Trans. Richard Miller. New York: Hill and Wang, 1998.

Barthes, Roland. 1989. *The Rustle of Language*. Trans. Richard Howard. Berkeley, CA: University of California Press.

Beauvoir, Simone de. 1949. *Le Deuxième Sexe*. Coll. "Folio." vol. 1. Paris: Gallimard.

Beauvoir, Simone de. 1989. *The Second Sex*. Trans. H. M. Parhsley (1952). New York: Vintage Books.

Beauvoir, Simone de. 2009. *The Second Sex*. Trans. Constance Borde and Sheila Malovany-Chevallier. New York: Alfred A. Knopf.

Bhaba, Homi. 1974. "The Commitment to Theory" in *The Location of Culture*. New York: Routledge, 2004.

Birkerts, Sven. 2000. "Death in Atlanta," review of *Those Bones Are Not My Child* by Toni Cade Bambara in the *New York Times*, January 2: 17.

Bloom, Harold. 1973 *The Anxiety of Influence: A Theory of Poetry*. New York: Oxford University Press.

Bluestone, George. 1957. *Novels Into Film*. Baltimore: Johns Hopkins University Press.

Booth, Wayne. 1988. *The Company We Keep: An Ethics of Fiction*. Berkeley, CA: University of California Press.

Boyd, Brian. 2009. *On the Origin of Stories: Evolution, Cognition, and Fiction*. Cambridge, MA: The Belknap Press of Harvard University Press.

Brooker, Peter. 2007. "Postmodern adaptation: pastiche, intertextuality and re-functioning" in *The Cambridge Companion to Literature on Screen*. Deborah Cartmell and Imelda Whehelan (eds.). New York: Cambridge University Press, 107–20.

Buckland, Warren. 1998. *Teach Yourself Film Studies*. New York: The McGraw-Hill Companies.

Butler, Judith. 1990. *Gender Trouble*. New York: Routledge.

Butler, Robert Olen. 2005. *From Where You Dream: The Process of Writing Fiction*. New York: Grove Press.

Cahir, Linda Costanza. 2006. *Literature Into Film: Theory and Practical Approaches*. Jefferson, NC: McFarland & Company.

Cartmell, Deborah and Imelda Whelehan, eds. 2007. *The Cambridge Companion to Literature on Screen*. New York: Cambridge University Press, 2007.

Chandler, Daniel. 2009. "Introduction." *Semiotics for Beginners*. January 13, 2009. MCS (Media and Communication Studies). http://www.aber.ac.uk/media/Documents/S4B/sem02.html (accessed March 10, 2010).

Chandler, Daniel. 2009. "Signs." *Semiotics for Beginners*. January 13, 2009. MCS (Media and Communication Studies). http://www.aber.ac.uk/media/Documents/S4B/sem02.html (accessed March 10, 2010).

Chatman, Seymour. 1990. *Coming to Terms: The Rhetoric of Narrative in Fiction and Film*. Ithaca, NY: Cornell University Press.

Children of Men. 2006. Dir. Alfonso Cuarón. Perf. Clive Owen, Julianne Moore, and Michael Caine. Universal Studios.

The Cider House Rules. 1999. Dir. Lasse Hallstrom. Perf. Toby Maguire, Charlize Theron, and Michael Caine. Miramax.

Cixous, Hélène. 1991. *Coming to Writing and Other Essays*. Deborah Jenson (ed.). Cambridge, MA: Harvard University Press.

Cixous, Hélène. 1997. "The Laugh of the Medusa" in *Feminisms: An Anthology of Literary Theory and Criticism*. Robin R. Warhol and Diane Price Herndl (eds.). New Brunswick, NJ: Rutgers University Press, 347–61.

The Constant Gardener. 2005. Dir. Fernando Meirelles. Perf. Ralph Fiennes, Rachel Weisz, and Danny Huston. Potboiler Productions.

Corrigan, Timothy. 1999. *Film and Literature: An Introduction and Reader*. Upper Saddle River, NJ: Prentice-Hall.

Corrigan, Timothy. 2007. "Literature on screen, a history: in the gap" in *The Cambridge Companion to Literature on Screen*. Deborah Cartmell and Imelda Whelehan (eds.). New York: Cambridge University Press, 29–43.

Corrigan, Timothy. 2010. *A Short Guide to Writing About Film*. 7th ed. New York: Pearson Education.

Creed, Barbara. 2000. "Film and Psychoanalysis" in *Film Studies: Critical Approaches*. John Hill and Pamela Church Gibson (eds.). New York: Oxford University Press, 75–88.

Culler, Jonathan. 1997. *Literary Theory: A Very Short Introduction*. New York: Oxford University Press.

Cunningham, Michael. 1998. *The Hours*. New York: Picador.

The Curious Case of Benjamin Button. 2008. Dir. David Fincher. Perf. Brad Pitt, Cate Blanchett, and Taraji P. Henson. Warner Brothers Pictures.

Dalley, Jan. 1992. "INTERVIEW/Mistress of morality tales: P D James: Jan Dalley meets the celebrated crime writer whose latest novel examines evil from a different perspective." *The Independent*. September 20, 1992. http://www.independent.co.uk/opinion/interview — mistress-of-morality-tales-p-d-james-jan-dalley-meets-the-celebrated-crime-writer-whose-latest-novel-examines-evil-from-a-very-different-perspective-1552435.html (accessed September 15, 2010).

Damrosch, David and Kevin J. H. Dettmar. 2006. *The Longman Anthology of British Literature: Volume 2A*. 3rd ed. New York: Pearson Longman.

Dargis, Manohla. 2008. "Is There a Real Woman in This Multiplex?" *New York Times*. May 4, 2008. http://www.nytimes.com/2008/05/04/movies/moviesspecial/04dargi.html (accessed May 25, 2008).

Derrida, Jacques. 1978. "Structure, Sign and Play in the Discourse of the Human Sciences" in *Writing and Difference*. Chicago: University of Chicago Press, 278–93.

Derrida, Jacques. 1997. *Of Grammatology*. Trans. Gayatri Chakravorty Spivak. Baltimore, MD: Johns Hopkins University Press.

Desmond, John M. and Peter Hawkes. 2006. *Adaptation: Studying Film and Literature*. New York: McGraw-Hill.

Dirks, Tim. 2010. "Timeline of Greatest Film Milestones and Important Turning Points in Film History." *Filmsite*. American Movie Classics. http://www.filmsite.org/milestones (accessed March 25, 2010).

Dobie, Ann B. 2009. *Theory Into Practice: An Introduction to Literary Criticism*. 2nd ed. Boston, MA: Wadsworth Cengage Learning.

Doty, Alexander. 2000. "Queer Theory" in *Film Studies: Critical Approaches*. John Hill and Pamela Church Gibson (eds.). New York: Oxford University Press, 146–50.

Dunne, John Gregory. 1968. *The Studio*. New York: Vintage Books.

Dunne, John Gregory. 1998. *Monster: Living Off the Big Screen*. New York: Vintage Books.

Dyer, Richard. 2000. "Introduction to Film Studies" in *Film Studies: Critical Approaches*. John Hill and Pamela Church Gibson (eds.). New York: Oxford University Press, 1–8.

Eagleton, Terry. 2003. *After Theory*. New York: Basic Books.

Eagleton, Terry. 2008. *Literary Theory: An Introduction*. Minneapolis, MN: University of Minnesota Press.

Eakin, Emily. 2001. "The Untold Links between Biographer and Subject" in the *New York Times Week in Review*. June 24: 3.

Easthope, Anthony. 2000. "Classic Film Theory and Semiotics" in *Film Studies: Critical Approaches*. John Hill and Pamela Church Gibson (eds.). New York: Oxford University Press, 49–55.

Eliot, T. S. 1919. "Tradition and Individual Talent" in *The Best American Essays of the Century*. Joyce Carol Oates (ed.). New York: Houghton Mifflin Company.

Elliott, Kamilla. 2003. *Rethinking the Novel/Film Debate*. New York: Cambridge University Press.

Ellison, Ralph. 2000. *Juneteenth*. New York: Vintage.

Empson, William. 1966. *Seven Types of Ambiguity*. New York: New Direction.

Feeley, Gregory. 1999. "Invisible Hand" in the *New York Times Magazine*. May 23: 50–3.

Fish, Stanley. 1999. "Is There a Text in This Class?" in *The Stanley Fish Reader*. H. Aram Veeser (ed.). Malden, MA: Blackwell Publishers, 38–54.

Fitzgerald, F. Scott. 1920. *The Curious Case of Benjamin Button and Other Jazz Age Stories*. New York: Penguin Books, 2008.

Foote, Horton. 1988. "Writing for Film" in *Film and Literature: A Comparative Approach to Adaptation*. Wendell Aycock and Michael Schoenecke (eds.). Lubbock, TX: Texas Tech University Press, 5–20.

Foster, Thomas C. 2008. *How to Read Novels Like a Professor*. New York: HarperCollins.

Foucault, Michel. 1979. "What Is an Author?" in *The Foucault Reader*. Paul Rabinow (ed.). New York: Pantheon Books, 1984.

Frankenstein. 1931. Dir. James Whale. Perf. Colin Clive, Mae Clarke, and Boris Karloff. Universal Pictures.

Freedman, Diane P. and Olivia Frey, eds. 2003. *Autobiographical Writing Across the Disciplines: A Reader*. Durham, NC: Duke University Press.

Freedman, Diane P., Olivia Frey, and Frances Murphy Zauhar. 1993. *The Intimate Critique: Autobiographical Literary Criticism*. Durham, NC: Duke University Press.

Freud, Sigmund. 1900. *The Interpretation of Dreams*. New York: Random House, 1978.

Frey, Hans-Jost. *Interruptions*. 1989. Trans. Georgia Albert. Albany, NY: State University of New York Press.

Fuss, Diana. 1989. *Essentially Speaking: Feminism, Nature and Difference*. New York: Routledge, Chapman and Hall.

Geiger, Jeffrey and R. L. Rutsky, eds. 2005. *Film Analysis: A Norton Reader*. New York: W.W. Norton & Company.

Genette, Gerard. 1972. *Narrative Discourse: An Essay in Method*. Ithaca, NY: Cornell University Press, 1983.

Geraghty, Christine. 2008. *Now a Major Motion Picture: Film Adaptations of Literature and Drama*. Lanham, MD: Rowman & Littlefield.

Gilbert, Sandra M. and Susan Gubar, eds. 1984. *The Madwoman in the Attic: The Woman Writer and the Nineteenth-Century Literary Imagination*. New Haven, CT: Yale University Press.

Gioia, Dana and R. S. Gwynn. 2006. *The Art of the Short Story*. New York: Pearson Longman.

Godwin, William. 1987. *Memoirs of the Author of The Rights of Woman*. Wollstonecraft, Mary. *A Short Residence in Sweden, Norway, and Denmark*. Richard Holmes (ed.). New York: Penguin Books, 204–310.

Gone Baby Gone. 2007. Dir. Ben Affleck. Perf. Casey Affleck, Michelle Monaghan, Morgan Freeman, and Amy Ryan. LivePlanet.

Greenblatt, Stephen. 1989. "Towards a Poetics of Culture" in *The New Historicism*. H. Aram Veeser (ed.). New York: Routledge, 1–14.

Guerrasio, Jason. "A New Humanity." *Filmmaker*. December 22, 2006. http://filmmakermagazine.com/news/2006/12/a-new-humanity-by-jason-guerrasio/ (accessed September 15, 2010).

Hill, John and Pamela Church Gibson. 2000. *Film Studies: Critical Approaches*. New York: Oxford University Press.

Holmes, Richard. 1987. "Introduction" in *Memoirs of the Author of The Rights of Woman*. William Godwin. New York: Penguin, 1–55.

The Hours. 2003. Dir. Stephen Daldry. Perf. Meryl Streep, Nicole Kidman, Julianne Moore, and Ed Harris. DVD. Paramount Home Video.

Hutcheon, Linda. 2006. *A Theory of Adaptation*. New York: Routledge.

Irigaray, Luce. 1987. "Sexual Difference" in *French Feminist Thought: A Reader*. Toril Moi (ed.). New York: Basil Blackwell, 118–30.

Irigaray, Luce. 1990. *This Sex Which Is Not One*. Trans. Catherine Porter. Ithaca, NY: Cornell University Press.

Irving, John. 1985. *The Cider House Rules*. New York: Ballantine Publishing Group.

Irving, John. 1999. *The Cider House Rules: A Screenplay*. New York: Garp Enterprises.

Irving, John. 1999. *My Movie Business: A Memoir*. New York: Ballantine Books.

Itzkoff, Dave. 2009. "Watchmen Skulk the Same." January 30, 2009. http://www.nytimes.com/2009/02/01/movies/01itzk.html (accessed January 30, 2009).

James, P. D. 1992. *The Children of Men*. New York: Vintage, 2006.

Jensen, Deborah. 1991. *"Coming to Writing" and Other Essays*. Cambridge, MA: Harvard University Press.

Jones, Ann Rosalind. 1997. "Writing the Body: Toward an Understanding of L'Écriture Feminine" in *Feminisms: An Anthology of Literary Theory and Criticism*. Robin R. Warhol and Diane Price Herndl (eds.). New Brunswick, NJ: Rutgers University Press, 370–83.

Kaplan, Cora. 1986. "Wild Nights: Pleasure/Sexuality/Feminism" in *Sea Changes: Essays on Culture and Feminism*. London: Verso, 31–56.

Kawin, Bruce. 1992. *How Movies Work*. Berkeley, CA: University of California Press.

Kincaid, James R. 2000. "You Jane?" *New York Times Book Review*. December 3: 62–3.

King, Lynnea Chapman, Rick Wallach, and Jim Welsh. 2009. *No Country for Old Men: From Novel to Film*. Lanham, MD: Scarecrow Press.

Klages, Mary. 2001. "Humanism and Literary Theory." August 29, 2001. http://www.colorado.edu/English/courses/ENGL2012Klages/humanism.html (accessed February 20, 2010).

Krevolin, Richard. 2003. *How to Adapt Anything into a Screenplay*. Hoboken, New Jersey: John Wiley & Sons.

Kristeva, Julia. 1986a. "Revolution in Poetic Language" in *The Kristeva Reader*. Toril Moi (ed.). New York: Columbia University Press, 89–136.

Kristeva, Julia. 1986b. "The System and the Speaking Subject" in *The Kristeva Reader*. Toril Moi (ed.). New York: Columbia University Press, 24–33.

Kristeva, Julia. 1986c. "Stabat Mater" in *The Kristeva Reader*. Toril Moi (ed.). New York: Columbia University Press, 160–86.

Kristeva, Julia. 1986d. "Women's Time" in *The Kristeva Reader*. Toril Moi (ed.). New York: Columbia University Press, 187–213.

Kristeva, Julia. 1986e. "Word, Dialogue and Novel" in *The Kristeva Reader*. Toril Moi (ed.). New York: Columbia University Press, 34–61.

Lacan, Jacques. 1977. *Écrits: A Selection*. Trans. Alan Sheridan. New York: W. W. Norton & Company.

LeCarre, John. 2001. *The Constant Gardener*. New York: Scribner.

Lee, Harper. 2002. *To Kill a Mockingbird*. New York: Perennial.

Lehane, Dennis. 1998. *Gone, Baby, Gone*. New York: HarperCollins.

Lehane, Dennis. 2001. *Mystic River*. New York: HarperCollins.

Leitch, Thomas. 2003. "Twelve Fallacies in Contemporary Adaptation Theory." *Criticism* 45.2 (Spring 2003). http://findarticles.com/p/articles/mi_m2220/is_2_45/ai_n6143332/ (BNET.com, accessed January 23, 2008).

Leitch, Thomas M. 2007. *Film Adaptation and Its Discontents: From Gone with the Wind to The Passion of the Christ*. Baltimore, MD: Johns Hopkins University Press.

Leitch, Vincent B., ed. 2001. *The Norton Anthology of Theory and Criticism*. 1st ed. New York: W. W. Norton & Company.

Lessing, Gotthold Ephraim. 2005. *Laocoon: An Essay upon the Limits of Painting and Poetry*. New York: Dover Publications.

Lodge, David. 1992. *The Art of Fiction*. New York: Penguin Books.

The Lovely Bones. 2009. Dir. Peter Jackson. Perf. Saoirse Ronan, Mark Wahlberg, Rachel Weisz, and Stanley Tucci. DreamWorks SKG.

Mary Shelley's Frankenstein. 1994. Dir. Kenneth Branagh. Perf. Kenneth Branagh, Helena Bonham Carter, Tom Hulce, and Robert DeNiro. TriStar Pictures.

Larkin, Merre. 2002. *Sentences*. Draft of unpublished novel by author of this book (pen name for creative work).

Lynn, Steven. 1998. *Texts and Contexts: Writing about Literature with Critical Theory*. 2nd ed. New York: Addison-Wesley Educational Publishers.

Marx, Karl and Friedrich Engels, 1848. *The Communist Manifesto*. New York: Oxford University Press, 2008.

McCarthy, Cormac. 2006. *No Country for Old Men*. New York: Vintage.

McCarthy, Cormac. 2006. *The Road*. New York: Vintage.

McFarlane, Brian. 1996. *Novel to Film: An Introduction to the Theory of Adaptation*. New York: Oxford University Press.

McFarlane, Brian. 2007. "Reading film and literature" in *The Cambridge Companion to Literature on Screen*. Deborah Cartmell and Imelda Whelehan (eds.). New York: Cambridge University Press, 15–28.

McGinn, Colin. 2007. *The Power of Movies: How Screen and Mind Interact*. New York: Vintage.

McEwan, Ian. 2003. *Atonement*. New York: Anchor Books.

Mellor, Anne K. 1989. "My Hideous Progeny" in *Mary Shelley, Her Life, Her Fiction, Her Monsters*. New York: Routledge, Chapman & Hall, 52–69.

Mellor, Anne K. 1994. "Introduction" in *Maria, or The Wrongs of Woman*. Mary Wollstonecraft. New York: W.W. Norton & Company, v–xviii.

Mellor, Anne K. 1996. "Choosing a Text of Frankenstein to Teach," in *Frankenstein, or the Modern Prometheus*. J. Paul Hunter (ed.). New York: W. W. Norton & Company, 160–6.

Memento. 2000. Dir. Christopher Nolan. Perf. Guy Pearce, Carrie-Anne Moss, and Joe Pantoliano. Newmarket Capital Group.

Metz, Christian. 1977. *The Imaginary Signifier: Pschoanalysis and the Cinema*. Bloomington, IN: University of Indiana Press.

Meyer, Michael. *The Bedford Introduction to Literature*. 8th ed. New York: Bedford/St. Martins, 2008.

Miller, J. Hillis. 1979. "The Critic as Host" in *Deconstruction and Criticism*. Harold Bloom (ed.). New York: The Seabury Press, 217–53.

Miller, Toby and Robert Stam. 1999. *A Companion to Film Theory*. Malden, MA: Blackwell Publishing.

Millett, Kate. 1969. *Sexual Politics*. Chicago, IL: University of Illinois Press.

Million Dollar Baby. 2004. Dir. Clint Eastwood. Perf. Hilary Swank, Clint
        Eastwood, Morgan Freeman, and Jay Baruchel. Warner Brothers Pictures.

Moi, Toril. 1985. *Sexual/Textual Politics: Feminist Literary Theory*. New York:
        Routledge.

Moi, Toril, ed. 1986. *The Kristeva Reader*. New York: Columbia University Press.

Moi, Toril. 1999a. "(Mis)Reading The Second Sex: Questions of Equality and
        Difference Prefaced by Some Reflexions on the General Tendency to
        Debasement of Beauvoir." Legacies of Simone de Beauvoir. Penn State
        Beauvoir Conference. State College, PA. November 19–21, 1999: 4.

Moi, Toril. 1999b. "I Am a Woman" in *What is a Woman? And Other Essays*.
        Oxford: Oxford University Press, 121–250.

Mottram, James. 2002. *The Making of Memento*. New York: Faber and Faber.

Mottram, James. 2002. "Memento Mori: A Short Story by Jonathan Nolan" in *The
        Making of Memento*. New York: Faber and Faber, 183–95.

Mullan, John. 2006. *How Novels Work*. New York: Oxford University Press.

Munro, Alice. 2002. "The Bear Came Over the Mountain" in *Hateship, Friendship,
        Courtship, Loveship, Marriage*. New York: Vintage.

Mystic River. 2003. Dir. Clint Eastwood. Perf. Sean Penn, Tim Robbins, and Kevin
        Bacon. Warner Brothers Pictures.

Nance, Kevin. 2009. "Anything Can Happen." *Poets & Writers Magazine*.
        November/December, 2009: 54–60.

Naremore, James. 2000. *Film Adaptation*. New Brunswick, NJ: Rutgers University
        Press.

No Country for Old Men. 2007. Dirs. Ethan and Joel Coen. Perf. Javier Bardem,
        Tommy Lee Jones, Josh Brolin, and Kelly Macdonald. Paramount Vantage.

Nolan, Christopher. 2001. "How *Memento* Began" in *Memento & Following*. New
        York: Faber and Faber, 233–4.

Nolan, Christopher. 2001. *Memento & Following*. New York: Faber and Faber.

Oates, Joyce Carol. 2003. *The Faith of a Writer: Life, Craft, Art*. New York:
        HarperCollins.

O'Neill. 1987. "Foreword" in *Long Day's Journey into Night*. Harold Bloom. New
        Haven, CT: Yale University Press, v–viii.

Orlean, Susan. 1998. *The Orchid Thief*. New York: Ballantine Books.

Payne, Michael. 1997. *A Dictionary of Cultural and Critical Theory*. Malden, MA:
        Blackwell.

Payne, Michael. 2000. "The Survival of Truth after Derrida." *Journal for Cultural
        Research* 4, 127–34.

Payne, Michael and John Schad. 2003. *life. after. theory*. New York: Continuum.

Precious. 2009. Dir. Lee Daniels. Perf. Gabourey Sidibe, Mo'Nique, and Paula
        Patton. Lee Daniels Entertainment.

Propp, Vladimir. 1968. *The Morphology of the Folktale*. Austin, TX: University of
        Texas Press.

Proulx, Annie, Larry McMurtry, and Diana Ossana. 2005. *Brokeback Mountain:
        Story to Screenplay*. New York: Scribner.

Rabinow, Paul, ed. 1984. *The Foucault Reader*. New York: Pantheon Books.

Ray, Robert B. 1985. *A Certain Tendency of the Hollywood Cinema, 1930–1980*. Princeton, NJ: Princeton University Press.

Richards, I. A. 1929. *Practical Criticism*. New York: Harcourt Brace & Company.

The Road. 2009. Dir. John Hillcoat. Perf. Viggo Mortenson, Kodi Smit-McPhee, and Charlize Theron. Dimension Films.

Rodin, Christine. 2010. Email correspondence, April 14.

Rousseau, Jean-Jacques. 1979. *Emile or On Education*. Trans. Allan Bloom. New York: Basic Books.

Said, Edward. 1993. *Culture and Imperialism*. New York: Vintage.

Said, Edward. 1994. *Orientalism*. New York: Vintage.

Sallis, James. 1993. "The Decline and Fall of the Human Race." *The Los Angeles Times*. April 4, 1993. http://articles.latimes.com/1993-04-04/books/bk-18765_1_human-race (accessed August 29, 2010).

Sanders, Julie. 2006. *Adaptation and Appropriation*. New York: Routledge.

Sapphire. 1996. *Push*. New York: Vintage.

Saussure, Ferdinand de. 1972. *Course in General Linguistics*. Peru, IL: Open Court.

Sebold, Alice. 2002. *The Lovely Bones*. New York: Back Bay Books.

Sedgwick, Eve Kosofsky. 1985. *Between Men: English Literature and Male Homosocial Desire*. New York: Columbia University Press.

Seger, Linda. 1992. *The Art of Adaptation: Turning Fact and Fiction into Film*. New York: Owl Books.

Shelley, Mary. 1996. *Frankenstein, or The Modern Prometheus*. J. Paul Hunter (ed.). New York: W.W. Norton and Company.

Shelley, Mary. 1992. *Frankenstein, or The Modern Prometheus*. New York: Penguin Putnam.

Shelley, Percy. 1996. *A Defence of Poetry* in *British Literature 1780–1830*. Anne K. Mellor and Richard E. Matlak (eds.). New York: Harcourt Brace & Company, 1167–78.

Showalter, Elaine. 2001. *Inventing Herself: Claiming a Feminist Intellectual Heritage*. New York: Scribner.

Shulevitz, Judith. 2001a. "Ahead of Her Time." *New York Times Book Review*. July 1, 2001: 23.

Shulevitz, Judith. 2001b. "The Wound and the Historian." *New York Times Book Review*. July 15, 2001: 31.

Sidney, Sir Phillip. 1580. "An Apology for Poetry" (or "A Defence of Poetry") in *The Norton Anthology of Theory and Criticism*. Vincent B. Leitch (ed.). New York: W. W. Norton & Company, 2001.

Sielke, Sabine. 1997. *Fashioning the Female Subject: The Intertextual Networking of Dickinson, Moore, and Rich*. Ann Arbor, MI: University of Michigan Press.

Spender, Dale. 1986. *Mothers of the Novel*. New York: Pandora.

Spivak, Gayatri Chakravorty. 2006. *In Other Worlds: Essays in Cultural Politics*. New York: Routledge.

Stam, Robert and Alessandra Raengo. 2005a. *Literature and Film: A Guide to the Theory and Practice of Film Adaptation*. New York: Blackwell.

Stam, Robert and Alessandro Raengo. 2005b. *Literature through Film: Realism, Magic, and the Art of Adaptation*. New York: Blackwell.

St. Clair, William. 1989. *The Godwins and the Shelleys: A Biography of a Family*. Baltimore, MD: Johns Hopkins University Press.

Stevens, Dana. 2006. "The Movie of the Millenium." *Slate*. December 21, 2006. http://www.slate.com/id/2155950/ (accessed September 1, 2010).

Taylor, Barbara. 1992. "Introduction" in *A Vindication of the Rights of Woman*. Mary Wollstonecraft. New York: Alfred A. Knopf, vii–xxxi.

"Tim Dirks." http://www.rottentomatoes.com/author/author-2/ (accessed March 25, 2010).

Todd, Janet. 1992. "Introduction" in *Mary/Maria/Matilda*. Mary Wollstonecraft and Mary Shelley. New York: Penguin, vii–xxvi.

Tompkins, Jane. 1980. "An Introduction to Reader-Response Criticism" in *Reader-Response Criticism: From Formalism to Post-Structuralism*. Jane Tompkins (ed.). Baltimore, MD: The John Hopkins University Press.

Tompkins, Jane. 1980. "The Reader in History: The Changing Shape of Literary Response" in *Reader-Response Criticism: From Formalism to Post-Structuralism*. Jane Tompkins (ed.). Baltimore, MD: The John Hopkins University Press.

Tompkins, Jane. 1997. "Me and My Shadow" in *Feminisms: An Anthology of Literary Theory and Criticism*. Robin R. Warhol and Diane Price Herndl (eds.). New Brunswick, NJ: Rutgers University Press, 1103–16.

Toole, F. X. 2005. *Million Dollar Baby: Stories from the Corner*. New York: HarperCollins.

Troost, Linda V. 2007. "The nineteenth-century novel on film: Jane Austen" in *The Cambridge Companion to Literature on Screen*. Deborah Cartmell and Imelda Whelehan (eds.). New York: Cambridge University Press, 75–89.

Villarejo, Amy. 2007. *Film Studies: The Basics*. New York: Routledge.

Voynar, Kim. "Interview: Children of Men Director Alfonso Cuaron." *Cinematical*. December 25, 2006. http://www.cinematical.com/2006/12/25/interview-children-ofmen-director-alfonso-cuaron/ (accessed August 29, 2010).

Wittig, Monique. 1986. "The Mark of Gender" in *The Poetics of Gender*. Nancy K. Miller (ed.). New York: Columbia University Press, 63–73.

Wollstonecraft, Mary. 1975. *Maria, or The Wrongs of Woman*. Anne K. Mellor (ed.). New York: W.W. Norton & Company.

Wollstonecraft, Mary. 1989. *The Works of Mary Wollstonecraft*. Marilyn Butler and Janet Todd (eds.). New York: New York University Press.

Wollstonecraft, Mary. 1992. *A Vindication of the Rights of Woman*. Barbara Taylor (ed.). New York: Alfred A. Knopf.

Woolf, Virginia. 1981. *Mrs. Dalloway*. New York: Harcourt.

Woolf, Virginia. 1989. *A Room of One's Own*. New York: Harcourt.

Wordsworth, William. 1996. "Preface from Lyrical Ballads" in *British Literature 1780–1830*. Anne K. Mellor and Richard E. Matlak (eds.). New York: Harcourt Brace & Company, 580.

Index